Y0-CWP-806

Studies in Eighteenth-Century Culture

VOLUME 15

Studies in Eighteenth-Century Culture VOLUME 15

EDITED BY *O M Brack, Jr.*
Arizona State University

PUBLISHED for the
AMERICAN SOCIETY FOR EIGHTEENTH-CENTURY STUDIES
by THE UNIVERSITY OF WISCONSIN PRESS

Published 1986

The University of Wisconsin Press
114 North Murray Street
Madison, Wisconsin 53715

The University of Wisconsin Press, Ltd.
1 Gower Street
London WC1E 6HA, England

Copyright © 1986
American Society for Eighteenth-Century Studies
All rights reserved

First printing

Printed in the United States of America

LC 75-648277

ISBN 0-299-10430-3

Editorial Readers for Volume Fifteen

PAUL K. ALKON / English / University of Southern California
W. JOHN ARCHER / Humanities / University of Minnesota
JERRY C. BEASLEY / English / University of Delaware
DAVID BLEWETT / English / McMaster University
J. DOUGLAS CANFIELD / English / University of Arizona
MICHAEL CARTWRIGHT / French / McGill University
W. J. ECCLES / History / University of Toronto
WILLIAM EDINGER / English / University of Maryland, Baltimore County
CHRISTINE FERDINAND / History / Tempe, Arizona
BEATRICE FINK / French / University of Maryland
MARY E. GREEN / English / Arizona State University
BASIL J. GUY / French / University of California, Berkeley
PHILLIP HARTH / English / University of Wisconsin
DANIEL HEARTZ / Music / University of California, Berkeley
PATRICK HENRY / French / Whitman College
ROBERT D. HUME / English / Pennsylvania State University
REGINA JANES / English / Skidmore College
THOMAS KAMINSKI / English / Loyola University of Chicago
WILLIAM KINSLEY / English / University of Montreal
WULF KOEPKE / German / Texas A & M University
LIESELOTTE E. KURTH / German / Johns Hopkins University
MAURICE LE BRETON / English / Université de Toulouse-Le Mirail
JAMES B. MISENHEIMER / English / Indiana State University
MELVYN NEW / English / University of Florida
MAXIMILLIAN NOVAK / English / University of California, Los Angeles
CATHERINE N. PARKE / English / University of Missouri
HARRY PAYNE / History / Haverford College
JEAN A. PERKINS / French / Swarthmore College
JANE PERRY-CAMP / Music / Florida State University
WILLIAM BOWMAN PIPER / English / Rice University
JOHN C. RIELY / English / Boston University
BETTY W. RIZZO / English / City College of New York
IAN ROSS / English / University of British Columbia
JOHN F. SENA / English / Ohio State University
FRANK SHUFFELTON / English / University of Rochester
PETER J. STANLIS / English / Rockford College
PHILIP STEWART / French / Duke University
ALBRECHT B. STRAUSS / English / University of North Carolina
MADELEINE B. THERRIEN / French / University of Maryland

vi / Editorial Readers

JAMES THOMPSON / English / University of North Carolina
VIRGIL W. TOPAZIO / French / Rice University
BRUCE TUCKER / History / University of Cincinnati
SIMON VAREY / English / Rijksuniversiteit Utrecht
ARAM VARTANIAN / French / University of Virginia
CARMELO VIRGILLO / Portuguese / Arizona State University
VICTOR WEXLER / History / University of Maryland, Baltimore County
JAMES F. WOODRUFF / English / University of Western Ontario

Contents

Preface xi
O M BRACK, JR. / *Arizona State University*

Presidential Address: The First Fifteen Years of the American Society for Eighteenth-Century Studies 3
JEAN A. PERKINS / *Swarthmore College*

Diderot and the Technology of Life 11
ARAM VARTANIAN / *University of Virginia*

Diderot and Reader-Response Criticism: The Case of Jacques le fataliste 33
KATHRYN SIMPSON VIDAL / *Houston, Texas*

Voltaire's Fables of Discretion: The Conte philosophique in Le Taureau blanc 47
THOMAS M. CARR, JR. / *University of Nebraska*

Continuing Education and Other Innovations: An Eighteenth-Century Case Study 67
REED BENHAMOU / *Washington State University*

The Changing Meaning of "Sensibilité": 1654 till 1704 77
FRANK BAASNER / *Universität Tübingen*

Savages, Noble and Otherwise, and the French Enlightenment   97
MICHELLE BUCHANAN / *University of Southern California*

Teresa Margarida da Silva e Orta and the Portuguese Enlightenment   111
MONICA LETZRING / *Temple University*

Christina Dorothea Leporin (Erxleben), Sophia (Gutermann) von La Roche, and Angelika Kauffmann: Background and Dilemmas of Independence   127
PETER PETSCHAUER / *Appalachian State University*

A Scottish Middle-Class Family and Patronage: The Ancestors of Sir John Moore   145
HENRY L. FULTON / *Central Michigan University*

Dryden's Definition of a Play in An Essay of Dramatic Poesy: *A Structuralist Approach*   161
CHARLES H. HINNANT / *University of Missouri*

Calista and the "Equal Empire" of Her "Sacred Sex"   173
J. M. ARMISTEAD / *University of Tennessee*

Defoe, Political Parties, and the Monarch   187
MANUEL SCHONHORN / *Southern Illinois University*

The Word and the Thing in Swift's Prose   199
DAN DOLL / *Purdue University*

Song Form and the Mind in Christopher Smart's Later Poetry   211
MARK W. BOOTH / *Virginia Commonwealth University*

Samuel Johnson, The Vanity of Human Wishes, *and Biographical Criticism*   227
THOMAS JEMIELITY / *University of Notre Dame*

Johnson and Hume: Of Like Historical Minds   241
JOHN A. VANCE / *University of Georgia*

Images of the Orient: Goldsmith and the Philosophes   257
SAMUEL H. WOODS, JR. / *Oklahoma State University*

Is God Really Omniscient? or What Does God Know about Pain?   271
GEORGE B. WALL / *Lamar University*

Learning, Virtue, and the Term "Bluestocking"   279
SYLVIA H. MYERS / *Berkeley, California*

Executive Board, 1984–85   289

Institutional Members   291

Sponsoring Members   293

Patrons   295

Preface

There is "some pleasure," Johnson reminds us, in reflecting that those who have only "trifled till diligence was necessary" might still congratulate themselves upon the "superiority to multitudes who have trifled till diligence is vain." Months are spent selecting and editing the essays before sending them off to the press in November. The necessity of producing a preface did not concentrate my mind wonderfully then, and I now find myself in danger of joining the multitudes. The decreasing size of the volume has made it difficult for the editor to attempt to relate the essays to each other in a meaningful way. But what can be said, and with considerable pleasure, is that these essays are representative of the best scholarship in the eighteenth century.

O M Brack, Jr.

Arizona State University
June 27, 1985

Studies in Eighteenth-Century Culture

VOLUME 15

Presidential Address: The First Fifteen Years of the American Society for Eighteenth-Century Studies

JEAN A. PERKINS

The American Society for Eighteenth-Century Studies was incorporated in 1969 and held its first annual meeting in 1970. On this occasion, the fifteenth annual meeting, it seems appropriate to look backwards at the hopes and aspirations of the founders and to measure the accomplishments of these fifteen years against their ideas.

According to a recent survey compiled by Beatrice Fink, a member of the American Society as well as Secretary of the International Society for Eighteenth-Century Studies, there are currently fifteen national societies that belong to the International Society for Eighteenth-Century Studies. They cover the whole world on a geographical basis and include the Australian and Pacific Society, the Japanese Society, the Canadian and the American Societies, as well as most of the major European countries. Only three of these groups are older than ours: the Greek society was founded in 1962, but it has fewer than 200 members, although its annual journal *Ho Eranistis* has a circulation of approximately 300; the French came along in 1964, and are currently the second largest group with 1200 members; and the Dutch Werkgroep was formed in 1968. The American Society is the largest of these societies. The International Society holds a congress every four years and, as I understand the story, it was at the Second Congress held at St. Andrews, Scotland, in 1967 that the idea of founding an American Society was conceived. Three people were primarily responsible: Jim Clifford, Lester Crocker, and Don Greene. By great good fortune both the MLA and the AHA met in New York City at the same time in December of 1968. Leaflets were distributed at appropriate sessions of both societies inviting interested people to attend an open meeting at the Americana Hotel on December 29. I remember how thrilled I was when I attended that session to find at least 200 other people there. We had all been drawn together by the prospect of an interdisciplinary society that would foster "communication and cooperation among scholars in various disciplines engaged in the study of the period," to quote from the first brochure. Lester Crocker chaired the meeting; a vote was taken that established a provisional committee consisting of Clifford, Crocker, and Greene with three charges: first, to establish a provisional Executive Committee; second, to write a constitution; and third, to organize the first annual meeting to be held in the spring of 1970 so as not to coincide with either the MLA or the AHA. The three "Founding Fathers" quickly coopted Owen Aldridge, Louis Gottschalk, Warren Kirkendale, Richard Popkin, Charles Ritcheson, Peter Stanlis, Robert Wark, and Roy Miles to act as a provisional executive board. You will note the all-male nature of the "Founding Fathers," but the Society has always been open to women and has made a special effort to insure the presence of women on the board ever since the first elected slate in 1970.

In any case, 1969 was a busy year for this pioneering group. Jim Clifford took charge of drawing up a constitution; Lester Crocker as provisional president was responsible for the forthcoming First Annual Meeting; Don Greene as secretary took charge of publicity; Peter Stanlis as treasurer was heartened by the steadily growing bank balance as new members sent in their dues. Notices of the new organization appeared in the *Johnsonian News Letter, Studies in Burke and his Time*, the AHA *Newsletter*, and *PMLA*. A blue flyer was sent out in April which evidently had the desired effect since by February of 1970 there were 630 members who had all paid their $7 dues. I would like to quote the paragraph that sets out the activities contemplated for the new society.

> The provisional executive board is making plans for the first annual general meeting of the Society, to be held in Cleveland, Ohio, April 17–18, 1970, and is exploring the possibility of such other activities of the Society as the sponsorship of a journal, the compilation of an annual interdisciplinary bibliography of eighteenth-century studies, and the awarding of prizes for publications dealing with the eigh-

teenth century. A *News Letter* of the Society will be issued two or three times a year and will be sent to all members, and a directory of the membership will be published from time to time.

This was truly a prescient statement, since all of these activities did indeed come to fruition in the years ahead.

The Provisional Board met in September at which time it discussed finances (an ever important item at any board meeting), appointed committees, and explored the possibility of affiliating with an already existent journal, namely *Eighteenth-Century Studies,* as well as an already existent bibliography, *English Literature, 1660–1800: A Current Bibliography,* the annual bibliography issue of *Philological Quarterly.* Both of these publications had specialized in English literature up to then, but both of them were open to becoming interdisciplinary.

On December 23, Don Greene mailed out the first newsletter along with the program for the first annual meeting. Being a stickler over terminology, Don refused to christen his brief two-page typed document a *News Letter,* so he called it *A News Circular.* Those of you who have read *News Circular,* no. 51 that was distributed during the winter will note how faithful the Society has been to his wishes! The most exciting announcement was the promise of $3000 "to help set up a fund for book prizes." In reconstructing the history of the finances of the Society, I found that an additional $3000 was donated by the same generous patron the next year but that it was impossible to handle these funds as endowment since expenses were running ahead of income. So the $6000 was used up, and we are only now in a position to restore this sum to a real endowment fund. It will join the $1000 left to the Society in a bequest from Shirley Bill.

Just before the First Annual Meeting Peter Stanlis, who had incorporated the Society in Illinois, received the welcome news from the IRS that the American Society for Eighteenth-Century Studies did indeed qualify for exempt status. All gifts to the Society can be deducted as a charitable contribution and let me urge all of you to consider including the Society in your last will and testament if you are not in a position to make a donation here and now. We are currently solvent and operating in a fiscally sound manner, but there is very little cushion to fall back on. If we wish to embark on new ventures, we will need new funds to back them up.

The First Annual Meeting sponsored by Case Western Reserve drew over 250 members to Cleveland. It set the pattern for future meetings in certain respects: excellent plenary speakers from a variety of disciplines, distinguished foreign guests, a musical program, an art exhibit, a book exhibit, and the presentation of an eighteenth-century play. The Business Meeting had a crowded agenda: adopting a constitution, election of the Executive Board, the report of the Treasurer who recorded dues from 775 members, the announcement of a new series of annual volumes containing papers given at the meetings of the Society to be entitled *Studies in the Eighteenth Century* and to be published by Case Western Reserve University Press; the announcement of an agreement with the editors of *Eighteenth-Century Studies* to the effect that this journal would become the official journal of the Society; the announcement of an agreement with Curt Zimansky, editor of *Philological Quarterly,* to convert his annual bibliography of English literature into an interdisciplinary volume, *The Eighteenth Century: A Current Bibliography.* Much had been accomplished since December of 1968. In addition I have a very distinct memory of two events connected with the banquet that was held in the antique car museum a few blocks from the motel. The first one was trying at the time, but quite amusing in retrospect. After greetings from the president of Case Western Reserve and a few remarks from Don Greene, the master of ceremonies, Jim Clifford, asked Roland Desné, the secretary of the French Society, to say a few words. That he did! In French for twenty minutes! I shall never forget the look of anguish on Jim Clifford's face during that peroration. The other memory is anything but funny. We had all been warned not to walk to the museum alone but to go in groups for safety's sake. One member ignored this warning and was mugged on the way back to the motel. Fortunately neither of these incidents established a precedent. As far as I am aware, we have had no lengthy impromptu remarks in a foreign language at any banquet or luncheon since 1970, nor have any of our members been attacked during an annual meeting.

By the fall of 1970 four regional affiliates had been established. The already existent Samuel Johnson Society of the Northwest became an affiliate member of ASECS and three regional organizations were organized: midwestern, north central, and east central. This phenomenon has continued to grow. The program for this year lists eight regional societies, including two Johnson groups, as well as a Goethe group and a Lessing group. There are also three separate groups in Canada. The ASECS board sometimes worries that the local societies are taking over the tasks of the parent body, but we all rejoice in the fact that these societies all speak to the continuing growing interest in eighteenth-century studies. Our intrepid secretary, Richard Peterson, has visited every one of these affiliate societies' meetings during the course of this academic year and can report far more fully than I on their activities. Obviously many people find it easier to attend a meeting in their own region.

In terms of attendance at our national meetings, it ran to about 250 until the time of the International Congress held at Yale in 1975 which drew some 700 American members. Since then the attendance at our annual meeting has settled down at about 400. However New York City proved to be more popular running to 500+. This year's figures are not yet complete, but Charlie Knight reports preregistration of about 360. Membership has varied from 1500 to 1700 since 1977.

The format of the Annual Meeting has changed over the years. In addition to plenary speakers the Second Annual Meeting held at the University of Maryland devoted one-half day to section meetings representing the various disciplines identified in the constitution. The problem that soon became apparent was that this hardly stimulated interdisciplinary work. Take Modern Languages as an example. Even at the first meeting it had split up into two sections, Slavic holding its own session. By the next year there were five different sections in Modern Languages alone. Two changes in format appeared in 1974: this was the first meeting at which people were housed in a hotel rather than on a campus; this was also the first meeting at which seminars were arranged. Dissatisfaction with the general format led to the formation of a Committee on the Annual Meeting under the leadership of Howard Weinbrot which eventually recommended the format under which we are still functioning today: plenary sessions plus a series of seminars and workshops that are chosen by the Program Committee from suggestions contributed by individual members who have obtained a certain number of signatures on a petition. The first meeting to move to this format was held at Virginia in 1976 at which there were five plenary sessions and thirty seminars. For the last five years the number of seminars has stabilized at about fifty; some people fear that this may be a threat to the interdisciplinary nature of our society since some of the seminars are on narrowly defined topics. However conference participants can easily attend seminars on topics outside their own speciality, so the interdisciplinary thrust is preserved.

The Chicago meeting of 1978 was a first in a number of different ways. First of all, the meetings themselves took place in a hotel rather than on a campus. It was also the first time that the national office rather than the host institution really ran the meeting. Over the years there have been various problems associated with this situation. We still rely on a host institution to sponsor the meeting: subsidies must be found; speakers must be found and remunerated; a program must be arranged; innumerable details have to be attended to on the spot—but the national office retains ultimate responsibility for its Annual Meeting both in terms of content and in terms of finances. After a few rocky moments I think the system is now running relatively smoothly. Unfortunately we are just too large to be able to meet completely on a single campus and just too small to be able to handle the whole affair ourselves, as do the MLA and the AHA. Chicago was also the first time that we met at a luncheon rather than an evening banquet. This choice was dictated purely and simply by financial considerations; prices for an evening meal in a hotel had reached astronomical heights. Judging by what we had to fork out to eat together today, the luncheon may soon be displaced by a tea! Those of you who were at the Chicago meeting will remember with delight and awe the marvellous performance of the then President, John Pocock, who regaled us with a witty mock-heroic epic on the subject of the society.

In 1975 ASECS held its annual meeting in conjunction with the International Congress that was held at Yale University. We sponsored seven section meetings and took part in many others. The Business Meeting was stormy, as tends to be the habit at the International Society. A slate of candidates for the Executive Committee was drawn up by the outgoing Executive Committee and it was soon noted that not a single woman was included on the list. A large group of American women met in the courtyard of one of the Yale Colleges and formed the Women's Caucus of ASECS. By dint of much heated argument and lobbying of members of the International Executive Committee, during which I was told personally by one man that there were no women of sufficient scholarly stature to be asked to serve on such a distinguished body, a few names of women were finally included. The voting was overwhelmingly in favor of all the women added to the list, and thus the Women's Caucus of ASECS both got its start and its first political victory. It has operated effectively since then in achieving its two major goals: representing the interests of women members to the board and promoting women's studies, particularly at the annual meeting.

In addition to being a member of the International Society for Eighteenth-Century Studies, ASECS joined ACLS in 1976. This has been a great help for our executive secretary who attends two conferences per year sponsored by this umbrella organization. We were fortunate indeed to be accepted into membership of this august body so soon after our founding. Most other societies have had to wait at least a decade before they are deemed worthy of membership. We are also members of the National Humanities Alliance, an association based in Washington, D.C., that is basically a lobbying group for anything that concerns the humanities.

The "Founding Fathers" built well; most of their ideas continue to play a major part in the life of the society. We still rely heavily on support from institutions of higher learning, either as sponsors of our annual meeting or as subsidizers of our various publications, or as sponsoring members of ASECS itself. In 1970 there were only twenty-five institutional members; today there are ninety-three and this figure should continue to grow. We have also had a lot of support from NEH. A small grant in 1975 enabled ASECS to conduct a survey of its members' needs for research tools. This in turn led to a series of feasibility studies in which ASECS participated to determine whether a short-title catalogue of eighteenth-century British imprints was possible. This venture picked up steam fairly quickly, involving the British Library, the Library of Congress, and a whole stable of people working at Louisiana State University under Henry Snyder, director and editor of *ESTC* for North America. The NEH also made two grants to ASECS to support the production of an enlarged interdisciplinary bibliography. The story of this venture is far too complex to go into now; suffice it to say that delays in production resulted in an intolerable drain on the financial resources of the society and so the bibliography was reluctantly dropped in 1980. Fortunately for our members, AMS Press undertook to continue publication of *ECCB* guaranteeing a substantial discount to members of ASECS.

In terms of finances, ASECS has been on a roller-coaster ride that we hope is now over. In the last decade the annual financial report has reported assets ranging from $14,943 in 1980, a real low point, to $66,151 in 1982. I am not using this year's figures since they represent an inflated balance due to a change in accounting procedures but it certainly looks as if financial health has been restored to the society. I can vividly remember the problem with cash flow at the time I was treasurer in the mid-1970s; indeed, it got so bad that I actually transferred money from my own personal checking account into that of the society, knowing that the society would again be solvent in a month or so. My accountant was absolutely horrified. Obviously that is no way to insure a stable organization!

A final goal of the Founding Fathers has also been accomplished, that of "the awarding of prizes for publications dealing with the eighteenth century." The first prize for a scholarly article was awarded in 1972 to Bob Darnton's "The High Enlightenment and the Low Life of Literature in Pre-Revolutionary France" published in *Past and Present*.

When Jim Clifford died in April 1978, a group of his friends and colleagues started an endowment fund in his memory which has been used to fund the James L. Clifford Prize for the best article in the field of eighteenth-century studies. The first recipient was Judith Colton for her article on "Merlin's Cave and Queen Caroline: Garden Art as Political Propaganda" published in *Eighteenth-Century Studies*. The Clifford fund is now large enough to support an occasional Clifford Memorial Lecture at our annual meeting. This will be inaugurated tomorrow by Don Greene. The society also awards a prize for the most distinguished book published on the eighteenth century. The first annual Louis Gottschalk award was made to Peg Jacob for *The Newtonians and the English Revolution, 1689–1720* (Cornell, 1976). The most recent award went to John Sitter's *Literary Loneliness in Mid-Eighteenth-Century England* (Cornell, 1982).

An innovative program to stimulate younger scholars was initiated in 1982. ASECS joined forces with three of the most eminent research libraries in the country, the Folger, the Newberry, and the Clark, to subsidize short-term fellowships for research at these institutions by members who have been in the profession for ten years or less. The first recipient was Ruth Salvaggio of Virginia Polytechnic who both did research and participated in a seminar at the Folger in 1983.

In addition to rewarding research and publication in the field of eighteenth-century studies, the board has been concerned to find ways in which to stimulate good teaching as well. Everyone shuddered at the thought of trying to determine the "best" teacher of any given year, but various other approaches to this concern are currently being addressed by a special committee.

I believe that the American Society for Eighteenth-Century Studies has been a positive force in keeping the eighteenth century a living period in contemporary life. It has provided a forum for interdisciplinary research and discussion, both in its publications and its annual meetings; through the affiliated societies it has brought the eighteenth century to the doorsteps of many isolated researchers; it has spun off a number of important research tools, including *ECCB* and *ESTC*; it has encouraged good research; it has acted as a catalyst for any number of people who appreciate the opportunity to widen their horizons; and it has acted as a watchdog to determine that interdisciplinary work meets the same standards as more specialized work. I believe that it has indeed lived up to the Founding Fathers' hopes and aspirations, and I trust that with the dedicated support of all its members, the Society will continue to do so for at least the next fifteen years.

Diderot and the Technology of Life

ARAM VARTANIAN

A machine can be modified or reconstructed at will so as to fulfill more efficiently the purpose it is expected to serve. Ordinarily, this cannot be done with an organism, whose "life" depends on a basic structure that must not be tampered with. I say "ordinarily" because we know that it is possible, by means of genetic engineering, organ transplants, and even the replacement of organs by man-made "spare-parts," to treat organisms in ways that were once suited only to mechanical artifacts. Biomedical technology has tended in recent times to invalidate the usual divorce made between machines and organisms, and to promote between them instead a sort of common-law marriage. My intention at present is to show how this development, of which the moral implications are often disquieting, had an early—perhaps the earliest—anticipation in the writings of Diderot, particularly in his *Le Rêve de d'Alembert*.

The idea that animate beings might be reconstructable and modifiable appears to have first occurred to Diderot, although as yet somewhat dimly, in the *Pensées sur l'interprétation de la nature* (1753), where it figured suppositionally as part of a sketch of organic evolution. The following portion of a longer passage is relevant here: "Il semble que la nature se soit plu à varier le même mécanisme d'une infinité de manières différentes. Elle n'abandonne un genre de productions qu'après en avoir multiplié les individus sous toutes les faces possibles. . . . Ne croirait-on pas volontiers qu'il n'y a jamais eu qu'un premier animal, prototype de tous les animaux, dont la nature n'a fait qu'allonger, raccourcir, transformer, multiplier, oblitérer certains organes?"[1] By its curious turn of phrase, this statement points to a veiled meaning, especially if at the same time one compares it with the main textual source from which Diderot borrowed its scientific content. He had come across the transformist hypothesis, worded straightforwardly and without mention of any active role played by "nature," in Maupertuis' inspired guess that the phenomenon of genetic mutation might be the general cause behind the diversification of organic species: "Ne pourrait-on pas expliquer par là comment de deux seuls individus la multiplication des espèces les plus dissemblables aurait pu s'ensuivre? Elles n'auraient dû leur première origine qu'à quelques productions fortuites, dans lesquelles les parties élémentaires n'auraient pas tenu l'ordre qu'elles tenaient dans les animaux père et mère. Chaque degré d'erreur aurait fait une nouvelle espèce; et à force d'écarts répétés serait venue la diversité infinie des animaux que nous voyons aujourd'hui."[2] Diderot's version of Maupertuis' theory introduced into it his own characterization of the process of continual mutation from which evolution had resulted. First, he "mechanized" the process ("la nature se soit plu à varier le même mécanisme"), as if the changes wrought by nature in the prototypic organism were like the redesigning of a machine into all its structural variants. Secondly, he personified nature, as if, like some demiurgic artisan, it had set deliberately to work reshaping its own substance ("la nature n'a fait qu'allonger, raccourcir, transformer, multiplier, oblitérer certains organes"). While the fact may not yet be apparent in the *Interprétation de la nature*, this creative nature which, having usurped the prerogative of God, fabricates life in new forms to "please itself" is the metaphorical mask worn by its own "literary" creator, the atheist and materialist Diderot.

That fact, however, became much more apparent, some fifteen years later, in the *Rêve de d'Alembert*, where the central problem was to expound the purely natural origin of organic beings. Diderot seized the occasion to speculate also on the possibility of their artificial origin. This auxiliary theme runs like a leitmotiv through the entire work, which explores its consequences in a series of "variations," each dealing with one of its many aspects.

The human urge to create life, rooted in physiology, has always found two different modes of expression. The more literal and concrete of these is the act of reproduction. But that by no means exhausts the need from which it springs. Procreation, which is a capability we share with every animal species, remains essentially passive, for its outcome is decided by impersonal laws of nature that obey their own, not our, ends. The power really to create life would be that of doing so in accordance with a conscious design. And so, since the earliest times, the sexual generation of life has had to be complemented by another method: that of its artistic creation. But while a painter, sculptor, or poet can bring into existence whatever objects he wills to exist, this ability is flawed to the extent that its products are only simulacra which, at their best, give the illusion of being alive. The sharing of creativity between, on the one hand, man as reproducer and artist, and, on the other, God, acting alone or through Nature, as the true and original creator of all things had persisted for millennia, legitimated and consecrated by the history of culture both primitive and civilized. This *entente,* which ratified an actual state of affairs in the distribution of powers, went unquestioned, except occasionally in myth, until the Enlightenment, when all kinds of traditional arrangements were subverted. It then finally became vulnerable to challenge as a result of two crucial developments typical of the eighteenth century in France: the rise of biology as a science independent of religion, and, closely related to that event, the success of atheistic materialism as a philosophical position. The thought could therefore emerge that it might be possible to "make" live beings, not merely in the reproductive or representational sense, but also in a more direct and ambitious manner—that is, to create life, if not absolutely (for that might prove too difficult), at least relatively, by deriving new forms of it from those already existing, as a technology invents new types of objects that cannot be said to have existed before. It was in this regard that Diderot felt tempted, like a latter-day Prometheus, to steal the "vital fire" of the Gods. The temptation found utterance as a "dream of science" in the *Rêve de d'Alembert,* where his friend, and co-editor with him of the *Encyclopédie,* became (as is common enough in a dream) the less inhibited *alter ego* of himself.

This subject first appears through the exchange of views about Falconet's statue in the "Entretien," which opens the triptych of dialogues.[3] Diderot's remarks on the art of sculpture, influenced by his materialist outlook, focus on the problem of converting nonliving into living matter. Falconet's work depicted Pygmalion in the act of conferring, with the miraculous aid of Aphrodite, the gift of life on his statue of Galatea. But this sculptural *mise en abîme* offers, in effect, a negative example of the process by which, according to the *Rêve de d'Alembert,* life is created. For we are told that a statue, however ingeniously executed, cannot even begin to approximate an animate body. Yet Diderot himself, earlier in the "Entretien," had based his materialism on a postulate that seems inconsistent with such a judgment: namely, *il faut que la pierre sente.* That condition—supposing a metamorphosis of unfeeling marble into feeling flesh—was precisely what the mythic feat of Pygmalion had satisfied. But Falconet, in trying to portray in his turn Pygmalion's achievement, had obviously failed to equal it. Thus Diderot's reference to his statue makes the fundamental point that, with respect to the problem of the creation of life, myth and science, or art and nature, are not to be confused and that, moreover, nature takes precedence over art. And so, to support his argument experimentally, Diderot proposes that Falconet's masterpiece be shattered, pulverized, mixed with soil, and ultimately turned into cabbage! As a metaphor signifying the displacement of myth by science, or, more exactly, the transformation of one into the other as the statue itself is transformed into an organic substance, this scene from the "Entretien" could hardly be improved.[4]

The myth it evokes, however, can be read also in reverse, to give both sides of the same allegorical coin. The statue, despite its imagined recycling into food, remains a symbol of human, in contrast to natural, creativity. Although Diderot does not identify in the text the actual subject of what he calls simply Falconet's "chef d'oeuvre," he does not have to, because the statue in question, no less than that of any sculptor aiming at lifelike imitation, suggests the ancient myth and the general truth implied by it, especially in the setting, as here given, of a discussion about the creation of life. Now the underlying truth of the Pygmalion story, beyond what it reveals figuratively about the artist's relationship to his art, has to do with an awareness of the lurking desire in man to rival God and Nature by creating, not just lifelike artifacts, but life itself. The reference to Falconet's statue thus adumbrates a notion that will be intimately linked to Diderot's exposition of materialism—the notion of actualizing by scientific means the legendary project of Pygmalion, and in so doing to wrest from Nature, along with its greatest secret, some of its power as well. Falconet was on the right track, but he had employed the wrong art; for to animate stone what is needed is not hammer and chisel, but biotechnology.[5]

Diderot thereupon tells a skeptical D'Alembert how the sculptor's failure to elicit life from stone may be redeemed by recourse to organic chemistry: "Lorsque le bloc de marbre est réduit en poudre impalpable, je mêle cette poudre à de l'humus ou terre végétale; je les pétris bien ensemble; j'arrose le mélange, je le laisse putréfier un an, deux ans, un siècle. . . . Lorsque le tout s'est transformé en une matière à peu près homogène, en humus, savez-vous ce que je fais? . . . J'y sème des pois, des fèves, des choux, d'autres plantes légumineuses. Les plantes se nourrissent de la terre, et je me nourris des plantes."[6] In this account of how the statue (or at least some small part of it) can be brought to a living state, Diderot's purpose is to show that the production of life, or the "animalization" of matter, is not an incomprehensible mystery, but a sequence of chemical reactions which we are able to not only observe and analyze, but also to set in motion and control. The syntax and rhetoric of the passage are, philosophically, inseparable from its message. The assimilation of inert matter to living tissue is expressed in language that depicts less an external process of nature than an operation that is manipulated, from beginning to end, by a personal will. Diderot's insistence on the first-person pronoun as the subject of a string of transitive verbs—"je mêle," "je pétris," "j'arrose," "je le laisse putréfier," "j'y sème des pois," "je me nourris"—conjures up, cumulatively, the image of a *homo faber* who, in the concluding sentence, steps proudly forth as the "cause" of life and *sensibilité:* "Je fais donc de la chair ou de l'âme . . . une matière activement sensible" (p. 264). The innuendo of this text— that "living matter" can be fabricated—sets the stage for the unfolding of the theme of biotechnology in all three dialogues.

The next episode makes, from another angle, the same point as that made by Falconet's statue. It consists of a description of D'Alembert's formation in his mother's womb. Diderot explains how, from the seminal "molécules" in the "jeunes et frêles machines" of his parents to the famous mathematician that was the end-product, the creation of D'Alembert was carried out "en mangeant et par d'autres opérations purement mécaniques" (p. 265). But behind the obviously materialist meaning of this embryological biography, there is a deeper and bolder implication present. It comes noticeably to the fore in a statement that, although purporting to summarize the physiology of reproduction, manages to sound more like a set of rules for the manufacture of human beings: "Voici en quatre mots la formule générale: Mangez, digérez, distillez *in vasi licito, et fiat homo secundum artem.*" This oddly framed bit of advice has been called a "parodie moliéresque d'une ordonnance médicale," and a joke on the chemico-mechanical approach to the origin of life: "il n'y a pas seulement de la drôlerie à assimiler la génération à un processus d'ordre chimique. Diderot veut insister sur le caractère purement mécanique de l'opération."[7] While it is true, as we shall see, that Diderot has in mind the "purely mechanical character" of generation, the humorous point of his prescription has nothing to do with either medicine or Molière. As for the Latin formula, it is indeed a parody—but of the Bible. The *fiat homo*, which echoes a group of pronouncements in the Vulgate: *fiat lux, fiat firmamentum, fiant luminaria,* and the accompanying *secundum artem*, which mimics language found in the same place, such as *sementem secundum speciem suam* and *omne volatile secundum genus suum*, transport us back to the opening pages of *Genesis*. As in the history of Pygmalion, we are thus confronted again by a myth about the creation of life. But in rendering the parodic thought as *fiat homo secundum artem*, rather than, in the style and spirit of Scripture, as something like: *fiat homo secundum speciem suam*, Diderot has distinguished between natural generation within the species and what will interest him in particular: artificial production outside it. His recipe, which translates with admirable precision the idea of a technology having man as its object, allows us to glimpse the *arrière-pensée* of the entire passage in which it occurs, and of which it is in fact a summing up: "voici en quatre mots la formule générale." The "quatre mots" that count especially are, of course, *fiat homo secundum artem*.[8]

Later in the "Entretien," the embryological proof of materialism is repeated, this time concerning the formation *in ovo* of a bird or fowl. The antireligious and naturalistic aim of this text is announced from the start: "Voyez-vous cet oeuf? C'est avec cela qu'on renverse toutes les écoles de théologie et tous les temples de la terre." There follows a sketch of how the egg, "une masse insensible avant que le germe y soit introduit," is by degrees converted into a full-fledged animal. We observe, once more, that no extramaterial factors are involved in reproduction, the nascent organism being visibly the outcome of "la sensibilité, propriété générale de la matière, ou produit de l'organisation," and of the physical conditions that favor its maturation. From these data, a broad philosophical inference is drawn: "on en conclura . . . qu'avec une matière inerte, disposée d'une certaine manière, imprégnée d'une autre matière inerte, de la chaleur et du mouvement, on obtient de la sensibilité, de la vie, de la mémoire, de la conscience, des passions, de la pensée" (p. 376). Here, too, the way this conclusion is put is not indifferent to what it is meant to convey. Who, the reader may well wonder, is this "on" who, not content merely to describe what he sees, also "obtains"—that is, brings into being—a whole sequence of phenomena peculiar to higher organic life? "On" cannot be nature, for grammatically it designates a personal, even if unidentified, subject; nor, in view of the author's atheism, can it be God. This "on" is apparently the same person who commenced the passage with the prediction: "C'est avec cela qu'on renverse . . . etc." "On" is Diderot himself, along with his ideal reader, both of whom learn the same lesson from a hypothetical experiment, the purpose of which is to confirm that animal life and behavior are "derivable" from matter. The experimenter is shown not only as observing the facts of such a derivation, but also as its *metteur en scène*.

The topic of foetal growth recurs on two other occasions. It comprises the exordium of D'Alembert's oneiric speculations on organic nature: "Un point vivant. . . . Non, je me trompe. Rien d'abord, puis un point vivant. . . . A ce point il s'en applique un autre, encore un autre; et par ces applications successives il résulte un être un, car je suis bien un" (p. 287–88). The amplification of these remarks transcribes in a different key the two descriptions already given of the reproductive process. The main difference is that now the events referred to are more ostensibly a product of D'Alembert's (i.e., Diderot's) own mind. For we realize that while he is dreaming his consciousness is not subordinated to the real world of sense impressions, and that what he says about the organism taking shape from its basic elements must therefore, in large part, be imagined by him without the benefit of empirical control. The oneiric medium, among its various functions in the "Rêve" dialogue, permits Diderot in this scene to transpose ontogenetical phenomena from the sphere of normal scientific discourse to that of subjective evocation. In proportion as the gulf between subjectivity and objectivity is diminished in sleep, the dreamer is more at liberty to rearrange the natural world as he sees fit. While D'Alembert assembles mentally his "points vivants" until they compose a living organic entity, we cannot but feel that what he beholds is as much a creature of his own devising as it is something known to him independently of his "poetic" will. At the same time, his speech assumes the oracular tone of a visionary who, no longer bound by "mere" reality, sets over against it a reality of his own. D'Alembert *dreams* of the immanent production of life: the dream provides here not only the outward vehicle of his monologue, but also its inward metaphorical sense. Diderot, by the clever use of a dreaming spokesman who remembers and develops the opinions that he himself has stated in the "Entretien," has found in the role played by D'Alembert a suitable *porte-parole,* or rather a "porte-rêve," for the articulation of what is in effect his own dream of creating life.

Elsewhere in the "Rêve," Dr. Bordeu traces an embryonic history of Mlle de l'Espinasse, which is the counterpart of D'Alembert's history previously given: "D'abord vous n'étiez rien. Vous fûtes, en commençant, un point imperceptible, formé de molécules plus petites, éparses dans le sang, la lymphe de votre père ou de votre mère; ce point devint un fil délié, puis un faisceau de fils" (p. 320). As Mlle de l'Espinasse is brought gradually to the moment of her birth, the accent falls on the ramifications of her nervous system and its organs of sensation. No subject in the *Rêve de d'Alembert,* we notice by now, is treated with such persistence as that of ontogeny. The enigma of the emergence of life *ex molecula* was for Diderot the principal obstacle that a materialist philosophy had to surmount. But why "solve" the problem four different times, and each time by giving a similar embryological answer? Diderot's perseverance indicates that he did not consider it solved altogether to his satisfaction; that, beyond the puzzle of the reproduction of life, there remained for him the far more stubborn one of its *creation,* which continued to resist his efforts and to excite his curiosity. To know what a living thing really is, one should know also how it got that way in a universe that appears overwhelmingly nonliving, for the logical imperative of biology is preeminently genetic. Such was the kind of knowledge that Diderot pursued relentlessly through the embryogenetic narratives of the *Rêve de d'Alembert*. But the test of possessing that knowledge with certainty depends, in turn, on the ability to simulate life "experimentally," that is, on the verification by synthesis of its natural origin. The ultimate challenge to biology is therefore the fabrication of life in the laboratory. Diderot recognized, intuitively, that just this challenge was the supreme issue not only of biology, but also, in consequence, of a materialism which, like his, rested squarely on that science. His preoccupation with ontogenesis was not merely an attempt to understand the mechanics of reproduction; it was, much more than that, an attempt to grasp the secret of nature by virtue of which organic beings might be "created." Totally lacking, of course, any practical means with which to attain so remote a goal, Diderot utilized the sole means at his disposal: language. In the episodes already encountered, all of which presume to explain how an organism is constituted from its primary building blocks, the philosophe has taken on himself the task of a poet-scientist who strives to prod into being (as if behind *omne ex ovo* there is an older maxim: *omne ex verbo*) the elusive phenomenon of life.

An important aspect of this aspiration was Diderot's faith in the claim advanced by Needham, and accepted for a time by many contemporary scientists, that it was possible, with infusions of macerated animal and vegetable substances, to produce at random a whole assortment of primitive, usually microscopic, organisms. The experiments on which Needham had based his case for spontaneous generation were, of course, faulty and misleading, as Spallanzani demonstrated in 1765. But Diderot continued to believe in what Voltaire had meanwhile facetiously dubbed Needham's "eels" because these agreed all too well with his own "system." He therefore gave the subject a prominent place in D'Alembert's dream. Spontaneous generation, if it were true, would mean that the elementary materials—Buffon had called them "molécules organiques," a concept favored also by Diderot—out of which all living things are made could, under the proper conditions, be combined by experimental art into "animalcules." This manipulated spontaneity amounted, in effect, to a fabricated heterogenesis, even if only at the lowest levels. Thus spontaneous generation, besides implying the virtuality of life in matter, a postulate fundamental to Diderot's materialism, also indicated in matter a biotechnological potential—more precisely, the convertibility of dead organic substances into altogether new and unrelated species. In the paragraph of the "Rêve" where D'Alembert ruminates on the results obtained by Needham, he expands their implications to the farthest limit, imagining by analogy the origin of life on earth, and even in the cosmos: "le vase où il apercevait tant de générations momentanées, il le comparait à l'univers; il voyait dans une goutte d'eau l'histoire du monde. Cette idée lui paraissait grande; il la trouvait tout à fait conforme à la bonne philosophie qui étudie les grands corps dans les petits. Il disait: 'Dans la goutte d'eau de Needham, tout s'exécute et se passe en un clin d'oeil. Dans le monde, le même phénomène dure un peu davantage'" (p. 299). The entire passage is a myth of Creation retold materialistically, and a scientific substitute for its religious version in *Genesis*. Here God is conspicuous by his absence, while it is man—i.e., Needham himself, or anyone caring to repeat his experiments—who, with a test tube of suitably prepared matter in his hand, can transform a "drop of water" microcosmically into a kind of "world," thereby recapitulating, as if by a *fiat animalcula*, the creative act of Nature.

Any doubt that might still linger about the general theme being scrutinized in the *Rêve de d'Alembert* is dispelled by Diderot's extraordinary interest in the polyp. Trembley's discovery, in 1744, of the amazing behavior of that zoophyte was a scientific event that had wide repercussions on eighteenth-century thought, and perhaps no one felt those effects more radically than Diderot. The fresh water hydra, a plant like animal that could regenerate as a complete organism from each of the pieces into which it was cut up, seemed to render palpable the vital principle itself. Not only did it undermine the traditional dichotomy between vegetation and animality; it went against the preformationist theory of the origin of life, with which the more conservative sector of the Enlightenment shored up its faith in the teleological fixity of organic forms. But, more specially, the polyp's regenerative powers came to represent for the scientific imagination of the period the rough equivalent of what the artificial creation of life would represent for that of our own age. To an inventive and speculative materialist like Diderot, all this suggested that life might be an inherent property of matter which, along with its properties of extension and motion, could be modified at will in ways that would make the scientist a party to the creation—or rather, the re-creation—of organic beings. Such, it would seem, was the reason why the polyp so fascinated Diderot that he made of it, in the "Rêve," a symbol of the recombinant potential of living matter, that is, a symbol of biotechnology itself.

The privileged status of the polyp in the "Rêve" is brought out clearly through Diderot's well-known image of the swarm of bees as a model for the organism. That analogy had already been mentioned by both Maupertuis and Bordeu. However, Diderot's motive for borrowing it from them is disclosed in the novel use to which he put it. To make the image even more concretely "organic," he first supposed, rather surrealistically, that the bees would merge into one continuous body. He then pictured that this unified living mass would be severed, like a polyp, into many pieces: "Prenez vos ciseaux. . . . Approchez doucement, tout doucement, et séparez-moi ces abeilles, mais prenez garde de les diviser par la moitié du corps, coupez juste à l'endroit où elles se sont assimilées par les pattes. . . . Voyez-vous comment elles s'envolent chacune à son côté? Elles s'envolent une à une, deux à deux, trois à trois. Combien il y en a!" (p. 294). This fantasy reveals the dreamer D'Alembert/Diderot engaged in the activity of creating new combinations of life out of the protoplasmic stuff that his cluster of bees has now become. The very conceivability of such a substance is owing to the example of the polyp: "ce tout, formé d'abeilles imperceptibles, sera un véritable polype que vous ne détruirez qu'en l'écrasant."

But the best is yet to come. Diderot's flight of fancy has in prospect no merely apiarian goal; more enterprisingly, it will be concerned with ameliorating his own race. Before long, the talk gets around to "human polyps." Although these, it is admitted, cannot be found anywhere on earth, D'Alembert conjectures that they might well reside extraterrestrially: "Dans Jupiter, ou dans Saturne, des polypes humains! . . . L'homme se résolvant en une infinité d'hommes atomiques, qu'on renferme entre des feuilles de papier comme les oeufs d'insectes . . . une société d'hommes formée, une province entière peuplée des débris d'un seul, cela est tout à fait agréable à imaginer" (p. 297). This method of rapidly increasing the population corresponded to the demographic policy of Diderot's France. But statistics were not his chief interest. It would be even more desirable, he felt, to create people with highly specialized aptitudes. This result, surmises D'Alembert, might be achieved by an *ex vitro* production of new strains of humanity with samples of living matter selected from particular areas of the body: "la dissolution de différentes parties ne donne-t-elle pas des hommes de différents caractères? La cervelle, le coeur, la poitrine, les pieds, les mains, les testicules. . . . Oh! comme cela simplifie la morale! . . . Une chambre chaude, tapissée de petits cornets, et sur chacun de ces cornets une étiquette: guerriers, magistrats, philosophes, poètes, cornet de courtisans, cornet de catins, cornet de rois" (p. 298). It is in this situation that the somewhat bemusing formula: *fiat homo secundum artem* acquires its full significance. Diderot's hallucinatory excursus into science fiction removes all restraints from his projected technology of life. In doing so, it brings together and harmonizes his various talents as a novelist, moral philosopher, *amateur* of science, and editor of the *Encyclopédie*. The spectacle he has called forth is a laboratory where the raw material of human beings, neatly arranged in test tubes, waits to be manufactured into finished products designed to perform in a superior fashion whatever their social duty requires. Diderot's thinking, or rather fantasizing, however fugitive and bizarre it may seem, is nonetheless at this point a reflection of the solid and sober volumes of the *Encyclopédie* that he had devoted to the "arts et métiers." His synthesis of biology and technology, with its aim of contriving human types that can function with the efficiency of machines, is a recognizable, though farfetched, expression of the Enlightenment idea of "perfectibilité," transposed from machinery to the organism. The "Rêve" betrays, in this portion of text, the unbridled ambition of a philosophe turned momentarily *Dieu artisan!* To be sure, none of this can be taken verbatim, for it all happens in a "dream." Yet we know that a dream, even when it is purely literary or philosophical, communicates its own kind of truth—that of wishes, ulterior motives, and sometimes also of prophecies.

Diderot's vision of genetic engineering, thus stimulated by the polyp's strange malleability and Needham's theory of spontaneous generation, is taken up later in the "Rêve" in a less unreal but still largely fictive manner. He supposes that, as the embryo matures, its structure is differentiated under the influence of a bundle of what he calls "brins" that are present already in the fertilized ovum; and, moreover, that each of these filaments is responsible for the formation of a specific part of the fetal anatomy. The notion of such a genetic apparatus prompts Diderot, voicing himself through Bordeu, to try to direct its operations in such a way as to determine predictably the effects obtained. It is explained, for instance, that if the "brin qui formera les yeux" is mutilated, the resulting organism will be eyeless or perhaps a "Cyclops." Other manipulations will induce corresponding changes in the foetus, which is perceived, consequently, as something to be constructed—or "deconstructed," as the case may be—by the will of an artificer: "Supprimez un autre brin du faisceau, le brin qui doit former le nez, l'animal sera sans nez. Supprimez le brin qui doit former l'oreille, l'animal sera sans oreilles, ou n'en aura qu'une. . . . Continuez la suppression des brins et l'animal sera sans tête, sans pieds, sans main" (p. 325). The syntax of this quotation, consisting of a sequence of imperatives, is, we discern, similar in its thematic intent to what we found earlier in the dictum: "Mangez, digérez, distillez *in vasi licito, et fiat homo secundum artem.*" It, too, leaves an impression that we are dealing with a set of instructions on how to fabricate a human being, as if the word sought to become flesh, but in a technological, not a theological, sense. Diderot was enchanted by the organic combinations that mastery of the genetic mechanism made possible. He went on: "Ce n'est pas tout. Doublez quelques-uns des brins du faisceau, et l'animal aura deux têtes, quatre yeux, quatre oreilles, trois testicules, trois pieds, quatre bras, six doigts à chaque main. Dérangez les brins du faisceau, et les organes seront déplacés: la tête occupera le milieu de la poitrine, les poumons seront à gauche, le coeur à droite. Collez ensemble deux brins, et les organes se confondront; les bras s'attacheront au corps; les cuisses, les jambes et les pieds se réuniront, et vous aurez toutes les sortes de monstres imaginables." The entire passage plays freely on the theme of a technical, man-made creation of life-forms.

Diderot is aware that if the organism can be restructured according to a variety of specifications, it would in the end resemble a machine, for both would be perfectible products of human skill rather than stable effects of natural forces. This affinity is stressed in the comments of Mlle de l'Espinasse on Bordeu's genetic hypothesis: "Mais il me semble qu'une machine aussi composée qu'un animal, une machine qui naît d'un point, d'un fluide agité . . . une machine qui s'avance à sa perfection par une infinité de développements successifs; une machine dont la formation régulière ou irrégulière dépend d'un paquet de fils minces, déliés et flexibles, d'une espèce d'écheveau où le moindre brin ne peut être cassé, rompu, déplacé, manquant, sans conséquence fâcheuse pour le tout, devrait se nouer, s'embarrasser encore plus souvent dans le lieu de sa formation que mes soies sur ma tournette." In these lines, the anaphoric highlighting of "machine" to denote the organism in general, as well as the parallel drawn between the mechanism of heredity and a "tournette"—which was a spinning device that figures among the plates of the *Encyclopédie*—

leave little doubt as to how closely the technological was allied in Diderot's mind with the creation of life. Those who maintain that his materialism was vitalistic to the point of excluding the mechanistic paradigm from biology would do well to ponder this and comparable statements in his works. Diderot's receptivity to vitalism, although an essential feature of his natural philosophy, did not in fact prevent him, when it suited his purpose, from conceiving mechanistically of organic systems, that is, from defining the organism as literally a "machine vivante." In the example just cited, the technological ideal invades and encompasses the central phenomenon of life, and perforce mechanizes it, in proportion as Diderot feels a need to exercise control over the forms and functions of living things—and especially those of the human species.

The model of a genetic weaving device by means of which animate beings could be, as it were, unraveled and rewoven to order appealed so much to Diderot that, near the end of the "Rêve", he returned to it in a lengthy recapitulation. Mlle de l'Espinasse is led to the following conclusion from Bordeu's *exposé:* "D'après vos principes, il me semble que, par une suite d'opérations purement mécaniques, je réduirais le premier génie de la terre à une masse de chair inorganisée, à laquelle on ne laisserait que la sensibilité du moment, et que l'on ramènerait cette masse informe de l'état de stupidité la plus profonde qu'on puisse imaginer à la condition de l'homme de génie" (p. 366). This, we readily guess, can be done by eliminating, restoring, or otherwise tinkering with the genelike "brins": "Exemple, j'ôte à Newton les deux brins auditifs, et plus de sensations de sons; les brins olfactifs, et plus de sensations d'odeurs; les brins optiques, et plus de sensations de couleurs; les brins palatins, et plus de sensations de saveurs; je supprime ou brouille les autres, et adieu l'organisation du cerveau, la mémoire, le jugement, les désirs, les aversions, les passions, la volonté, la conscience du soi, et voilà une masse informe qui n'a retenu que la vie et la sensibilité." The repetitiveness of actions recounted in the first person singular sets in relief, as in the incident of Falconet's statue, the willfulness with which Diderot, speaking through Mlle de l'Espinasse, sees generation as an event under the management of a human agent. His use of language is here inappropriate for giving a neutral account of a natural process; instead, it intervenes deliberately into a process of nature with the aim of determining and modifying the outcome. Diderot's syntax, at the service of his technological consciousness, has become manifestly a tool for acting upon, rather than representing, the biological reality that interests him.

Mlle de l'Espinasse, after having taken Newton apart, puts him back together again by reversing the procedure just described. The vitalist metaphor of the spider spinning its web, with which she had previously characterized the formation of an organism, is thus in the end technologized and mechanized without reserve. One may wonder why Newton, of all people, was chosen for this purpose. The choice makes good figurative sense, if it is recalled that his name had become, in eighteenth-century France, synonymous with mechanical and experimental philosophy itself. What could have been more fitting than to deconstruct and reconstruct Newton by his own scientific method, doing with his person what he had done, for example, with light?

One may wonder, also, about the provenance of Diderot's genetic model. Almost all the opinions in the *Rêve de d'Alembert* pertaining to biology, physiology, and medicine are traceable, despite literary distortions, to his reading of contemporary authorities, such as Haller, Buffon, Maupertuis, Bordeu, La Mettrie, Whyte, and others. But in the case of his genetic weaving machine, there is no source but Diderot's own ingenuity. It would appear that, having found nothing in the relevant literature that could help him to envision, from the standpoint of genetics, how a technology of living things might be feasible, he devised a hypothesis of his own which was eminently suited to precisely such an objective. Moreover, in yielding to that motive and to his imagination, Diderot also hit, coincidentally, on an explanation of the workings of heredity that strikes the historian of science as far more plausible and promising than any others that were current at the time.[9]

The "Suite de l'entretien," the brief third dialogue of the *Rêve de d'Alembert*, has never been related satisfactorily to the architecture of the work as a whole. After the philosophical and scientific density of the preceding sections, it could be taken as a casual anticlimax, or a mere appendage. Yet its linkage to the "Entretien" and the "Rêve," as well as its intrinsic value, become clearer in the light of what has been said about Diderot's quest for a biotechnology. That theme, which had been partly obscured by several others peculiar to his materialist philosophy in the two main dialogues, emerges at last as the conversational focus of the "Suite," when Mlle de l'Espinasse raises the issue that is its point of departure and arrival: "Que pensez-vous du mélange des espèces?" Hybridization, it goes without saying, is also a technique for the production of new forms of life—a technique not mentioned until now in the *Rêve de d'Alembert*, but which, in the eighteenth century, was the only practical means available for modifying the patterns of organic nature. Bordeu informs Mlle de l'Espinasse that she has asked a "question de physique, de morale, et de poétique." Especially of poetics, because "l'art de créer des êtres qui ne sont pas, à l'imitation de ceux qui sont, est de la vraie poésie" (pp. 374–75). But such a goal, which was presented in the dream-context of the "Rêve" as fantasy, now becomes, on the disappearance of D'Alembert and, with him, of the work's oneiric dimension, something more like an experimental project. In answer to Mlle de l'Espinasse, who repeats her query: "Que pensez-vous du mélange des espèces?" Bordeu asserts: "je vous dirai que, grâce à notre pusillanimité, à nos répugnances, à nos lois, à nos préjugés, il y a très peu d'expériences faites, qu'on ignore quelles seraient les copulations tout à fait infructueuses . . . quelles sortes d'espèces on se pourrait promettre de tentatives variées at suivies . . . si l'on ne multiplierait pas en cent façons diverses les races des mulets" (pp. 381–82). It turns out that one of Bordeu's (or rather Diderot's) fond utilitarian hopes of this type is the creation of a new breed of "chèvre-pieds," a cross between goat and *homo sapiens*, which will be "vigoureuse, intelligente, infatigable, et véloce." This new species, an offshoot of the satyrs of antiquity, would replace the poor wretches condemned to employment as domestics or as "beasts of burden" in the colonies. The prospect of such a zoological marvel causes Mlle de l'Espinasse to exclaim: "Vite, vite, docteur, mettez-vous à la besogne, et faites-nous des chèvre-pieds." This demand: "faites-nous des chèvre-pieds" rhymes, of course, with the general formula: *fiat homo secundum artem,* of which it is a particular application.

The exchange between the two interlocutors of the "Suite" may be regarded as an *interpretation* of D'Alembert's dream, whereas in the "Rêve" their remarks were an amplifying commentary on it. The word "suite" has here the double meaning of a "continuation" of the preceding dialogues, and of the "consequence" to which the argument in them leads. In keeping with the latter sense, the "Suite de l'entretien" pursues in the daylight of the next afternoon the murky nightthoughts of D'Alembert's fitful sleep; that is, it offers a conscious, post-oneiric association to the content of the dream that has just taken place. If it thus provides a key for deciphering the "Rêve," then the dream-strategy of the middle portion of the trilogy would seem to have, besides the epistemological and artistic functions which critics have recognized, that of a visionary wish-fulfillment. The author's dark desire, verbalized as psychodrama through the characters he has put on stage, would in that event be an assertion of power over phenomena that are, ordinarily, held to lie beyond human reach. This makes D'Alembert's dream, as dreams frequently are, an act of over-reaching—a transgression of conventional limits. The hybris of biotechnology, which, because Diderot did not believe in God, was therefore directed against Nature, called for moral justification and reassurance. Hence in the "Suite" we find the unconditionally self-absolving maxim: "Tout ce qui est ne peut être ni contre nature ni hors de nature" (p. 380). This grants to man the right, provided he can do so, to recreate as he pleases animate no less than inanimate objects. Still, Diderot remained vaguely aware of an infringement, from which, nevertheless, he was resolved not to recoil. This ambivalence of uneasiness and willfullness is expressed *sexually* in the "Suite" through a discussion of various practices prohibited as being "contrary to nature." Bordeu, however, is at pains to defend them as useful, or at least to excuse them as harmless. Because sexuality is the universal symbol, not to say the actual instrument, for both the production and the perversion of life, the lure of biotechnology and erotic impropriety are joined together in the "Suite," in order that both kinds of transgression against Nature might be destigmatized as triumphs of human resourcefulness over moralistic taboos. In connection with D'Alembert's dream, the final dialogue is thus *apologia* as well as interpretation.

How and why did the biotechnological theme find its way into the *Rêve de d'Alembert?* Serving as a corollary and support of materialism, it undercuts the basic claim made by deists (like D'Alembert) and more orthodox thinkers that the "mystery" of living things could not be clarified except by assuming that only God, soul, and final causes—the stock-in-trade of metaphysics—had the power to endow matter with animate form. A science of biology able to attain the same result demystifies the phenomenon of life and, simultaneously, such an argument based on it. More broadly, Diderot's wish to refashion life may even be understood as a global metaphor for the Enlightenment itself. In this respect, the re-forming of man by science, like the re-forming of society by other intellectual means, sprang at different levels of consciousness from the same outlook typical of *Lumières.* The truly original element in that outlook—the one which, at any rate, defined it more fatefully than any other—was that, for the first time, the human individual was seen by some less as a creature of God or Nature, than as the object of a self-creative intention. The motto of the Enlightenment, too, could have been: *fiat homo secundum artem.*

Several other factors predisposed Diderot to his dream of biotechnology. One of these was the concept of a transformistic nature which itself exemplified, as a universal law, that organic beings were modifiable indefinitely. Science no less than art could thus be expected to pursue an *imitatio naturae*. Another factor was Diderot's teratology. His interest in abnormally constituted persons, for whom he felt a sympathetic attraction, has been much studied. In the *Lettre sur les aveugles*, the mathematician Saunderson, born sightless, was made the touchstone (so to speak) of an epistemological inquiry into the sensory, cognitive, moral, and metaphysical world of the congenitally blind. In the *Lettre sur les sourds et muets*, Diderot examined the bearing of another kind of physical anomaly on problems of language, expressivity, and poetic discourse. The *Rêve de d'Alembert*, following the same method, is so full of references to "monsters" of all sorts that it resembles, at times, a freak show. In these instances, as in the multiplication of ontogenetic vignettes, the emphasis by repetition is in itself significant. Diderot's preoccupation with physical abnormalities reinforced, to be sure, the antifinalistic basis of his materialism; but it also owed much to the fact that the prevalence of *monstres* offered living proof of the plasticity and pliability of the organism. The freak was not for him an unfortunate creature who excited pity or consternation; his deformity was, rather, an encouraging sign (hence Diderot's reluctance to drop the subject) that biotechnology was no illusion, but an ongoing enterprise. If the monster was a haphazard experiment by nature that had little or no value to society, could one not, in taking nature's cue, experiment more wisely with man's own good in view? It was some such reflection as this, present in the back of Diderot's mind, that lent a paradoxically sanguine tone to his catalogue of teratological data.

A third factor was the philosophy of organism prevalent in his milieu. Once Descartes had launched on its polemical career the animal-machine idea, a convergence between the two terms of that equation became a theoretical aim of biology. To perceive the organism as a machine of sorts meant, inevitably, to perceive it sooner or later as also subject to modification and even fabrication. In the eighteenth century, the *bête machine* doctrine had mostly ceased to denote that animals were actual automata, for that opinion seemed patently false. Instead, it came to signify that their behavior as living, feeling, and thinking organisms could be explained by reference to mechanical causes. La Mettrie, in particular, expanded this hypothetical equivalence from the case of animals to that of what, consequently, he termed the man-machine. Diderot's scientific and philosophical attitudes were formed initially in the ambiance of this French school of mechanistic psychophysiology. Later, he fell under the sway of a more recent vitalist current that, by contrast, emphasized the specificity and irreducibility of the organic. By the time he wrote the *Rêve de d'Alembert,* his position lay somewhere between the opposing paradigms of mechanism and vitalism—in other words, between La Mettrie and Bordeu—although his writings show that he did not consider these two outlooks mutually exclusive or necessarily at odds. Diderot's conciliatory approach allowed him, when it served his purpose, to treat mechanistically, that is, technologically, the kind of phenomena which to others might well have implied the presence of an inviolable and unitary "life force" in animate beings. In fact, his desire to technologize life was, in spirit and method, profoundly antivitalist. The Montpellier physicians, who best represented French vitalism, had typically so strong a respect for the integrity—indeed, almost the sacredness—of the living organism that they were loathe not only to experiment with it, but even to intervene with too much therapeutic vigor in its illnesses. The biotechnological aspect of Diderot's materialism was an outcome, greatly magnified, of the impact on him of iatrophysical and chemiatric tradition. Both mechanics and chemistry, as combinatorial sciences, were notably oriented toward experimentation and invention. It would be superfluous to prove this with respect to mechanics in eighteenth-century France, where Vaucanson's automata, for example, were famous for their simulations of live animals. As for chemistry, it had always been, ever since its alchemical beginnings, a science that aspired to control over nature through the manipulation and transformation of substances. Already in the "Prospectus" of the *Encyclopédie,* Diderot had spoken of it in just that manner: "La *Chimie* est imitatrice et rivale de la nature; son objet est presque aussi étendu que celui de la nature même: ou elle *décompose* les êtres; ou elle les *revivifie;* ou elle les *transforme.*"[10] His hopes for a biotechnology at the disposition of *homo faber* were thus intimately tied to a physico-chemical conception of life itself.

Finally, other and more personal reasons contributed to this aspect of Diderot's thought. Foremost among these was, probably, his taste for experimentation, which in science no less than in the arts made him eager to alter existing forms. At the same time, he was fervently committed to utility as an overriding criterion in all spheres of endeavor—a commitment which was manifestly behind the unprecedented importance he gave to the "arts et métiers" in the *Encyclopédie,* and which also, it would seem, carried over into his biological materialism. That his family origins placed him in the class of industrial artisans must no doubt have reinforced his willingness to treat organisms as "manufacturable" artifacts. What came at last to the surface from this composite of traits and tendencies proved to be unique in the Enlightenment. At least, there is nothing like it among those of Diderot's contemporaries whose advocacy of mechanism, materialism, atheism, utility, and experimental science came closest to his own, such as La Mettrie and D'Holbach.

In conclusion, what is one to make, after more than two hundred years, of Diderot's precociously technological vision of life? Scholars have preferred to dismiss, or at least to minimize, the entire subject by relegating it to the rich vein of fantasy that traverses the *Rêve de d'Alembert*. Diderot was himself conscious, indeed self-conscious, about this peculiarity of his philosophical testament, and drew attention more than once to what he disarmingly called his "extravagances" and "folies".[11] But when he did so, it was in a dialectical fashion and with an eye on posterity, for he invariably proclaimed in the same breath that his fantasies would be appreciated someday as among the most worthwhile and farsighted of his ideas. About the *Rêve de d'Alembert*, he remained in general convinced that: "cela est de la plus haute extravagance et tout à la fois de la philosophie la plus profonde. . . . Il faut souvent donner à la sagesse l'air de la folie afin de lui procurer ses entrées."[12] There is no valid motive for not applying Diderot's self-appraisal also to his expectation that, in the future, the structures of living matter would be brought within the scope of human will and art. We are compelled by the evidence here adduced to acknowledge that, once again, he foresaw a whole program of scientific progress reserved to a distant age, and that his "dream of D'Alembert" was, in that regard, of the prophetic type. Of course, his foresight consisted in little more than simply imagining the possibility of a biotechnology and asserting, in defiance of prohibitions, a readiness to pursue it wherever it might lead. Yet, even if only that much credit is given to Diderot, his *Rêve de d'Alembert* remains, on the theme we have explored, a striking illustration not merely of the truism that yesterday's science fiction is often today's science, but also of the Faustian gamble that inheres, for better or for worse, in the association of curiosity about nature with the inevitable dream of power over it.

NOTES

1 Denis Diderot, *Oeuvres complètes* (Paris: Hermann, 1975–), vol. 9, *L'Interprétation de la nature*, éd. crit., Jean Varloot (1981), p. 36.
2 *Système de la nature*, xlv, in Maupertuis, *Oeuvres* (Lyon, 1756) 2: *148.

3 Hereafter, the three components of the *Rêve de d'Alembert* will be designated separately as the "Entretien," the "Rêve," and the "Suite."
4 For a fuller analysis of the rhetorical significance of the "Falconet's statue" incident, see Suzanne L. Pucci, "Metaphor and Metamorphosis in Diderot's *Le Rêve de d'Alembert:* Pygmalion Materialized," *Symposium* 35 (Winter 1981–82): 325–40.
5 That Diderot, on this occasion, was thinking specifically of his "Pygmalion aux pieds de sa statue qui s'anime" is borne out by external evidence. The allusion to it as "le chef d'oeuvre de Falconet" accords with the fact that, more than any other, this work had established the sculptor's reputation. Diderot himself reviewed it enthusiastically in the *Salon de 1763* (*Oeuvres*, ed. J. Assézat & M. Tourneux, 20 vols. [Paris: Garnier, 1875–77], 10: 221–23), where we find several clues that foreshadow the use he later made of it in the *Rêve de d'Alembert*. For example, he remarked: "Voilà le morceau que j'aurais dans mon cabinet, si je me piquais d'avoir un cabinet"; and this wish is fulfilled when Falconet's "masterpiece" turns up in Diderot's study during his discussion with D'Alembert. He also judged the statue in terms of the illusion it gave of having transformed marble into flesh: "quelle mollesse de chair! Non, ce n'est pas du marbre; appuyez-y votre doigt, et la matière qui a perdu sa dureté cèdera à votre impression." Finally, he saw in the depiction by Falconet of Pygmalion's miraculous creation of life an attempt to rival the Gods: "Emule des dieux, s'ils ont animé la statue, tu en as renouvelé le miracle en animant le statuaire . . . mais crains que, coupable du crime de Prométhée, un vautour ne t'attende aussi." Both of these considerations, adapted to the requirements of a materialist thesis, reappear in the "Entretien." Jean Varloot, in his edition of the *Rêve de d'Alembert* (Paris, 1962), p. 6, was right to identify the anonymous "chef d'oeuvre de Falconet" as the statue of Pygmalion and Galatea.
6 Diderot, *Oeuvres philosophiques*, ed. Paul Vernière (Paris: Garnier, 1964), p. 263. Page references to the *Rêve de d'Alembert* from this edition will be given in the body of the essay.
7 Vernière's footnote, ibid., p. 265.
8 The only scholar who, to my knowledge, has descried the subtext of D'Alembert's prenatal history is Jean Starobinski, in "Le philosophe, le géomètre, l'hybride" (*Poétique* 21 [1975]: 8–23), which offers a remarkably careful reading of the whole episode in question. He states (p. 17): "la formule latine . . .établit un battement sémantique entre l'image de la procréation naturelle (*vas licitans* étant alors l'utérus) et celle, évidemment chimérique, de la fabrication artificielle de l'*homo in vitro*, selon une recette savamment exécutée. (On ne peut s'empêcher d'évoquer ici le *Second Faust*.)" If Starobinski does not develop further the relationship between this *aperçu* and the biotechnology of the *Rêve de d'Alembert*, it is, first, because the latter theme is not his subject, and secondly, because he has assumed, like almost everyone, that the proposal of a "fabrication artificielle de l'*homo*

in vitro," present in Diderot's Latin formula, is "évidemment chimérique."
9 Among these, the principal approaches were preformationism, of which there were several variants; Buffon's theory of *molécules organiques,* according to which the elementary units in the developing foetus were seen as positioning themselves under the action of "moules intérieurs"; and Maupertuis' attribution of psychic properties, such as memory, desire, and aversion, to the particles of matter that, as a result, combined in predetermined ways to form the organism.
10 Diderot, *Oeuvres,* ed. Assézat & Tourneux, 13: 155. Twenty-five years later, in the *Plan d'une université,* his estimate had not changed: "La chimie analyse, compose, décompose; c'est la rivale du grand ouvrier. L'athanor du laboratoire est une image fidèle de l'athanor universel"; ibid., 3: 463. These words, in turn, are reminiscent of Needham's "vial" in which a world could be produced from a drop of water. On the chemical foundations of Diderotian natural philosophy, see Yvon Belaval, "Sur le matérialisme de Diderot," *Europäische Aufklärung* (München, 1967), pp. 9–21.
11 The exposition of D'Alembert's dream and Bordeu's gloss on it are situated rhetorically in a zone between sense and nonsense, reality and fantasy, without this prejudicing their ultimate "truth." The central dialogue is replete with remarks like: "Cela m'a paru si fou . . ."; "Il n'est donc pas fou?" "Cette extravagante supposition . . ."; "Docteur, et vous n'appelez pas cela de la déraison?" "J'appelle cela des folies . . ."; "Docteur, délirez-vous aussi?" "Mais voici bien une autre extravagance qui me vient"; "Il faut que vous ayez un merveilleux penchant à la folie"; and so forth. Thus nothing serious is argued against the scientific or philosophical value of any opinion in the *Rêve de D'Alembert* merely by saying it is irrational or "wild," for Diderot was the first to concede that.
12 In a letter to Sophie Volland, 31 August 1769; Denis Diderot, *Correspondance* (Paris: Minuit, 1955–) vol. 9, ed. Georges Roth (1963), pp. 126–27. The same letter advises the reader how to read the work: "J'aime mieux qu'on dise: Mais cela n'est pas si insensé qu'on croirait bien, que de dire . . . voici des choses très sages."

Diderot and Reader-Response Criticism: The Case of Jacques le fataliste

KATHRYN SIMPSON VIDAL

In the "Eloge de Richardson," Diderot praises the English novelist for his dramatic impact upon the reader and describes how, while reading, he had the sensation of the acquisition of experience, of having played a role in the work.[1] Through an examination of his own reactions as a reader, Diderot attempts briefly to discern how Richardson's art provokes such a compelling feeling of involvement within the text. Modern critics have equally turned towards the phenomenon of the reader's response as an essential dimension of the literary text, and Wolfgang Iser, one of the more prominent theoreticians in this domain, echoes Diderot's concept of "experience" in his analysis of reader activity. Diderot's novels themselves exhibit a good deal of experimentation with respect to the reader's role, but it is his final novel, *Jacques le fataliste,* which directly overturns convention in order to focus upon the presence of "the reader in the text."[2] Iser's concept of the implied reader, whose role he analyzes at length in the English novel,[3] provides some surprising parallels with the frustrated and frustrating *lecteur* in *Jacques le fataliste*.[4] This fictive reader is quite an unusual and problematic presence because of his very flagrant role and the frequency of his interruptions. In effect, his questions supply the very first sentences of the novel, and from that point on he is everywhere, unannounced and often unidentified, constantly accompanied by his respondent, the narrator. Even the novel's conclusion is left up to the faithful reader; for his own satisfaction, he is

33

asked to choose among the three possible endings salvaged by the "editor" after the narrator's disappearance.

The playful, nonchalant tone which characterizes the intrusive dialogue between narrator and reader disguises a paradoxical interrogation into the premises of the novel itself. *Jacques le fataliste* dismantles its own powers of illusion while destroying the reader's faith in such powers, and thus effectively demonstrates one of Iser's axioms, that fiction "possesses none of the criteria of reality and yet it pretends that it does."[5] Within this complex novel, Diderot's *lecteur* has often been dismissed as a parody of the typical eighteenth-century reader, avid for the mimetic illusion the novel purported to produce. Critical attention generally focuses upon the narrator, whose disdain for the reader's requests and outright refusal to respond seem to confirm the weaknesses of the *lecteur*. This narrator's apparent drive to dominate both reader and text, his unpredictability and his unreliability, all render him a more fascinating and inscrutable figure.[6]

The fictive reader's role is more complex than a simple parody, however. He is not totally submissive. Not only does he begin and end the novel, it is his response which triggers the narrator's commentary. We must also take into account the fact that the entire novel is built upon a series of narrative situations which largely mirror the tendencies present in the initial narrator-reader relationship. Storytelling is the essential activity of the novel, and all of the main characters have stories to tell. They, too, comment upon the comportment of their audience just as those listening intervene to criticize the speakers' respective techniques. This commentary complements that of the explicitly inscribed *lecteur*. Jacques's master, the most avid listener, most often exhibits the same failings and is equally frustrated in his quest for a story. Such interaction is the foundation for my comparison of the novel and Iser's inquiry into the reader's response.[7] *Jacques le fataliste* offers fertile ground for a very active response by the implied reader. It is even more striking to find in the novel a theoretical awareness of the reader's role which resembles the basic premises of today's audience-oriented criticism.

Iser invites us to view the implied reader as a construct "which makes it possible for the structured effects of literary texts to be described," a presence devoid of any predetermined character or historical context.[8] His attention to the reader's response is derived from his conviction that the meaning of a literary text is only realized through the act of reading itself, and he thus examines the means by which the novel initiates such a "performance of meaning," rather than autonomously supplying a message.[9] The implied reader is neither real nor ideal. He is distinct from the fictive reader who is directly addressed as such and clearly inscribed in the text as a character on a par with the other characters in the novel.[10]

In *Jacques le fataliste* both narrator and fictive reader play preponderant roles, for on over forty occasions their dialogue interrupts what is traditionally considered the mainstream of the action, the travels of Jacques and his master and the stories they tell along the way. The initial exchange between the two, which forms the first paragraph of the novel, sets the tone for most of their subsequent appearances: the narrator evasively offers only the vaguest responses to his reader's queries and denigrates his desire for an introduction to the story. When the reader merely requests the characters' names and the destination of their journey, he retorts: "Que vous importe?" and "qu'est-ce que cela vous fait?" (pp. 23 and 25). He persistently refuses any semblance of a framework and withholds the expected perspective. The fictive reader, desperate for solid ground, thus interrupts at will, interjecting his own questions and comments. Both narrator and reader are uncooperative, and this marks a vital breach of their traditional compliance.

The eighteenth-century convention of the fictive reader in the novel served to reinforce the validity of the text in a budding genre still defending its pretentions to the truth.[11] Such an inscribed reader established an explicit narrative situation and provided a witness to the narrator's veracity so that the story could be told. Direct address to this reader is usually limited to specific moments in the novel: a clearly defined introduction to the action and to the characters; well-delineated moments of introspection; and judgment meant to offer the desired perspective. This reader is essentially passive, and the convention serves its purpose when the implied reader identifies with the fictive reader and believes the narrator.

Diderot's *lecteur* is obviously unconventional in this respect, and herein lies the initial rapport between this novel and the general focus of Iser's work. As a clue to a descriptive analysis of the reading process, Iser follows the breakdown of this conventional passivity as the perspectives of both narrator and reader are blurred and final judgment is withheld. In Fielding's novels, for example, Iser shows how the more dynamic role attributed to the fictive reader increases interaction between text and implied reader. The narrator merely guides the fictive reader in completing descriptions on his own or in formulating his own conclusions about the action. Here the implied reader must intervene, becoming an actor in the novel as he constructs his own conception of this reality.[12] Fielding's narrator is explicit about his points of divergence with commonly held moral norms, yet he leaves the conclusions open, in the hands of the fictive reader. The inscription of the reader in the novel constantly triggers an impulse to complete and comprehend the text on the part of an implied reader, and this "production of meaning" constitutes what Iser designates as the "unformulated text."[13] Furthermore, when the fictive reader's moral judgment is thus questioned, the implied reader is engaged in the text to an even greater extent. If he identifies with his fictive counterpart, he likewise endures such "critical scrutiny," and is forced to reevaluate his position. Thus the reader actively creates the meaning of the text for himself.[14]

The pattern of reader response Iser traces in Fielding's novels offers a few initial parallels with *Jacques le fataliste*. The similarities are obvious on the moral level of the narrator-reader relationship. Diderot's narrator also criticizes the fictive reader's judgment, yet refuses to formulate conclusions for him. An excellent example is the lengthy commentary following the tale of Madame de la Pommeraye. Indeed, the problematic relativity of any public judgment of private actions is a constant backdrop to the moral clashes in the novel, and accordingly the narrator refuses to take a stand. The treatment of the theme of fatalism fulfills a similar function. In the case of *Jacques le fataliste*, however, the floundering moral position of the fictive reader is merely one of many symptoms of the increased instability of the entire premise of his conventional presence in the text. No longer a passive figure, this reader finds that the commonly held norms of the act of reading are demolished and he must aggressively reinstate himself. The consequences for the implied reader's role are complex. First of all, I will briefly examine the means by which the fictive reader's role triggers a response, according to the patterns suggested by Iser. The second portion of my analysis deals with the impact of this process. Essentially, *Jacques le fataliste* is not only a "novel about the novel," it is a novel about the act of reading itself.

Two of the most predominant linguistic features of the dialogue between narrator and reader are negation and the use of the past conditional tense to suggest, and then revoke, entire sequences of the action. Consequently, the interventions take on the air of a confrontation rather than a dialogue, and the mutual conventions of storytelling are thwarted by constant refusal and interruption. Negative connotations are, by extension, consistently associated with the fictive reader. Iser's studies link such negation with what he terms "blanks" in the text, which spur the implied reader to infuse them with meaning. In the case of *Jacques*, the process is complicated by the overt destruction of traditional patterns of reader response through the seemingly inept performance of the *lecteur.* In essence, the fictive reader constitutes one of the major blanks in the text.

What, then, is destroyed? As a presence in the novel, the fictive reader is usually a voice whose requests are denied and whose comments are stifled. Through this voice, Diderot's *lecteur* appears as an intertextual construct, a distorted combination of both the passive fictive reader who accepts the narrator's assurances that the novel is truth and the reader whose numerous expectations consist of sheer illusion. The recurrent phrase, "un autre auteur que moi," announces the infinite possibilities of the romanesque, geared to such expectations, but in each case, these hopes are dashed. The narrator continues to be quite explicit in signaling his divergence from the desired norm (and thus implicitly defines an expectation of the norm), typically by denying that his text is a novel at all: "Il est bien évident que je ne fais pas un roman, puisque je néglige ce qu'un romancier ne manquerait pas d'employer" (p. 35). Judging from the narrator's regular allusions to the classics, to contemporary novels, and to generally accepted narrative techniques, the fictive reader takes form as an entity well-versed in literary currents and strategies, highly critical at times, and alert to "art" as well as to the truth. Among the other characters, the master most often fills a similar role, and to similar ends, that is, to denounce the equation of art and truth. For example, he criticizes the artistic merits of the *hôtesse*'s tale:

> Notre hôtesse, vous narrez assez bien, mais vous n'êtes pas encore profonde dans l'art dramatique. . . . Quand on introduit un personnage sur la scène, il faut que son rôle soit un; or je vous demanderai notre charmante hôtesse, si la fille qui complote avec deux scélérates est bien la femme suppliante que nous avons vue aux pieds de son mari? Vous avez péché contre les règles d'Aristote, d'Horace, de Vida et de le Bossu.
>
> L'hôtesse — Je ne connais ni bossu ni droit, je vous ai dit la chose comme elle s'est passée sans en rien omettre, sans y rien ajouter. Et qui sait ce qui se passait au fond du coeur de cette jeune fille? [Pp. 169–70]

The fictive reader is also expected to be familiar with specific weaknesses of contemporary authors. Prévost's *Cleveland* is one target of such mockery:

> Telle fut à la lettre la conversation du chirurgien, de l'hôte et de l'hôtesse; mais quelle autre couleur n'aurais-je pas été le maître de lui donner, en introduisant un scélérat parmi ces bonnes gens? Jacques

se serait vu ou vous auriez vu Jacques au moment d'être arraché de son lit, jeté sur un grand chemin ou dans une fondrière. — Pourquoi pas tué? — Tué, non. J'aurais bien su appeler quelqu'un à son secours, ce quelqu'un-là aurait été un soldat de sa compagnie; mais cela aurait pué le *Cleveland* à infecter. La vérité, la vérité, la vérite, me direz-vous, est souvent froide, commune et plate. [P. 56][15]

Techniques generally intended to appeal to readers, such as romanesque plots and outlandish coincidence, are the most common victims of the narrator's sarcasm. Likewise, this narrator gleefully admits he has no memory for word-for-word transcriptions of conversations and documents lost far in the past.[16] He readily invokes his ignorance and forgetfulness, to the reader's further despair.[17]

Another essential element of the reader's expectations which surfaces in this novel is the need for order and meaning, a framework and a progression for the action at hand. On this point the dialogue between narrator and reader is especially laced with the denial of the "story" and a refusal to signify. The tempting sequences of plots and coincidences reveal themselves outlandishly false when revoked at such frequency. In contrast, what little plot that exists (the journey) appears banal, and the narrator frankly admits to the sparseness of his text because of his commitment to the truth. As each technique of illusion is denounced, a reexamination of exactly what constitutes "reality" in the novel becomes the role of the implied reader. This is essential in the reformulation of the latter's expectations.

The constant interruptions which occur on all of the major narrative levels have a significant function in this regard. The novel's halting rhythm forms numerous gaps in the plots and subplots, heightening the fictive reader's dissatisfaction and defying the implied reader's attempts to link the pieces together. Perhaps the two most frustrating series of such interruptions are those provided at one point by Jacques's horse, which keeps leaving the road while he is telling a story, and later those at the inn, in which the *hôtesse,* just commencing her tale quite dramatically, is continually called away by her duties. In both cases, the interrupting actions are described repetitively and with great precision. This forces the reader to join the other characters who are also waiting for the storyteller to return. In this manner, the telling of the story becomes more real than the story itself. As the narrator so often reminds his wayward reader, this is the only reality to which the teller can be true; the innkeeper's wife must necessarily see to her functions; Jacques, on horseback, must follow his horse's whims; similarly the narrator sleeps when he is tired and his personal existence disrupts the story.[18] These overtly blank spaces in the action call attention to themselves in their frequency and further heighten the impression of disorder in the novel.

Iser is particularly attentive to gaps of this sort as triggers for increased reader activity. In *Jacques,* gaps in the action are complemented by thematic blanks which defy synthesis and thwart the production of meaning. Several isolated incidents illustrate the narrator's general reluctance to interpret reality in any absolute sense. A prominent example is that of the château where Jacques and his master "supposedly" spend the night. The paradoxical inscription at the entrance defies logic within the context of their immediate situation or even in the text as a whole, and thus, for that very reason, seems of vital significance. Moments later, however, the narrator dismisses his allegory as "la ressource ordinaire des esprits stériles" (p. 43). Similarly, other apparently profound statements are tossed out nonchalantly and rarely followed through.[19] Jacques equally indulges in such a refusal to interpret or signify, especially when it is a question of coming to terms with his fatalism:

> C'est que, faute de savoir ce qui est écrit là-haut, on ne sait ni ce qu'on veut ni ce qu'on fait, et qu'on suit sa fantaisie qu'on appelle raison, ou sa raison qui n'est souvent qu'une dangereuse fantaisie qui tourne tantôt bien, tantôt mal. [P. 33]

The reader comes away with many choices, but no sense of meaning. Once again, such a strategy negates the passivity of the typical reader's expectations of an ordered explanation. Order, in effect, is denied up to the end, for neither Jacques nor the narrator ever finishes his respective tale.

The fictive reader's comments upon this inconclusiveness and refusal to signify serve as cues for the implied reader's own sense of disorientation. Furthermore, the constant interventions and questions simply increase the irregularity of the novel's pace, further deterring comprehension. The multiple hindrances to the production of meaning also suggest the uncontrollable aspect of reality in its raw state. As readers, we are forced, as Iser states, "to reject our habitual orientations as inadequate."[20] The act of reading itself, the progressive attempt to formulate some kind of meaning from the text, becomes part of the subject matter of the novel. Guidelines for a new reader appear only as the negation of the conventional reader. Such guidelines must be constructed implicitly as both the means of and the end to the reading process.

Iser reaches a similar conclusion in his analysis of reader response in the modern novels of Joyce and Beckett. In these texts, he focuses upon the greater frequency of "gaps of indeterminacy," as he labels the hindrances to comprehension. Such gaps are essential to the communicative value of the literary text, for they stimulate and increase reader participation by forcing him continually to reformulate meaning while reading. As the aforementioned examples illustrate, the presence of the fictive reader in *Jacques* not only elicits but also underlines obstacles to any clear formulation of meaning. In this novel, order is but another illusion of the romanesque. Characters and plot sequences are linked at random; the protagonists (Jacques and his master) meet by chance ("par hasard") and their actions and stories offer none but the most arbitrary progression in the course of an unspecified journey to an unspecified location. The formula of fatalism, "c'était écrit là-haut," which is echoed by Jacques throughout the novel, is equally empty of thematic, moral, or formal significance. As Otis Fellows so succintly reminds us, it explains at once everything and nothing with equal grace.[21] Nothing but the chance association of ideas determines each shift in the action or the various narrative levels, yet each gap creates the need for a synthesis. Perhaps the strongest illustration of this need is the persistent critical search for such a synthesis.[22]

The fictive reader's interruptions, coupled with the negative pressure of the narrator, trigger the strongest hindrances to consistency in *Jacques le fataliste*. The projections and conclusions of the fictive reader are brought to the surface of the novel in order to confront the implied reader with the entire process of consistency building which is engaged in reading. The dialogue between narrator and reader continually returns to Iser's concept of the "nonfulfillment of functions," that is, those functions which satisfy traditional expectations. It is in order to compensate for this loss that the reader becomes more productive.[23] Hence the exaggerated presence of the fictive reader in *Jacques* heralds the vastly intensified role delegated to the implied reader. Here, as in the modern novel, the only authentic experience of reality is the experience of the text itself, for the narrator's project, "être vrai," is realized only through the act of reading.[24]

Once the matter of meaning is left open to virtualization by any individual reader, what limits are then set by the text? Iser applies the precepts of speech-act theory in an attempt to identify various elements in the novel (designated as "strategies") which guide the reader's response.[25] One such strategy concerns the degree of control exerted explicity by the fictive narrator. After a chronological examination of English novels from Fielding to Beckett, Iser concludes that a decrease in the narrator's direct control leads to an increase in gaps of indeterminacy. In *Jacques*, however, we have an exception, an increase in narrative control and an increase in the gaps. On the surface, the narrator in *Jacques* exhibits the same penchant for domination which Iser sees in Fielding's narrators. He would readily echo the narrator of *Tom Jones*, for example, "I am indeed, set over them, [the readers] for their own good only, and was created for their use and not they for mine."[26] Nevertheless, there are other moments in which the same narrator withdraws unexpectedly, feigning disinterest. The narrator's need to challenge and redirect the fictive reader seems exorbitant; in contrast, more than once he offers the same reader a choice in wrapping up the plot to his own satisfaction. As I have previously suggested, such a refusal to signify is usually quite explicit, but everywhere represents an abdication on the narrator's part. In the light of this contradiction within the strategy of narratorial intervention elaborated by Iser, I would suggest that *Jacques le fataliste* presents more of a theoretical precedent to, rather than a mere illustration of, the dynamics of reader response.

The narrator's paradoxical comportment is mirrored by Jacques in his relationship to his master, and a brief examination of this character's narrative role offers clues to an understanding of the behavior of the narrator. Jacques's duties as a servant are largely limited to his storytelling, for the continuation of his tale is the master's most frequent command. Yet he, like the narrator, also taunts his listener with his own power as the sole proprietor of the truth. His story is at once a means of emancipation and the emblem of his servitude. Jacques feels the liberating effect of speech, and exploits it, for the pleasure of storytelling also provides mastery of a situation:

> Avez-vous oublié que Jacques aimait à parler et surtout à parler de lui, manie générale des gens de son état; manie qui les tire de leur abjection, qui les place dans la tribune, et qui les transforme tout à coup en personnages intéressants? . . . Il [le peuple] va chercher en Grève une scène qu'il puisse raconter à son retour dans le faubourg, celle-là ou une autre, cela lui est indifférent, pourvu qu'il fasse un rôle, qu'il rassemble ses voisins et qu'il s'en fasse écouter. [P. 189][27]

The above passage also underlines the need for an audience to effect the full realization of the story. This need is the basis for the narrator's creation of the fictive reader just as it renders Jacques and his master inseparable. Like Jacques, the narrator, in his derision and proclamations of control over his reader, also reveals the weakness of his position, for he is still obliged to respond to the questions and criticism of his audience. The narrator's paradox coincides with Jacques's status as a servant, for narration is always his task before the reader, yet is also a form of liberation. In choosing to withdraw from the text, neither the narrator nor Jacques definitively gains the upper hand in the confrontation.

The true power of the reader's projections is suggested in a relatively long digression on obscenity situated near the end of the novel (pp. 229–31). The passage specifically illustrates that the real nature of obscenity lies in the mind of the individual and not in the text itself, but the narrator goes on to reveal his inherent frustration at his dependence upon the reader for a final interpretation. His intentions, he insists, are pure: "Si mon ouvrage est bon, il vous fera plaisir; s'il est mauvais, il ne fera point de mal. Point de livre plus innocent qu'un mauvais livre" (p. 230). The only danger lies in the text's falling into the hands of the misguided reader:

> Lecteur, à vous parler franchement, je trouve que le plus méchant de nous deux, ce n'est pas moi. Que je serais satisfait s'il m'était aussi facile de me garantir de vos noirceurs qu'à vous de l'ennui ou du danger de mon ouvrage! [P. 230]

In essence, the reception of the text carries numerous ambiguities which the narrator can never ultimately resolve to his satisfaction. In any narrative relationship, the reader has his own individual power of projection and interpretation. Therein lies the paradoxical and reversible nature of any verbal exchange. When the master demands that Jacques "tell things as they are" ("dis la chose comme elle est"), the servant not only echoes the narrator's mocking reminders that the novel is never the mimetic mirror it claims to be, he also concludes that the audience's response is just as problematic:

> Cela n'est pas aisé. N'a-t-on pas son caractère, son intérêt, son goût, ses passions, d'après quoi l'on exagère ou l'on atténue? Dis la chose comme elle est! . . . Cela n'arrive peut-être pas deux fois en un jour dans toute une grande ville. *Et celui qui vous écoute est-il mieux disposé que celui qui parle?* Non. [P. 73, my emphasis]

Throughout the novel, the narrator consistently insists that he is telling the truth in order to create a reader so "disposed" to listen and believe. His failure and eventual abdication further highlight the reader's impulse to create the text for himself. As the narrator states before his disappearance, "on ne peut s'intéresser qu'à ce qu'on croit vrai" (p. 288). The fictive reader's presence is a rich reminder of the power of the individual reader, and each of his interventions implicitly triggers an evaluation of the reader's response, thus effectively thematizing the problem of the role of the reader. While *Jacques le fataliste* characteristically offers no answers, it raises questions about narration and reception which bear a striking resemblance to theoretical preoccupations of today.

NOTES

1 The original text reads: "On prend . . . un rôle dans tes ouvrages," and further on: "je sentais que j'avais acquis de l'expérience." "Eloge de Richardson," in *Oeuvres complètes,* ed. Jean Varloot (Paris: Hermann, 1980), 13: 193.
2 The title of a recent collection of essays devoted to audience-oriented criticism, which includes an excellent overview of the question: *The Reader in the Text: Essays on Audience and Interpretation,* ed. Susan R. Suleiman and Inge Crosman (Princeton: Princeton University Press, 1980).
3 Wolfgang Iser, *The Implied Reader: Patterns of Communication from Bunyan to Beckett* (Baltimore: Johns Hopkins University Press, 1974).
4 *Jacques le fataliste et son maître,* in *Oeuvres complètes,* ed. Jacques Proust (Paris:Hermann, 1981), 23: 21–291. Further references to the novel will be indicated in parentheses in the text.
5 Wolfgang Iser, *The Act of Reading: A Theory of Aesthetic Response* (Baltimore: Johns Hopkins University Press, 1979), p. 181. References to this work will subsequently be abbreviated as *Act.*
6 To date, no critical study has focused specifically upon the activity of the *lecteur* within *Jacques le fataliste,* nor the implications for readers of all sorts. The closest study one might cite in passing is that of Christie McDonald, "Fractured Readers," *Modern Language Notes* 97 (1982): 840–48, which hypothesizes "clues" for the reader's role in the associations surrounding Jacques's knee. Otherwise, interest has largely been concentrated upon the narrator's interventions with little emphasis upon the activity of the fictive reader, who, in his ignorance, is most often relegated to a minor role. In general, such analyses are found within the context of studies intent upon finding the "keys" (i.e., synthesizing meanings) to *Jacques,* whether philosophical, moral, thematic, or formal and structural.
7 See Gabriel J. Brogyanyi, "The Function of Narration in Diderot's *Jacques le fataliste,*" *Modern Language Notes* 89 (1974): 550–59. Brogyanyi, however, examines narration in terms of the narrators with less attention to their respective audiences.

8 *Act*, pp. 38 and 34, respectively.
9 Ibid., pp. 20–27.
10 I have simplified terminology somewhat, following W. Daniel Wilson's argument that Iser, for one, fails to clearly distinguish among the reader clearly inscribed in a text, his abstract notion of the implied reader, and the actual reader confronting a text. Wilson correctly emphasizes the fictivity of both of the first two concepts, the inscribed or fictive reader and the implied reader. Once this is clarified it is unnecessary to continually repeat the terms he suggests, "characterized fictive reader" and "implied fictive reader." See his article, "Readers in Texts," *PMLA* 96 (1981): 848–63.
11 See *Act*, pp. 152–53.
12 Ibid., pp. 32–42.
13 Ibid., pp. 225–26.
14 Ibid., pp. 151–53. The best illustration of the application of these patterns in analysis is found in the individual chapters of Iser's *The Implied Reader.*
15 Other specific references to literary works and authors occur on pp. 37, 81, 101, 117, 229–34, and 255.
16 For example: "Lecteur vous suspendez ici votre lecture; qu'est-ce qu'il y a? Ah! je crois vous comprendre, vous voudriez voir cette lettre. Madame Riccoboni n'aurait pas manqué de vous la montrer" (p. 252). The narrator goes on to demonstrate how easily such letters are compiled, effectively destroying their illusory value before paradoxically stating: "On les lit avec plaisir, mais elles détruisent l'illusion" (p. 253).
17 For example, pp. 48 or 145.
18 In one instance (p. 174), no one actually saw what happened when the candles were extinguished, so the narrator offers two "versions" as conjectures for the reader. See also pp. 45 and 81.
19 The speaker remains anonymous and the narrator again pleads ignorance to the reader (pp. 128–29 and 235). Iser singles out such moments as "irritants," most especially in the case of the distorted use of allegory, in *The Implied Reader*, p. 176.
20 *Act*, p. 18
21 "*Jacques le fataliste* Revisited," *L'Esprit créateur* 8 (1968): 47.
22 See note 6.
23 *Act*, pp. 207–8.
24 In a different manner, Thomas M. Kavanagh reaches a similar conclusion, to the effect that *Jacques* shows us how the literary text "comes to mean" rather than intrinsically containing a meaning. See his excellent study, *The Vacant Mirror: A Study of Mimesis through Diderot's "Jacques le fataliste,"* Studies on Voltaire and the Eighteenth Century, vol. 104 (Banbury: The Voltaire Foundation, 1973).
25 Iser's discussion is complex and would be difficult to summarize. See *Act*, chapter 3, "The Repertoire," and chapter 4, "Strategies," pp. 53–103. Further parallels with *Jacques* and Diderot's concepts of aesthetic perception are evident here, but beyond the immediate scope of this paper.

26 *Tom Jones*, vol. 1, bk. 2, chap. 1, p. 39, quoted by Iser, "Indeterminacy and the Reader's Response in Prose Fiction," in *Aspects of Narrative: Selected Papers from the English Institute*, ed. J. Hillis Miller (New York: Columbia University Press, 1971), pp. 25–26.
27 Jacques's past experiences confirm that he has often used speech to extricate himself from dependence and take control over his fate.

Voltaire's Fables of Discretion: The Conte philosophique in Le Taureau blanc

THOMAS M. CARR, JR.

> *Je voudrais surtout que, sous le voile de la fable, il laissât entrevoir aux yeux exercés quelque vérité fine qui échappe au vulgaire.*
> Amaside on the conte

Le Taureau blanc (1774)[1] offers remarkable insight into Voltaire's use of the *conte* as persuasive discourse for two reasons. First, as the purest example of the genre among his last *contes*, it is in many ways the quintessence of his talents as a *conteur*. This tale does not cover any new ideological territory in its treatment of the Old Testament, a preoccupation found in much of his production of the Ferney period; nor does it introduce any technical innovations. But unlike Voltaire's last tragedies, where his reworking of the themes and dramatic conventions of his dramatic successes of the 1730s and 1740s gives the impression of self-parody, his handling of fantasy, irony, and philosophic commentary in Le Taureau blanc remains fresh. Study of this *conte*, which has been neglected more because its subject excites little passion today than for any flaws, can help us isolate key components of the *conte philosophique* in a way more problematic *contes* like Candide or more experimental ones like L'Ingénu cannot. Second, Le Taureau blanc contains some of the most explicit commentary on persuasive discourse to be found in the corpus of his imaginative works. Moreover, the rhetorical situation of the characters within the tale offers certain parallels to Voltaire's own situation as a persuader. An examination of the various modes of persuasive speech, especially narrative and eloquence, within what might be called his *méta-conte*, will afford a better understanding of why narrative proved a more effective weapon on behalf of enlightenment in Voltaire's hands than eloquence.

Critics have elucidated the religious significance of this work, showing how Voltaire presents biblical discourse as arising from the same process of fabulation which produced the myths of all ancient cultures. However the political and social setting in which he places this demystification of scripture has been somewhat neglected, even though politics is an essential component of the rhetorical situation within the *conte*.[2] *Le Taureau blanc* explores a gamut of registers available to the would-be sage: prophecy and eloquence, biblical narrative and the moral or philosophical tale, but all of these modes of discourse on display have in common the fact that they are enunciated by courtiers.

In contrast with other tales of Voltaire which take as their setting a Baedeker of Oriental, American, or European lands, if not the galaxies, all the action of this tale unfolds in the confines of the court of Amasis, king of Tanis. While the tale does offer vistas open on the ancient Orient—Babylon, Memphis, Israel—it is only because representatives of these outside worlds make their way to the court of Amasis. Nabuchodonosor, who has been transformed into a white bull, arrives in the custody of the witch of Endor. The priests of Memphis travel in great pomp toward Tanis in search of a replacement for their god-bull who has just died. Finally, the prophets Daniel, Jérémie, and Ezéchiel journey from the Holy Land. All the characters are either royalty like Nabuchodonosor, Amasis, and his daughter, Amaside, or they are courtiers. The sage Mambrès is counsellor to the king and superintendant of the household of the princess. The serpent, who displays a perfect mastery of courtly graces, recalls his reputation as a disgraced favorite (21: 491), a reference to the fall of Lucifer from the celestial court. Even the prophets have less a religious aura than the political character of courtiers; they are presented as ambitious upstarts who covet the rank of their royal masters.

Discretion is the hallmark of all discourse in the court of the superstitious tyrant of Tanis. This discretion involves, on the one hand, the guarded use of language necessitated by an environment where distrust and suspicion are a condition for survival. It also implies the aristocratic exclusiveness (as seen in Amaside's description of the ideal *conte*) that is the mark of a self-conscious elite eager to preserve its secrets from outsiders it considers unworthy. I would argue that in the course of Voltaire's efforts to promote enlightenment he had to come to terms with similar expectations that all discourse be discreet. In a regime such as that of Louis XV where discretion was all the more imperative if any criticism of the official ideology was contemplated, eloquence in its enlightened forms could hardly exist.

Amasis' attitude toward language illuminates why discretion is a necessity for all who live in the court of such a despot. His vow to have his daughter executed if she speaks the name of his enemy Nabuchodonosor doubly illustrates the irrevocable nature of the word for him. In his eyes, for Amaside even to pronounce Nabuchodonosor's name is to surrender herself body and soul to the king of Babylon because, for the superstitious Amasis, a word *is* the reality it is supposed to represent. Likewise, once he has given his word to have her killed if she transgresses his taboo, he cannot gainsay himself. Thus it is not surprising that his advisors tell him only what they think he wants to hear. For example, aware of the king's ire when he learns of his daughter's affection for the white bull, "tous les ministres d'état conclurent que le taureau était un sorcier. C'était tout le contraire" (21: 494). As the princess remarks elsewhere, "tant de ministres ont été punis d'avoir donné de bons conseils" (21: 491). In such a world where the mere enunciation of a word can carry such grave consequences, discretion must mark all discourse. Little wonder that the wise Mambrès suggests that his pupil be wary of the potential indiscretion of her ladies-in-waiting. Indeed, in spite of their devotion to the princess and their promise of silence, they only manage to keep the secret of her interest in the mysterious white bull a single day. Worse, perfidious souls like the crow, "une bête si difficile et si bavarde" (21: 500), stand ready to denounce Amaside when she eventually breaks her father's taboo. Thus Mambrès recommends to the princess the cult of the god Harpocrate, who is presented as the god of discretion. "Vous n'avez pas été élevée dans la sagesse égyptienne pour ne savoir pas commander à votre langue. Songez qu'Harpocrate, l'un de nos plus grand dieux, a toujours le doigt sur sa bouche" (21: 484). The tale's entire plot turns on this effort to control Amaside's tendency toward indiscretion. During the first part of the *conte* Mambrès struggles to keep Amaside from uttering her lover's name. In the second part, when the secret is out, he attempts to soften the consequences of her inability to remain silent after her father condemns first the bull and then her to death.

The first comedy of Voltaire, *L'Indiscret* (1725) had already brought a similar analysis of indiscretion to the stage. The court in this play, "ce lieu tout rempli d'injustice," "ce dangereux séjour" (2: 247–48), could almost be that of Amasis. In *L'Indiscret* we find the same warning against feminine indiscretion, the same stress on the absence of freedom of expression at court, the same advice to hold back secrets. However, *L'Indiscret* only deals with discretion in the context of fashionable Parisian society where a young fop loses his amorous conquests by bragging too loudly about them. In the court of Amasis, discretion was a matter of life and death, a situation not without parallel to that of a *philosophe* like Voltaire who challenged the ideology of the Ancien Régime.

Before proceeding further, some reflections on the notion of discretion can be useful. While in its broadest sense, discretion implies prudence in both action and speech, only discreet discourse is at issue here. Such discretion is ultimately a defensive strategy, motivated by fear that full and open disclosure will in some way leave a speaker vulnerable. The audience is the enemy. Thus discretion commonly involves some degree of self-censorship ranging, on the one hand, from partial disclosure to the extreme of absolute silence. An alternate form of this self-censorship is to conceal not so much what the speaker believes as the speaker's identity. Rather than seek self-protection by censoring discourse itself, such discreet speakers make use of stratagems such as a pseudonym or anonymous publication to speak their mind while not revealing their name. They suppress their identity, not their thoughts. At the other extreme from such tactics involving some degree of silence we find another mode of address that might loosely be labeled discreet—effusive flattery. A flatterer speaks openly and publicly but at the loss of the congruence that should exist between one's self-identity as a speaker and one's discourse. Rather than enunciate what they truly believe, such speakers allow the expectations of their audience to become their norm.

II

Two broad categories of persuasive discourse can be distinguished within *Le Taureau blanc*, the first centering around eloquence and the second around narrative. Both are conditioned by the requirements of discretion, and Voltaire's handling of both within the *conte* sheds light on how he adapted his own discourse to the discretion imposed by eighteenth-century expectations.

Voltaire was well aware of the old rhetorical topos[3] on the incompatibility of true eloquence and lack of freedom. He wrote in an article prepared for the *Encyclopédie*, "L'éloquence sublime n'appartient, dit-on, qu'à la liberté: c'est qu'elle consiste à dire des vérités hardies, à étaler des raisons et des peintures fortes. Souvent un maître n'aime pas la vérité, craint les raisons, et aime mieux un compliment délicat que de grands traits" ("Eloquence," 18: 516). Without a free forum, discretion smothers true eloquence. In *Le Taureau blanc* Voltaire presents two forms of such false eloquence; the first is the empty verbiage of the Hebrew prophets, the second is the courtly eloquence best exemplified by the serpent, but also practiced to some extent by Mambrès.

Voltaire assimilates prophecy to defective eloquence by portraying the prophets as verbose buffoons, whose figured style conceals an absence of solid reasoning. Prophecy is reduced to the ability to manipulate a splendid, although empty eloquence. "Ezéchiel et Jérémie parlèrent aussi très-longtemps dans un fort beau style qu'on pouvait à peine comprendre" (21: 503). The variants of the last chapter point out the precise path the prophets must follow to practice true eloquence: "on leur enjoignit seulement de parler moins et de parler mieux."[4] Of course, their garrulous discourse is neither innocent nor harmless. For Voltaire, the prophets are ambitious political upstarts who aspire to privileges of their royal masters. Sprung from the people, their false eloquence is a means of self-promotion. Elsewhere Voltaire describes them as demagogues, bent on deceiving the people.[5] In *Le Taureau blanc,* where Nabuchodonosor's metamorphosis into a bull is presented as the work of Daniel, the accent is on the danger they pose for their sovereigns.

Given this natural enmity between the monarch and prophets, it is not surprising that Daniel, Ezéchiel, and Jérémie are attacked by Nabuchodonosor who is enraged to find that they can discourse so freely while he is deprived of language and imprisoned in the body of a bull. The three are only saved from death when they are themselves transformed into chattering magpies. Mambrès reads into this metamorphosis a lesson of discretion: the empty eloquence of the prophets must give way to a wisdom that never forgets to be discreet. "Ce nouvel incident produisait de nouvelles réflexions dans l'esprit du sage Mambrès. 'Voilà, disait-il, trois grands prophètes changés en pies: cela doit nous apprendre à ne pas trop parler, et à garder toujours une discrétion convenable.' Il concluait que sagesse vaut mieux qu'éloquence" (21: 503).

The courtly eloquence of Mambrès and the serpent is, in a sense, more discreet than the pompous eloquence of prophecy, but only because it is controlled by a worldly wisdom that has less regard for truth than for what its audience wants to hear. As we have seen in the article "Eloquence," Voltaire had noted the preference of tyrants for flattery over authentic eloquence. In fact, he singles out oriental oratory designed to flatter some despot as being particularly prone to hyperbole: "Les Orientaux étaient presque tous esclaves: c'est un caractère de la servitude de tout exagérer: ainsi l'éloquence asiatique fut monstrueuse" (18: 515). This use of exaggeration makes courtly eloquence a close relative of the figure-laden style of prophecy.

In *Le Taureau blanc* the serpent is the acknowledged master of this rhetoric of flattery. The princess identifies his talent with the art of pleasing: "vous avez le talent de persuader tout ce que vous voulez, et c'est régner que de plaire" (21: 491). Yet the danger that such a rhetoric can pose for its public is seen in the consequences for the princess of her dealings with the serpent. Even though he insists that he only wants to please and aid her, after each interview with him she moves one syllable closer to uttering the complete name of her lover and bringing down upon herself her father's sentence of death. A rhetoric that sets up the pleasure of its audience as its standard ultimately appeals to the passions of its listeners, not necessarily their best interests.[6]

Even Mambrès, whose intentions are above suspicion, must adapt his eloquence to the restrictions imposed by discretion. For example, in his efforts to save the bull from Amasis' wrath, he discreetly adapts his arguments to his audience and sets bounds on his objectives: "Le sage Mambrès ne voulut point choquer l'opinion du roi et du conseil" (21: 494-95). Instead of attempting to gain a pardon for the bull who was accused of bewitching the princess, he only aims at postponing the date of the execution, citing an excuse designed to appeal to the piety of the king—they should delay until a new god-bull is named in Memphis. In doing so, he invents a sort of prophecy of his own to which he adds a liberal dose of courtly flattery. "O roi! vivez à jamais. Le taureau blanc doit être sacrifié, car Votre Majesté a toujours raison; mais le Maître des choses a dit: 'Ce taureau ne doit être mangé par le poisson de Jonas qu'après que Memphis aura trouvé un dieu pour mettre à la place de son dieu qui est mort'" (21: 504). This discreet eloquence is only effective in so far as it uses *ad hominem* arguments that do not merit this closet deist's own adhesion, and even then its goals are limited.[7] As Amaside reminds Mambrès bitterly, he is unable to soften the heart of the king with words alone: "Eh bien! mon cher Mambrès, lui dit-elle, vous avez changé les eaux du Nil en sang, selon la coutume, et vous ne pouvez changer le coeur d'Amasis mon père" (21: 509).

Even though the eloquence of Mambrès is clearly superior to that of the prophets or even the serpent, it does not reach the ideal dreamed of by Voltaire.[8] How could it be otherwise in a courtly setting where discretion, whether silence or flattery, rather than open truth, was the order of the day? Voltaire had summed up this requirement of discretion in *L'Indiscret* where he had noted that at court, "L'art le plus nécessaire / N'est pas de bien parler, mais de savoir se taire" (2: 248). Appropriately, in *Le Taureau blanc* the full use of speech is restored only when the characters leave behind the constraints of the court. Amaside does not drop the mask of discretion and openly defy her father until she has crossed beyond the boundaries of his kingdom: "Mon cher père, allez couper le cou à qui vous voudrez; mais ce ne sera pas à moi" (21: 511). At this precise moment, when for the first time someone dares address the king frankly, the seven years of the metamorphosis of Nabuchodonosor are completed, and he recovers first his voice and then his human form.

Likewise, in the regime of Louis XV where liberty of expression was also frustrated, the true "art de bien parler," the most authentic eloquence, was too dangerous to practice. Like Amaside, Voltaire had left the court, even if he could not bring himself to establish himself permanently outside of France, choosing instead to hover on the Genevan border at Ferney. Fortunately, the path of the "discrétion convenable" recommended by Mambrès remained open. For eloquence, this meant that the speeches which Voltaire acknowledged publicly such as his 1746 *Discours de réception* upon entrance into the Académie française are guarded. His most forceful eloquence had to take refuge in the world of fiction. It is in the Blueridge Mountains of Virginia that Freind's oratory in the *Histoire de Jenni* brings back his son to virtue and converts the atheist Birton, and Voltaire sets his *Quatre Homélies sur la religion* of 1765 in London. Only in a fictional setting could the philosopher display the full power of the enlightened word. His eloquence must imagine itself far from Paris to be free.

III

In *Le Taureau blanc* Voltaire brings into play a second mode of persuasive discourse, in the form of the narratives which Mambrès and the serpent relate to console the princess. However, Amaside rejects the Old Testament stories of the serpent in a sweeping critique that attacks them as boring, lacking verisimilitude, taste, and morality. An elitist brand of discretion is especially prominent in her capsule summary of the ideal *conte* that appears at the center of her tirade: "Je voudrais surtout que, sous le voile de la fable, il laissât entrevoir aux yeux exercés quelque vérité fine qui échappe au vulgaire" (21: 506). In this formula Voltaire offers perhaps his most complete description of the *conte philosophique* since he alludes to the message ("vérité fine"), the mode of discourse ("le voile de la fable"), and to its public ("yeux exercés," "qui échappe au vulgaire"). It would place too heavy a burden on this formulation, which is situated within a broad attack against Old Testament narrative, to expect that it should provide an adequate definition of all Voltaire's performance as a *conteur*. Just the same, if we examine these components in light of the discretion Voltaire used in his philosophic propaganda we can better understand how the *conte* can be seen as his own fable of discretion.

In fact, Voltaire saw fable, or at least Aesopian fable, as a discreet form of discourse. In his article "Fable" Aesop's tales are presented as a medium which the weak, obliged to "se garantir des forts autant qu'ils peuvent" (19: 61), employ to conceal their thoughts from their masters: "Il est vraisemblable que les fables dans le goût de celles qu'on attribue à Ésope, et qui sont plus anciennes que lui, furent inventées en Asie par les premiers peuples subjugés; des hommes libres n'auraient pas eu toujours besoin de déguiser la vérité; on ne peut guère parler à un tyran qu'en paraboles, encore ce détour même est-il dangereux" (19: 59). There is certainly an element of Aesopian caution in Voltaire. For example, in public works like *Mahomet* or *Alzire*, the imaginary action on the stage is often a veil that allowed him to allude to religious issues which otherwise would have been off limits.

The *contes*, however, make fewer concessions to the official ideology; their fictional elements in no way diverted the authorities from recognizing their subversive nature, and thus even the occasional *permission tacite* foolishly granted to a work like *L'Ingénu* was quickly withdrawn. The clandestine distribution of the *contes*, and above all the fact that Voltaire refused to acknowledge them publicly, freed him from the need to disguise his criticism from the officials charged with monitoring the book trade by using some fictional screen *à la Ésope*. Yet while the fiction found in the *contes* is only one of the many genres Voltaire cultivates in his clandestine propaganda, it is in many ways his most successful. As we shall see, this is because the particular Voltairean brand of fable is uniquely suited to the public he addressed as well as to the targets against which his philosophic propaganda was aimed.

But if the discretion offered by the fable of Voltaire's *conte philoso-*

phique is not Aesopian caution, where does it lie? Amaside's description of an audience composed of those with "yeux exercés" and her references to "quelque vérité fine qui échappe au vulgaire" suggest that the genre, at least as she conceives it, is the aristocratic counterpoint of Aesopian fable. If Aesop's fables are the expression of popular wisdom using fiction to disguise the truth from tyrannical rulers, does a *conte* by Voltaire embody an esoteric truth reserved for an elite and from which "le vulgaire" is excluded?

Two views of Voltaire's audience come into play, one which sees it as primarily composed of aristocratic *initiés*, and the other as encompassing a wider public. The first view has recently been summed up by H. A. Stavan. "The *initiés* all use the same or very similar turns of sentences, expressions and allusions. The social milieu of the salon predominates and shapes this language. For the *initiés* it was certainly one of the greatest attractions to understand the sous-entendus of the letter-writer and author for this flattered their vanity whereas he used the jargon learned partly from them. He wrote his tales for them foremost and only in second place for the general public (the lower middle class)."[9] Stavan acknowledges his debt to the concept of Voltaire's audience as a series of concentric circles which Geoffrey Murray identified through his analysis of the correspondence of the period of *Candide*. Murray found that Voltaire had groups of initiates, intimate correspondents, to whom he offers the first fruits of his writings and who share with the master a language of personal allusion and above all a knowledge of the multitude of roles (*jardinier, vieillard, laboureur, militant,* etc.) which Voltaire constantly adopts. At times Voltaire accompanies the printed texts with letters that act as keys directing his intimates to certain resonances of the text; in any event, their contacts with Voltaire position the *initiés* to grasp references which readers not in the know might miss.[10]

On the other hand, Roland Mortier, who studied the tension found among all the *philosophes* between their zeal for enlightenment and their uncertainty about to whom and how this message should be addressed, minimizes the tendency toward what he calls "esotérisme" in Voltaire. Mortier does concede that Voltaire gives widest diffusion only to his religious and moral ideas—his desire to see Christianity replaced by natural religion: "Voltaire distingue, sans le dire toujours expressément, entre les vérités qu'il est urgent de divulguer et celles qu'il convient de réserver au 'petit troupeau' des gens de 'la bonne compagnie.'" Still Mortier concludes in favor of a much broader audience: "Au fond, Voltaire n'a cessé d'écrire pour le grand public, sinon peut-être pour les cordonniers et les servantes, et encore! Le tout est de s'entendre sur le processus et le rythme de cette diffusion."[11]

These views of Voltaire's audience are not mutually exclusive, and the notion of discretion can help us discriminate between the strategies Voltaire uses in dealing with his various publics. First, the discretion of the *contes* is not the form we saw in the analysis of courtly eloquence where speakers use some measure of silence to conceal their true thoughts or misrepresent them with lies or flattery. Nor is it the Aesopean caution that uses fiction as a mask to allegorize some "vérité fine;" by adopting the discretion of clandestine distribution, Voltaire was freed from the need to disguise the "vérités" he dealt with from the censors. Yet the discretion of that clandestinity posed certain dilemmas at the same time. Rather than deny his "vérité" by disguising or deforming it, Voltaire denied authorship, but in doing so violated the bond of congruence that links speaker and utterance. Thus if Voltaire manages to assuage the established authorities charged with censorship and protect himself by publicly denying paternity of his works, it is, in a very real sense, at the price of a measure of his own identity.

However, his relationship with his most intimate readers, his *initiés*, allows him compensation. Even if he publicly denied a work, they could recognize his signature in his stylized disavowals. Indeed, with the *initiés*, he fostered an aura of connivance so that the text was for them testimony that they belonged to a chosen elite thanks to the network of allusions they shared with him through their correspondence. The implication is that among members of this inner circle there was no need for discretion since there are no secrets among friends. Discretion is rather directed by this self-conscious elite against outsiders. Thus, on the one hand, withholding his identity from the state's officials is justified: after all, he has in any case revealed it to those who count, the *initiés*. On the other hand, this discretion implies an aristocratic scorn for another group of outsiders, "le vulgaire" of Amaside, who are pictured as unworthy of the secrets of the elite.

Nonetheless, this concept of Voltaire's audience does not necessarily transform a work like *Le Taureau blanc* into a code that is indecipherable for the noninitiates, like the "symboles de l'antiquité" which Voltaire mentions in the article "Emblème" as reserved exclusively for a privileged minority (18: 520). Voltaire's relation to the readers of his *contes* beyond the *initiés* might be thought of as a sort of calculated indiscretion. The initial public may be the aristocratic insiders, exemplified in the case of *Le Taureau blanc* by the readers of Meister's

Correspondance littéraire which was reserved for princely subscribers and where the tale first appeared in late 1773 and early 1774. However, from the beginning, a much wider diffusion of the *conte* was calculated as seen in the good number of editions which followed in late winter of 1774. Indeed, Voltaire manages to flatter all segments of his audience. The initiates can take pleasure in the fact that the first fruits are reserved for them, while the broader public in this hierarchical society is delighted to be let in on what passes for an interchange among the elite.

But the best indication that the indiscretion involved in reaching this wider audience is calculated rather than real can be seen if we examine what Voltaire requires from his readers. A letter to De Lisle who couriered *Le Taureau blanc* from Ferney to Meister, the Parisian editor of the *Correspondance littéraire*, is revealing. De Lisle was also in contact with Mme Du Deffant, a longtime correspondent of Voltaire who was afraid that the *conte* would not please her: "Je ne sais si vous l'amuserez avec vôtre boeuf, car il faut être un peu familiarisé avec le stile oriental, et les bêtises de l'antiquité, pour se plaire un peu avec de telles fadaises, et Madame Du Deffant ne se plait guères à cette antiquité respectable. Je n'ai jamais pu lui persuader de se faire lire l'ancien Testament, quoi qu'il soit à mon gré plus curieux qu'Homère" (Best D. 18583). Even though Mme Du Deffant counts among the more intimate correspondents of Voltaire, the knowledge of scripture and ancient history he expects from his reader is accessible to a much wider audience. The Bible, of course, is always available, but Voltaire has in mind not so much indiscriminate reading of the Old Testament as familiarity with the sections he considers *curieux*. Indeed, an acquaintance with rather obscure episodes he alludes to, such as the sexual tastes of Oolla, or the "confitures" of Ezéchiel (21: 502), which were the frequent butt of his ridicule, facilitates an appreciation of *Le Taureau blanc*.

Yet a reader need not be an *initié* like Mme Du Deffant to be acquainted with these points of scripture. The many *facéties* in which he picks apart the Bible, published since his installation in Ferney, furnished a less intimate reader with a course of directed readings in Voltairean exegesis. In a sense, the fact that these works were available to any reader who took the trouble and expense to procure Voltaire's clandestine propaganda is an indication of how the effective circle of *initiés*, at least as far as his religious interests are concerned, had been expanded by the 1770s by dint of frequent repetition. The allusions to Constantinople, the *vieillard*, etc., in the correspondence, which according to Murray add resonance to *Candide* for the *initiés* have been replaced to a large extent by the much more widely diffused biblical allusions found throughout his propaganda and crystalized in this *conte*. The fact that the saws have become common currency explains some of the poor reception accorded by the *initiés* to such later works. Mme Du Deffant complains that Voltaire offers nothing new: "Il fait depuis q̄q̄ temps un bien plat usage de ses talents. Je ne comprends pas quel projet il a eu en composant son conte du Taureau blanc: ce ne peut être que pour mettre au même niveau la Bible et la fable. Cela valait il la peine d'écrire?" (to De Lisle, 24 October, 1773, Best. D. 18596). This is, in a sense, a protest against Voltaire's indiscretion in sharing his "vérité fine" with a wider audience. Once outsiders have been let in on the game, the intimates begin to lose interest.

But what Voltaire requires chiefly of his reader is not so much knowledge of a code gained either as an intimate correspondent, as a frequent reader of his propaganda, or even from general knowledge of scripture acquired independently. The elite reader differs from "le vulgaire" of Amaside above all by sharing the "petit fonds de philosophie" which Sadi attributes to the sultana Sheraa in the dedicatory epistle of *Zadig* (21: 32). This elite is characterized by its open critical mind, and by being already won over, at least in part, to enlightenment. Voltaire does not exclude completely those he calls in a letter to Marmontel "les hiboux" with "leur haine pour la lumière" (Best D. 11667), but rather than convert the devout, he seeks to influence those who already lean towards enlightened values. This elite is distinguished from "le vulgaire" by its willingness to discern that there is more to the *conte* than the whimsical adventures of the plot. "Le vulgaire" is not so much those who cannot decode the "vérité fine" as those who do not choose to do so, preferring to be amused alone. For them, the fanciful intrigue of the tale is a veil of entertainment they have no desire to lift.

IV

"Les voiles de la fable" do not exist to conceal the "vérité fine" from some official censor or the unworthy masses any more than they exist to merely provide entertainment for the reader. Voltaire's unique brand of fable is rather a particularly apt instrument for fostering the critical spirit he prized, a fact we can better appreciate if we examine the fable in the context of the range of eighteenth-century meanings of the term.[12] In its most fundamental sense, fable is fiction. It is an account of events presented as false, "le récit des faits donnés pour faux" (19: 346), in contrast to historical accounts that purport to relate events faithfully. Voltaire often refers to two particular forms of fiction, also identified as fable. We have already noted his reference to Aesopian fable. Fable could also refer to what we today label myth or legend. Winnowing authentic history from the mass of ancient legends that passed for history had long been part of the philosophic enterprise. Voltaire was especially sensitive to the fact that fable in this sense had often been used to convey moral or religious doctrine.[13] Allegorical interpretation of pagan myths allowed them to be used as ethical instruction; Christian dogma itself is prefigured in the Old Testament and embedded in the events of the life of Christ. Voltaire, who dreamed of a purified religion with fewer concessions given to man's anthropomorphic tendencies, addressed the issue of using fable or legend as a bearer of truth in the article "Fraude" of the *Dictionnaire philosophique,* where the ideal of indoctrinating the masses in the central principles of moral law without recourse to myth or legend is defended: "on peut enseigner la vérité au peuple sans la soutenir par des fables" (19: 207).

Whatever success Voltaire might have had in propagating the core tenants of his deistic credo—the existence of God and the reality of natural law—without embodying them in an imaginative frame of fable, his own personal form of fable, the *conte philosophique,* was an especially effective medium for denouncing the doctrines of his enemies. Voltaire objected to the sacred history of the *Infâme* found in the Bible because it satisfied him neither as true history nor as fable capable of bearing some moral interpretation. The Old Testament for him was a web of improbabilities; the events it recounts are so mixed with legend and preposterous happenings that they could not be considered an authentic history of the past. But the scriptures fail as well as legend or myth because they are so filled with cruel or immoral happenings that it is often difficult to read into them any edifying lesson. The Bible is "ce détestable amas de fables qui outragent également le bon sens, la vertu, la nature, et la Divinité" (26: 212).

Le Taureau blanc thus denounces the Old Testament as a fable or myth of the worst sort. Voltaire's method, however, is far from the one used in a work of eloquence like *Le Sermon des cinquante,* where he ponderously judges scripture against two of the same standards used in this *conte*—*vraisemblance* and moral value. In *Le Taureau blanc,* rather than examine the Hebrew histories with discursive argumentation, he merely juxtaposes a fable of his own invention with the personages of scripture. Voltaire's own fanciful version of Egyptian legend is not presented as an alternative to the history the Church recognized; in fact, Voltaire assumes that the reader only considers the pagan stories as fiction. It is the juxtaposition of the two that reduces the Hebrew accounts which are supposedly inspired by God to the level of the mythologies of other ancient peoples. Or more precisely, the Hebrew stories come off as inferior versions of the legends that infested the ancient Middle East. To this end, the Hebrew prophets are not presented as complete impostors. They are recognized as colleagues of the Egyptian sage Mambrès and share the same magical powers; however, they are less urbane, less successful, and far less wise. Similarly, Voltaire uses a character of his own creation, the heartless despot Amasis who condemns his daughter to death rather than break a vow, in order to highlight what Voltaire considers the barbarous morality of the Old Testament deity by drawing attention to Jepthé's sacrifice of his daughter to fulfill a vow to God. The story of the Fall is ridiculed by the parallelism between Amaside and Eve: the well-meaning serpent is less to blame for leading Amaside to commit the crime of pronouncing her lover's name than is her father who had established such an absurd taboo.

This strategy of destroying traditional myths with fables of his own invention that Voltaire directs against scripture in *Le Taureau blanc* works equally well against other widely accepted beliefs which have attained the status of cultural icons and is at the heart of his critical method in the *contes*.[14] Beginning with his first *conte*, *Micromégas*, in fact, he had aimed it at other myths of his day. In one of the most elegant discussions to date of Voltaire's use of *fable*, Oscar Kenshur proposes what he calls "counter-hypothetical fictions" as the basis of that first tale.[15] Such a counter-hypothetical fiction, "while making no truth claims of its own, undermines the plausibility of the original hypothesis" (p. 45). In *Micromégas*, according to Kenshur, "instead of opposing man's complaints about his limitations (and the implicit assumption that he could be happier than he is) with the positive metaphysical claims of the *Discours* [*sur l' homme*], that everything is as it must be, and that our limitations are necessary, we have a counter-hypothesis, according to which those imaginary beings that we imagine to be better off than ourselves see themselves as equally shackled with limitations" (p. 49).

Although Kenshur specifically refuses to claim "that Voltaire's *conte philosophique* is an intrinsically counter-hypothetical genre" (p. 50), I think an argument can be made that the juxtaposition of official myth with Voltaire's own fable is at the core of the critical enterprise in the *contes*, and that in large measure it provides their narrative coherence as well. In *Le Taureau blanc*, the plot centers around the consequences of Amasis' arbitrary taboo against uttering the name of his conqueror, which, as we have seen, provides numerous parallels with Voltaire's notion of the cruel Hebrew god. In *Candide* the action is structured around a parody of fictional genres with happy endings, whether the quest for a lost lover or the novel of adventures through which Voltaire satirizes optimistic visions of the world which minimize the presence of evil. In *L'Ingénu* he shows that the vaunted civilization of Europe has as much need of the sound judgment of the noble savage as the noble savage needs the experience accumulated over the centuries on the old continent. The focus of *Le Taureau blanc*, limited primarily to subverting Old Testament discourse, allows this strategy of juxtaposition to be perceived more clearly than in works like *Candide* where complexity of the issues raised can obscure the fundamental pattern. Such an exercise in critical reading constitutes the real "vérité fine" of Voltaire's fable. It also explains why the philosophic storyteller wins out over the philosophic orator in his clandestine writings. In the long run, fiction with its base of an imagined action serves Voltaire's satiric "vérité fine" more effectively than eloquence, even if eloquence with its affinity with argumentation seems more direct, and somehow more philosophic. If one compares, for example, the *Sermon des cinquante*, which like *Le Taureau blanc* is aimed against the Bible, the advantage of the ironic method of the *conte* is clear. The solemn tone of the *Sermon* may be more effective in establishing respect for the positive elements of Voltaire's deism, but in terms of the two works' subversive dynamics, the *conte* scores the same points as the *Sermon* against the immorality and implausibility of scripture, but in a more engaging, if not more telling way by leaving it to the readers to make explicit the "vérité fine" themselves.

V

If Voltaire adapted his discourse so successfully to the requirements of discretion it is perhaps because a fundamental tension in his thought impelled him to remain discreet. His militancy against the *Infâme* was tempered by a political and social conservatism. He placed his hopes on royal absolutism as the ultimate promoter of enlightenment, and although he envisaged a society with more personal liberty and where the rule of law would be respected, he did not contemplate upsetting radically the prevailing social arrangements. Unwilling or unable to acknowledge that the monarchy could not disentangle itself from the Church, he was forced into a stance of discretion. To speak his mind publicly against the *Infâme* would call down upon him the wrath of the civil authorities he struggled not to alienate. Not that he was unaware of the fragility of enlightenment that depended on absolutism. Witness his own experience with Frederick the Great, Louis XV, and Catherine of Russia, none of whom fulfilled his expectations about how a philosopher-prince should reign. In his late fiction, even when he tries to portray an ideal ruler, there is almost always a note of doubt impinging on the paean as seen in the refrain, "Vive notre grand roi, qui n'est plus boeuf" which closes the portrait of Nabuchodonosor in the last paragraph of *Le Taureau blanc*. On the surface, the description of the king of Babylon reigning over a vast empire with peace and justice seems to validate the concept of enlightened absolutism. But the fact that this curious acclamation becomes a tradition in Babylon reminds the reader on further reflection that kings are singularly susceptible to being deceived by their entourage, and that even the exemplary rule of Nabuchodonosor is more an exception than the norm.

Voltaire's discretion is thus just one manifestation of a powerful impulse toward accommodation with the powers-that-be to be found throughout his works, but which is especially evident in the *contes*. From Ituriel's "Tout est passable" (21: 16) in *Le Monde comme il va* to Candide's garden, from the Ingénu's socialization into the army of Louvois to Amaside's passivity in the face of her father's absurd sentence, Voltaire's characters prefer to adapt themselves to the status quo, even if they remain ideologically undaunted.

A comparison with Rousseau can be instructive at this point. The theoretical deism of both men was quite similar, as Voltaire's high regard for the *Profession de foi du vicaire savoyard* shows, but since the Citizen of Geneva placed no hopes in the French monarchy and was profoundly distrustful of the aristocracy, he hardly felt bound by the same requirements of discretion as Voltaire. He insisted on signing his works, even those like *Emile* that contained material thoroughly offensive to the Church. Indeed, Rousseau was forced out of France for this indiscretion against the gentlemen's code regarding *permissions tacites*.[16] Voltaire, on the other hand, chose the path of discretion by publishing clandestinely, and above all anonymously. Thus Voltaire's discretion allowed him to assert intellectual revolt without suffering the extreme consequences that Rousseau brought upon himself by openly avowing *Emile*. Yet it was by refusing the conventional discretion of his day which limited free expression that Rousseau created the most potent eloquence heard in eighteenth-century France.

Voltaire seems to have recognized that fiction adapts itself much better to the requirements of discretion than of eloquence. In a letter to Marmontel, in which he advises the younger writer who was famous for his *Contes moraux* to add *contes philosophiques* to his repertoire, Voltaire points to the potential of the genre as a discreet mode of discourse: "Vous devriez bien nous faire des contes philosophiques, où vous rendriez ridicules certains sots, et certaines sotises, certaines méchancetés et certain méchants; le tout avec discrétion en prenant bien vôtre temps, et en rognant les ongles de la bête quand vous la trouverez un peu endormie" (Best D. 11667). Voltaire's achievement was to turn fable against the fables of authority. He expropriated the *conte*, a form of fable that normally sought only to amuse, or in political terms to divert the readers' attention from the restraints on free expression by offering an escape into the world of fantasy. In Voltaire's hands, this discourse of diversion became persuasive fable that unmasks the mythic fables of the powerful. The amusement Voltaire proposes is above all philosophical, the delight that his readers/accomplices discover in using their critical faculties to expose error and stupidity.

Thus *le vulgaire* of Amaside's definition is not so much those readers who lack some insider's information available only to the experienced eyes of the *initiés* as those who refuse to assume the critical frame of mind every reasonable reader is summoned to assume. If Voltaire chose "le voile de la fable," it is not so much to trick the censors or to mystify the masses as because fiction, as an imaginary story, can become counterexample revealing the portion of the imaginary in the official fables. The *conte* may be a less direct mode of discourse than eloquence, but, because it is more discreet, it is a more effective instrument for a *philosophe* in a regime where discretion was the *via media* between obsequious acquiescence and the defiance that could lead to expulsion.

NOTES

1 The point of departure for any analysis of *Le Taureau blanc* is the critical edition of René Pomeau (Paris: Nizet, 1957). Other studies that treat the *conte* will be mentioned in passing. Two of the best are Maureen F. O'Meara, "*Le Taureau blanc* and the Activity of Language," *Studies on Voltaire and the*

Eighteenth Century 148 (1976): 115–75, which analyzes the *conte* in great detail in terms of various eighteenth-century theories of language, and Douglas A. Bonneville who discusses the book as a highly self-conscious work in *Voltaire and the Forms of the Novel,* Studies on Voltaire and the Eighteenth Century, vol. 158 (Banbury: The Voltaire Foundation, 1976) p. 114. The *Correspondence* is cited from the definitive edition in the Besterman *Complete Works of Voltaire,* 51 vols. (Oxford: The Voltaire Foundation, 1968–1977). All other references to Voltaire's writings are cited from the Moland edition of the *Oeuvres complètes,* 52 vols. (Paris: Garnier, 1877–1882) unless otherwise indicated.

2 One of the few commentators to point to the political implications of the *conte* is Hadyn T. Mason, "A Biblical 'Conte Philosophique,' Voltaire's *Taureau blanc*," in *Eighteenth-Century French Studies: Literature and the Arts,* ed. E. T. Dubois (Oriel Press: Newcastle upon Tyne, 1969): "What counts more than all these marvellous and fairy-tale metamorphoses is the reality of human happiness, supported and encouraged by the conduct of a good and wise king" (p. 68). My reading stresses the consequences for discourse of the fact that such wise and good rulers are the exception rather than the norm.

3 For the evolution of this *topos* in the eighteenth century see Jean Starobinski, "Eloquence and Liberty," *Journal of the History of Ideas* 38 (1977): 195–210.

4 Pomeau, p. 65.

5 *La Bible enfin expliquée* makes an interesting parallel between the Hebrew prophets and Greek demagogues: "les prophètes étaient chez la nation juive ce qu'étaient les orateurs dans Athènes; ils remuaient les esprits du peuple. Les orateurs athéniens employaient l'éloquence auprès d'un peuple ingénieux; et les orateurs juifs employaient la superstition et le style des oracles, l'enthousiasme, l'ivresse de l'inspiration, auprès du peuple le plus grossier, le plus enthousiaste, et le plus imbécile qui fût sur la terre" (30: 246).

6 The serpent's ultimate appeal is to the passions. Voltaire notes elsewhere that for the Church fathers the serpent of the Garden of Eden was "une expression figurée qui peint sensiblement nos désirs corrumpus. L'usage de la parole . . . est la voix de nos passions qui parle à nos coeurs" (26: 339). Certainly the net effect of his intervention with Amaside is not to calm, but to excite her passion.

7 This passage from the *Dictionnaire philosophique* ("Apis") makes clearer the significance of Mambrès' hidden deism: "Le boeuf Apis était-il adoré à Memphis comme dieu, comme symbole, ou comme boeuf? Il est à croire que les fanatiques voyaient en lui un dieu, les sages un simple symbole, et que le sot peuple adorait le boeuf" (18: 286).

8 For a description of the potential of authentic eloquence see Thomas M. Carr, "Voltaire's Concept of Enlightened Eloquence," *Nottingham French Studies* 19 (1980): 22–32.

9 H. A. Stavan, "Are Voltaire's tales narrative fantasies? A reply to Wolper," *Studies on Voltaire and the Eighteenth Century* 215 (1982): 283.
10 Geoffrey Murray, *Voltaire's Candide: The Protean Gardener, 1757–1762*, Studies on Voltaire and the Eighteenth Century, vol. 69 (Geneva: Institut et musée Voltaire, 1970), pp. 36–38, 180–87.
11 Roland Mortier, "Esotérisme et lumières," in *Clartés et Ombres au Siècle des lumières* (Geneva: Droz, 1969), p. 76.
12 For a comprehensive examination of the semantic field of such terms as *fable, conte, roman, nouvelle* based on definitions given in eighteenth-century dictionaries, periodicals, and literary manuals, see Nicole Gueunier, "Pour une définition du conte," in *Roman et lumières au XVIII siècle* (Paris: Editions sociales, 1970), pp. 422–36. See pp. 426–28 for the opposition *fable, conte*.
13 He treats moral and dogmatic interpretation of scripture in the *Homélie sur l'interprétation de l'Ancien Testament*, 26: 338–49. As might be expected he has no use for interpretations that see in each event of scripture "un emblème historique et physique." It is much better to "tirer de tous les faits des instructions pour la conduite de la vie" (26: 346). He deals in more detail with the issue of Hebrew and Christian fable in the *Examen important de Milord Bolingbroke*, (26: 195–300).
14 A number of critics recently have pointed to Voltaire's use of fable. Jean Sareil groups together all short didactic texts that Voltaire variously called *diatribe, conte, fable, apologue, historiette* under the label *apologue*, "Les Apologues de Voltaire," *Romanic Review* 67 (1977): 118–27. "L'apologue est donc toujours militant chez Voltaire, en ce sens qu'il vise un but immédiat auquel tous les effets littéraires sont subordonnés. La plupart du temps il est simple et naif, mais la simplicité et la naïveté sont des procédés comme la sophistication" (p. 127). Jean-Michel Raynaud underscores Voltaire's denunciation of human fabulation by means of fiction in "Mimésis et philosophie: approche du récit philosophique voltairien," *Dix-Huitième Siècle* 10 (1978): 407. Paul Lecocq assimilates *Candide* to fable in "Un apologue de l'éternel séisme: *Candide*," *Informations littéraires* 35 (1983): 77–78. One might also add P. C. Mitchell who shows how Voltaire manipulates inconsistencies and absurdities to develop a critical awareness in the reader in "An Underlying Theme in *La Princesse de Babylone*," *Studies on Voltaire and the Eighteenth Century* 137 (1975): 31–45.
15 Oscar Kenshur, "Fiction and Hypothesis in Voltaire," *The Eighteenth Century: Theory and Interpretation* 21 (1983): 46.
16 For an account of the affair see Lester G. Crocker, *Jean-Jacques Rousseau: The Prophetic Voice* (New York: Macmillan, 1973), 2: 118–27. Crocker notes, "If Rousseau had followed the usual practice of anonymous publication followed by denial of authorship, he would probably not have been personally molested" (p. 127).

Continuing Education and Other Innovations: An Eighteenth-Century Case Study

REED BENHAMOU

In many areas, theoreticians draw a wider audience than do practitioners. In the case of education in eighteenth-century France, for example, those who debated the societal effect of universal literacy, or proposed approaches to taming the human cub, are remembered and discussed, while those who founded schools, published textbooks, and imparted skills are rarely remembered. This, at least, is the conclusion that might be drawn from the case of Jacques-François Blondel, architect, member of the Académie Royale d'Architecture, founder of the Ecole des Arts, and author of the textbook *Cours d'Architecture*.[1]

Blondel first came to the attention of the Parisian architectural community with the publication of his *Distribution des maisons de plaisance* in 1737.[2] In this work, Blondel presented five plans for country estates which, though never built, allowed him to illustrate, by his own good example, the shortcomings he discerned in the work of his fellows. Blondel nowhere mentions the reception accorded this covertly didactic work, but shortly thereafter he took more direct approaches to architectural education, opening a private school in 1740[3] and, in 1743, offering the first of a series of public courses.

He built little;[4] but through his teaching, which occupied him twelve hours a day, seven days a week, for over 30 years,[5] he restructured

French architecture. His influence is taken for granted; but, strangely, little attention has been given to the means by which this end was achieved: to date, although his private school is mentioned in a variety of texts,[6] only one brief article has been devoted to his life as an educator.[7]

Blondel's exclusion from general works on French education history, such as those by Barnard, Snyders, or Léon,[8] may be readily explained. His goal was to make architectural techniques, theory, and criticism accessible to a public which included the artisan and laboring classes; and he ignored, or dismissed, the larger question debated by many of his contemporaries concerning the effect of intellectual growth on social stability.[9] On the other hand, it is difficult to see why he has not been included in works dealing with technical and vocational education, such as those by Chartier et al., Artz, or Chisick.[10] The oversight is unfortunate. His approach to teaching, incorporating techniques which have since become standard practice in many classrooms, qualifies him for our attention, as does his position at the forefront of two trends in eighteenth-century France: vocational training and public education.

Let us begin with his school, the Ecole des Arts, which he founded to train architects. Nothing of the kind had existed before. Pierre Patte, the architect who completed *Cours d'Architecture* after Blondel's death in 1774, makes this clear:

> Before 1740, there was no school in Paris where a young architect could receive his training, and learn what he had to know about drawing, ornament, perspective, mathematics, stone-cutting, surveying, or any of the infinite details involved in constructing a building. He had to go to one artisan after another to learn each of these specialties. Not only did this prolong his study, it usually meant that once he produced a plan, he neglected everything else.[11]

To rectify this situation, Blondel developed a curriculum drawn from fifteen years of reflection on the nature and needs of architecture, and assembled a specialized faculty to teach it. This group was chosen for its expertise—Blondel described its members as "known for their skills"[12]—an approach which ignored class differences to mix the bourgeois professional with the artisan. In addition to Blondel himself (who taught theory, drafting, and the professional aspects of architecture), the faculty included an engineer (mathematics and hydraulics), artists (life-drawing, graphic symbolism, perspective drawing, and model-making), and craftsmen (such as the stone-cutters and carpenters who developed three-month practicums in their trades).[13]

As time went on, advanced students also joined the faculty, certainly an early instance of the undergraduate teaching assistant.[14]

Courses at the Ecole were arranged in a three-year cycle, so that all aspects of architecture could be covered and ability could be developed through material of increasing complexity. Most of the young men who enrolled paid 1500 *livres* a year for tuition and board; but day-students were also accepted, their fees depending on the season of the year and on whether they were residents of the Paris region. The royal treasury contributed to the support of students who were meeting their architecture requirements for the Ecole des Ponts et Chaussées (the royal school of engineering) through Blondel's classes. And Blondel himself underwrote twelve full scholarships so that a promising architect would not be kept from the profession for financial reasons.[15]

Although the Ecole eventually provided private lessons in fencing, music, and dance—skills Blondel thought necessary to young men who, as architects, were "destined to live in polite society"[16]—its major emphasis was on the practical. Competitions and outside juries[17] (basic components of today's design education) were used as motivation. And from the beginning, Blondel provided courses in professional practice (that is, the business aspects of architecture), the supervised work experiences we now call internships,[18] and field trips ("conférences sur les lieux"[19]) during which classroom theory could be related to actual practice.

The Ecole des Arts brought Blondel little money—toward the end of his life he wrote of his students, "only ten pay me, the others are free"[20]—but its example inspired others both in the provinces and in Paris. In 1763, the Académie des Arts of Toulouse asked him for course descriptions (he refused, saying they were not yet ready for publication); and in 1765, former students from the royal academies of architecture and painting petitioned to establish their own Ecole des Arts, its curriculum to be copied from that of Blondel (their request was denied).[21] Blondel professed himself "more flattered than offended" by these events, but he sought to protect his approach by appointing an associate director who would continue the Ecole after his death.[22] His efforts were seemingly in vain. Dumont, a colleague of Soufflot, took it over in 1774, maintaining its links with the Ecole Royale des Ponts et Chaussées. In 1775, it passed to Daubenton, one of Blondel's former students and a professor at Ponts et Chaussées, who called himself Blondel's "successor."[23] After 1775, the Ecole disappeared from public notice, perhaps to be absorbed into Ponts et Chaussées, which was not officially recognized until that year.[24]

The Ecole des Arts provided solid instruction in the theoretical and technical aspects of building, but the number of architects it could train was obviously limited. Moreover, Blondel had a holistic view of architecture, believing that only the informed interaction of designer, builder, and client could produce an excellent structure. Consequently, in 1743, he began his famous series of public courses ("cours publics"), trying by this means to reach all members of the architectural constellation. It is here, even more than in his Ecole, that he revealed the full range of his educational philosophy and methods.

Cours publics in a wide range of subjects were popular in an era disposed toward self-enlightenment.[25] Blondel did not invent this kind of instruction, but he brought a dimension to it unmatched by any of his contemporaries. Whereas they tended to offer general lectures to general audiences, Blondel targeted certain groups, devised specific approaches for them, and provided part-time and continuing education for those in the building trades. Blondel's dedication to both architecture and teaching can be inferred from his willingness to analyze his material and delivery for their relevance to his audience, and from his equal willingness to develop innovative approaches to instruction.

When the *cours publics* began in 1743, Blondel followed the model set by the academies, inviting the public to attend the three-hour lectures on architectural theory which he gave each Tuesday and Friday afternoon to his students. This practice lasted a comparatively brief time: "We conducted only four public courses, the last of which ended in 1748. We soon saw their inadequacy. Being completely theoretical, they were appropriate only to artists. We felt it was necessary to suspend them for a few years, until we found how to make them useful."[26] After six years, he was ready to start again.

The courses which Blondel inaugurated on June 15, 1754, were revolutionary. Audiences were defined, and his lectures designed to accommodate individual interests and backgrounds. Dividing his listeners into three groups, he pledged "to speak to each in appropriate language." This involved reorganizing his material: "while the principles remained the same, we saw that to make them accessible to all students, we had to present them differently [and] distribute them into a number of different courses."[27]

One of the changes this approach entailed was in scheduling. Because of their occupations, artists, artisans, and workers could not attend the earlier set of lectures on Tuesday and Friday afternoons. To adapt to their needs, Blondel taught on Sundays. A course in theory ("cours de théorie") for artists and practicing architects presented and then tested architectural principles through applied problems in the classroom and direct examination in the field. Artisans and workers had their own course, the "cours de pratique," in which they received training in drafting, mathematics, and the applied geometry basic to wood and stone construction.[28] These early examples of continuing education were without cost to the student; and their value may be assumed from the fact that up to eighty workers devoted their one free day a week to perfecting their skills through these classes. It was also possible for them to follow a more focused curriculum, using the three-month intensives at the Ecole des Arts to gain architectural training on a part-time basis.[29]

Blondel's last course, the "cours élémentaire," was dedicated to the third member of the architectural triumvirate, the client, particularly those who would commission buildings for the State. Blondel made a direct appeal to the chauvinism of these potential clients,

> wishing them to know enough about art to be able to conceive of grand ideas, respond to beauty, appreciate worthy projects, . . . encourage talent and reward it, and, finally, reach that degree of discernment . . . that can distinguish . . . the mediocre from the excellent. It is not enough to order that . . . public buildings and roads be maintained. These expenses are praiseworthy, but if the works are undistinguished by style, proportion, or taste, our . . . cities will be buried in buildings which bring no glory to the nation.[30]

Blondel's purpose in the elementary course was, obviously, to build an informed market in which his newly trained architects and re-trained craftsmen could operate with profit. His technique was to give his wellborn students solid but somewhat simplified information about all aspects of architecture, and to back up his lectures with blackboard illustrations, cutaway models, field trips, and a continuing stream of written material.[31] These all served to stress the architectural principles which Blondel had developed after years of study and observation.[32] To Blondel, however, great principles were valid only in so far as they could be applied. He therefore took pains not only to provide theory but also the occasion to use it. Fréron, who took the elementary course in 1757, reported that:

> Our zealous professor was not content with purely speculative lessons. He took us to visit the principal buildings of this city and the surrounding countryside. . . . It was here that he allied his theory to practice, by comparing these buildings to one another, [and by] making us distinguish the truly beautiful from the unfortunate but

necessary compromise. . . . M. Blondel led us to see . . . how important it is that we not indiscriminately applaud . . . parts of a work without recognizing their effect on the whole.[33]

The elementary course opened in 1754 as forty lessons, beginning with a historical survey; progressing through space planning, decoration, landscape, and construction; and ending with field trips to famous buildings in the Paris region.[34] By 1756, the course had been divided into the three parts to which Blondel would remain faithful over the years: decoration, space planning, and construction. In 1757, the course expanded to fifty lessons in three parts; and in 1759, there were sixty lessons in four parts, the fourth being devoted to field trips.[35]

In 1758, Blondel began charging a fee for the elementary course, which had previously been "public and free."[36] He was in the happy position of choking on his own success. Attendance had risen to about eighty persons per session; and some of those were "simple workers, artisans, masters, and apprentices [who] left their shops, willing to sacrifice a day's wages to receive an education."[37] Fréron was charmed by this, but others were not. Hearing complaints about having to share instruction with "all sorts of auditors," Blondel formed small-group tutorials. For seventy-two *livres*, enrollment could be restricted to twelve or fifteen well-bred students, and they would have the advantages of multiple sections and a voice in course content.[38]

Blondel's approach remained so popular that he was able to raise tuition by a third in 1761, from seventy-two to ninety-six *livres*.[39] The following year, however, he was named to direct the teaching program of the Académie Royale d'Architecture. Because he brought the same dedication to this program as he did to his private school, he lacked the time to offer the elementary course in its entirety. The elaborate sequence of sixty lessons disappeared, replaced by more narrowly focused explorations that the public shared with the students of the Academy. The courses in theory and practice developed for artists and artisans were still taught by the faculty of the Ecole, and do not seem to have been affected by Blondel's new position.

As has been shown, Blondel was innovative in both his approach to education and in his implementation of that approach. He brought a new kind of school into existence, and inspired others to include architecture in their vocational curricula. He developed the discipline of comparative architecture. He held short-courses, intensives, and workshops. He used lectures, drawings, models, field trips, handouts, teaching assistants, and small-group discussions to make his points. He introduced architectural competitions, and brought in outside juries to judge them. He was capable of flexible scheduling and, within limits, flexible content. Pragmatically egalitarian, he underwrote the continuing education of artists and craftsmen with tuition collected from their potential employers. In joining seventeenth-century aesthetics to eighteenth-century enlightenment, he developed a thoroughly modern pedagogy.

His efforts were not universally welcomed, especially by those who saw in a general enlightenment some dimming of their own prospects. His colleagues in architecture applauded his efforts to raise the standards at the academy and to increase the level of competence among artisans; but they denounced his policy of educating craftsmen and clients in architectural theory.[40] Their reaction reveals them as fearing that the broad range of knowledge and experience made available by Blondel would erode the distinction they were endeavoring to create between themselves as professional architects and the master-masons who handled construction. They also feared that an educated client might assume himself to be the equal of any architect he hired (or, worse, might ally himself with a master-mason and dispense with the architect altogether). It is of interest that, although these views are still with us, it is becoming an article of architectural faith that educated consumers and workers help, rather than hinder, the creation of great buildings. In this as in the classroom, Blondel's legacy survives.

NOTES

1 Jacques-François Blondel, *Cours d'Architecture*, continued by Pierre Patte (Paris: Desaint, 1771–1777). Blondel (1705–1774), no relation to seventeenth-century architect François Blondel, was elected a member second-class of the French architectural academy in 1755. In addition to the *Cours* and the works cited below, he wrote *Architecture française* (Paris: Jombert, 1764), and collaborated with Cochin on three works, among them *L'Homme du monde éclairé par les arts* (Paris: Monory, 1774), a work which Fréron characterized as "un assemblage assez bizarre" (*Année littéraire* 5 [1774]: 187). He also produced over 400 articles on architecture for the *Encyclopédie*.
2 (1737; rpt. Westmead: Gregg Press, 1967). The work was analyzed by E. Schlumberger, "L'Art de bâtir à la campagne selon Jacques-François Blondel," *Connaissance des Arts* 181 (1967): 74–81.
3 Although he generally used the date 1743, Blondel gave 1740 in the article

"Ecole, (*Archit.*)," which he wrote for the *Encyclopédie*. The discrepancy arises from the fact that he founded the school before he received permission from the Académie Royale d'Architecture to do so (Henry Lemmonier, *Procès-verbaux de l'Académie royale d'Architecture*, vol. 5 [Paris: Champion], pp. 314–15 and 342–43).

4 Plans for buildings in Metz and Strasbourg were developed but not executed. Daniel Rémy, "Urban beautification in 18th century France: Blondel in Metz and Strasbourg," *Lotus International Quarterly* 39 (1983): 95–101.

5 Blondel's course descriptions, published between 1743 and 1774 in journals such as *Année littéraire* and *Affiches de Paris*, and the sequence of courses established for his students, confirm this ambitious schedule. See, for example, Blondel, "Discours sur la manière d'étudier l'architecture," included as an appendix to his *Discours sur la nécessité de l'étude de l'architecture* (Paris: Jombert, 1764), pp. 140–47; and Blondel, *De l'utilité de joindre à l'étude de l'architecture celle des sciences et des arts qui lui sont relatifs* (Paris: Desaint, 1771), pp. 75–80. References to specific journal articles will be made below.

6 See, for example, Louis Courajod, *Histoire de l'Ecole des Beaux-Arts au XVIIIe siècle: L'Ecole royale des Elèves protégés* (Paris: Rouam, 1874); Lemmonier (see note 3, above), particularly vols. 5–7; Louis Hautecoeur, *Histoire de l'architecture classique en France*, vol. 3 (Paris: Picard, 1947).

7 Jeanne Lejeaux, "Jacques-François Blondel, professeur d'architecture (1705–1774)," *L'Architecture* 50 (1927): 23–27. A second article by this author ("Un architecte français: Jacques-François Blondel," *La Revue de l'Art* 52 [1927]: 223–33) deals with Blondel's pedagogical achievements as part of a general biography.

8 H. C. Barnard, *The French Tradition in Education* (Cambridge: University Press, 1922); George Snyders, *La Pédagogie en France aux XVIIe et XVIIIe siècles* (Paris: PUF, 1965); Antoine Léon, *Histoire de l'enseignement en France* (Paris: PUF, 1972).

9 It is clear from comments in *Distribution des maisons de plaisance* and other works that Blondel respected class differences; it is equally clear that his desire to better architectural production caused him to seek talent, regardless of the social class in which it might appear. See, in this regard, the article "Ecole, (*Archit.*)" in the *Encyclopédie*.

10 Roger Chartier, Dominique Julia, and Marie-Madeleine Compère, *L'Education en France du XVIe au XVIIIe siècle* (Paris: SEDES, 1976); Frederick Artz, *The Development of Technical Education in France, 1500–1850* (Cambridge: MIT Press, 1966); Harvey Chisick, *The Limits of Reform in the Enlightenment* (Princeton: Princeton University Press, 1981).

11 Patte, *Cours*, 5: v.

12 Blondel, "Discours sur la manière d'étudier l'architecture," p. 127.

13 See above, note 5.

14 Blondel, *De l'utilité*, p. 80.

15 *Année littéraire* 5 (1754): 341. This was done throughout Blondel's lifetime,

despite the financial difficulties he experienced through mismanagement and a tendency to live beyond his means. See Lejeaux, "Jacques-François Blondel," p. 25; on p. 27 of this article, she quotes Blondel's widow who, in asking that she be awarded a pension, stated in a letter to the Marquis de Marigny that "'Loin d'augmenter sa fortune, il a sacrifié le peu qu'il en avoit et même celle de sa femme'" to maintain his school and his students.

16 Blondel, *De l'utilité*, p. 79.
17 "Les projets . . . furent jugés par les Académiciens & les Artistes les plus célèbres, par les amateurs & les connoisseurs les plus éclairés, que le Professeur avoit invités chez lui." (*Mercure de France*, June 1755, p. 199).
18 "[L']on choisera un temps propice . . . pour conduire les élèves dans les divers ateliers de cette capitale, afin qu'ils y acquierent la pratique du bâtiment. . . . Ils ne quitteront point ces bâtimens, depuis l'excavation des terres, jusqu'à ce que l'édifice soit achevé." ("Discours sur la manière d'étudier l'architecture," p. 148).
19 Ibid., p. 130.
20 Blondel, letter to the Directeur des Bâtiments, April 7, 1773, quoted by Lejeaux, "Jacques-François Blondel," p. 25.
21 Ibid., pp. 25 and 26.
22 Blondel, *De l'utilité*, pp. 72–73.
23 Pierre Saddy, "Un élève de Soufflot: Bartélemy Jeanson (1760–1820), architecte-ingènieur," in, *Soufflot et l'architecture des Lumières, Cahiers de la Recherche Architecturale* 6–7 (supplement [1980]): 193; *Mercure de France*, December 1775, p. 189.
24 Léon, *Histoire de l'enseignement*, p. 38. Daubenton, who was still associated with Ponts et Chaussées, continued to advertise for private architectural students as late as 1777. Although he no longer described himself as Blondel's successor, his curriculum and approach remained Blondelian (*Mercure de France*, April 1777, pp. 184–85).
25 More information on such courses will be found in my article, "*Cours Publics:* Elective Education in the Eighteenth Century," to appear in *Studies on Voltaire and the Eighteenth Century*, 1985.
26 Blondel, *Discours sur la nécessité*, pp. 7–8.
27 Ibid., pp. 14–15.
28 Ibid., pp. 117–20.
29 See above, note 5. If a would-be architect were to enroll only in the intensive courses, he would emerge with what we might now call paraprofessional status, that is as an architectural technician. Blondel welcomed listeners of any class into his courses on architectural theory, however; and so the determined worker could eventually amass architectural training.
30 *Année littéraire* 5 (1754): 343–44. It is worth noting that this extract from a long article is just one example of Blondel's ability to put the press to good use. The consistent content and phrasing of the articles about the Ecole and the various public courses which appeared between 1754 and 1772 in

the *Mémoires de Trévoux*, the *Mercure de France, Année littéraire, Affiches de Paris*, and the article "Ecole, (*Archit.*)" in the *Encyclopédie* show Blondel to be one of the first users of the news release, and should interest anyone studying the history of public relations.
31 Blondel, *Discours sur la nécessité*, pp. 110–17; see also, *Année littéraire* 7 (1758): 135.
32 The aesthetic merit of his views can be debated. Suffice it to say that they were rooted in ancient Greece and seventeenth-century France; and that he was credited by his contemporaries with having abridged France's flirtation with the rococo and hastened her reconciliation with the classic (Patte, *Cours*, 5: vii).
33 *Année littéraire* 6 (1757): 350–52.
34 The "Paris region" was loosely interpreted: Fréron mentions a nine-leagues' walk (ibid., p. 352).
35 See above, note 5; and Lejeaux, "Jacques-François Blondel," p. 24.
36 *Année littéraire* 6 (1757): 347.
37 Ibid., p. 352.
38 Ibid., p. 353, and 8 (1757): 235–37. Blondel also tried one section of field trips alone, but twenty-five days of peripatetic lectures were perhaps too much for elite students; the experiment does not seem to have been repeated (ibid., 3 [1759]: 19–23).
39 *Affiches de Paris*, January 12, 1761 (n.p.).
40 Blondel, *Cours*, 1: xvi.

The Changing Meaning of "Sensibilité": 1654 till 1704

FRANK BAASNER

The word "sensibilité" was one of several key concepts of eighteenth-century French literature and philosophy. Its frequent and varied use make it difficult to assign a precise meaning to the word. Like "raison" or "lumière,"[1] "sensibilité" can mean a number of different things, and the word was used in such diverse disciplines as ethics, medicine, aesthetics, etc.

This study focuses on one particular meaning of "sensibilité," namely when it was used to describe the new notion of human nature as this began to take hold during the first third of the eighteenth century in France. Throughout the seventeenth century "sensibilité" had held a neutral or even negative connotation. But in the course of the eighteenth century it became an expression of the highest of all moral values. The new notion of man's nature derived from the firm belief that we are good by nature and natively sociable. In this context, "sensibilité" took on the meaning of a virtuous love between the sexes, as well as every kind of benevolent feeling towards one's fellow human beings. It came to denote our innate sociability, and thus the very foundation of human society. "Sensibilité," in the period under consideration, refers to the innate capacity in man to produce virtue or humanity: "Vous ne pouvez avoir ni humanité ni générosité sans sensibilité. . . . La sensibilité secourt l'esprit et sert la vertu,"[2] states Madame de Lambert in 1727, and about 1750 the identification of "sensibilité" with the total of social virtues is well established and seems broadly accepted. Let us have a look at the most famous expression of the French Enlightenment, Diderot's *Encyclopédie*. Apart from a long article on the medical meaning of sensibility we find a short one giving the moral definition. The entry is based upon Duclos's *Considérations sur les moeurs de ce siècle* published in 1751. Duclos's definition of "sensibilité" was representative enough to find its way into the *Encyclopédie* as follows: "L'esprit seul peut et doit faire l'homme de probité; la sensibilité prépare l'homme vertueux."[3]

The history of the term "sensibilité" leading up to this high moral appreciation remains unwritten.[4] Such a complex history cannot possibly be the subject of a short article. This study focuses on some of the aspects of the many-sided development of "sensibilité" which led to its identification with social virtue.

Generally, the middle of the eighteenth century is considered the moment when "sensibilité" became a central concept in French literature.[5] John S. Spink, in a recent article, is right in pointing out that essential elements of "sensibilité," as it was praised later on, were part of the term from the very beginning of the eighteenth century. In this article I will take a further step back in history and try to show how new connotations became part of "sensibilité" in the second half of the seventeenth century, and thus help to explain the further success of the term. It is not my purpose to prove that there has been, as early as in the seventeenth century, a "préromantisme" which has often been mistakenly identified with the word "sensibilité."[6] What I would like to do is to explain the change in the evaluation of "sensibilité" which took place at the beginning of the eighteenth century by analyzing the meaning and implications of the term in the seventeenth century. We shall see that many elements of the eighteenth-century definition of "sensibilité" were inherent in the seventeenth-century connotations, although the positive evaluation was to be fully developed only in the eighteenth century.

Two texts shall be in the center of our inquiry: the popular novel *Clélie* (1654), which is partly a treatise on "honnêteté" and partly a love-novel, by Madeleine de Scudéry, and the less widely acclaimed treatise *Le Système du Coeur* (1704) by the Abbé Gamaches.[7] Several other texts of different literary genres will help to illustrate our main points.

The English and German equivalents of "sensibilité" (sensibility and Empfindsamkeit) did not come into use before the eighteenth century. But "sensibilité" and the adjective "sensible" had been part of the French language much earlier. Derived from Latin "sensibilitas"/ "sensibilis" both words were used as early as in the fourteenth century.[8] On the one hand "sensibilité" was a medical term, on the other it was an expression of Aristotelian and scholastic psychology, represented by Brunetto Latini for instance. In spite of these early instances "sensibilité" was not in frequent use until the seventeenth century, and it was used most of the time as a technical term.

Through the seventeenth century "sensibilité" takes on a much broader range of meaning. Apart from the general definition of "sensibilité physique" ("Disposition des sens à recevoir les impressions des objets")[9] several figurative meanings are mentioned in the dictionaries of the time:

> *Sensibilité*: Ce mot se dit de bonne part et signifie ressentiment de quelque bénéfice reçu. La sensibilité marque qu'un homme est bien né et il faut en avoir.[10]
>
> Il a de la sensibilité pour tout ce qui regarde la gloire. La sensibilité du coeur.[11]

The article "sensible" in Furetière's *Dictionnaire Universel* (1690) sums up the different significations:

> Se dit figurément en choses morales, et en parlant de l'émotion de l'âme et des passions. Cet homme est fort délicat et *sensible* sur le point d'honneur. . . . Cette femme a l'âme tendre et sensible, ce qui se dit tant de l'amour, que de la compassion, et de la reconnaissance.

First of all it must be emphasized that the context of love (this is true for the noun as well as for the adjective) is the most normal and frequent one in the use of "sensibilité" and "sensible" during the seventeenth century.[12]

A few examples may illustrate this predominant signification. Malherbe, the major poet of early seventeenth-century France, writes in one of his love-poems:

> Elle, auparavant invincible,
> Et plus dure qu'un diamant
> S'apercevoit que cet amant
> La faisoit devenir sensible.[13]

The most famous novel of the first half of the century, *L'Astrée* written by Honoré d'Urfé who was strongly influenced by the neo-stoic authors of the late sixteenth and early seventeenth centuries, does not speak often of the "sensible" love of its heroes.[14] But many other novels of the time know "sensible" lovers: in *Polexandre* (1629–45) by Gomberville it is the "sensible Iphidamante"[15] and in *Scanderberg* (1644) by Chevreau a male hero defines himself as follows: "je suis sensible et je suis amant."[16] The unhappy Mariane of the *Lettres portugaises* too defines her love given to the unfaithful Frenchman as a "sensibilité qu'il (le coeur) ne retrouve plus."[17] Probably the most famous example is the following: "Hippolyte est sensible et ne sent rien pour moi"[18] exclaims Phèdre when discovering Hippolyte's love to Aricie.

The great number of examples—others could easily be quoted[19]—shows that "sensible" in the meaning of "being in love" was frequently used and had become part of the semantics of love during the seventeenth century.[20]

In Madeleine de Scudéry's novels "sensibilité" is part of the love-theory as well. In her novel *Clélie* we will understand better, thanks to her relatively precise definitions of "sensibilité," some essential aspects of the mid-seventeenth-century notion of "sensibilité."

In the very first of the ten-volume novel the protagonists discuss the nature of ideal love and friendship. They regret that everyone speaks of "tendresse" without there being any agreement about what *precisely* has to be understood by that term. In the following discussion about the right definition of "tendresse," where important ideas of Mlle de Scudéry's "honnêteté"—and love—theory are developed, "sensibilité" is one of the key words. "Tendresse" is the condition *sine qua non* of the ideal lover, in love as well as in friendship. Aronce first defines "tendresse" in friendship:

> Mais pour bien définir la tendresse, je pense pouvoir dire, que c'est une certaine sensibilité de coeur, qui ne se trouve presques jamais souverainement, qu'en des personnes qui ont l'ame noble, les indications vertueuses et l'esprit bien tourné; et qui fait que lors qu'elles ont de l'amitié, elles l'ont sincère, et ardente.[21]

"Sensibilité" is not only a guarantee for the sincerity and intensity of the relationship, it is further a quality to be found only in morally outstanding, virtuous individuals. In addition, "sensibilité" is hardly to be found where there is no "esprit bien tourné." Consequently it is false to conclude that praise of "sensibilité" indicates antirationalism. "Esprit" and "coeur" are simply two complementary parts[22] of the perfect "tender" lover or friend. The same conviction is expressed a little later when the discussion turns to ideal love. Aronce emphasizes that love can sometimes be very far from reasonable behavior. It is therefore of the utmost importance that "tendresse" attenuates the passion and guarantees virtuous behavior:[23]

> pour l'amour, Madame, qui est presque toujours incomparable avec la raison, et qui du moins ne luy peut jamais estre assujettie; elle a absolument besoin de tendresse pour l'empescher d'estre brutale, grossiere, et inconsidérée. En effet, une amour sans tendresse, n'a que des désirs impetueux, qui n'ont ni bornes ni retenue.[24]

After all, it is "sensibilité" that makes the perfect lover:

> En effet, . . . toutes les actions d'un amant qui n'a point le coeur tendre, sont entièrement differentes de celles d'un amant qui a de la tendresse; car il a quelquefois . . . de l'amour mesme, sans une certaine sensibilité délicate, . . . qui est enfin la plus véritable marque d'une amour parfaite.[25]

According to its high value "sensibilité" can be found on the famous allegorical "Carte de Tendre": it is situated on the road to "Tendresse sur Reconnaissance" immediately before "tendresse."

This love-"sensibilité," as it is defined by Mlle de Scudéry, occurs often in late seventeenth- or eighteenth-century texts. The comedies of Marivaux provide a considerable number of examples, and in a comedy of Dufresny from 1702 the tender love is even explicitly defined as a sincere love not similar to other more superficial kinds of affection. Dorante, the lover of the piece, explains his ideal conception of "sensibilité" which unfortunately does not correspond to the behavior of his beloved Thérèse.

> Je ne confonds point cette gaieté dissipée avec le plaisir sensible et passionné que doit causer la vue de ce qu'on aime. Moi, par exemple, que son abord a pénétré, je suis resté immobile; un saisissement . . . une langueur . . . mon coeur palpite . . . ma vue se trouble . . . Ah! C'est ainsi que devroit s'exprimer sa passion; mais elle est incapable de cet amour solide et sensible.

Frosine's (the servant) irreverent objections to this noble sort of love do not trouble Dorante's conviction. He insists: "Je veux de la sensibilité. . . . On peut être sensible et avoir de la vertu."[26]

But let us return to the seventeenth century. If we consider the positive moral value of "sensibilité" and "tendresse" the question arises why Mlle de Scudéry put such emphasis just on *these* human qualities. The answer to that question becomes clear when we look at one of the *Conversations sur divers sujets* (1682), where Mlle de Scudéry summarizes once more the main points of her moral teaching. The title is clear: *Contre l'indifférence*.[27] In the name of "sensibilité" and "tendresse" the participants of the discussion attack indifference represented here by Cleocrite. Making use of stoic philosophical ideas she defends herself against the reproach that her only fault were indifference:

> Veritablement, si je n'estimois pas mes Amies autant qu'elles méritent de l'estre; que je ne les servisse pas quand elles ont besoin de mon assistance; . . . je souffrirois qu'on me condamnast comme on fait. Mais parce que je ne donne pas mon coeur tout entier; que je ne l'ay pas sensible de la derniere sensibilité, et que je ne mesle pas dans tous mes discours les mots de tendresse, d'ardente amitié, et autres semblables, je passe pour indifférente. . . . C'est ce que je ne puis endurer. En effet, poursuivit-elle, en riant; n'est-il pas vray, que ces Sages, dont on parle dans le monde, font consister la sagesse en un détachement de toutes choses?[28]

An important distinction is made between the *assistance* of a friend, which Cleocrite too considers to be a duty, and the *feeling* with the partner. For Aronce, who represents Mlle de Scudéry's own opinion, does not agree with the stoic detachment from all emotions. On the contrary, he prefers any passion at all to indifference:

> En effet, dit Aronce, toutes les passions peuvent produire de bons effets: mais l'indifférence universelle jamais. Il ne faut donc plus bannir les passions. Il faut seulement les combatre, pour les regler.[29]

The anti-stoic position of Mlle de Scudéry[30] is the background that has to be kept in mind in order to explain her praise of "sensibilité." Actually, the polemic against neo-stoic authors[31] from the early seventeenth century is part of the term "sensibilité" as it was used not only by Mlle de Scudéry but by many authors from the second half of the century, as the following pages will illustrate.

Dictionaries represent the general and most current definitions of words, and Furetière's (1690) entries on "insensibilité" and "insensible" support our hypothesis:

> Cette orgueilleuse secte qui se paroit d'*insensibilité* a été blâmée de toutes les autres, de vouloir metamorphoser tous les hommes en statues.

The following quotation from St. Evremond is even more explicit:

> Que les Stoiciens vantent tant qu'ils voudront l'insensibilité de leur secte.

And s.v. "insensibilité" we read:

> se dit figurément, et signifie, dur; qui ne se laisse point toucher; qui n'est émû par aucune passion. Un Stoique est *insensible* aux injures, aux assauts de la fortune.

Thus the negative opposite of "sensibilité" is at the time associated with the stoic philosophers. Among the seventeenth century authors of love-novels Mlle de Scudéry is not the only one to add an anti-stoic element to her praise of "sensibilité." Madame de Villedieu, whose best known novels appeared from 1669 to 1680, makes Théocrite, one of her heroes, cry out:

> C'est vous, ridicule Philosophie, c'est vous qui m'avez forcé à ce combat: vous m'avez persuadé que l'amour et la sagesse sont incompatibles; comme si la sensibilité n'était pas un attribut de l'homme, aussi inséparable de sa nature que l'est sa propre raison.[32]

The defense of passion (in which the scholars have seen the first flowering of romanticism)[33] turns out to be first and foremost a reaction against the reign of stoicism which reached its climax during the first half of the seventeenth century.

In his excellent article on "Le classicisme français et l'expression de la sensibilité"[34] Jean Mesnard points out that the attack on stoicism becomes stronger about 1650: "La mentalité se transforme vers le milieu du siècle. Le sévérité du jugement porté sur les passions s'atténue au fur et à mesure que progresse la critique du stoicisme."[35] Sénault, whom Mesnard chooses as his main source, was an Augustinian. His major work, *De l'usage des passions* (1641), is an anti-stoic treatise, as appears from the title of the first chapter: "Apologie pour les passions contre les stoiques". In fact many religious authors agreed with the condemnation of *insensibilité* even if they did not necessarily praise *sensibilité* because of its sensual implications. Bérulle, whose work was of great importance for the further development of Jansenism, advocates a proper quantity of "sensibilité";[36] by "sensibilité" he means "capacity of feeling pain", just the opposite of the stoic insensibility toward external stimulation or pain. Similarly, an anonymous conduct-book from 1685 demands "Qu'il faut garder le milieu entre la trop grande sensibilité, et la trop grande insolence."[37] The Jansenist Pierre Nicole condemns "insensibilité": "L'indifférence, et l'*insensibilité*, est un état de secheresse, et de froideur, qui fait perdre cette affection humaine qui fait le lien de la société civile."[38] And Bourdaloue, one of the best known preachers of the late seventeenth century, regrets the lack of charity among the people, using the following words: "Quelle image, Mesdames, et quel caractère! Des âmes dures comme des pierres, des âmes insensibles et que rien ne peut émouvoir, des âmes sans pitié, sans humanité."[39] But the same Bourdaloue is skeptical about our natural "sensibilité" because the corrupt human nature spoils all native goodness: "Quoi qu'il en soit, la sensibilité du coeur n'est point un crime en elle-même, mais c'est le principe de bien des crimes: car aisément elle se change en sensualité."[40] A similar ambiguity, namely a eulogy of "sensibilité" and skepticism about human nature, characterizes Massillon's use of "sensibilité." For him it is above all a sign of weakness: "Ces sensibilités vulgaires que les faiblesses déshonorent, et où, à force de donner tout à la tendresse, on ne donne rien à la raison et au devoir."[41] In later years his attitude toward "sensibilité" seems much more positive. In a long passage from his *Sermon sur l'aumône* "sensibilité" and humanity are the primary duties of a Christian: "Oui, mes frères, offrons du moins aux malheureux des coeurs sensibles à leurs misères." Unfortunately many Christians leave that precious capacity of commisération, which is "sensibilité," in the theater where they "honorent les malheurs feints d'une véritable sensibilité." Massillon is afraid there will be no "sensibilité" left for the miseries of real life. "Ame inhumaine, avez-vous donc laissé toute votre sensibilité sur un théâtre infame?"[42] Both Bourdaloue and Massillon show that for the clerical authors an anti-stoic polemic against "insensibilité" is not necessarily identical with an unconditioned faith in the power of "sensibilité." In a recent article on "Augustinisme et épicurisme," Jean Lafond sees certain similarities between those two philosophical parties. The main point they have in common is an opposition to "stoicism". The history of "sensibilité" has led us to the same result, but it shows at the same time that the difference between secular authors such as Scudéry, St. Evremond, or Méré and clerical ones such as Nicole, Bourdaloue, and Massillon remains evident.

In brief: Mlle de Scudéry's praise of "sensibilité" is part of a large anti-stoic reaction which is significant for the moralistic discussion of the second half of the seventeenth century.

Looking over the quotations from the foregoing pages we notice that "sensibilité" was often used in connection with pity or compassion, except when used in the context of virtuous love. This is true, of course, for the clerical writers but also for quite a number of lay authors, among whom we can find again Mlle de Scudéry. This third aspect of "sensibilité" was to become very important for the further history of the term in the eighteenth century.

One of the definitions of "sensible" from Furetière's dictionary quoted at the very beginning is that: "se dit tant de l'amour que de la compassion." It is exactly in this latter signification that "sensibilité" is considered an important Christian virtue similar to charity by the clergymen. In Mlle de Scudéry's *Conversations morales* (1686) we find an interesting discussion where the close relation between "sensibilité" (in the sense of love) and compassion becomes evident. Belinde and Alcionide discuss the never ending subject of true love. Belinde defends herself by saying that she feels only compassion for Poliante. Alcionide then explains that the feeling of compassion is always at the beginning of a tender love. The "bienveillance"—benevolence—which is the origin of a compassionate emotion is not identical with love or friendship but "elle peut devenir l'une et l'autre, et cette bienveillance qui nous porte déjà à une sensible compassion pourra bien devenir une amitié tendre."[43] This "sensible" compassion is of some importance not only in the discussion about love but in other contexts too. In the theory of the "honnête-homme" in the second half of the century the compassionate "sensibilité" is an essential element. There is no "honnête-homme" without this kind of "sensibilité." Mitton in his "Description de l'honnête-homme" gives a list of what a gentleman requires:

> L'Honneste Homme remplit tous les devoirs; il est bon sujet, bon mary, bon père, bon amy, bon citoyen, bon maistre; il est indulgent, humain, secourable et sensible aux mal-heurs des autres.[44]

And La Rochefoucauld expresses the same opinion in his 434th maxim:

> Quand nos amis nous ont trompés, on ne doit que de l'indifférence aux marques de leur amitié, mais on doit toujours de la sensibilité à leurs malheurs.[45]

The Princesse de Clèves, and this will be our last example, shows a compassionate trouble when the Duc de Nemours is slightly hurt during the tournament. "J'ai reçu aujourd'hui des marques de votre pitié, Madame." With these words the duke thanks the princess for the attention which she has paid to his accident. Now she knows that the duke noticed her reaction. "Mme de Clèves s'était bien doutée que ce prince s'était aperçu de la sensibilité qu'elle avait eue pour lui." A short time afterwards she regrets to have shown "sensibilité" because the compassionate "sensibilité" is also witness for the other form of tenderness she wanted to hide: "elle s'était reproché comme un crime de lui avoir donné des marques de sensibilité que la seule compassion pouvait avoir fait naitre."[46] As in the passage from Mlle de Scudéry's Conversations it is compassion which leads immediately to the discovery of her love. "Sensible" love and "sensible" compassion are intimately linked.

In summary, during the second half of the seventeenth century "sensibilité" is a morally outstanding capacity of tender love which can be found only in few individuals. This "sensibilité" guarantees a virtuous and sincere love, excluding all kinds of dissimulation so common at the court of Louis XIV.[47] This signification of "sensibilité" is almost synonymous with "tendresse"—the link of the two terms remained unbroken throughout the eighteenth century. On the other hand, "sensibilité" is a compassionate feeling for other individuals, similar to charity. Both connotations are closely related and share an anti-stoic implication. This anti-stoic element constitutes the third noteworthy connotation of "sensibilité." At that time "sensibilité" was, in spite of the skepticism of some clerical writers, a positive value not opposed to rational and virtuous behavior. The Chevalier de Méré expresses the belief of his time when he defines as the highest human scope "[de] vivre en toutes les passions que peut avoir une âme sensible et raisonnable."[48] "Sensibilité" is generally seen as a passive quality—and this is one of the important differences between the seventeenth century definitions of "sensibilité" and its subsequent development which will be the purpose of the second part of this study.

The second important text, Gamaches's *Système du coeur*, will help to illustrate the similarities as well as the differences in the meanings of "sensibilité" which emerge at the beginning of the eighteenth century. This relatively unknown text has been chosen instead of better known ones—one could think of Marivaux or Dubos[49]—because *Le Système du coeur* demonstrates in one *single* text that there is, on the one hand, much continuity in the history of "sensibilité" and that there are, on the other hand, new aspects to the term "sensibilité" which were to become current only later in the eighteenth century. First, we point out the parallels between Gamaches's text and the seventeenth century connotations of "sensibilité" mentioned above. Second, we show that "sensibilité" undergoes a significant change at the beginning of the eighteenth century.

The *Système du coeur* is divided into three discourses with the following titles: "De l'Amour en général," "De l'Amour et de l'Amitié," and "De l'Amour propre." In the preceding "Avertissement" the author explains his general position, emphasizing that reason is the principle of a moral life. "Comment sauver son coeur de la tirannie des passions, si l'on ignore la maniere de le conduire."[50] In the first discourse he repeats several times that reason is very important for the control of the human passions. These preliminaries provide the general context for a eulogy of "sensibilité", which is the subject of the second and third discourse. Like Mlle de Scudéry Gamaches does not cancel reason as a moral principle when praising the miraculous "sensibilité."

The second discourse, "De l'Amour et de l'Amitié," contains the most interesting statements about "sensibilité." Professor Spink, who has pointed out the importance of Gamaches's text for the history of "sensibilité," does not mention that the context in which the first definition of "sensibilité" occurs is that of love. Gamaches uses "sensibilité" for the first time in order to define a certain love:

> Je restrains icy la signification de ce terme [i.e., Amour]; je ne m'en sers plus que pour marquer ce tribut de sensibilité, que la beauté semble exiger de nous. Tout le monde éprouve assez quelle est cette sorte de sensibilité dont je parle.(66)

So the first association which appears as soon as "sensibilité" is mentioned is the same as in the seventeenth century: "sensibilité" as a special quality of love remains a part of the semantics of love.

In the second part of the second discourse Gamaches continues his reflections about "sensibilité," adding several other elements to the definition of the term.

> La sensibilité est le fondement de toutes les dispositions de l'âme qu'il nous est avantageux de trouver dans les autres et qui peuvent nous disposer à les aimer; en effet, sans elle on ne peut au plus avoir que les simples dehors des qualitez du coeur, c'est-à-dire, de celles qui sont utiles aux interests de la société. Il faut être sensible pour être véritablement généreux, complaisant, doux, traitables, officieux; ni les soins, ni les déferences, ni les assiduitez, ni les bons offices ne peuvent gagner le coeur, dès qu'on les soupçonne d'avoir quelque autre principe que la sensibilité.(180)

We will have to return to this very important paragraph in more detail, but two points have to be underlined here in order to show the similarity to what has been said about the seventeenth century definition: "sensibilité" is a quality owned by all persons worthy of love because (and this is the second point) it guarantees sincerity and authenticity of the feeling. Another important connotation of "sensibilité" is also part of Gamaches's definition. On page 197 he says explicitly: "car la compassion fait une partie considérable de cette sensibilité dont nous avons besoin pour les interets d'autruy."

Finally the third element of the seventeenth century "sensibilité," the anti-stoic polemic, constitutes an important aspect of Gamaches's book. He takes five pages to attack strongly the stoic philosophers. He informs the reader about the subject to follow: "Et c'est icy le lieu d'attaquer certains Philosophes qui font gloire de donner tout à la raison." He then summarizes the main sentences of the stoics which are opposed to his own belief. The stoics mock "sensibilité" which they consider to be opposed to reasonable behavior: "nous ne pouvons estre sages et raisonnables avec cette sorte de sensibilité."(200) For them compassion for a friend is ridiculous: "quand nous devenons sensibles à ses peines, quand par la compassion nous souffrons avec luy, c'est folie."(200) The conclusion of this passage condemns once more the stoic lack of "sensibilité": "Voilà . . . la langage que tiennent ceux qui prennent plaisir à se moquer des qualitez du coeur, parce qu'ils sentent qu'il leur manque quelque chose de ce côté-là."(205) These parallels to texts of the seventeenth century demonstrate that there is a noticeable continuity in the history of "sensibilité." There has not been an abrupt change in the meaning of the term with the beginning of the eighteenth century.

Let us now have a look at the differences between the seventeenth- and eighteenth-century meanings. The decisive new aspect in the definition of "sensibilité" is the following: what for Mlle de Scudéry was the quality of only a few aristocratic souls becomes a basic anthropological value in Gamaches's text and is therefore of great importance for the question of human sociability. "Amour" and "Amitié" were first used to designate the relationship between two individuals, but soon the signification is widened to include the affairs of humanity in general.[51] This amplification of the definition includes necessarily "sensibilité" which becomes the basis for all human society:

> C'est-elle comme on le voit, qui fait le lien le plus ferme de la société, qui nous en facilite les devoirs; sans elle nous ne pourrions jamais estre sûrs de les remplir, et si la raison n'empruntoit son secours, ce seroit inutilement qu'elle voudroit se mêler de nous conduire.(194)

This political aspect of the term appeared already in the long passage from page 180 where Gamaches said that the best qualities of the heart are those which are useful for society: "les qualitez du coeur . . . qui sont utiles aux interests de la société." It is precisely this utility which constitutes the high moral value of "sensibilité":[52]

> c'est pourquoy il faut convenir, que de ce côté-là notre sensibilité est toujours véritablement estimable, puis qu'elle nous met et qu'elle nous affermit dans les dispositions où nous devons estre pour les interests de la société.(206)

In the third discourse Gamaches tries to show that "amour-propre," in spite of his theory of natural "sensibilité," from which derive altruism and sociability, is the only motive of human activity. Gamaches does not go as far as saying that "sensibilité" is an innate virtue that makes man naturally good and altruistic. There is, however, a great difference between Gamaches's statements on self-love and the current seventeenth century definition: La Rochefoucauld discovers the omnipresent amour-propre in order to criticize the aristocratic society while Gamaches and the big majority of the eighteenth-century thinkers accept the fact that all derives from amour-propre and try to explain nonetheless that there can be a communal life, that there can even be a happy society.

Thus the most important new aspects of the definition of "sensibilité" at the beginning of the eighteenth century is the generalization of the quality "sensibilité" which becomes anthropological and grows into an important element of the ethical and political problem of sociability. This amplification has another consequence. Now "sensibilité" is looked upon as a useful, *active* quality from which social behavior can be derived. "Il faut estre sensible pour estre véritablement généreux, complaisant, doux, traitable, officieux."(180) One of the most frequent associations of the eighteenth century, however—that of "bienfaisance"—cannot be found in Gamaches. When he wrote his *Système du coeur* this term was not yet so generally used as it was some years later. The Abbé de Saint Pierre is looked upon as the one who is responsible for the high prestige the eighteenth century attributed to "bienfaisance." For Voltaire "bienfaisance" was synonymous with virtue: "Qu'est-ce que la vertu? Bienfaisance envers le prochain."[53] Thus, our study shows that all the new connotations which Gamaches added to the seventeenth-century definition of "sensibilité" ("sensibilité" as an anthropological fact; "sensibilité" as the basic condition of all human societies; "sensibilité" as the origin of *active* moral behavior) are exactly those that constitute the high moral value of "sensibilité" in the eighteenth century.

In the last part of this article we have to give an answer to the question why "sensibilité" became such an important notion only in the eighteenth century, although essential parts of the positive definition had been developed during the seventeenth century. One possible answer to this question (too complex to be completely resolved here) derives from an analysis of our texts. We mentioned that the continuity in the history of "sensibilité" is marked. And yet it seems clear that "sensibilité" could only develop the full provocative strength of its already existing positive meaning when transferred to a new context—that of natural law. There was hardly any other subject as pressing and as controversial as natural law at the end of the seventeenth century. The publication of Hobbes' *Leviathan* in 1651 had provoked a wave of indignation in England and on the Continent. Many different philosophers did not agree with Hobbes' pessimistic view of human nature. In England it was the clergy that postulated natural sociability and goodness of man. Among the predecessors of the theory of "moral sense," made popular by the works of Shaftesbury, one of the most important was Richard Cumberland whose *De legibus naturae disquisitio philosophica* was published in 1672. The central category of his theory is that of natural "benevolence." In France, however, his work did not provoke much immediate reaction.[54] The opposite happened to the books of the German professor Samuel Pufendorf whose *De jure naturae et gentium libri octo* was published in the same year. A shorter version followed in 1673 (*De officio hominis et civis*). Barbeyrac translated both books into French in 1706 and 1707.

These important works have one thing in common which is of interest here: they try to derive from nature—and not from divine law or providence—the constitution of human society and its basic laws. Because Hobbes' theory could not be empirically refuted, the speculative supposition of natural goodness and sociability became the central point of the reflection.[55] It is in this context that "sensibilité" assumes a key position: "sensibilité" could be made use of as an anthropological entity in order to explain the spontaneous constitution of society. Dubos expresses this conviction in a passage of his famous *Réflexions critiques sur la poésie et la peinture* (1719):

> La nature a voulu mettre en lui (le coeur) cette sensibilité si prompte et si soudaine, comme le premier fondement de la société. . . . La nature a donc pris le parti de nous construire de manière que l'agitation de tout ce qui nous approche eût un puissant empire sur nous, afin que ceux qui ont besoin de notre indulgence ou de notre secours, puissent nous ébranler avec facilité. Ainsi leur émotion seule nous touche subitement; et ils obtiennent de nous, en nous attendrissant, ce qu'ils n'obtiendroient jamais par la voie du raisonnement et de la conviction.[56]

The eighteenth century saw in "sensibilité," like Dubos, a stimulus contrary to self-love.

There is another point that may help us to answer our question. In the seventeenth-century texts, as well as in Gamaches's *Système*, there is one element missing which was to become an important part of the term "sensibilité": the belief in natural goodness of mankind.[57] When "sensibilité" is considered the human quality which can make *every* man a virtuous and well-mannered citizen if he only listens to his natural disposition, a number of revolutionary ideas follows from this. The objections to "sensibilité" formulated by Bourdaloue and other clergymen will no longer be possible because man is good and not necessarily inclined to a corrupt sensual life. The optimism inherent in "sensibilité" thus defined joins some of the general ideas and convictions of the Enlightenment. This is why the eighteenth-century authors such as Voltaire, Diderot, and many others could integrate "sensibilité" into their own philosophical systems and thus give this term a key position in the thinking of the Enlightenment.

It has become evident that the seventeenth century developed some of the essential aspects of the later definitions of "sensibilité." The wide-spread anti-stoicism is constitutive for the positive evaluation of "sensibilité." The further rise of sentimentalism would never have been possible in the way it happened without this critic of the stoic philosophy. Critics dealing with the anti-stoic movement in seventeenth- and early eighteenth-century England have come to the same conclusion. Although sensibility was not used in England as early as the seventeenth century, other key words like "benevolence," "humanity" or "good-nature" had the same function as "sensibilité" had in France. M. W. Sams concludes his study on "Anti-Stoicism in 17th and Early 18th-Century England" with the following sentences: "The attack on apathy of necessity preceded sentimentalism, but sentimentalism did not of necessity follow the attack on apathy."[58] The same conclusion follows from the history of "sensibilité" in France. The associations which exist in the seventeenth century, above all that of virtuous love with an anti-stoic element, are *necessary* presuppositions of the further history. The amplification and generalization which the term undergoes in Gamaches's text is immediately based upon the preexisting definition. Mlle de Scudéry seems to be the contemporary author who was most concerned with a definition of "sensibilité" and "sensible." She not only uses these terms, but she defines "sensibilité" in the context of her moralistic love-theory. None of the allegorical maps published after the success of her *Carte de Tendre*—fifteen of them are known from the seventeenth century alone![59]—concedes a place to "sensibilité" in the geography of love like Mlle de Scudéry had done. "Sensibilité" in the signification described in the first part of our paper can be called an "invention" of Mlle de Scudéry—although the word had already existed for a long time.

Without the contribution of the seventeenth century, "sensibilité" would never have become the key term which, together with reason, stands for a new human ideal whose general characteristics Roland Mortier outlines in such an impressive way:

> "Sensibilité" et lumières appartiennent à des ordres différents, mais elles peuvent se fortifier mutuellement, elles vont dans le même sens et tendent vers la réalisation d'un type humain complet dont le bonheur consistera, non à se mutiler d'une part de soi-même (comme la princesse de Clèves), mais à assumer pleinement *tous* les aspects de son "moi".[60]

NOTES

1 See Roland Mortier, "'Lumière' et 'Lumières', histoire d'une image et d'une idée" in *Clartés et ombres du siècle des lumières*, (Genève, 1969), pp. 13–59.

2 Marquise de Lambert, *Reflexions nouvelles sur les femmes* (Paris, 1727), p. 155.

3 Charles Pinot Duclos, *Considérations sur les moeurs de ce siècle* (Lausanne, 1970), p. 235

4 Apart from a few short articles we have only one work on the subject: 4 volumes of Trahard's *Maîtres de la sensibilité française* (Paris, 1931), which unfortunately lacks a systematic approach. Among the articles two have to be mentioned. Arthur M. Wilson, "Sensibility in France in the 18th

Century: A Study in Word History," *French Quarterly* 13 (1931): 35–46; John S. Spink, "Sentiment, sensible, sensibilité: les mots, les idées d'après les moralistes français et britanniques du début du 18e siècle," *Zagadnienia Rodzajów Literackich* 20 (1977): 33–46.
5 One of the innumerable examples is the anthology, used in French high schools, of the "grands auteurs français du programme" (3d volume: *Eighteenth century*) by A. Lagarde and L. Michard. Geoffroy Atkinson with his book *The Sentimental Revolution: French Writers of 1690–1740*, (Washington, 1965), was one of the first to correct this erroneous view.
6 Critics have often tried to identify "sensibilité" and romanticism: cf. Emile Deschanel, *Le romantisme des classiques*, 6 vols. (Paris, 1886–91) and more recently Maurice Magendie, *Le roman français au XVIIe siècle. De l'Astrée au Grand Cyrus* (Paris 1932), chap. 13: "Le romantisme dans le roman."
7 The Abbé Gamaches (1672–1756) had become famous thanks to his astronomic works. He was a member of the Académie des Sciences since 1735. There was a second edition of the *Système du coeur* in 1708.
8 For the early history of "sensibilité/sensible" see Eugen Lerch "Sinn, Sinne, Sinnlichkeit," *Archiv für die gesamte Psychologie* 103 (1939): 446–95 and Hildegard Kruchen, "Sensus" in *Europäische Schlüsselwörter*, hrsg. vom Sprachwissenschaftlichen Kolloquium Bonn, Bd. 2 (München, 1964), pp. 141–66.
9 Antoine Furetière, *Dictionnaire Universel de la langue française* (Paris, 1690).
10 César Pierre Richelet, *Dictionnaire François* (Genève 1680).
11 *Dictionnaire de l'Académie Française*, 1694.
12 The big *Dictionnaire* of Larousse (1971) calls this signification the "classique" one.
13 François de Malherbe, *Oeuvres*, éd. Lalanne (Paris, 1869), 1:12; vv. 252–54.
14 Honoré d'Urfé, *L'Astrée*, ed. H. Vaganay (Genève, 1966). The opposite of "sensible," that is, "insensible," is used more often and is always related to love: "insensible bergère" (1.1, p. 29), "le coeur n'est pas insensible aux coups de l'amant" (1.8, p. 319).
15 Marin Le Roy de Gomberville, *Polexandre* (Paris, 1629–45), 4:7.
16 Urbain Chevreau, *Scanderberg* (Paris, 1644), 1:421.
17 Guilleragues, *Lettres portugaises*, éd. F. Deloffre (Genève, 1972), p. 172.
18 *Phèdre*, 4:5; v. 1203.
19 For more examples see Raymond Lebègue, "La sensibilité dans les lettres d'amour au XVIIe siècle," *Cahiers de l'Association Internationale des études françaises*, no. 11 (1959), pp. 77–85.
20 In his book with the promising title *Langue et sensibilité au 17e siècle. L'évolution du vocabulaire affectif* (Genève, 1975), Pierre Dumonceaux does not analyse the use of "tendresse" or "sensibilité." His interest is focused on terms like "charme," "ravir," "ennui," "gêne," etc.
21 Madeleine de Scudéry, *Clélie, histoire romaine* (Paris/Amsterdam, 1660–61), 1:211.
22 The connection of "esprit" and "coeur" was quite frequent in the seven-

teenth century. The theorists of the "honnête-homme" saw an important condition in the link of these two qualities: "Pour avoir cette Honnesteté au plus haut degré, il faut avoir l'esprit excellent et le coeur bien fait, et qu'ils soient tous deux de concert ensemble" (Mitton in St. Evremond: *Oeuvres meslées* [Paris, 1680], 6:4), and Chevalier de Méré: "L'honnêteté, comme j'ai dit, est le comble et le couronnement de toutes les vertues: Car peu s'en faut, que nous ne comprenions sous ce mot, les plus belles qualitez du coeur et de l'esprit" (Chevalier de Méré: *Oeuvres complètes* [Paris 1930], 3:77).

23 A quotation from the third volume *Clélie* (p. 1408) shows how much Mlle de Scudéry was concerned with the compatibility of true love and virtue: "Une parfaite amour ne peut jamais naistre dans le coeur d'une personne sans vertu."

24 Ibid., 1:215–16.
25 Ibid., p. 220.
26 *Le double veuvage* 1.1, in *Oeuvres de Dufresny* (Paris, 1747), 2:16–18; cited from Garapon, "Sensibilité et sensiblerie dans les comédies de la seconde moitié du XVIIe siècle," *Cahiers de l'Association Internationale des études françaises*, no. 11 (1959), pp. 67–76.
27 Mlle de Scudéry, *Conversations sur divers sujets* (Amsterdam, 1682), 2:51ff.
28 Ibid., pp. 53–54.
29 Ibid., p. 64.
30 See also *Nouvelles conversations morales* (Paris, 1688), 1:123.
31 On the subject of the combat between "passion" and "reason" and the role of the neo-stoics in it see Anthony Levi, *French Moralists. The Theory of the Passions, 1585 to 1649* (Oxford, 1964).
32 Mme de Villedieu, *Oeuvres complètes* (Paris, 1720; rpt. Genève, 1971), 3:187f. For more examples see Shirley Jones, "Examples of Sensibility in the late 17th Century Feminine Novel in France," *Modern Language Review* 61 (1966): 199–208.
33 Beside n. 6 see also Antoine Adam, *Histoire de la littérature française au XVIIe siècle*, 2:139.
34 Jean Mesnard, "Le classicisme Français et l'Expression de la Sensibilité," in Ronald G. Popperwell, ed., *Expression, Communication and Experience in Literature and Language* (Modern Humanities Research Association, 1973), pp. 28–37.
35 Ibid., p. 31.
36 Pierre de Bérulle, *Oeuvres complètes* (Paris, 1644; rpt. Montsoult, 1959–60), 2:1059f.
37 *Les règles de la sagesse ou la manière de se conduire saintement dans la vie chrétienne* (Paris, 1685), Règle X.
38 Cited from Furetière's *Dictionnaire* (1690) s.v. "insensibilité."
39 Louis Bourdaloue, *Oeuvres complètes* (Paris, 1890), 4:13.
40 Ibid., p. 451. Both Malebranche and Fénelon used "sensibilité" in the sense of "sensualité" and therefore disparaged this quality. This may be the reason why Fénelon did not use "sensibilité" even once in his very suc-

cessful novel *Télémaque* although other terms like "tendresse," "bonté," "humanité" are of great importance in the text, so that several critics rightly have cited *Télémaque* as an important text in the history of sentimentalism.
41 Massillon, *Oeuvres* (Paris, 1769–1780), 9:192.
42 Ibid., 3:131. The polemic against the theater is typical of the position of the church in that time.
43 Mlle de Scudéry, *Conversations morales* (Paris, 1686), 2:975.
44 Published in Charles de St. Evremond, *Oeuvres meslées* (Paris, 1680), 6:8.
45 La Rochefoucauld, *Maximes et réflexions diverses* (Paris, 1976), no. 434, p. 114.
46 Mme de La Fayette, *La Princesse de Cléves et autres romans* (Paris, 1972), pp. 209 and 235. Other quotations from Mme de La Fayette's work underline what has been said. In *Le triomphe de l'indifférence,* for instance, Mlle de La Tremblaye asks: "Mais pourquoi . . . le coeur a-t-il été fait si sensible, s'il ne doit pas aimer?" (p. 31).
47 In addition to the cited passage, see Scudéry, *Conversations sur divers sujets,* 1:164ff., *De la dissimulation et de la sincérité.* For this subject in the work of Mme de La Fayette see Roland Galle, "'Aveu' und Intimitätsbildung. Das Geständnis der Princesse de Cléves als Abschied von der höfischen Gesellschaft," *Poetica* 12 (1980): 182–204.
48 Chevalier de Méré, *Lettres* (Paris, 1682), 2:561.
49 Dubos will be cited later. For Marivaux see Ruth Kirby Jamieson, *Marivaux: A Study in Sensibility* (New York, 1941).
50 Abbé Gamaches, *Le Système du coeur* (Paris, 1704). The numbers in brackets give the page numbers for this edition.
51 We can not follow here the rather complex development of "Amour" and "Amitié" in the seventeenth century. Perrault's short *Dialogue de l'Amour et de l'Amitié* may illustrate the relation between the two terms. For the subject in general see two recent studies: Jean-Michel Pelous, *Amour Précieux—Amour galant (1654–1675)* (Paris, 1980) and Niklas Luhmann, *Liebe als Passion. Zur Codierung von Intimität* (Frankfurt/Main, 1982), especially chap. 7.
52 On p. 194 Gamaches says: "pour cela il est necessaire que nous ayons de la sensibilité, et nous retombons encore dans le principe des avantages et de l'utilité de cette première qualité du coeur."
53 *Dictionnaire philosophique,* Art. "vertu" in *Oeuvres complètes,* éd. Moland (Paris, 1877–1885), 20:573.
54 The only noteworthy article on the work in the reviews of the time is in Leclerc's *Bibliothèque Universelle et Historique,* 1686, 3:494.
55 See J. S. Spink, "Sentiment, sensible, sensibilité." Recently a German dissertation on the rise of English sentimentalism appeared in Tübingen: Jochen Barkhausen, *Die Vernunft des Sentimentalismus* (Tübingen, 1983).
56 Jean Baptiste Dubos, *Réflexions* (1755; rpt. Genève, 1970), p. 39–40.
57 Spink emphasizes this aspect too: "Pour doter la sensibilité naturelle et instinctive du nouveau prestige dont elle allait jouir par la suite. . . . il fallait l'adjonction de la conception optimiste de la nature humaine," p. 37.

58 M. W. Sams, "Anti-Stoicism in 17th and Early 18th-Century England," *Studies in Philology* 41 (1944): 65–78, here p. 78.
59 See E. P. Mayberry Senter, "Les cartes allégoriques romanesques du XVIIe siècle," *Gazette des Beaux Arts* 119 (1977): 133–44. At the beginning of the nineteenth century "sensibilité" itself was to become the object of an allegorical representation.
60 Roland Mortier, "Unité ou scission du siècle des lumières?" in *Clartés ou Ombres du siècle des lumières* (Genève, 1969), p. 123.

Savages, Noble and Otherwise, and the French Enlightenment

MICHELLE BUCHANAN

The notion of the French philosophes' humanistic view of the savage continues to find wide acceptance, along with the belief in the capital role played by Montaigne and Rousseau in the development and concretization of the concept of the Noble Savage. Both commonplaces, having too long served as a springboard for studies of philosophical, aesthetic, political, and economic issues, should now take their place among the myths which underpin the thesis of the nobility of Man in Nature.

The belief in the importance of the Noble Savage in the thought of the Enlightenment gave rise to the corollary belief in its conversion into a notable element of fiction and drama in the literature of eighteenth-century France. Setting aside the possible relationship between life in nature and utopistic or socialistic societies, which is the chief premise of René Gonnard's *La Légende du bon sauvage* (1946), and accepting the reality of a continuing interest in exoticism which Gilbert Chinard endeavors to prove in *L'Amérique et le rêve exotique dans la littérature française au XVIIe et au XVIIe siècle* (1913), an attempt must be made to determine whether "le bon sauvage" is indeed an important link in the chain of philosophical and psychological elements which so decisively change the substance of French literature during the eighteenth century, or whether he is one of many stock characters used by writers much as they did "le bon mari," "la bonne mère," "le bon père" (Marmontel), "le père de famille" (Diderot), among others.

From de Lisle's *Arlequin sauvage* (1721) through Marmontel's *Les Incas* (1777) to the end of the century when Chateaubriand's *Atala* (1801) heralds the dawn of Romanticism, who are those savages and what role are they given in the literature of eighteenth-century France?

In Voltaire's *Candide* (1759) Cacambo is of mixed-blood, from Mexico, but hardly a savage. At one point in the story, master and servant find themselves prisoners of fifty Oreillons, a savage tribe in Paraguay. The naked savages are getting their cooking pots and spits ready to roast the two men whom they have mistaken for Jesuits. Fortunately Cacambo speaks some Oreillon and persuades the savages that Candide is not a Jesuit and has in fact just killed one. Adds Cacambo "I am persuaded you are too well acquainted with the principles of the laws of society, humanity, and justice, not to use us courteously, and suffer us to depart unhurt."[1] The scene is farcical: Cacambo extolling the Oreillons' civic virtues while they are all standing before boiling cauldrons. Indeed the Oreillons release the two prisoners and show them "all sorts of civilities: offer them girls, give them refreshments, and reconduct them to the confines of their country, crying before them all the way, in token of joy, 'He is no Jesuit, he is no Jesuit!'"[2]

L'Ingénu of Voltaire, first published in 1767, becomes in one English translation *The Child of Nature*, in another *The Simple Soul*, again in another *The Huron*. The hero is a Huron and a fine lad he is: "His head was uncovered, and his legs bare; instead of shoes, he wore a kind of sandals. From his head his long hair flowed in tresses, while a small, close doublet displayed the beauty of his shape. He had a sweet and martial air."[3] He speaks excellent French, and the first thing his French hostess notices is his complexion of lilies and roses. The Huron delights everyone with his pleasant manners taught him, along with the language, by a Frenchman. But early in the second chapter, we find out that l'Ingénu is really his hosts' nephew. Voltaire has fun with his pseudo-Indian who needles his new-found family and friends about their religious practices and love problems. We are not surprised to see that in the end l'Ingénu, who now lives in Paris under a different name, becomes an excellent officer in the king's army and is "respected by all honest men, being at once a warrior and an intrepid philosopher."[4]

The Tahitians in Diderot's *Supplément au voyage de Bougainville*, published posthumously in 1796, are directly borrowed from Bougainville's own *Voyage autour du monde* (1771), and the old Tahitian's warning to his people that they will rue the day they welcomed foreigners to their beautiful island is based on an encounter that Bougainville had with a Tahitian chief. The captain of the king's navy had written many pages describing the loveliness of the South Pacific islands he had discovered, but philosophes and "beaux-esprits" chose to focus their attention on the few which recounted the islanders' sexual freedom. In the *Supplément* Diderot praises Tahitians, above all, for their lack of religious binds and sexual restraints. Diderot's spokesman is the Tahitian Orou who argues for the Tahitian way of life against a French priest whose counterarguments, based on the narrowest of religious constraints, lose the debate. The priest's forensic loss simply reinforces, metaphorically, his actions; he has already, before his discussion with Orou, slept with Orou's Number One daughter, now sleeps with Number Two, then on the third night with the third daughter, often crying out in the dark "but what of my religion! What of my priesthood!" And on the fourth night, he sleeps with his host's wife so as not to displease him.

Towards the end of the century, in 1788, Bernardin de Saint-Pierre published *Paul et Virginie,* often cited among works dealing with the notion of a simpler life in the midst of nature's bounty. *Paul et Virginie* does have an exotic island setting, but for all the simple life Paul's and Virginie's families lead, social distinctions remain as rigid as in Parisian society. Virginie's well-born mother is "Madame de la Tour," while Paul's unwed mother is "Marguerite." The two servants, Domingo and Marie, are blacks, one from Senegal, the other from Madagascar, and they spend their days seeing to the comfort of their mistresses and young charges. They are slaves who, like Paul's dog Fidele, are totally devoted and loving with Paul and Virginie. After Virginie, Paul, and their mothers die, we are told that "the Governor took care of Domingo and Marie, who were no longer able to labour, and who survived their mistresses but a short time. As for poor Fidele, he pined to death soon after he had lost his master."[5] The death of the slaves, symbols of kind devotion and utter simplicity of mind, and the dog's death are noted together in one short paragraph.

So, where in eighteenth-century French literature are the "noble" or "bons" savages who stand before the malevolence of civilized society, reminding morally bankrupt men and women of the lifeforce they forfeited when they forgot the ways of nature? Are they to be found, or are they only a too-long abused literary cliché?

Preliminary research to establish a bibliography revealed the paucity of works dealing with the subject. There seems to have been no study of the savage until 1911 when Gilbert Chinard brought out his *L'Exotisme américain dans la littérature française au XVIe siècle,* followed in 1913 by the aforementioned *L'Amérique et le rêve exotique.* In 1928,

Hoxie Neale Fairchild published *The Noble Savage, a Study in Romantic Naturalism in English Literature,* in which the fourth chapter is devoted to some eighteenth-century travelers, among them Rousseau. As a starting point for his short analysis of Rousseau's role in the development of the concept of the Noble Savage, Fairchild uses Lovejoy's statement that Rousseau's *Discours sur l'origine de l'inégalité* represents "a movement away from rather than towards primitivism."[6] More recent scholarship on the *Discours* has consistently defended the position that Rousseau's primitive condition is not the natural state of the "bon sauvage," but rather a mythical state, which therefore never existed, and to which, if it had existed, we should not want to go back.[7]

In 1946, René Gonnard's *La Légende du bon sauvage* deals with the legend's important contribution to the development of communistic and socialistic forms of government, as the lack of concept of property in the "bon sauvage" environment maintained the principle of equality between all savages. A couple of Gonnard's examples can lead to the conclusion that he has not read carefully some of the works he mentions.

In 1950, John Kennedy's *Jesuit and Savage in New France* gives interesting historical information on the Jesuit missions and on the relationships between Jesuit and savage in the New World.

In 1971, when Michèle Duchet published her study *Anthropologie et histoire au siècle des Lumières,* she acknowledged that her initial idea had been to study the theme of the "bon sauvage" from Montaigne to Raynal, to determine its permanence and its variants "à l'intérieur de l'espace littéraire" (p. 11). Very soon her research led her to face the problem of investigating the reality of the savage which she sees inextricably caught in the web of Christian thought and at the same time obscured by the myth of a world free of masters, priests, and laws, products of the disenchantment of civilized man with his own world. Initially she considers the "bon sauvage" within the parameters of his literary configuration, but then turns to explore the concept of the savage as "Other," to denounce the ideological nature and function of the anthropology of the French Enlightenment, and to desacralize the myth of the philosophes' humanistic virtues.

Finally, in 1976, Ronald Meek's *Social Science and the Ignoble Savage* studies the four stages—hunting, pasturage, agriculture and commerce—in the development of society. The third chapter, "The French Pioneers of the 1750's," deals with the writings of Turgot, Rousseau, Quesnay, Helvetius, and Goguet. What interests Meek in Rousseau is the evolution in his thinking from the *Discours sur l'origine de l'inégalité*, published in 1755, to his little-known *Essai sur l'origine des langues* written between 1761 and 1763.

Each of the above books deals with the savage through its own particular bias. The most comprehensive study is undoubtedly Gilbert Chinard's. His erudition is staggering, which is perhaps the reason no one seems to have seriously challenged some of his interpretations—especially his enthusiastic conviction that we must see in Montaigne the defender of Indians, a man whose lips have tasted of "le lait de l'humaine tendresse" (p. 214), and whose words announce "les pages les plus hardies des philosophes du XVIIIe siècle" (p. 218).[8]

In the final chapter of *La Légende du bon sauvage*, René Gonnard capsulizes the history of the legend in the following manner: "Nous avons vu la légende du bon sauvage prendre naissance dans les récits des voyageurs et des explorateurs s'installer dans les traités des géographes, s'introduire ensuite dans la littérature et la philosophie, pénétrer enfin dans les systèmes d'économie sociale" (p. 111).[9] Although Gonnard's and Meek's interest in the savage and his legend resides mainly in the role they play in the elaboration of the concept of social equality, both writers join Chinard in assigning two basic features to the world of the savage: natural goodness and the absence of private property. While upon the discovery of the New World, men living in "natural state" were first thought inferior for their ignorance of Christian beliefs, it would not be long before "libertins," freethinkers in religious matters, would attack the European foundation of religious superiority. Soon the idea of natural goodness of Americans served to underline the vices of civilized Europe, and was itself confirmed in the absence of the concept of private property. Then the popularity of utopias encouraged their visionary builders to seize upon the legend and let their imagination supplant close study of reality.

René Gonnard defines the savage, beyond its etymological meaning of "silvaticus," the man of the forest, mostly by opposing him to civilized man: "Le sauvage est l'homme qui vit d'une existence simplifiée, ignorante ou dédaigneuse de presque tout ce qui constitue la civilisation" (p. 12). The savage is, at the same time, better and happier than civilized man. He lives in a superior state because he lives according to the laws of nature.

The first travelers and missionaries to the New World had noted the existence in American natives of some virtues which had led them to equate the Indians with the Golden Race, long sung by Greek and Roman poets in their telling of the legend of the Golden Age. French missionaries, in particular, whose main goal was to Christianize the newly discovered peoples were happy to find them virtuous, when they had feared to find them damned without the light of Christian faith. Savages were also found to be intelligent, especially in Mexico and Peru where their magnificent civilizations astounded Europeans.

Another consideration enters into the appreciation of American natives. Hoxie Fairchild writes "the physical beauty of the Indians delights Columbus no less than their moral attractiveness" (p. 9).[10] Chinard had already mentioned this strong aesthetic element which he explained as deeply rooted in folklore, to wit, that the body is the clothing of the soul. American Indians were described as naturally and extraordinarily beautiful. Their physical beauty had to be proof of their moral beauty. This conviction was so firmly rooted in travelers' minds that they scorned negroes as a perverse and inferior race, often referring to them as "ugly blackbirds" while they admired the splendid and graceful Indians. Fairchild reminds us that even Bartolomé de las Casas "did not hesitate to advocate the importation of negro slaves to lighten the burden of his beloved Caribbeans." For Fairchild, the restriction of the term "Noble Savage" to the American Indian has no logical basis. Negroes, among other sorts of savages, should be able to qualify as "Noble Savages," but he recognizes that only when the Romantic movement develops will negroes be granted, at least in English literature, the qualities and virtues until then reserved to American Indians. According to Fairchild "the Noble Savage is . . . originally a Carib and in the early stages of his development he owes much to his 'beaux yeux'" (p. 10).

Gilbert Chinard tells us that the first Indians to be brought to France, in 1509, did not inspire much admiration. Seven of them had been captured by a seagoing captain and brought back to France, much as he had brought back some curious looking birds. Chinard quotes a description of the visiting Indians: "ils sont couleur de suie, leurs lèvres sont épaisses. . . . Leurs cheveux sont noirs et rudes comme du crin de cheval. Ils n'ont jamais de barbe et n'ont de poil ni sur le pubis, ni en aucune partie du corps" (*L'Exotisme américain*, p. 6). In spite of a less than glowing first impression, the American Indian soon becomes fashionable in France and in 1550, 1554, 1565, Indians participated in royal entries and other festivities. Chinard relates that in 1554, under Henry II, 300 naked Indians paraded in Rouen. It is said that the King had a good laugh at the spectacle, while the Queen did not seem at all shocked by the nakedness of so many men, fifty of whom were real Indians and the rest French sailors dressed or undressed as savages. It was also in Rouen in 1562, under Charles IX, that Montaigne had occasion to see and speak with one of three Indians who had come to pay their respects to the King of France. From that encounter between Montaigne and an Indian, in Fairchild's words "the Noble Savage . . . arrived in literature" (p. 21). In 1580 the first book of Montaigne's *Essais* was published and its thirty-first chapter is entitled "Des Cannibales." In it, Montaigne writes of one of his manservants who had spent over ten years in a settlement established by French Protestants in a newly discovered country, Antarctic France, today's Brazil. From what he has been told Montaigne finds "qu'il n'y a rien de barbare et de sauvage en cette nation, . . . sinon que chacun appelle barbarie ce qui n'est pas de son usage."[11] Montaigne adds that had Greek philosophers known or seen such countries they would have found them to exceed all the pictures with which poetry had embellished the descriptions of the Golden Age. After several observations about Indian practices and customs in fighting wars, Montaigne ends his essay by relating his meeting with the three savages who had been brought to Rouen in 1562. French ways had astounded them, especially the sight of overfed men while many others were starving, and they had found it strange that the needy people would not take the others by the throat and set fire to their houses.

Although Chinard believes that in "Des Cannibales," probably written in the late 1570s, Montaigne systematically gives his contemporaries a lesson in morality and tolerance, he finds in "Des Coches" written in the mid-1580s a remarkable transformation in the essayist's mind on the subject of the New World's peoples. He sees in the latter essay a sort of "engagement" on Montaigne's part against the colonization of the New World, "devant certains crimes et devant certains spectacles il a senti battre son coeur et a courageusement crié son indignation" (*L'Exotisme américain,* p. 216). Chinard's enthusiasm appears to have kept him from an objective reading of the two essays. In "Des Cannibales" Montaigne, while describing the savage and his lifestyle, finds little practical or profitable reason to go in search of new worlds as "nous avons plus de curiosité que . . . de capacité" (p. 200)—capacity for developing such regions, we should read. In "Des Coches" Montaigne does not lament the conquest of Peru or Mexico. He only wishes that such a "noble conquête" had been accomplished by Alexander, or by Greeks or Romans, all so superior to bloodthirsty Spaniards.

Careful reading of not only "Des Cannibales" and of "Des Coches" but also of "De la Modération" which immediately precedes "Des Cannibales" confirms the difficulty of clearing up all ambiguity from Montaigne's writings, but they seem to be much less passionate on the subject of American natives than Chinard and others have felt. There appears to be no other link between the bloodthirsty savages in "De la Modération," the contented natural men in "Des Cannibales," and the Peruvian and Mexican kings in "Des Coches" than the fact that they all live in "ce monde-là," the world over there.

Montaigne had read the travel books of his time, and by mentioning the Golden Age and Antiquity when he writes of Indians he discreetly espouses convictions and reflects attitudes of many of his contemporaries. That his essays are a deliberate expression of indignation, as Chinard would have it, is highly debatable. What is generally accepted is that Montaigne does introduce the American Indian into French literature, but, as René Gonnard reminds us after Gabriel Hanotaux, "sans y prendre garde" (p. 49). Ever enthusiastic Gilbert Chinard writes "il a fixé et pour longtemps . . . le type littéraire du sauvage américain" (p. 216). This time Chinard is right, but he should have written "les types littéraires" because it appears unquestionable that Indians in eighteenth-century fiction and drama in France follow the typecasting set in the two major essays of Montaigne. The few novels and plays which present American heroes and heroines offer natural men and women brought to Europe where they are subjected to incomprehensible customs and prejudices, or they dramatize the plight of the civilized Peruvians under the barbaric rule of Spaniards.

Before briefly studying such works, it should be mentioned that a third type of American appears in interminable adventure stories, to the probable delight of seekers of stronger emotions: the marauding Indian, burning, stealing, scalping, finally conquered by only one victor, firewater. That type is directly borrowed from travelers' relations: Lescarbot's *Histoire de la Nouvelle-France,* published in 1606; Lahontan's *Nouveaux voyages* in 1702, where Indian courtship rules are carefully explained and illustrated; Lafitau's *Moeurs des sauvages américains* in 1724, which seeks to prove that Indians are the descendants of Greeks. Jean-Bernard Bossu's *Nouveaux voyages aux Indes occidentales* published in 1768 adds little to the fund of knowledge about Indians according to contemporary opinion.

Alain-René Lesage, whose novel *Histoire de Gil Blas de Santillane* and several tightly structured plays count among the best literary works of eighteenth-century France, published in 1732 *Les Aventures de Monsieur . . . de Beauchêne.* The novel is based on the adventures of one Robert de Beauchêne, French Canadian by birth, fierce savage by inclination. Born violent, the young boy has for playthings knives, arrows, swords, and assorted weapons which he uses to kill all dogs, cats, and pigs in the neighborhood. Only living among Iroquois, the most cruel and violent of Indians, will permit him to satisfy his love of killing and maiming. Iroquois violence during their habitual raids on Montreal is graphically described. When Robert manages to get himself kidnapped during one of the raids, he is adopted by an Iroquois woman, and he goes to live with his new people. A comical note: Robert is so cruelly evil that even the Iroquois are appalled and are often tempted to send him back to his real parents. We expect at this point to learn how Iroquois live, but the only Iroquois activities we are permitted to follow in detail are their warring practices. We find out that they love to attack but will run when attacked, that they drown in groups of seven or eight whenever a raiding party uses canoes, and that they easily get lost in the woods.

Eventually, running out of territory to burn and loot, Robert turns to the sea and finds himself in Santo Domingo, in a plantation where negro women vie with their white mistresses for their masters' favors. The only interest in that adventure is the number of times the words "monster" and "monstrous" are used to describe negroes. We leave Robert as he returns to his buccaneering activities.

While Lesage's novel represents a minor attempt to fictionalize material abundantly available in travel relations, the list of eighteenth-century French works of greater importance and worth which present on stage or in novels characters of American birth is woefully limited. Two revive the theme of the destruction of the kingdom of Peru by fanatic Spanish invaders: Voltaire's play *Alzire* in 1736 and Marmontel's *Les Incas* in 1777. Nothing in *Alzire* recalls a Peruvian background. The Peruvians in the play could be any people fighting for freedom. Even the name of the heroine, Alzire, it has been said, sounds more Arabic than Inca. The plot is trivial and its development without surprise or suspense. The new Spanish governor, Guzman, is the arrogant son of the kind, Inca-loving former governor, Alvarez. Guzman speaks of breaking the will of the fierce Americans who behave as savage monsters, while his father laments the implacable destruction of the Inca civilization which has already begun. A timid Inca maiden, Alzire, and her renegade Inca lover, Zamore, complete the cast. Guzman wants to marry Alzire in spite of her "coeur sauvage." By Act 3 the wedding is to take place, and Zamore and his followers are about to attack. When they do, they suffer defeat but not before Guzman is mortally wounded. Zamore is sentenced to die and only if he converts to Catholicism will he be spared. As he hesitates, Guzman who is dying forgives everyone. His last words befit him:

> Américains, qui fûtes mes victimes,
> Songez que ma clémence a surpassé mes crimes.
> Instruisez l'Amérique, apprenez à ses rois
> Que les chrétiens sont nés pour leur donner des lois.[12]

The curtain falls as Zamore, overwhelmed by emotion, cries out his love and admiration for Guzman.

Marmontel's *Les Incas* was written, he tells his readers, in the hope of establishing a clear distinction between fanaticism and true religion. Somehow, in spite of the description of Inca festivities in honor of the Sun, the arrival of Mexicans fleeing conquering Spaniards, Pizarro's inability to control the rapacity of his officers, the hatred between the two sons of the late Emperor of Peru, the eruption of a volcano, the doomed love story of a young Spaniard and an Inca virgin, Marmontel's work remains without dramatic force. We are not convinced that Marmontel's Spaniards are fanatics who kill Indians in the name of religion. Gold and riches seem more the reason for the killings, even if the novel's last sentence reads "Et le Fanatisme, entouré de massacres et de débris, assis sur des monceaux de morts, promenant ses regards sur de vastes ruines, s'applaudit, et loua le ciel d'avoir couronné ses travaux."

Less ponderous are the works presenting Northern American natives. In 1721 La Drevetière de Lisle gave a play, *Arlequin sauvage*, which in its English translation of 1758 received the title *Tombo-Chiqui*, much more exotic sounding than Arlequin, with the subtitle *The American Savage*. The character is a fusion of two traditions, the literary tradition which allows the use of a foreigner to criticize customs and institutions, and the theatrical tradition of the Arlequin character. Tombo-Chiqui has arrived from his native land with his master, Clérimond, who has carefully kept the American ignorant of European manners. As Tombo-Chiqui is perceptive and shrewd, Clérimond promises himself much amusement at the expense of his servant in his new environment.

The subplot involves the postponed betrothal of the same Clérimond to his beloved Silvia, now promised to Mirabel. The outcome of this "pas de trois" is never in doubt, so we can give all our attention to Tombo-Chiqui, who is on a collision course with almost everyone he meets. "Sauvages insolents," he calls them, as he mocks the French and their clothes, and supposes that those who travel in carriages must all have broken legs. Clérimond's fun has begun. He informs Tombo-Chiqui that what makes people civilized is their need for laws to be wise and honest, which seems to the American proof that all around him are knaves if they need laws to be honest. From an encounter when he wants to make love rather than talk about it, to his troubles with a peddler who expects payment for goods which Tombo-Chiqui thought were his for the taking, to the upsetting discovery of arrogant wealth callously flaunted before abject poverty, Clérimond's servant gets an education in the customs and manners of "civilized" men. He will return to his country, he says, where he will once more be his own king, master and servant, but love will keep him from returning to the land where one needs no money to be happy, no laws to be wise. He will remain in the employ and care of Clérimond who has, all along, been vastly amused by Tombo-Chiqui's misadventures. Thus continues to prevail white man's paternalism towards the "savage."

Chamford's *La jeune Indienne,* a slight comedy in both length and substance, was first produced in 1764. The play may have been a success or a total failure depending on whose review of the time one reads. In any case, its success would not have been due to the presence of an Indian on stage, even an Indian maiden, but rather to the fact that the one-act play is a "drame bourgeois" in miniature, and that its real hero is a favorite of French anglophiles, the Quaker Mowbray. Neither the young Englishman Belton, nor the Indian heroine with the unlikely name of Betti are particularly appealing characters, while Mowbray is portrayed with the traits of a conventionally wise and loving father-figure. It is Mowbray whose daughter Belton wants to marry to gain social status and money, who finally arranges for Betti to become Belton's wife. He has seen Betti's grief before the younger man's apparent disloyalty and touched by it, he brings, as expected, the play to its righteous and moral conclusion.

What is strikingly similar in the works which have been discussed is the lack of individuality, the absence of personal characteristics in the Indians portrayed. Alzire in Voltaire's play, Cora in Marmontel's novel, Tombo-Chiqui who is more Arlequin than American, or Betti who yearns to be back in her dark cave in the thick of her forest but knows the value of a signed marriage contract—all are two-dimensional marionettes with no particular life of their own. What happens to them does not evolve from any specific delineation of Indian character or psychology. Their expressions of love or suffering bear no idiomatic Indian imprint, and a change in the origins of the American hero or heroine would not create the need to recast the character. As we get to know those Indians so briefly and so superficially, it is impossible to label them "noble" or "bons." Their contribution as "savages" to the unfolding of the plot, and to the development of relationships between characters is too slight to sustain an in-depth study. We can then perhaps divest the notion of the "savage" in eighteenth-century French fiction and drama of the overlay of philosophical trappings and view him as a faintly picturesque example of the diversity of characters which French writers of the times created for the enjoyment of their public.

Are we to conclude that there is not one "noble" or "bon" savage in eighteenth-century French literature? There is one, but few readers have met him or heard of him: Kador in *Florello,* a novel by Loaisel de Tréogate, published in 1776. The influence of Prevost, Baculard d' Arnaud, and Richardson is undeniable in the novel, but it is impossible to state precisely where Tréogate had found the inspiration for the creation of such a character. Tréogate, by profession a soldier in the King's Guard, devoted to literature when not on duty, had already written several works, most of them ignored or ridiculed by critics past and present. Reading the novel today affects one rather curiously, as, setting chronology aside, one would seem to be reading a blurry imitation of Chateaubriand's *Atala,* which was not published until 1801, twenty-five years after *Florello.*

After a shipwreck, Florello, who is fleeing the civilized world, finds himself on an island where Nature has laid out all its marvels. The beautiful Orenoco river, majestically winding its course through the green valley, serves as setting for the unfolding of Florello's story. An old man, Kador, welcomes him. To console the despairing young man, Kador leads him to admire the beauty of his enchanting valley. He advises him to forget the past and his old destructive passions. The study of nature will cure his moral sickness. The old Indian teaches his European guest the workings of the universe by contemplating the stars and many other manifestations of the greatness of the Supreme Being. Florello soon finds happiness in the peace and splendor of the island, while Kador wants him to remember that humanity will forever remain suspended between light and darkness.

When Kador offers shelter to Florello and helps him overcome the despair caused by what Kador calls "le mal moral de la civilisation,"[13] he is indeed a Noble Savage, a free being embodying wisdom, great and true humanity, virtues which he has drawn directly from nature. The story of Florello does not need to be told. Loaisel de Tréogate was undoubtedly a writer of limited talent, and it is regrettable that his mediocre skills have denied Kador an honorable ranking among fictional American natives, but, at the end of the eighteenth century, somehow Loaisel de Tréogate appears to have glimpsed the aesthetic and psychological wealth offered by the artistic representation of the Savage at his Noble best. However, only Chateaubriand's *Atala,* the jewel of pre-Romantic literature, will blend landscapes, adventures, and emotions through the artistry and lyricism of the writer we call "l'Enchanteur," the Sorcerer, to fashion the Savage into a sensitive and poignant human being for the enjoyment and the edification of the readers of the early nineteenth century.

NOTES

1 *The Writings of Voltaire* (New York: Wm. H. Wise, 1931), p. 123.
2 Ibid.
3 Ibid., p. 66.
4 Ibid., p. 162.
5 Bernardin de Saint-Pierre, *Paul and Virginia* (Boston: Estes and Lauriat, n.d.), p. 186.
6 A. O. Lovejoy, "The Supposed Primitivism of Rousseau's *Discourse on Inequality*," *Modern Philology* 21 (1923): 169.
7 "Le sauvage de Rousseau n'est qu'une abstraction, sa bonté purement négative est celle d'un être isolé, situé dans un temps antérieur à l'existence des sociétés." Michèle Duchet, *Anthropologie et histoire au siècle des lumières* (Paris: Flammarion, 1977), p. 169.
8 Gilbert Chinard, *L'Exotisme américaine dans la littérature française au XVIe siècle*.
9 René Gonnard, *La Légende du bon sauvage*.
10 Hoxie Neal Fairchild, *The Noble Savage, A Study in Romantic Naturalism in English Literature*.
11 Montaigne, *Essais* (Paris: Bibliothèque de la Pléiade, 1967), p. 203.
12 Voltaire, *Alzire*.
13 Loaisel de Tréogate, *Florello*.

Teresa Margarida da Silva e Orta and the Portuguese Enlightenment

MONICA LETZRING

Although the Portuguese Luzes were as concerned as the rest of enlightened Europe with the issue of good government, few of their writings on the subject were published in the eighteenth century, and, of those few, fewer still were published in Portugal.[1] Thus, despite the fact that it was widely read in manuscript form, Dom Luís da Cunha's *Testamento Político* (1747–49), addressed to Dom José, who was soon to succeed his father to the throne, did not actually appear in print until 1812, when the colony of Portuguese expatriots in England adopted da Cunha as their master and published it serially in their *Investigador Portuguez em Inglaterra* (1812–16). The anti-absolutist *Aventuras de Diófanes* of Teresa Margarida da Silva e Orta is then especially significant because it is the only work of its kind representing Portuguese ideas on enlightened government to be published in Portugal in the eighteenth century, and, as the dates of the four early editions suggest, corresponding as they do with current political crises, it was considered to be specifically relevant to political issues. The *Aventuras*, furthermore, stands out in eighteenth century Portuguese literature for its feminist stance.[2]

Teresa Margarida da Silva e Orta (1711/12–1793) was not, strictly speaking, Portuguese, but Brazilian, daughter of an exceptionally wealthy Paulista who emigrated to Portugal when she was five years old and there added prestige and power to his wealth in the post of Superintendent of the Mint in Lisbon. She and her sister were placed in the Convent das Trinas do Mocambo, one of the best convents available for the education of girls. Whether through the efforts of the nuns of the Convent das Trinas or through her own, Teresa Margarida received an education exceptional enough to lead Barbosa Machado to remark in his *Biblioteca Lusitana* on her accomplishments in the "linguas mais polidas da Europe,"[3] at a time when knowledge of European languages, especially French, was a special mark of culture in Portugal, and when Portuguese women were generally illiterate.[4] She herself, in the "Prologo" to the *Aventuras,* alludes to her knowledge of Spanish, French, and Italian literary works as well as a number of classical works.

Through her own and her husband's family as well as through her friendships, she was in touch with individuals and offices of considerable power. Her father was a familiar of the Holy Office, her father-in-law, Judge of the Court of Appeals, and her brother-in-law, a prosecutor of the Court of the Holy Office of the Inquisition. Alexandre Gusmão, private secretary to the king, João V, was a close friend and godfather of one of her twelve children; the Infante D. Manuel was godfather of another. Correspondence published by her biographer, Ernesto Ennes, indicates that even Pombal (then the Conde de Oeiras) enlisted her to write for his campaign against the Jesuits. Some of these connections, especially those in the Holy Office, were no doubt useful when she was ready to publish her book.

The *Adventuras de Diófanes* is a loose, instructive narrative carrying, as its first title (*Máximas de Virtude e Formosura*) suggests, maxims on conduct and morality. As its model, Fénelon's *Télémaque,* it provides at the same time lessons on enlightened rule for the heir to the throne, Dom José, and a critique of the regime during which it was written, that of João V, although by the time it had passed through the required readings by the Holy Office and gone to press, José I had already been on the throne for two years. Most of the instruction in the *Aventuras* appears in two distinct lessons on good government: a series of lectures by Antionor (Diófanes, King of Thebes, in disguise) to Anfiaráo, the young king of Corinth, who has allowed his kingdom to fall into ruin, and an example of a government formed by Prince Arnesto on the ideas in Antionor's lectures.

The first of these, Antionor's lectures, serves as a virtual textbook based on the enlightened principles which Portuguese expatriots, emissaries, or students living or traveling in the rest of Europe had come in contact with and on which they had based their arguments and projects for reforms at all levels. Corinth, as Antionor sees it, has been reduced to a miserable state: "não ha nelle caminho algum, que seguro seja; não ha lugar privilegiado, nem quem queira cultivar os campos; o commercio está arruinado, porque se lhe quebrantão os privilegios, e não ha verdade; os que admittis no vosso agrado servem-se da vossa authoridade, arruinando os creditos, e corrompendo as vossas Leis" (p. 141). It was essentially the state of Portugal. As da Cunha, the celebrated diplomat, saw it, there was little that did not need reform: "a Corte, o exército, o ensino, os tribunais e, de um modo geral, todos os costumes e todos os ramos da nossa administração pública."[5]

As in Portugal, the economy of Corinth has all but collapsed. Industry and crafts have fallen into decline: "as fabricas estão paradas, o commercio está arruinado, labora a ociosidade." As a consequence, the entire nation suffers: "os sabios se retirão, os bem morigerados se escandalizão, os pobres padecem, os vicios se augmentão" (pp. 153–54). Attempts to deal with these problems in Portugal had begun in earnest in the last quarter of the seventeenth century, the basic text for the mercantilist policy of the day being provided by Duarte de Macedo, ambassador to France when the ideas of Colbert were beginning to make their impact. His *Discurso sobre a Introducção das Artes no Reyno* (1675) argues the need to balance external trade and obtain gold by developing national crafts for export, but the incentive to do so was lost when the tons of gold arriving from Brazil made it easier to buy well-made, fashionable goods and to bring artisans in from foreign countries, and the economic problems of the reign of Pedro II persisted in that of João V. It is such thinking as Macedo's which lies behind Antionor's warning to Anfiaráo that the flow of money out of the country must be checked: "mandai que não saia para fóra a vossa moeda" (p. 141). His advice echoes that of Gusmão to the king, as his recommendation that Anfiaráo punish fraud, negligence, and ostentation (p. 148) reflects the concerns leading to the passage of the sumptuary law of 1749.[6] Antionor's argument that companies must be given special privileges and that laws giving complete freedom to trade be passed in order to encourage trade and the development of industry (p. 148) is that of many Portuguese.[7]

As urgent as the need for economic reform, in Corinth as in Portugal, was the need for educational reform. To inspire his people to a love of letters and to instill in them a desire to learn, Anfiaráo must recognize and reward skill and intellectual achievement, providing prizes and pensions for craftsmen and artists, but especially high honors and privileges for scientists (pp. 147, 152); he must send young nobles abroad to gain experience that will make them useful to Corinth (p. 152) because Corinth, as Portugal, does not have the means to provide that experience. Portuguese who had the opportunity to travel abroad soon became aware of the weakness of Portugal's educational system, still dominated by Jesuit scholastics ignorant of or antipathetic to the ideas of Descartes, Bacon, Locke, and Newton, to developments in science and medicine, and to new methods of instruction. The ideas on education that appear in the *Aventuras* can be found in the writings of a number of Portuguese: Martinho de Mendonça de Pina e Proença, who learned about the principles of Leibnitz and Newton from Wolff in Saxony and s'Gravesande in Holland and argued the need for observation and experimentation in his *Apontamentos para a Educação de um Menino Nobre* (1734), advocating specifically the integration of mathematics, history, geography, and the living languages into the secondary school system; António Nunes Ribeiro Sanches, disciple of Boerhaave and physician at the court of Russia, who called for the secularization of education in his *Cartas sobre a Educação da Mocidade* (1760) and provided a basis for the reform of the medical school at the University of Coimbra in his *Método para Aprender e Estudar a Medicina* (1763); and, above all, Luís António Vernei, in his *Verdadeiro Método da Estudar* (1746–47), a scathing, sweeping attack on all those individuals and institutions that did not wholeheartedly reject the old in favor of the new, enlightened way of thinking.

Some of these recommendations João V had followed, even if, perhaps, only at the urging of others more enlightened than he. It was under his patronage that Vernei went to Italy to study, that Bartolomeo Gusmão, brother of Alexandre Gusmão, went abroad to gain the experience that led to his experimentation in aerostatics, and that José Bonifácio de Andrade e Silva went abroad to study metallurgy, serving his country when he returned as superintendent of mines. It was under his patronage as well that the Académia Real da História was founded and that the Oratorians were granted permission to set up a school where they taught experimental philosophy, providing the first real threat to Jesuit domination of education in Portugal.

At mid-century, however, those who owed their own enlightenment to the patronage and good will of the king were speaking out against the movement toward absolutism that had begun under Pedro II and was growing under João V with the increased centralizing of power and development of the cabinet system, the decline of the role of the nobles and the weakening of the Cortes. In the *Aventuras*, this absolutism is a central point in Antionor's instruction to Anfiaráo, a ruler who has chosen his counsellors unwisely, heeded bad advice, failed to check the spread of "luxury," and, largely through negligence, brought his state to the condition it is in. We are given no evidence of his actually having acted arbitrarily on prerogative or set aside the laws, perhaps because he could too easily be identified with João, but the wise Antionor again and again counsels him that he must choose for ministers those subjects who demonstrate talent, wisdom, and good moral principles because "o supremo governo só consiste em governar os que governão," that the ruler is himself subject to the laws, which are based on reason, and should rule as he would wish to be ruled. He must not act in everything "como senhor absoluto," not only because "o Soberano se faz amavel pela bondade, e não pela authoridade," but because no mortal has so great an authority that he does not have over him the immortal gods. At times one may disobey the king in order to obey a higher law to which the king himself is subject (pp. 135, 138, 145, 151). These are commonplace maxims that might have been found in many places, even explicitly in the *Télémaque* as well as in advice of Gusmão to the king.[8]

The second "lesson" provides not more criticism and theory but a model of good government. Following the example of Fénelon, Teresa Margarida applies her theory by placing Prince Arnesto among a tribe of lazy, warlike, anarchic, mountain barbarians and showing how he turns them into a civilized society, applying at all stages the principles expounded by Antionor earlier. Unable to escape, Arnesto and his companion, Antreo, make the best they can of the situation. To make their lives more comfortable, they shear sheep and sow grain—neither of which the mountain people had ever done. They experiment with plants, water, and fruit, always sharing what they have with the people. They teach them such skills as spinning when they show an interest, conciliating when they can, conducting themselves entirely as reasonable human beings. By the end of the second year, all the people are looking to Arnesto with respect to solve their problems and have become tractable enough to pay some attention as he teaches them the importance of living according to reason and the advantages of subjecting themselves to a head rather than living in the disorder created by their absolute liberty. Having come to the realization that Arnesto is right, they ask him to be their ruler. He declines, reluctant to take on the burden and unconvinced that they are sufficiently aware of the responsibilities they will have to bear or of the necessity of conducting themselves according to reason. Although they do not persuade him to become their ruler, they do bring him to agree to write laws for them. When he has done so, he is again asked to become their ruler and this time accepts, on the condition that he govern for four years and then be allowed to retire, the government being left to whomever they should elect. In this Lockean exercise in government by social contract, the relation of the individuals to the law is carefully defined. The impetus for the creation of the laws—according to reason—comes from the people. Once drawn up, the laws are offered to the people, who choose to accept them; that is, they agree to subject themselves to the laws. Only then do they subject themselves to an executor of them. For his part, Arnesto demonstrates his virtue as a potential ruler by first offering the laws to the people and then, only after they have accepted them, assuming the charge of governing them according to those (now their) laws, thus subjecting himself to the laws of those he rules. In both cases, the primacy of the law is affirmed. After four years Arnesto retires and Antreo is elected to take his place. Under their rule the country prospers. As if following a checklist prepared for them by Antionor, they send the most capable subjects to tour the world to learn languages, the sciences, and military, mechanical, and other arts. To assure that business is carried out honestly and successfully they teach the people the horror of lying and they institute harsh punishments for those who do not heed the teachings. They establish colleges for outstanding students and others for inferiors. They bring experts from other countries.

Finally able to return to their own countries after many years of forced exile, both Arnesto and Diófanes immediately set to righting affairs, providing a sort of recapitulation of the major principles presented theoretically by Antionor/Diófanes and worked out practically by Arnesto and Antreo. They free their slaves, set up colleges and academies that admit both girls and boys, initiate investigations into the military and ministries, and punish criminals and reward the good lavishly, both of them demonstrating the qualities of the enlightened ruler.

By the time that Teresa Margarida's book appeared in 1752, José I had been ruling for two years, not showing any signs of having taken to heart the lessons offered to him in the *Aventuras*. His prime minister, Sebastião José de Carvalho e Melo, a man who had spent time abroad himself and learned just how out of step Portugal was with the rest of Europe, had not yet begun the experiment in enlightened despotism that would follow his rise to power after the earthquake of 1755. When he did, he would make use of many of the ideas of da Cunha, Ribeiro Sanches, Vernei, Gusmão, and the other Luzes whose ideas Teresa Margarida represents in her book.

It may have been because he saw so many similarities between the ideas in the *Aventuras* and the ideas of Gusmão, well known though not published, that the editor of the third edition in 1790 attributed it to Gusmão. His doing so has resulted in a considerable amount of discussion on the question of its authorship, more perhaps than the question merits. The most thorough and convincing evidence that Teresa Margarida is indeed the author is presented by Ernesto Ennes, who, having presented it, then rejects the conclusions it necessarily leads him to on the grounds that a woman educated in eighteenth century Portugal, burdened with a variety of domestic responsibilities, could not possibly have produced a work of its intellectual caliber.[9] Given the evidence, there is little reason to question that Teresa Margarida is the author.

If the question of authorship does not merit much more attention, the attribution to Gusmão is, however, very useful in interpreting and assessing the significance of the work, for Gusmão was a recognized liberal, much distrusted by the conservative court. At the end of João's reign, even association with him was enough to raise suspicion: when Bento de Moura Portugal was brought before the Inquisition in 1748, his friendship with Gusmão was used as evidence against him.[10] In itself, the attribution to Gusmão thus stands as evidence that the *Aventuras* represents the enlightened thinking of the liberals, of whom Gusmão, da Cunha, and Vernei were leaders. The evidence provided by the attribution is buttressed by the editor's evaluation of the book in his prefatory note: "Porém como a Obra he de tanto merecimento, e tão correspondente ao sublime engenho do seu Author [i.e., Gusmão], e tem conseguido a mais distincta reputação entre os Sabios, não parece justo, que havendo de sahir ao público novamente impressa, entre as Aventuras de Diófanes se conte a de se negar a gloria a quem por tantos titulos a merece, e he seu dono" (pp. iii–iv). On the basis of the similarity between Gusmão's ideas and those in Vernei's *Verdadeiro Método*, there was speculation that Gusmão was the author of that anonymous work also.[11] Thus, by the irony of syllogism, we find Teresa Margarida's work identified with that of two of the major thinkers of the Portuguese Enlightenment.

The relevance of the ideas in the *Aventuras* to political realities is apparent in the coincidence of the publication of each of the editions with a political event of marked significance. The first edition left Teresa Margarida's hands at the end of João's reign. In general, in its antiabsolutist stance and its discussion of good government, it appeals to the successor of João for enlightened rule. Specifically, in the recognizable correspondence between the thinking of Gusmão and the enlightened attitudes of Diófanes and Arnesto, it may be offering a portrait of Gusmão as the ideal counsellor and thus advancing his candidacy for a cabinet post, perhaps as a response or counterproposal to Luís da Cunha's *Testamento Político*, which was in circulation at the time that Teresa Margarida was writing the *Aventuras* and which includes the recommendation that Sebastião José de Carvalho e Melo be called to government. Gusmão, one of the most powerful figures in government at the time, had proven also to be one of the most enlightened. His influence on the king was extraordinary. That the Oratorians could establish a school, that even limited dissemination of liberal ideas could be tolerated, that books and scientific instruments could be made available for use in Portugal were all owing to the influence of Gusmão. His private writings reveal the extent to which he struggled intellectually with the superstition and ignorance of his countrymen and the growing absolutism of João V. According to Jaime Cortesão, by the middle of 1747, Gusmão had turned against the king and was leading a secret movement against him and the absolutist regime. There were those who hoped and expected that he would become prime minister under the next king.[12] Teresa Margarida, his close friend, through the *Aventuras*, speaks for them.

In 1777, the year of José's death and of the publication of the second edition, Gusmão, having died in 1753, was out of the picture. The theoretical arguments of the *Aventuras*, however, were as timely as they had been at the end of João's reign. Under Pombal, significant advances had been made, many of the kind recommended in Teresa Margarida's book. The entire system of instruction had been revised and the system of taxation reorganized. Industries had been developed and dependence on Great Britain reduced. But with these gains had come increasingly repressive measures and even Teresa Margarida, who had contributed to his anti-Jesuitical campaign, found herself in prison along with members of Portugal's leading families and other political enemies.[13] It was an appropriate time for the reissue of an appeal for enlightened government. The change in title from *Máximas* to *Aventuras* takes greater advantage of the esteem and popularity of Fénelon's *Télémaque* and at the same time suggests more explicitly the antiabsolutist content.

The third edition, in 1790, when Teresa Margarida was seventy-eight years old, does not coincide with the end of a reign—Dona Maria lived on for two more years—but with the enactment of the law of 1790 which unified jurisdiction, further infringing on feudal privilege and strengthening the sole authority of the crown. At such a time, an antiabsolutist statement would seem once more in order, and the attribution to Gusmão in this edition leaves no question about the political nature and particular point of view of the book. Somehow the editor managed to get the work by the censors, now under the authority of the state, at a time when any writing that reflected liberal thinking was suspect. Attaching the book to the illustrious name of Gusmão may have relieved the author of some risk.[14]

The fourth edition, in 1818, is a curious, truncated version including only the first two chapters, thus omitting virtually all of the political and moral content, and leaving what appears to be only the beginnings of a pastoral romance. The number of romances in the bookseller's list at the end of the volume contributes to the impression that in this abbreviated *Aventuras* the editor is offering the public nothing more than a light piece appealing to romantic taste, which would not, we must assume, care that the incidents introduced in those two chapters were never brought to any conclusion. Stripping from the title page any reference to Fénelon's *Télémaque* and substituting for Teresa Margarida's anagrammatic pseudonym simply "escrita por huma Senhora Portugueza" removed the edition even further from the original with its serious themes. And yet the times are precisely those that would call for an edition of the work as it had appeared earlier, with its full explanation of what constitutes enlightened government. Portugal was in a true state of crisis, with no settled government, a king who refused to come home from Brazil, order-keeping in the hands of an English commander, and revolutionaries calling for a constitution. In England, the political expatriates, looking for a mentor, turned back to Teresa Margarida's contemporary, Luís da Cunha, who, with her, had spoken to the political crisis of the late 1740s, at the end of the reign of João V. By 1816, they had seen his *Testamento Político* into print for the first time—in England, however, not in Portugal where, even the following year, conspirators were still to be executed. In 1820, the situation had changed. A junta had been formed, British officers had been expelled from the army, and a constitution was ready for the king to return to. And in this year, the year of the constitution, da Cunha's *Testamento* was published in Portugal for the first time. It was between the English (1816) and the Portuguese (1820) publications of da Cunha's broad plan for enlightened government, when reform was in the air but not yet safely on the streets, that the fourth edition of Teresa Margarida's own plan appeared, in its curtailed form. What prompted the publication we can only speculate, but the coincidence of the political situation, the revival of da Cunha's enlightened *Testamento,* and the appearance of the *Aventuras* is too intriguing to rest with the assumption that this work which had consistently been associated with political reform should at this time be offered to the public as an incomplete pastoral romance.

Anticipating attacks on her work and on herself, Teresa Margarida defends herself in her "Prologo" with the platitude that the forces of ingenuity may destroy the forces of reason but never defeat the splendor of truth (p. viii) and with the less lofty plea that those who find fault with the book remind themselves that the author is a woman (p. vi). The plea for tolerance on the basis of her womanhood is out of character with the rest of the book itself, for an important element of the political and moral content is feminist. The three women in the *Aventuras*—Clymenea, wife of Diófanes; Bereniza, Princess of Athens; and Hemirema, daughter of Clymenea and Diófanes—serve in different ways to present statements on the situation of women.

Of the three, it is Clymenea who speaks out against injustices to women. Women, she argues, have the same right to be educated as men do: souls have no sex, "temos igualdade de almas, e o mesmo direito aos conhecimentos necessarios." To conclude that women's intellectual powers are no more than the refuse of men's because women don't know how to learn or form opinions is "insoffrivel semrazão." If the brilliant light of knowledge doesn't shine in all women, the reason is that they don't have the opportunity for education that men do: "Não resplandece em todas a luz brilhante das sciencias; porque elles occupão as aulas, em que não terião lugar, se ellas as frequentassem" (p. 80). Even if they are not admitted to the classroom, they can and should improve themselves by reading books and applying themselves to the sciences appropriate to their sphere of activity (p. 75).

Clymenea's own concerns are mainly domestic, however, and her severest remarks, delivered at the celebration of a shepherd wedding, are reserved for the domestic scene where women, subject first to fathers and then to husbands, suffer the most immediate oppression and injustice. Fathers, out of avarice and self interest, hand their daughters over to husbands so disgusting from their profligate living that they should be led to the sickbed rather than to the altar. Some are so violent that when they come home they beat their children and abuse their wives; not even other men can stand them. And there are those who save their good humor and attention and pleasure for the neighbors' wives and make use of their own only to provide food for them, bear children, and keep the house clean. Others are simply lazy, undisciplined, distrustful, talkative, boastful, and not very clean (p. 85). And what can a woman do about this? Not much but be patient and suffer their incivilities with good grace because there is little alternative: men came first into the world; they made the laws, and they take the privileges for themselves. The little consolation that is offered lies in remembering that unless they mend their ways, as they have been warned, they will drown in the Styx, while the women who fulfill their responsibilities will rest tranquilly in the fragrant shades of Elysium (pp. 86–87). Clymenea's own behavior provides a model of the virtuous, prudent, loyal, industrious wife and mother.

In Bereniza, Princess of Athens, we find quite a different model. The advice she offers, as the life she leads, has nothing to do with childrearing or household management but combines, rather, the qualities of the wise ruler and wise counsellor. She is a "Heroine" so highly respected for her sovereign thinking and judiciousness, for her "varonil" spirit, that in any political negotiations no decisions are made without consulting her (p. 199). Her passionate dedication to educating herself stems not simply from a great love of learning, but from a sense of her responsibility as a potential ruler ("os encargos dos Soberanos não ha distinção de sexo") (p. 203). Unlike Anfiaráo, who must be instructed by Antionor, Bereniza recognizes that the charge of governing includes the responsibility of choosing public servants in whom the public good can be entrusted. Thus the study of history has for the ruler a very practical use; from it a ruler can learn of the diversity of human nature and be better prepared to choose wisely. There are cases, Teresa Margarida shows, when women can be better rulers than men; the great worry of the people of Athens is that Bereniza's hours of study will ruin her health and they will lose a princess far more capable than her brother who must be taught— by Bereniza—that there is more to kingship than playing the hero on the battlefield (pp. 199–206). If, in dedicating her work to Dona Maria, Teresa Margarida is expressing her intention that the book serve to educate a princess as well as a prince, Bereniza would be a model designed specifically for her edification. Critics, however, tend not to take the dedication very seriously, seeing Bereniza's education as a description of Teresa Margarida's, without reference to the princess. In playing Mentor to her brother, Bereniza also reflects the role that Teresa Margarida plays as author of the book.

The education of Hemirema, the third female character, is generally interpreted also as a description of the author's own ("Fui . . . instruida . . . em a Musica, Poesia, e alguma parte da Astronomia") (p. 21),[15] but her interest for the reader lies more in her role as the central character of the subversive fantasy of the fiction itself. In this textbook for the education of the prince, the prince dies in battle and is thus disposed of on page three, and Hemirema, the princess, steps in to take his place. When her parents are overcome with grief at both the death of their son and the prospect of being sold into slavery, Hemirema takes charge, and throughout the narrative she continues to be the strong center that draws all the lost ones together and leads them home. She does all those things that princes, not princesses, are supposed to do. She goes off to fight in the war in Corinth. She engineers her mother's escape from prison. She saves her mother and Arnesto from shipwreck, like a valiant soldier battling the heavy seas: "Não parecia . . . dama delicada porque como robusto soldado, animando os companheiros, se pegava com incrivel valor ao seu ramo" (p. 229). And when she has them all together, she takes them home, back to their proper places, restoring her father to his throne in Thebes and Arnesto to his in Delos. She is not only the force that restores integrity to the family, but that which restores wholeness and order to the state.

Hemirema's "proper place" we are not given to know. Throughout the book she shares with Diófanes, Clymenea, and Arnesto some aspects of the role of Fénelon's Mentor, but she is an anomaly in her fictional world, as is Bereniza, who takes her into her care. When Bereniza's death leaves Hemirema to fend for herself, she must disguise herself as a young man to do so, thus complicating her identity, for the virtues she demonstrates as "Bellino," that is, the new qualities she adds to her personality, are ones which society interprets as masculine and thus cannot be carried back into her role of Hemirema after she drops her masculine disguise. Clymenea is, in fact, the only woman left with a "place" at the end of the book, and that is in her old role as wife and mother. Bereniza dies and Hemirema, as Fénelon's Mentor-turned-Minerva, who wraps herself in an azure cloud and fades away into the heavens, simply disappears from the work after she has brought her group home. Both Bereniza's death and the failure to draw the character of Hemirema to a conclusion may represent the inability of Teresa Margarida as a writer to deal with this social/psychological problem of the anomalous woman and of her own problem of placement as an intellectual woman in eighteenth-century Portuguese society.

One of the obstacles she had to overcome in presenting her book on enlightened government to the public was, Teresa Margarida says, the voices that warned her of her incapacity to deal with such a subject (p. v). Whether the voices were those of others or her own is not clear and doesn't matter. What matters is that history has shown they were wrong: the *Aventuras* was recognized in its own time as a valuable resource for ideas representative of the thought of the most knowledgeable and respected thinkers of the period of the Enlightenment in Portugal. Her "incapacidade" is belied by the very unusual reissuing of the book four times in little more than half a century, each time (even the fourth, I suggest) because it was known to be a work that spoke to the concerns of the moment in such a way as to be, if not in each instance a useful guide for practical action, an important emblem because of what it stood for.

NOTES

1 Various articles in the *Dicionário de História de Portugal*, gen. ed. Joel Serrão (Lisbon: Iniciativas Editores, 1975) provide a good survey of the Enlightenment in Portugal, e.g., "Estrangeirados" and "Luzes" (both by António Coimbra Martins) as well as articles on specific enlightenment figures and topics. Other useful works include José Sebastião de Silva Dias, *Portugal e a Cultura Europeia* (Coimbra, 1953); Hernani Cidade, *Liçoes de Cultura e Literatura Portuguesas* (Coimbra, 1968); António Alberto de Andrade, *Vernei e a Cultura do Seu Tempo* (Coimbra, 1965); and Manoel Cardozo, "The Internationalism of the Portuguese Enlightenment: The Role of the Estrangeirado, c.1700—c.1750," in *The Ibero-American Enlightenment*, ed. A. Owen Aldridge (Urbana: University of Illinois Press, 1971), pp. 141-207.
2 The book appeared in four editions, the full titles of which are *Maximás de Virtude e Formosura, com que Diófanes, Clymenea, e Hemirema, Principes de Thebes, Vencêrão os Mais Apertados Lances da Desgraça* (1752); *Aventuras de Diófanes, Imitando a Sapientissimo Fénelon na sua Viagem de Telemaco* (1777, 1790); *Historia de Diófanes, Clymenea, e Hemirema, Principes de Thebas* (1818). The 1790 edition was reprinted with a preface and biographical study by Rui Bloem in 1945 (Rio de Janeiro: Imprensa Nacional). All my references will be to the 1790 edition. The only full study of Teresa Margarida da Silva e Orta is that by Ernesto Ennes, *Teresa Margarida da Silva e Orta e o Primeiro Romance Brasileiro* (São Paulo: Companhia Editora Nacional, 1952). This is the second volume of Ennes' *Dois Paulistas Insignes*, the first volume containing biographies of her father, José Ramos da Silva, and her brother, the noted philosopher, Matias Aires Ramos da Silva de Eça. Ennes' work is especially valuable for the number of documents it reprints. Ennes is the source of my biographical information. Most of the other studies of Teresa Margarida and the *Aventuras* consider the work in terms of its place in the history of the Brazilian novel. Rui Bloem's "O Primeiro Romance Brasileiro," first published in 1938 and reprinted with his 1945 reissue of *Aventuras,* is mainly concerned with establishing the work as the first Brazilian novel and Teresa Margarida as the author of it. He does not discuss the work itself. Ivana Versiani's "The New World's First Novelist," published in *Luso-Brazilian Studies* (Bloomington: Indiana University Press, 1946), 1:15-27, compares the *Aventuras* with Fénelon's *Télémaque* and with her brother's philosophical essay, *Reflexões sobre a Vaidade dos Homens,* finding significant differences in both cases and concluding that, contrary to

the assertions of some critics, there is no evidence to show that her thinking was influenced by her brother's. Her essay is, in part, responding to the enthusiastic essay by Tristão de Athayde (Alceu Amoroso Lima), "Teresa Margarida da Silva e Orta, Precursora do Romance Brasileiro," in *O Romance Brasileiro de 1752 a 1930)*, ed., Aurélio Buarque de Hollanda (Rio de Janeiro: Edições O Cruzeiro, 1952), pp. 13–20; reprinted from *Revista do Brasil* 35 (May 1941). Athayde argues that Matias Aires passed on to his sister the political ideas and the taste for natural science that he acquired while studying in France and that from Fénelon she gets her ideas on social legislation and economic liberalism. José Brasileiro Vilanova, "Teresa Margarida Moralista Portuguêsa" (Recife: Editora Nordeste, 1953), measures *Aventuras* against definitions of the novel by Ortega y Gasset and others and concludes that it cannot be called a novel and, furthermore, that Teresa Margarida is not Brazilian but Portuguese.

3 Diogo Barbosa Machado, *Biblioteca Lusitana* (Lisbon, 1759), 4:271.

4 Susan A. Soeira considers the position of women in eighteenth-century Portuguese as well as Brazilian society in "A Baroque Nunnery: The Economic and Social Role of a Colonial Convent, Santa Clara do Desterro, Salvador, Bahia 1677–1800" (Ph.D. diss., New York University, 1974).

5 Silva Dias, p. 121.

6 The most thorough study of Gusmão is that of Jaime Cortesão, in eight volumes, *Alexandre de Gusmão e o Tratado de Madrid* (Rio de Janeiro: Instituto Rio Branco, 1950–60); the first two volumes are biographical-historical, the other six reprint documents and writings by Gusmão. Cortesão notes some of the similarities between Gusmão's ideas and those in the *Aventuras* in 2:220–21.

7 See Carl A. Hanson, *Economy and Society in Baroque Portugal, 1668–1703* (Minneapolis: University of Minnesota Press, 1981). Hanson's discussion of the late seventeenth century also gives a very good picture of Portugal during the reign of João V.

8 Cortesão, 2:221.

9 Ennes, pp. 184–95.

10 Silva Dias, p. 166.

11 Silva Dias, p. 166n.

12 Cortesão, 1:113; 2:221.

13 Documents discovered and reprinted by Ennes indicate that in 1768 she was apparently involved in a variety of anti-Jesuitical projects. In a letter of 1768 she alludes to some notes she is sending on, a paper laying out some "errors" of the Jesuits, and a "work," a "Diálogo," and a "relação," the last two possibly the "work" in two different forms. None of these has come to light. They could not have been contributions to either the *Relação Abreviada*, an account of acts supposedly committed by the Jesuits in South America against Portuguese sovereignty, which had been published ten years earlier, or the *Dedução Cronológica*, another attack on the Jesuits giving a detailed chronological account of their disastrous influence on Portuguese history, which was published at the same time that the letter was

written. Teresa Margarida was imprisoned in 1770, ostensibly for having lied to the king, but perhaps for political reasons. She was released in the general pardon at the beginning of Dona Maria's reign in 1777, together with so many other prisoners that, according to one observer, it was "una especie de resurrección de muertos" (Ennes, p. 166).

14 Cortesão, p. 115.
15 Most critics read the descriptions of Hemirema's and Bereniza's educations as descriptions of Teresa Margarida's own. See, for example, Ennes, p. 15, and Athayde, p. 13.

Christina Dorothea Leporin (Erxleben), Sophia (Gutermann) von La Roche, and Angelika Kauffmann: Background and Dilemmas of Independence

PETER PETSCHAUER

Independence was not a word men and women liked or tended to apply with as much fervor in the eighteenth-century German setting as we do in ours.[1] All too many persons at best smiled about women one might today consider emotionally and mentally mature enough to achieve personal and financial nondependence. The vast majority of the population lauded those women who were prepared for and accepted the profession of housemother or housewife which was thought to have been specifically designed by nature for them. The debate for most women did not revolve around being dependent or nondependent, about marrying or not marrying, about having a voice in marriage or not; by the end of the century most who left a record felt comfortable that some progress had been made through the introduction of choice in the selection of marriage partners. Indeed, the ready transition of the majority of women from the ideal of housemother to housewife later alerts us that most women were delighted to have gained at least a say in the choice of whom to marry and, potentially, a closer relationship with their partner.[2] In addition, few men or women had the slightest idea that the family was changing from a unit of production to a unit of consumption and that the role of women and the upbringing of children was about to head into uncharted directions.[3]

For the purpose of this essay, I assume the meaning of independent to be similar to that of self-reliant; that is, the independent woman was not part of the majority. She was an individual who could, as a maximum, perceive marriage itself as a choice and, as a minimum, see it not as her only fulfillment. Although I will not discuss independence within marriage, I hope to make clear that a trend in this direction was one reason, if not the principal one, that women could be more free in other areas of their lives as well. That a certain secular success accompanied such independence makes Angelika Kauffmann, Sophie von La Roche, and Christina Dorothea Leporin all the more fascinating examples for discussion.[4] But let us not mistake the self-reliance of the eighteenth century with feminist ideals of the twentieth. Even if these women served occasional later and younger women as examples, they cannot be considered to have been feminists; at most, they cleared the way for feminists of later periods. Precisely because these three women were exceptions in their isolated independence, future generations of feminist women could look back and perceive them as precursors.

How did a woman become independent when almost everyone else in the society, specifically in the circle of family and friends, was geared to dependence? Several key factors overlapped for Leporin, Kauffmann, and La Roche and seem to have had significance for many other women who achieved independence in the eighteenth century. Each of these three was born with sufficient intelligence and drive to take advantage of the opportunities that arose in her environment. Then too, the family into which each was born belonged either to what we today consider the middle classes or the elite. The birth order either placed the individual at the head of a generally small group of siblings or allowed her to become the principal sibling upon whom love and attention was showered. This caring is one of the best indicators that the families had entered a more advanced childrearing mode than the majority of families in the society.[5] Probably in conjunction with this advanced mode, the parents, and this applies more to fathers than mothers, were peculiarly interested in the development of a daughter and encouraged the exploration of her talents in every way emotionally, societally, and financially possible.

I chose the three women not because they fit this list of criteria from the outset, but because they were sufficiently famous to have remained recognizable as individuals and to point me to them. But upon comparing these to other recognizable German females of the period, these criteria began to leave their speculative, hypothetical, frame of reference. At first glance Kauffmann (1741–1807) seems to be the only one of the three who does not fit into the social hypothesis. Her father was an itinerant church painter and portraitist near Chur, Switzerland, and had that remained the case, Angelika might never have known success and independence. Yet through the work he undertook for churches and leading individuals, he gained sufficient access to a middle-class style of life for us to say confidently that he and his family behaved as if they were in that social class.[6] No such initial doubt arises in regard to Leporin (1715–1762) and La Roche (1731–1807); both were born into the households of successful city doctors, the first in Quedlinburg (today's German Democratic Republic) and the second in Kaufbeuren (today's Württemberg) from which the family moved to Augsburg in the early 1740s when Georg Friedrich Gutermann became dean of the medical faculty.[7]

One can contrast the origins of these women and their later success with that of the poetess Anna Louise Karsch(in). In spite of her unrivalled talent, of being lauded by many leading contemporaries for the beauty of her work and being offered a pension, albeit small, by Frederick II of Prussia, she could not make the transition from the poverty of her parents (and their lack of support for her talents) to the comfort which should have come with success.[8] The jump within one generation from the lower to the middle class, or beyond, was too difficult, maybe too traumatic.

Birth order, the second criterion, was no doubt also significant, but not more so than the amount and intensity of the parental attention devoted to each of the women. La Roche was first born; Leporin, though not first born, received as much attention and training as her older brother; and Kauffmann was an only child. Nevertheless and aside from the aspirations that fathers and mothers projected onto their daughters, the size of the families may provide the most telling clue about the kind of parental infant care that probably emerged in them, even if not for the first time in German history. Lloyd de Mause stated that in the course of the gradual progress in the western world's infant care, some eighteenth-century German families were about to leave the ambivalent and enter the intrusive mode of child rearing. Put differently, while many families were still in the ambivalent mode—sending out their children, beating them regularly, seeing them as wax which needed to be formed—some were moving beyond this stage. De Mause characterized this intrusive mode as follows:

> The child raised by the intrusive parents was nursed by the mother, not swaddled, not given regular enemas, toilet trained early, prayed with but not played with, hit but not regularly whipped, punished

for masturbation, and made to obey promptly with threats and guilt as often as with other methods of punishment. The child was so much less threatening that true empathy was possible.[9]

Yet while this transition was taking place in parts of the Holy Roman Empire, a few parents, including those of Sophie, Christina, and Angelika, were already moving on to the next modes of childrearing, those of socializing and helping.[10] Thus, while some eighteenth-century German parents were now telling their children what to do when and where, the parents of these three give every indication of having explored the next childrearing modes with their daughters and sons. In doing so, they probably applied some of the experiences of their own parents' intrusive mode and simultaneously catapulted with some of their practices to the socializing, even the helping mode.

Christina Dorothea Leporin's parents not only permitted her to express the desire to study medicine, but also backed her up when that wish called for more than one of the children to follow in the footsteps of the father. In somewhat different fashion but in expression of a similarly supportive childrearing mode, it is said that Angelika Kauffmann was never beaten by her parents and that most of her upbringing was geared to exploring as best as possible her talents and wishes. And this, too, in the positive setting of the father's guild. The same modern childrearing is demonstrable for Sophie von La Roche; that is, her parents had also reached at least the intrusive if not the socializing mode before they were separated by the mother's death during La Roche's late teens. After that event, her otherwise enlightened father changed completely; it is still rather terrifying to read how this generous man, under the pressure of this death, the difficult adjustment to a new and younger wife, and the possibly related inability to cope maturely with the Roman Catholicism of Sophie's first betrothed, reverted to the ambivalent childrearing mode.[11] But by that time La Roche was already shaped by her earliest exposure to the more advanced mode.

In general then, the three complete sets of parents responded often enough to the needs of their children for us to recognize more than two hundred years later their love, their willingness to listen, and their acceptance. Although this accommodation was broken in La Roche's teens, it was not undone, and it is confirmed in the willingness of all three sets to lay the groundwork for their daughters' plans for adulthood. In the midst of the emerging fashion of intrusive parenting, a new psycho-class was taking off and its then unusual patterns of parenting gave each girl the inner resiliency and emotional strength to resist their societies' scarcely favorable view of independent women. One needs to emphasize that such a stance took considerable courage on the parents' part. Also, the two women who had children of their own apparently brought them up with at least as much openness as their parents had afforded them. That La Roche failed by arranging the marriages of her daughters in spite of her other successes with them, tells us no more than that the new patterns of childrearing had not been fully accepted in her paternal household, that she was not able in one critical area to undo the traumatic rejection that her father had imposed on her, and that new patterns of childrearing are as fraught with difficulty as most other innovations. While considering this, however, one should not overlook the wonderful training which at least one of those daughters gave Sophie's grandchildren; Maximiliane and Peter von Brentano would have been impossible without it.[12]

If Karsch served as a model of a woman who could not overcome her surroundings, another, Dorothea Schlözer, can serve as a model of a person who enjoyed the appropriate social background, was trained in the emerging intrusive mode, and yet gained the emotional independence to match her intelligence. Pushed, rather than helped, by her father to perform from toilet training to Latin, she became not quite a puppet which attained at age seventeen one of the highest academic honors, the Ph.D. But five years later, in 1792, she married against her father's wishes and with this step overcame his leadstrings soon enough and emerged as the leading intellectual personage of her husband's household in Lübeck.[13] While La Roche was able to shape her own life in spite of her father's reversal primarily because of the positive experiences of early youth, Schlözer was able to do so because of her intelligence and the training her father had forced upon her.

At the outset, I also mentioned size of families and birth order as peculiar in the background of these independent women. As a minimum and however much debated such points are today, each of their parental households establishes them as having been on the road toward the widespread nuclear families of Western industrialized societies. While Kauffmann was an only child, Leporin seems to have had no more than three to four siblings, and La Roche was the first-born of twelve girls and one boy, few of whom seem to have reached adulthood. Each in turn did not revert fully to an extended household, or a larger core family size, although Leporin married a widower with four children and they in turn added another four brothers and sisters.[14] More significant, two of these women were first- or only-born and in the case of Leporin, the parental treatment was as supportive as it might have been if she had been first-born. Being first- or only-born was important for the direct interest fathers and mothers almost per force took in each child; for the fathers it was as if they perceived their eldest as sons, thus transferring on daughters many of the hopes that they would have expended on sons.

One must be careful, however, to differentiate the overwhelming attention afforded in cases such as Schlözer's from that offered to the women discussed in detail here. Although Leporin, Kauffmann, and La Roche became the expression of many parental hopes, initially it was not pressure, but understanding, support, and gentle directing which built in the emotional strength and professional know-how essential for independence. Principal aspects of this support and guidance were the deep affection with which the daughters were enveloped, the careful basic education that fathers, more so than mothers, either provided or made possible, and the extensive contacts through friends and travel which they furthered.[15] One can summarize this paternal role with the words of M. Kay Martin and Barbara Voorhies. They observed that

> when men are actively involved in the rearing of their children there is a tendency for the youngsters to develop self-reliance. . . . Under special circumstances . . . the father may be atypically involved in her [the daughter's] development. This can provide the girl with an available model for self-reliant adult behavior as well as his paternal encouragement to develop this trait.[16]

With such support, each of the women became proficient in oral and written German expression and more than adequate in several foreign languages (particularly French, the colloquial language of their social class), acquired skills essential for later survival and success, and made friends in their own circles and those of others. Just as important, each learned uniquely relevant skills: Kauffmann, Italian, French, English, and painting; Leporin, Latin, research skills, and writing; and La Roche, French, conversation, and writing. The relevancy of these skills explains itself further in the supportive social graces imbibed by Kauffmann and La Roche and the medical expertise attained by Leporin. It was said of the first two, especially Kauffmann, that one of the reasons for their success in the artistic and literary worlds of England and the Continent was directly connected with their feminine gift to attract and retain patrons and sponsors. To be specific, Kauffmann was perceived in London as "being the rage" because she wore "hoops of extra magnitude, toupees of superabundant floweriness, shoeheels of vivid scarlet and china monsters of superlative ugliness."[17]

The rather small size of families involved here, but also in the cases of other independent women, made possible and reinforced the attention that could be provided for each child. As several historians have shown, with a gradual decrease in the size and nuclearization of families, and the improvement of infant survival rates, parents could commit themselves emotionally and financially without the overwhelming risk of losing "their investment" through an all-too-early death. While life expectancies for all women in Germany still hovered around 34 to 40 years, they improved noticeably for the middle and upper classes; even if families were not fully conscious of such statistics, they would have had to notice the rising survival rates and improving life expectancies and planned their offsprings' futures accordingly.[18]

The last considerations highlight the parental capacity to direct efforts toward the training of a daughter. Aside from what appears to be the inability of these families to resolve the triangle of daughter, mother, and father into a ready identification of the daughter with the mother, one could explore the pronounced paternal need in the case of Kauffmann, Leporin, and La Roche to treat them in part as sons and trace several specific ways in which each family helped its prominent daughter to find a niche outside the role complex usually assigned to women. Since I have not yet been able to penetrate beyond what seems to be lack of interest on the part of the mothers, let me concentrate on the last two points.

Dr. Christian Polycarp (1689–1747), the successful city physician, headed a household in which learning, books, and discussion at table were ever prominent. Aside from that, he made sure that he and his friends helped his two most talented children to acquire the basics of Latin, German, and French and that they both read widely in the classics and the more recent natural sciences. Because medicine was in the first stages of professionalization, that is, was just emerging from its handicraft tradition, he could also permit these two youngsters to help him with patients. It is said, for example, that Christina accompanied him occasionally on his visits to the ill. Whether this statement is true or not, from all we know, she seems to have helped him as if she had been in an apprentice relationship to him.[19] When the time came for her to pursue her medical studies seriously, Leporin senior also had the unusual courage to ask the Prussian military establishment, and when it responded negatively, Frederick II, to relieve his older son of military duty so that his sister could accompany him to a probably not all too positive university environment. It is almost unnecessary to add that by then she had the emotional strength and the educational training to defend her unusual wish in one of the most feminist articulations of the eighteenth century. Although her *Thorough Investigation of the Reasons that the Female Sex is Restrained from Studies* never became a bestseller, it remains the most sophisticated statement of its kind in Germany before that of Theodor Gottfried von Hippel.[20] Several years later, after having married pastor Erxleben, she succeeded in her studies under the supervision of Professor Johann Junker, one of her father's friends and the head of the University of Halle, and in 1754 brilliantly passed her public defense for the M.D.

Kauffmann's father, Johann Josef (1707–1782), the painter and portraitist, had allied himself in his second marriage with the Swiss-Italian Cleopha Luz and is best presented as an individual comfortable in two cultural settings. Angelika thus from the very beginning grew up both in the German and Italian cultural patterns, in an understanding home environment, and in apprentice fashion, much like Leporin, learning early on the basics of painting. When her father later decided to enhance this ability and her social skills by living first in Como and then in Milan, he provided his daughter with what can only be considered a sophisticated education, however limited it is perceived by some historians and artists.[21] But she did not automatically become a painter; her talent in music was sufficient for her to consider seriously a career in it also. Only after having arrived at a decision about her career, came her additional sojourns in Milan, Parma, Bologna, Florence, Rome, Naples, and Venice.

La Roche's early training was not much different from that of the other two; even if she later ended up in a more traditional household. As early as Kaufbeuren, she expressed the wish to be trained like a boy so that she might acquire a great amount of wisdom (*Gelehrsamkeit*). As far as can be determined, by age three she was able to read, soon thereafter she was in charge of her father's extensive library, and in her early teens she learned Italian and knew a goodly range of Italy's cultural heritage through Bianconi, a young Italian assigned in Augsburg and her first betrothed. Because of this early start and the love given her, her father's vicious turn against Bianconi, following a trip to Italy, and Sophie's temporary exile within her rearranged paternal household did not crush but strengthen her. She matured to such an extent that she was able to cope well with the usual and not so usual situations of eighteenth-century adulthood.

The principal figure who continued her training after her subsequent move from Augsburg to Biberach was her cousin, Christoph Martin Wieland, just then emerging as a poet and writer. Once again she fell in love, became engaged, and through him discovered a different perspective of herself, Germany and German.

By their early twenties, Christina, Angelika, and Sophie had thus attained sufficient emotional, intellectual, and professional maturity to prevail as self-reliant human beings.

Finally, each was able to choose individuals as marriage partners who were supportive of their career aspirations, whether they brought them into marriage or discovered them, like La Roche, in marriage. Thus they achieved that marital independence mentioned at the outset. At the very least, none could have said of herself, as did one twentieth-century German woman: "and one day I noticed that I ceased to be myself; I had become my husband."[22]

Leporin married the otherwise unknown Erxleben, and theirs became a service-oriented marriage. Kauffmann first married an imposter who claimed to be the Swedish Count de Horn and only felt free to marry Antonio Zucci, a painter with whom her father and she had been working, years after the annulment of the first union and Horn's death in 1780.[23] Theirs was a mutually supportive marriage. La Roche married Georg Michael Frank von La Roche, the illegitimate son of Count Friedrich von Stadion, and entered the very public world of small German courts. Georg La Roche first worked as secretary for Stadion and then as chancellor for the Elector of Mainz. Their marriage can be characterized as a mutually supportive partnership, not a completely familiar form of marital arrangement in the aristocratic set.

One can argue that each of these women's fully developed inner strengths and subsequent physical and intellectual struggles allowed them to survive and succeed in the patriarchal world of their time. Such an argument would agree with a series of thoughts in Judy Chicago's *Through the Flower* which have at their core this characterization: "It is always a man who embodies the human condition."[24] One could add that in their world these women had to deny their feminine essence and thus had no hope of succeeding fully and attaining independence. Both of these statements get at part of the truth, but they do not elucidate at least one underlying issue. It is quite true that none of them succeeded completely in their world; yet each remained self-reliant by staying with those ideals and skills which they had worked out in the then available cultural and social context. And they did not succeed fully in the eyes of contemporaries and posterity for reasons that may be related only partially to their sex and having to adjust to a male world. Success is after all not necessarily related to independence; even more important, success in a field is not necessarily indicative of a person's aspirations. For some, the struggle to have arrived may be sufficient reward for many efforts. More to the point then, Leporin became and remained a women's doctor, Kauffmann a painter, and La Roche a writer.

All three succeeded as women first of all because they met the accepted standards in fields that did not generally find pleasure in female accomplishment. Very important, too, they chose their careers in medicine, writing, and painting themselves and with these pursuits rose beyond the role traditionally assigned to their sex. In a very real sense, they were motivated by the ownership of their decisions. They succeeded for other reasons as well, and most of them are connected to their chosen fields. Art and literature, as we know, have never become fully professionalized and medicine was just about then to enter full professionalization. In such an unstructured environment, a vigorous outsider could penetrate the very top ranks. Yet we must keep in mind the peculiarities of each specialization's tradition. Women were reluctantly accepted in art and literature, especially if their family and friends tolerated their participation in them; they were less likely to be accepted in medicine (or law), even if they could follow in the father's "guild" and had their family's and friend's support to do so.

Thus each woman had to struggle in her own way to be accepted; and it was a fierce struggle, in spite of the enlightenment of the age. That exuberant verbal exercising, unfortunately for them, and the majority of the others then excluded from practically all political and other meaningful participation in society, rarely left its elite frame of reference. This at a time when a number of fields fought for professionalization and middle-class men, like aristocrats earlier, left their households for non–home-related activities. The simultaneously emerging split into private and public spheres almost had to go poorly for women who tried to enter the second sphere (i.e., open doors to careers). They were to be wives, first and foremost. It was also too difficult mentally for most eighteenth-century persons to make the transition from the family in which everyone was part of a unit of production (an *Arbeitsgemeinschaft*), especially as this was still a period of heavy concentration on agriculture, to the family in which either the principal male or female member, or both, gathered outside of the household the funds for its survival. Women who were not perceived as nurturant could expect to encounter difficulties.[25] Nevertheless they never unlearned the so-called female household tasks without which, a point not be forgotten in our era of homes filled with labor-saving devices and roads lined with fast-food chains, an eighteenth-century household could not survive.[26]

But there is more to it. For the above and other reasons the three women discussed failed to some extent in the eyes of their peers.

We do not know how many patients Leporin treated, but we do know that her presence in history was obscured not so much by her femaleness but by her being a general practitioner. As a matter of fact, because she was a woman, we are today concerned about an otherwise unknown doctor.

The situation is more difficult with Kauffmann. Today she is perceived as a student of French rococo, particularly Boucher, to whom she added the rococo-classical elements of the Italian Batoni. A number of critics accept that her life-long ability to integrate into her oeuvre the work of other artists, together with her special ability with classical motifs, catapulted her onto the international stage as a renowned historical painter. She painted well, in other words, and had moved beyond being a mere dilettante, still providing clues about the international trends in late eighteenth-century European art. Yet to some extent her portraits continue to undo her.[27] Also, in the nineteenth and early twentieth centuries her somewhat sweet style and compositional weaknesses stood out more clearly than they do today; critics emphasized those who succeeded her and studied her less in the context of her contemporaries. Even today some commentators argue that in spite of her having had the ingredients of a great artist, including training and leisure to practice her craft, only some of her work can be considered excellent both from a compositional and feminist point of view.[28] I agree to this extent: she never rose above being a good artist of her time; it is as if she lacked that "certain something"; more important, she did not design a female form of expression. Unlike Leporin, however, she has not been ignored and her work has fared reasonably well in museums.

La Roche's fame was short-lived, but again I do not think this condition attributable only to her being a woman. Most characteristically, she was a transitional figure—Enlightenment versus Romanticism—and like most individuals caught in such a frame, she was forgotten in the rush to the next exposure. She was also less than an inspiring follower of Richardson in Germany. But, and more in her favor, which German authors have competed effectively with her contemporaries Schiller and Goethe? The problem has been all along that she, like most of her age-cohort, is compared to these giants in German literature.[29] She was not a poor writer; some of her work has been reprinted several times, especially of course *The History of the Maiden of Sternheim*,[30] and she inspired several good biographies. But the *Sternheim's* success drove her on to write too much in the same vein; she became set in a certain mode and thus incapable of staying with or ahead of her time.

Two interlocking questions arise at this point: did these three women see themselves as successful and did that perception have an impact on the intensity of their independence? There is no doubt that they thought themselves successful; if anything, they viewed those who denied them such standing as out of tune, out of date. There is another point. This was also, as indicated earlier, the age of fierce battles amongst German educators and bureaucrats over the degree of female access to education and public roles, and these three, together with many others, could serve as models of their gender's potential in public. It may even be that here and there a woman tried and was able to follow their lead.[31] But precisely because of their example, a few more males may have aligned themselves with those who would have changed traditional role assignments for and restraints on women. In other words, these women were successful in their perception of themselves and in their societal context; they probably felt as independent as anyone could feel. True, they did not beat the very best of men at their game, but they learned the game well enough to outdo the vast majority of them. Still more significant, their correspondence, or at least what is left of it, and their art and writing, indicate that they felt capable of changing, even improving, their situation; in other words, they felt *unabhängig* and *selbständig*.[32]

One must, however, add this modifier: from our perception of independence, that is, being self-sufficient women who designed a female or integrated approach to their fields and succeeded, they failed partially and thus cannot be considered fully independent or successful.[33] But then, very few of their contemporaries provided a glimpse of a possible future, our present. Among such women were Catherine II of Russia, Maria Theresa of Austria, and the *Great* Landgravine Caroline of Hesse-Darmstadt. Their training was poorer in some respects than that of the three women discussed here, but they had greater talent both at adjusting to male society and at using their social position to the fullest. Like the vast majority of those who sparkle for a time on the horizons of medicine, art, and literature, Leporin, Kauffmann, and La Roche were outshone by those who achieved even greater integration into their societies. If each of these other women thought of it, they would probably have wanted greater independence by avoiding marriage altogether and by bypassing those routine chores which Leporin chastized in her *Thorough Investigation* for their boredom and debilitation. And to some extent they did so through household help. It is no irony and rather a testimony to their awareness that, in the increasing professionalization of society and the conviction that women ought to have a nurturant role in it, all of them found it difficult to be housemothers and supervisors of households, except possibly Leporin later in life and La Roche who prided herself of this capacity for the sake of men.

The accomplishment of each of these women is that they recognized at least part of their *Zeitgeist* for what it was and worked within its context to achieve as much self-reliance as any male or female could then hope to achieve. Their tragedy was that each also had to pay more than lip service to the restraints imposed on women in order to do so. Leporin is an extreme example in this context. As much as she had spoken in her youth against the routines of womanhood, she spent a considerable proportion of her adulthood as the mother of eight children and the caretaker of a household. Only a woman of exceptional energy, so she had written, could overcome the drain that was (and is) associated with managing a large family's needs and pursuing a career; particularly doing both while dying of cancer.[34]

Because of the way eighteenth-century society functioned, few women wanted and could take on the double burden of home and profession. Aside from that, with more and more men leaving the household and women staying there, all too many men and women thought that a wonderful division of labor had been attained. It occurred only to a minute minority that women should have the same access to outside employment and self-realization as men.[35] Even an open-minded woman like La Roche had her heroine Sophie suggest employment outside the house only for women of the lower classes.[36] For the rest of womanhood, particularly its upper- and middle-class representatives, it was not considered feasible, even at the end of the eighteenth century, to contribute as much as men to the survival of a family.

NOTES

1 Translated into German, independence means *Unabhängigkeit* (not being dependent) and is usually connected with *von* to create the sense of being independent of something or someone; the word also means *Selbständig-*

keit (*selbständig*, that is, standing alone), and in the political connection, *parteilos* (without party). If there was a feminine ideal in Germany at the time, the discussion to create a new one was quite fierce, its key word was *Abhängigkeit* (dependency). *Cassell's German Dictionary*, ed. Herold T. Betteridge (London, New York, 1979), p. 1124.

The discussions about the appropriate female ideal were summarized in Peter Petschauer, "Opinions About Female Education in Eighteenth-Century Germany," presented at the Conference on the History of Women, St. Paul, Minn., October 1977, and to be published by *Central European History*. Consult also Silvia Bovenschen, *Die imaginierte Weiblichkeit* (Frankfurt a. M., 1979); Susanne Risse-Stumbries, *Erziehung und Bildung der Frau in der 2. Hälfte des achtzehnten Jahrhunderts* (Frankfurt a. M., 1980), especially pp. 29ff; and Sabine Jebens, "Das literarische Frauenbild in der Mitte des achtzehnten Jahrhunderts—Weibliche Bildung und Sexualität bei Richardson und Gellert," in *Beiträge zur feministischen theorie und praxis*, Sozialwissenschaftliche Forschung und Praxis für Frauen e.V. im Verlag Frauenoffensive (München, 1981), pp. 11–17.

2 Karin Hausen, "Die Polariesierung der 'Geschlechtscharaktere'—Eine Spiegelung der Dissoziation von Erwerb—und Familienleben," in *Sozialgeschichte der Familie in der Neuzeit Europas*, ed. Werner Conze (Industrielle Welt, XXI, Stuttgart, 1976), pp. 363–93; and Peter Petschauer, "From 'Hausmutter' to 'Hausfrau': Ideals and Realities in Late Eighteenth-Century Germany," *Eighteenth-Century Life*, n.s. 1 (October 1982): 72–82.

3 Edward Shorter, *The Making of the Modern Family* (New York, 1975) and Michael Mitterauer and Reinhard Sieder, *Vom Patriarchat zur Partnerschaft. Zum Strukturwandel der Familie*, 2d ed. (München, 1980), pp. 13–63.

4 For a more recent perspective, compare, e.g., Jo Freeman ed., *Women: A Feminist Perspective*, 2d ed. (Palo Alto, 1979) and Lisa Leghorn and Katherine Parker, *Woman's Worth: Sexual Economics and the World of Women* (Boston and London, 1981).

5 Lloyd de Mause, "The Evolution of Childhood," in *Foundations of Psychohistory*, ed. Lloyd de Mause (New York, 1982), pp. 1–83, and Peter Petschauer, "Growing Up Female in Eighteenth-Century Germany," *Journal of Psychohistory* 11 (Fall 1983): 167–207.

6 For Johann Josef Kauffmann's middle class status, see P. Walsh, *Angelica Kauffmann* (Ph.D. diss., Princeton University, 1968), pp. 13–15. About Kauffmann in general, refer also to Victoria Manners and G. C. Williamson, *Angelica Kauffmann, R.A., Her Life and Her Works* (London, 1924), Irmgard Smidt-Dörrenberg, *Angelika Kauffmann. Goethes Freundin in Rom* (Wien, 1968), and the more readily available Ann Sutherland Harris and Linda Nochlin, *Women Artists, 1550–1950* (New York, 1976), pp. 174–78, and Karen Petersen and J.J. Wilson, *Women Artists* (New York, 1976), pp. 43–46.

7 For Leporin, see especially Lotte Knabe, "Die erste Promotion einer Frau in Deutschland zum Dr. med. an der Universität Halle 1754," in *450 Jahre Martin-Luther-Universität Halle-Wittenberg*, 3 vols (Halle-Wittenberg, 1952), 2: 109–24, and compare her own *Gründliche Untersuchung der Ursachen, die*

das Weibliche Geschlecht vom Studiren abhalten (Berlin, 1742; rpt. Hildesheim and New York, 1975) and *Abhandlung von der gar zu geschwinden und angenehmen, aber deswegen öfters unsicheren Heilung der Krankheiten* (Halle: Gebauer, 1755). For La Roche, see especially Ludmilla Assing, *Sophie von LaRoche, die Freundin Wielands* (Berlin, 1859), Werner Milch, *Sophie LaRoche. Die Grossmutter der Brentanos* (Frankfurt a.M., 1935), Peter Petschauer, "Sophie von LaRoche, Novelist Between Reason and Emotion," *The Germanic Review,* 57, no. 2 (Spring 1982): 70–77, and Barbara Becker-Cantarino, "*Muse und Kunstdichter:* Sophie La Roche und Wieland," *Modern Language Notes* 99 (April 1984): 571–88.

8 On Karsch, see Elisabeth Hausmann, *Die Karschin. Friedrich des Großen Volksdichterin. Ein Leben in Briefen* (Frankfurt a.M., 1933).

9 de Mause, "Childhood," pp. 1–83, especially p. 62.

10 The socializing mode is practiced by most American parents today; the helping mode is the most recently introduced form of childrearing and practiced by a rather small psycho-class of middle-middle and upper-middle class American parents.

11 Assing, *die Freundin Wielands,* pp. 24–33.

12 In a more general context, the same is maintained in Elisabeth Badinter, *Die Mutterliebe. Geschichte eines Gefühls vom 17. Jahrhundert bis heute* (München, 1982).

13 Ludwig von Schlözer, *Dorothea von Schlözer, der Philosophie Doktor* (Stuttgart, 1923).

14 For the general eighteenth-century family context into which Leporin, Kauffmann, and La Roche must be fit refer to Shorter, *Modern Family;* Peter Laslett, "Characteristics of the Western family considered over time," in *Family and Illicit Love in Earlier Generations,* ed. Peter Laslett (Cambridge, 1977), pp. 12–49; and Mitterauer and Sieder, *Patriarchat,* pp. 13–63.

15 For Leporin, see Knabe, "Die erste Promotion," pp. 109–13; for Kauffmann, Walsh, pp. 13–45; for La Roche, Assing, *die Freundin Wielands,* pp. 9–26.

16 M. Kay Martin and Barbara Voorhies, *Female of the Species* (New York, 1975), especially the chapter entitled "Origins of Some Sex-Linked Traits" and pp. 65–66.

17 Quoted in Walsh, *Angelica Kauffman,* p. 48. The educational attainments of these three women is all the more admirable in view of the findings of such studies as Rolf Engelsing, *Analphabetentum und Lektüre. Zur Sozialgeschichte des Lesens in Deutschland zwischen feudaler und industrieller Gesellschaft* (Stuttgart, 1973), chapters 10–13, and *Das pädagogische Jahrhundert. Volksaufklärung und Erziehung zur Armut im 18. Jahrhundert,* ed. Ulrich Herrmann (Weinheim and Basel, 1981), chapters 3–5.

18 Louise Tilly, Joan W. Scott, and Miriam Cohen, "Women's Work and European Fertility Patterns," *Journal of Interdisciplinary History* 6 (Winter 1976): 447–76; Michael W. Flinn, *The European Demographic System, 1500–1820* (Baltimore, 1980), pp. 76–101; and in a more general sense Edward Shorter, *A History of Women's Bodies* (New York, 1982).

19 Knabe, "Die erste Promotion," p. 110.
20 See n. 7 above. For Hippel, see his *Über die bürgerliche Verbesserung der Weiber* (Berlin, 1792), trans. by Timothy F. Sellner as *On Improving the Status of Women* (Detroit, 1979). Hippel's discussion came out in the same year as Mary Wollstonecraft's *Vindication of the Rights of Women*.
21 Petersen and Wilson, *Women Artists*, p. 44, and n. 4, p. 169.
22 Ellen Diederich, *Und eines Tages merkte ich, ich war nicht mehr ich selber, ich war ja mein Mann* (Offenbach, 1981).
23 About some of the peculiarities that have often been ignored in the literature about her marriage, compare Susan Moller Okin, "Patriarchy and Married Women's Property in England: Questions on Some Current Views," *Eighteenth-Century Studies* 17 (Winter 1983–84): 137.
24 Judy Chicago, *Through the Flower: My Struggle as a Woman Artist* (New York, 1982), p. 128.
25 Tilly, Scott, and Cohen, "Women's Work." Compare both the ideological and practical sides. The first is reflected in the *Hausväterliteratur*, treated well in Otto Brunner, *Adeliges Landleben und europäischer Geist. Leben und Werk Wolf Helmhards von Hohberg, 1612–1688* (Salzburg, 1949); Heinrich Schmidlin, *Arbeit und Stellung der Frau in der Landgutwirtschaft der Hausväter* (diss. Heidelberg, 1940); and Mitterauer, "Vorindustrielle Familienformen. Zur Funktionsentlastung des 'Ganzen Hauses' im 17. und 18. Jahrhundert," in *Fürst, Bürger, Mensch. Untersuchungen zu politischen und soziokulturellen Wandlungsprozessen im vorrevolutionären Europa*, ed. Friedrich Engel-Janosi, et al. (Wiener Beiträge zur Geschichte der Neuzeit, II, München, 1976), pp. 132–85. The second may be followed in discussions such as Hans Medick, "The Proto-Industrial Family Economy: the Structural Function of Household and Family During the Transition from Peasant Society to Industrial Capitalism," *Social History* 3 (1976): 301–15.
26 This statement emerges from the context of the upbringing of women in eighteenth-century Germany; see Petschauer, "Growing Up Female." About the role of nurturance in general, compare notes 12 and 14 above.
27 See, e.g., David Irwin, "Angelica Kauffmann and Her Times," *Burlington Magazine* 110 (September 1968): 534.
28 About the problems faced by most women artists, cf. Linda Nochlin, "Why Are There No Great Women Artists?" in *Women in Sexist Society*, ed. Vivian Gornick and B. K. Moran (New York, 1971), pp. 480–511. In evaluating Kauffmann's work with some caution, I am balancing between Walsh, *Angelica Kauffman*; Peterson and Wilson, *Women Artists;* and the opinions of most late eighteenth-, nineteenth-, and early twentieth-century authors.
29 Becker-Cantarino, "La Roche und Wieland."
30 La Roche, *Geschichte des Fräuleins von Sternheim. Von einer Freundin derselben aus Original-Papieren und anderen zuverlässigen Quellen gezogen*, ed. C. M. Wieland (1771 and 1772, rpt. Leipzig, 1938, and Darmstadt, 1964).
31 See, e.g., Johanna Schopenhauer, as discussed in *Jugendleben und Wanderbilder*, ed. Willi Drost (Tübingen, 1958), pp. 97–98.

32 Much of this discussion has its origins in the considerations of Gerda Lerner, *The Majority Finds Its Past: Placing Women In History* (New York, 1973), p. 13.
33 At least that is what I gather from women who discuss their work, etc., in such books as *Working It Out,* ed. Sara Ruddick and Pamela Daniels (New York, 1977).
34 We know no more than that Leporin died of breast cancer. For the general context, compare the section "Cancer as a Woman's Disease" in Shorter, *Women's Bodies,* pp. 242–45.
35 One of the strongest defenders was Theodor von Hippel. Compare also Petschauer, "Opinions."
36 La Roche, *Sternheim,* 2: 193, and pp. 216–21.

A Scottish Middle-Class Family and Patronage: The Ancestors of Sir John Moore

HENRY L. FULTON

This paper proposes to describe the extent to which the careers and fortunes of a middle-class Scottish family were assisted from 1650 to 1800 by its connections and friendships with more influential families. Expectations, both fulfilled and denied, can be studied in the welfare of four generations of the male ancestors of General Sir John Moore (1761–1809), the hero of Corunna and the eldest son of Dr. John Moore, the author of *Zeluco* (1789). Although Sir John is by far the best known of all his family, his brothers were also eminent and deserve mention here. Next to Sir John in age was Dr. James Carrick Moore of Corsewall (1762–1860), who with Jenner introduced vaccination into Great Britain and succeeded Jenner as president of the National Vaccine Institute. The third son was Admiral Sir Graham Moore (1764–1843), knighted in 1815 for service in the Atlantic. The fourth brother, Francis (1767–1854), retired as Deputy Secretary of War in 1809.

That four brothers did so well was no accident.[1] Though much of their success occurred in the nineteenth century, the beginning of their rise lay with their father's efforts in the eighteenth, and it is with him that this paper will be principally concerned.

Dr. John Moore (1729–1802) was born in Stirling, but after the death of his father moved with his mother to Glasgow, her parents' city, where Moore resided until he was just past forty. He was trained as a surgeon and availed himself of travel and study on the continent, as did the best medical men of his time. He could do so because his mother had means. In 1772 he was chosen by the family and tutors of the young Duke of Hamilton to accompany the youth abroad and watch over his health until the youth was able to act responsibly for himself. Moore remained on the continent with his charge nearly five years. In 1777, Moore moved his family permanently to London, left off practice, and devoted his remaining twenty-five years to his sons' careers, his investments, politics, and books for the popular audience. His estate upon his death in 1802 was valued at more than £25,000,[2] a competence yielding £1000 per annum, which was roughly equivalent to what a judge of the Scottish Court of Session or the Professor of Chemistry at Edinburgh might have made in a year. Success like this comes from hard, sustained work, a little luck, and happy opportunities. In the Scotland of his day, moreover, the right connections were also necessary to bring such affluence to a man like Moore.

A Scottish middle-class family could live without the need of influence with "people above" so long as it drew income from land or made a simple merchant's livelihood. By contrast, any position in the church, the military, the university, or the government could be obtained only through the interest of powerful and invariably titled families who had connections with the ultimate source of patronage in London. The same situation applied also to any personal service such as a tutorship, a chaplaincy, etc. Employment came only through the favor of friendship, a long-standing family connection, or a personal recommendation. "To have stature and authority in Scotland," John Shaw has written recently, "the individual had to have a link with some Scottish political grandee or equivalent influential group in London. To be a success the individual had to be agent in the interest of such a southern master."

From the beginning of the century until the mid-1770s the Moores enjoyed a beneficial relationship with several figures upon whom they could draw for advancement. Primary among these were the chiefs of Clan Campbell, in particular the second Duke of Argyll until about 1725, and his younger brother, the Earl of Ilay, who dispensed virtually all the public offices, university chairs, and many livings in the church from 1725 until his death in 1761. The influence of the Dukes of Argyll in the first half of the eighteenth century was extensive. Shaw says that "central was the economic and political leverage provided by the Argyll estate and jurisdiction; but the strands of influence which extended beyond this were so extensive as to become indefinable."[3] The connection between the Moores and the Campbell interest can be traced back before the Restoration.

Moore's forebears were the Mores of Polkelly, an ancient family of Ayrshire, from which arose two distinguished lines, the Mures of Rowallen and Caldwell (see genealogical chart).[4] The subjects of this paper were descended from the Mures of Rowallen through Captain Alexander Mure, one of seven sons of William Mure the poet (d. 1657). This Alexander served under the sixth Earl of Eglintoun as part of the military forced hired by Parliament in London to quell the Irish Rebellion and protect the Scottish plantation in Ulster in the 1640s. Mure is listed as "ordinary receiver and proviant" in the New Scots Army in 1644 and most likely saw action in the Battle of Benburgh in 1646 against the victorious forces of Owen Roe, the only battle in which the Scottish forces engaged.[5] In 1650 Captain Mure's widow and children were among eleven Ayrshire families invited by the Marquess of Argyll to populate the Kintyre peninsula; it is likely that Argyll desired to settle more Presbyterian families in that area. This is the first traceable connection between this branch of the Mures and Clan Campbell, a connection that would prove viable for almost one hundred years. The Mure family consequently followed the marquess into war against the forces of James II in 1685, during which time William Mure of Kildarie was arrested by the Earl of Atholl and banished to Northern Ireland.[6] Kildarie's son Captain Charles Moore distinguished himself in the siege of Londonderry.[7] While in Ulster the family's name came to be spelled the Irish way, and after they returned to Scotland they retained this spelling, which differentiated them from the other Muirs, Mores, and Mures in western Scotland.

Captain Moore's son Charles, the only known descendent of Alexander Mure to return to Scotland, was born in County Armagh and sent over to Glasgow University in 1702 "to be educated Amongst his father's relations."[8] Chief of these was his first cousin once-removed, Jean Mure of Rowallen, who married the Earl of Glasgow. The kinship was further encouraged by their daughter Jane, "the heiress of Rowallen," as she was styled, who in 1720 married Sir James Campbell of Lawers (1667–1745), Lieutenant-Colonel of the "Scots Greys" and a military hero at the Battle of Malplaquet, as was the Duke of Argyll.[9] Dr. Moore said that his father "was bred a Presbyterian Clergyman"—a profession befitting a younger son. The younger Charles seems to have been the only Moore of his line to preach, the rest of the family traditionally following a military profession. He was probably one of many candidates admitted to the university from Northern Ireland specifically to be educated for the new Irish Presbyterian Church. Whether he intended to return to his birthplace or settle in Scotland is impossible to say; there were serious shortages in Presbyterian pulpits on both sides of the Irish Sea.[10] But after some years'

MORES OF POLKELLY

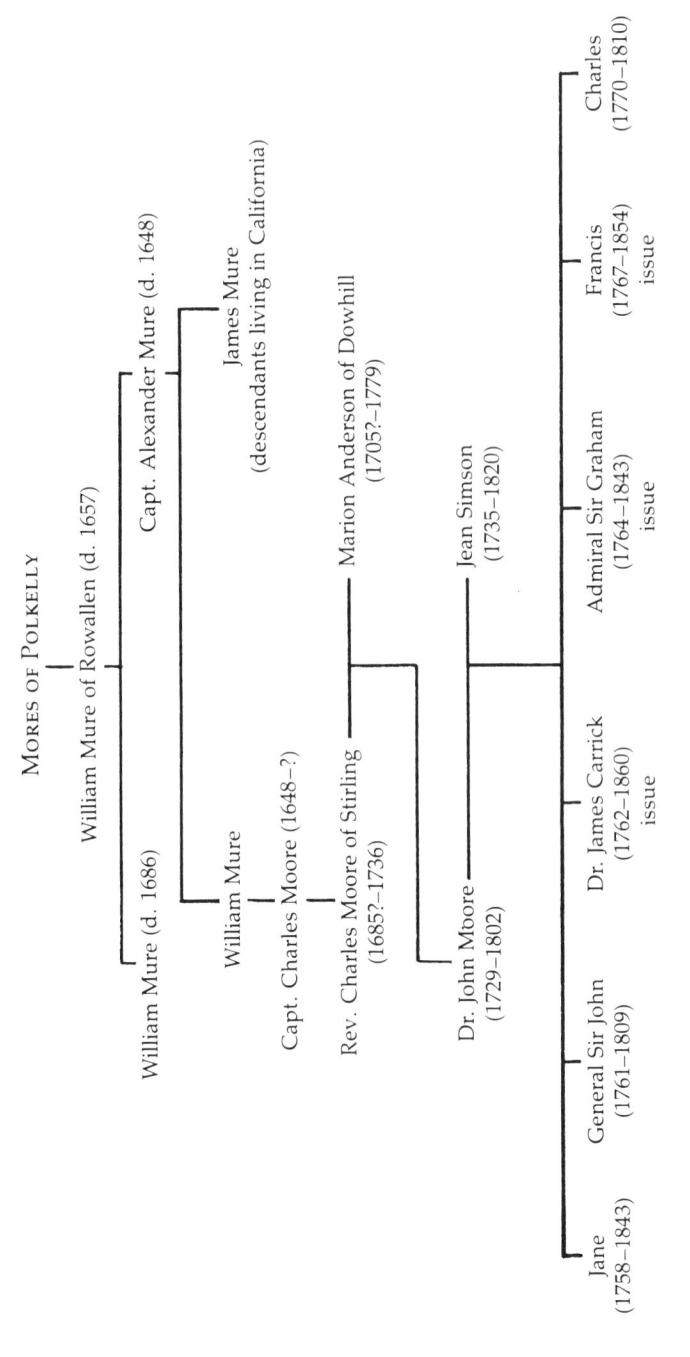

William Mure of Rowallen (d. 1657)
- William Mure (d. 1686)
  - William Mure
    - Capt. Charles Moore (1648–?)
      - Rev. Charles Moore of Stirling (1685?–1736) & Marion Anderson of Dowhill (1705?–1779)
        - Dr. John Moore (1729–1802) & Jean Simson (1735–1820)
          - Jane (1758–1843)
          - General Sir John (1761–1809)
          - Dr. James Carrick (1762–1860) — issue
          - Admiral Sir Graham (1764–1843) — issue
          - Francis (1767–1854) — issue
          - Charles (1770–1810)

No living descendants.

- Capt. Alexander Mure (d. 1648)
  - James Mure (descendants living in California)

148

study in the Lowlands and at the University of Edinburgh in Divinity, he was ordained at Dunfermline Presbytery in 1713.[11] He must have intended by then to settle in the land of his ancestors.

Not much is known about him, particularly because he died in 1736 when his only son was seven years old. Moore remembered that his father was tall, "of a Pale Complexion, of a pleasing Mild Countenance & remarkably genteel in his Manners." The boy also remembered being carried frequently by horseback up to the Lawers estate of Sir James Campbell, with whom his father was very close while he was at Stirling.[12] But as a ministerial candidate Charles Moore was stigmatized by a peculiar manner of speaking. An early source mentions that "he had a tone, and a singing voice, which disfigured his countenance, both in preaching and in prayer."[13] While sympathetic to the evangelicals, he was also, like many of William Hamilton's students, "an early Moderate" and a strong supporter of Argathelian politics, all which made him less than fully desirable in many "popular" pulpits. His two appointments, to the kirks at Culross and Stirling, were effected with the aid of Clan Campbell, and probably would not have gone through without their help.

John Moore wrote that his father received the call to Culross in 1715 through the direct intervention of Sir James Campbell of Lawers. If true, this could explain subsequent difficulties the elder Moore had with his heritors. Because of the opposition of one in particular, Colonel John Erskine of Carnock (1662–1743), who influenced the others, the minister was never paid his stipend the three years he served, presumably because he had not been freely called by the congregation as Erskine thought right.[14] (In other words, the colonel was expressing his opposition to the restoration of church patronage in 1712.) Moore put up with this unpleasant situation until late 1717, when it was arranged that he would be translated.

Early in 1718 the provost of Stirling and other dignitaries appeared before the Culross session with a call to translate Charles Moore to their city. In light of what their minister had already suffered at their hands, one would not expect any resistance from Culross to a move that would relieve them of a vexing problem. But those in the parish who had always favored Moore did protest, and the call seemed in jeopardy. More direct pressure was required. The next time the two parties met to deal with this issue, Stirling produced a letter from the Duke of Argyll, "bearing his Graces respect to the Church of Scotland and readiness to serve her Interests and craving that this Presby [sic] would comply with the Request of the Town of Stirling to have Mr.

150 / FULTON

Moor settled in Stirling."[15] This development is a good example of the increasing influence on Scottish affairs of the Duke of Argyll and his brother Lord Ilay (later third duke). Heretofore church patronage, in the words of one historian, "was exercised with considerable respect for popular opinion,"[16] which was frequently evangelical or reactionary, but this sensitivity declined as the duke withdrew from military life and the politics of St. James's. As Robert Wodrow remarked some years later, "The Duke of A and the Earl of Isla, take much pains to have some interest in all the various societies of Scotland and to have some thorough engaged to their side every where. Every body sees it in the Members of Parliament, the Lords of Session, the settlement of ministers, and particular presbyteries in the General Assembly."[17] The "patron" of the Church of the Holy Rude, Stirling, was, of course, the burgh council, but even here the Argyll interest was suasive. The provost of Stirling, James Christie, was the same person who acted years later as an agent and informer on behalf of Lord Milton, the third Duke of Argyll's (Ilay's) "sub-minister" in Edinburgh, when rumors of Jacobite activity began to reach London.[18] One infers from Dr. Moore's memoir of his family that in this instance Campbell of Lawers spoke to his chief, and the duke sought Christie's cooperation in this matter. The call to Moore, however, was not especially popular in Stirling, a town that favored evangelical, "popular" preachers. Such a man, Alexander Hamilton of Airth, was called in 1725, and five years later Ebenezer Erskine, who ultimately led the first secession from the church to protest the issue of patronage, was added to the ministry.

It is an axiom of patronage that such favor had a price, more than merely the minister's loyalty and gratitude. That Charles Moore recognized this is suggested by a letter of his (4 December 1734) to Captain Charles Campbell in Edinburgh, asking him to apologize to Lord Milton, in Edinburgh, for not being able to come over early in the winter—"nor will it be any loss to your Cause Since I'm told Several Concurring testimonys are given as to what I had to say." Then he goes on, "It's very good news y[e]^t the patriots [the Squadrone—the political opposition to the Duke] have their Languages confounded; may the Good Lord write disorders and disappointm[en]^t upon every measure tending to Sapp the foundations of what's dear to us as men & Christians."[19] These words show that once the Duke of Argyll retreated from the responsibilities of management in Scotland, the minister shifted his loyalty to the duke's brother Ilay and his man in Edinburgh, Lord Milton.

His only surviving son, Dr. John Moore, also followed a different family vocation, medicine, but on certain crucial occasions placed his reliance on Campbell favor.

The issue of patronage is central to an understanding and appreciation of his career because while he was certainly blessed with a good mind and a capacity for hard work, the success of his life depended on the right people recognizing these qualities in him. Although he lost his father when he was only seven, this did not seem to limit his opportunities. He achieved a degree of fame commensurate with his abilities.

The question of patronage arises with his choice of career once he matriculated at Glasgow University in 1742, for in following medicine he could hope to become successful only by the cultivation of crucial contacts with influential people who would recognize his ability and promote his vocation. This was indeed what transpired, but not quite as soon as Moore hoped.

According to the Glasgow custom of training physicians and surgeons he was apprenticed to two local practitioners, William Stirling and John Gordon (Smollett's masters five years earlier),[20] and took courses at the university in 1744 under William Cullen, who had just arrived from Hamilton to help establish a school of medicine at Glasgow to compete with Edinburgh's. In 1747 it was decided that Moore should continue his medical education abroad, as did nearly all Scottish professional aspirants who could afford to do so. A position was found for him as surgeon's mate in a Campbell regiment, the North British Fusiliers under the command of Colonel John Campbell of Mamore, seeing service in Flanders. After the truce of 1748 the commander of the British forces, the Earl of Albemarle, took up residence in Paris as ambassador, and invited the youthful Moore into his household as resident-physician. (This gave him opportunity to continue his medical study at several local hospitals.) In 1750, after further study in London, Moore was offered a place in the partnership with the aforementioned Stirling and Gordon. After debating whether to remain in the military profession, Moore chose the safer course, and settled in Glasgow, his future seemingly assured.[21] Disappointment lay directly ahead.

Moore, by his own admission, was never really enamoured of general practice,[22] though he worked extremely hard at it; so when an opportunity opened to broaden his career, he sought the interest of the Duke of Argyll to improve his prospects. On one occasion during his practice two chairs fell vacant at Glasgow University which Moore felt expressly qualified to fill, and he applied—unsuccessfully, it turned out—for one of them. This was the vacancy in Botany and Anatomy, which occurred in 1755 when Cullen moved to Edinburgh to assume the vacant chair in Chemistry, stipulating to Argyll that his prize pupil, Joseph Black, should be awarded a chair at Glasgow.[23] (Robert Hamilton, who held the chair in Botany and Anatomy, succeeded Cullen in Medicine, and it was determined that Black would assume Hamilton's old chair, for which he was not particularly qualified.) In the late summer of 1755 Moore also applied for one of these chairs, presumably approaching his father's old friend Lord Milton to intercede with the duke on his behalf. Cullen may have felt very uneasy in this situation. He cannot have made his own inclinations clear to Moore at that time or the younger man would have grasped how hopeless his own candidacy was. At any rate Moore got no encouragement from either Cullen or Milton so late in the fall he wrote desperately to his cousin Tobias Smollett in London to speak to the duke on his behalf. Smollett's reply was discouraging: "Far from being used to the Great, as you seem to imagine, I have neither Interest nor acquaintance with any Person whose countenance or Favour could be of advantage to myself or my friends. . . . I have not spoke to a Nobleman for some years."[24] Black got the chair the following year. Moore was shut out, even though a very strong case can be made that Moore was better qualified, having had medical training in Glasgow, London, and the Continent, as well as practice in surgery, which in spite of his bright promise, Black could not match. In 1755, Cullen's regard for Moore was high, but his regard and friendship for Black was higher. This instance is a good example of the shortcoming of Scottish public patronage where "the generality [of candidates] were selected for the social connections first, and their abilities and activities in business . . . second."[25] Cullen eventually made up for Moore's disappointment, but that lay ahead.

Moore attempted a second time to supplement general practice with a chair at Glasgow. This was in 1762. He was unsuccessful for an entirely different reason: the chair was withdrawn. Otherwise Moore certainly had the right connections for achieving his desire. In late 1762 the newly crowned George III made available £1000 "for the Encouragement of Arts and Sciences in Scotland"—doubtless a concession to Lord Bute. It was proposed that a Chair of Midwifery be added to the medical faculty at Glasgow to make that program competitive with Edinburgh's, and it was further proposed that Moore get this Chair. He was well qualified because under the auspices of the Faculty of Physicians and Surgeons of Glasgow he had been examining and instructing midwives in the city, and had studied the subject under Jean Astruc in Paris and William Hunter and William Smellie in London. Lord Milton's replacement as subminister in Scottish affairs was perhaps Moore's closest and most powerful friend, William Mure of Caldwell (1718–1776), whose family was, like Moore's, descended from the Mores of Polkelly. In 1761, after some time in Parliament, Mure of Caldwell was named one of the Barons of the Scottish Exchequer. He was an extremely capable and affable person; among his other close friends were Bute and David Hume. Pushing Moore's candidacy were, besides others, John Anderson (1726–1796), the controversial Professor of Moral Philosophy at Glasgow, who always interested himself in practical, up-to-date curricula, and John Graham of Dugaldston, who had been Rector of the university in 1746.[26] But the chair never materialized, and though Mure was made Rector of the university in 1764–65, Moore never found another opportunity to join the university. The major event in his otherwise uniform life at this time did not occur until 1769, and this involved Cullen directly (and the Campbells indirectly).

In 1769 the young Duke of Hamilton, George James, fell seriously ill, and his life was despaired of. The family physician of the Hamiltons since the 1730s had continued to be Cullen, probably advising a good deal by mail, but as treatment of the young man had not been effective, he must have decided that someone closer to Hamilton Palace was called for. He asked that Moore in Glasgow be designated physician in his place and that the desperate case be turned over to him. The young duke died on Moore's hands, but Moore's competence and gracious manner so captivated the duchess, her husband (the fifth Duke of Argyll), her surviving son, and the boys' tutors (Mure, Andrew Stuart, and the Earl of Galloway), that Moore was permanently retained, and continued for the next three years to advise the family on all medical matters and assisted Andrew Stuart in some pamphleteering related to the Douglas Cause.[27] In 1772 it was determined that the succeeding duke, Douglas, needed to be conveyed abroad for the tour; he seemed to be suffering from the same symptoms that took the life of his brother and, more embarrassing, had contracted a venereal infection in London. Several "governors" to accompany the young man were considered, among them Adam Smith, but Moore was settled on because the family viewed him as a father who knew how to instruct and handle young men, and they also realized that young Hamilton would, in any case, require a physician at all times.[28]

Moore spent close to five years' attendance upon the duke, for which extensive service he was paid £500 a year and an annuity of £300. This income, coupled with capital from the property of his mother's marriage portion, enabled him to make a major change in his career soon after he returned from the continent.

Within a year after he returned from Europe (1777) Moore moved his wife, six children, and mother-in-law to London, leaving Glasgow for good. There are a number of reasons why he made this drastic move, among which was chiefly the desire to leave off practice and write; he chose to reside near the best and most popular publishers. His output for the next twenty-five years consisted of three books of travels, three novels, a study of the French Revolution, a popular treatise on the medical profession, two plays, and an edition of Smollett's works. But an equally pressing reason was the vocations of his sons, in particular the need to find influential persons to advance their careers. Moore had a dread of idleness, and he often acted as though he suspected that all young people were susceptible to it unless specifically encouraged to exert themselves.

> I flattered myself [he wrote] that I should be able to push My Sons in different lines [than medicine], I thought they all had talents, I indeavoured to inspire them with energy, honourable Sentiments and ambition. . . . Vice & Misery are the children of Indolence, of disregard of character, and effeminate indulgences. . . . By enabling My Sons to follow Useful professions Successfully I thought I would do more for them than if I was to give them fortunes to tempt them to idleness, & indulgence in Uncomfortable comforts.[29]

Therefore, patronage had now become a necessity for his children, not for himself. The boys and their ambitious father had no interest in medicine, the church, or the Scottish professoriate; on the contrary, by 1776 Jack and Graham had already chosen military careers, and Jack had obtained an ensigncy at fifteen through the efforts of the Duchess of Argyll. James was to learn trade in London under Hutchinson Mure, a merchant (and a relative of the late baron). Frank and Charles were too young to be placed, although Frank was once expected to follow James in trade, and the family jokingly referred to young Charles as the "bishop."[30] The careers of all five required patronage, some private influence applied now and again to "the people above" when opportunities arose. But in London Moore was on foreign ground, with new rules to follow and new contacts to form.

Although Moore obtained the ensigncy for his eldest son through the direct application of the Duchess of Argyll to Lord Barrington, then Secretary of War, he did not continue to make further use of his Campbell connections. The current Duke of Argyll (the fifth) resided mostly in Inveraray, absorbed in town improvements. All of the

Moores, on the other hand, remained close to the Duke of Hamilton in London, and presumably through the duke's sister Lady Derby Moore was introduced to his next patron, the young and attractive Duchess of Devonshire.[31]

It is not known exactly when Moore first became a friend of the fashionable duchess, but his letters suggest that he first approached the Whig hostess on behalf of his boys early in 1782, when Fox's power and influence were on the rise. Both Jack and James had returned from service in the unsuccessful war with the American colonies, seeking further employment. During the summers of 1782 and 1783 Moore solicited her repeatedly to find Jack a lieutenancy in an "old" regiment not likely to be disbanded after the peace; Moore also asked her to approach General Henry Seymour Conway (1721–1795), a close friend, about nominating Jack as an aide-de-camp in Ireland. These petitions proved unsuccessful. On the other hand, the duchess was instrumental in procuring a clerkship in the Foreign Office through Fox and Charles Grey for Frank (1784),[32] who thus came to be permanently employed until, in 1803, he was named Deputy Secretary of War. Years later the duchess purchased Jack's promotion to major because he had always been, by her admission, a special favorite. On his side Moore advised her with her problems in conceiving and carrying a child to term;[33] in 1789 Moore helped her with a small loan when her indebtedness to the banker Thomas Coutts was precariously high.[34]

Yet her solicitations on behalf of Moore's family brought only modest success, considering the number of times Moore sought her help. Why was she not more successful?

She may have been too busy to advance his interest. Moore was one of many petitioners seeking her interest with Fox during a brief period when her influence was at its peak, the two years when the Rockinghams had power and Fox was not in Opposition. Moreover, after the defeat at the hands of the colonies, the military had few jobs to offer young men like the future Sir John Moore. How much Moore was sensitive to this it is difficult to say, but the tone of his letters to her suggests only that his duchess was diffident or negligent when acting on his most pressing entreaties. Moore always believed that she could carry any point with Conway, Fox, etc., so long as she pressed urgently enough; that is, Moore felt sure that had General Conway known giving Jack a commission in the foot guards would have obliged the Duke and Duchess of Devonshire (not just the Moores), he certainly would have acceded to her request. On other occasions it seemed to be just a lack of concern. In the summer of

1782 Moore asked her to speak to Fox about the clerkship for young Frank. Accustomed to waiting on her while she was on holiday, Moore followed her to the country in late August, only to find she had moved on. Divided between his deep affection for her and the most acute frustration, he sent a letter after:

> So you have run away, and left me in the Lurch, without Speaking to Mr F. or leaving any letter—But says you *the thing will be done*—O Duchess, Duchess, what reliance can I have in what you Say, remember how you served me about James,—on my Conscience if I had hold of you at this moment I would—God almighty only knows what I would do! As you have Saved yourself by a base perfidious flight I can only Curse and hate you—the first I have already done Most plentifully, the Second I am endeavouring to do as fast as I can.

There is some tongue-in-cheek in this, but it still seems a risky tone to take with a duchess in whom one had invested so much hope. Nevertheless, the following year Frank received the clerkship. Two years later Moore was importuning her again on behalf of James. The young man's private practice was improving, but he desired a more prestigious position—the next vacancy on the surgeons' staff of St. George's Hospital. Moore knew what was needed to forward his son's cause, and his directions to the duchess were explicit, almost to the point of rudeness:

> The Most essential Service the Duke or you can Possibly do him, after Employing him in your own Family, is to take the promise of as many People as you have influence with that they will Vote for him when a Vacancy happens—You had best begin with Drs Warren, Gisbourn, & Densman,[35]—then proceed to as many of the directors as you know. In Short let it be known that James will be earnestly Supported by the Devonshire family.

Then, lest in her charming way the duchess approach her friends with less than the utmost seriousness, he added, "Asking in a slight Jocular Manner will not be Sufficient to prevail on many to attend & vote who certainly will; the Duke & you must Show that you will take it as a favour." In short, "Since you have again Undertaken to interest yourself for them do it with energy or not at all, for to do it feebly gives you trouble and does them no Service." Nothing, incidently, came of this.

A third problem lay in the careless nature of the duchess herself. Throughout much of her life, her good intentions exceeded her performance, and as a patron and friend to Moore she had the fault of generously promising more than she could deliver. She was, however, sincere, unaffected, and wholly genuine in her desire to help the doctor. Moore had chosen his patron well; her influence, even when Fox was out of office, was enormous. But she served Moore less well than he expected from a person of her high station. A compulsive gambler, the hostess of an almost continuous open house in Devonshire House, and troubled with both her inability to carry her husband's heir to term and a new rival for her husband's affections, she was perhaps too disordered in her personal affairs to do justice to Moore's petitions.

A fourth problem lay in Moore's anxious expectation. All his life he was haunted with the dread of penury, an irrational fear inasmuch as his mother had been left well off, and Moore had prospered in London. But his autobiographical letter (c. 1800) devotes pages to his anxiety over the income tax and the chilling fear that Mrs. Moore would exceed her monthly allowance of £45 (she invariably did, giving much of it away) or that Charles, yet unemployed, would bleed him to subsistence.[36] The remote possibility that his sons could not find steady and profitable employment in their adopted country but might fall back on him for their maintenance drove him much of his London years to search out new opportunities for them—occasionally without their knowledge. Moore would have been gratified to know that his eldest son, as he advanced through the officers' ranks, became a patron to other young men seeking service under him. Sir John also obtained for his youngest brother Charles the office of auditor of the public accounts. By 1810 all the surviving sons were flourishing in their careers.

Several conclusions might be drawn from this brief history of a family. While, as A. S. Collins suggested many years ago,[37] direct literary patronage had almost completely disappeared by the end of the eighteenth century, other forms of patronage and interest were still essential for office and advancement. Patronage was not a way of avoiding competition; it was the competition. In addition, the blessing of patronage could not be taken for granted. Any application to the privileged and influential often required a good deal of "massaging" and persistence, which was aggravated by what J. Morgan Sweeney has termed the "assymetry, the inequality of status" between applicant and patron. Waiting on the benefit of such a condition could bring on high levels of stress and anxiety, if Dr. Moore's career is any valid example. Perhaps because the process was so personal, it brought more uneasiness and disappointment than the modern analogue of filling out applications and being interviewed by strangers. Patronage also implied responsibilities to both parties or "a degree of reciprocity, an exchange of good or services."[38] The patron expected, for his pains, that the applicant usually be qualified and, if successful, be able to render service or perform well to the honor of the patron. Such service might be as odious as Boswell's servility to the Earl of Lonsdale or as gratifying as Moore's service to the Duchesses of Argyll and Devonshire. But the benefit of patronage was not free. The connection established through patronage could bind socially disparate families together for several generations. Besides the connection between Moores and the Argyll interests, one can point to the connections between the Clerks of Penicuik and the Dukes of Queensberry or the friendship between the MacLaurins and the Campbells. Therefore switching patrons when he brought his family to London in 1777 probably caused Moore no little uneasiness. The dozen letters he wrote to the Duchess of Devonshire in the 1780s are only a specimen of the energy Moore devoted to this crucial concern throughout his career.

NOTES

1 A fifth son, Charles (1770–1810), was bred to the law but never found successful employment until his eldest brother obtained for him an auditorship of the public accounts during the last years of Pitt's administration (*The Farrington Diaries*, ed. James Grieg [London, 1926], 6: 178–79. I am indebted to Michael Collinge of the Institute of Historical Research, University of London, for this information). Charles died of a brain tumor.
2 According to his will in Somerset House.
3 John Stuart Shaw, *The Management of Scottish Society, 1707–1764* (Edinburgh, 1983), pp. 58 and 46. Another recent title on patronage and management is Alexander Murdoch, *The People Above: Politics and Administration in Mid-Eighteenth Century Scotland* (Edinburgh, 1980).
4 I am indebted to Hugh Moore of El Monte, California, for the major part of my information about the Mores of Polkelly and Dr. Moore's forebears in the seventeenth century.
5 David Stevenson, *Scottish Covenanters and Irish Confederates* (Belfast, 1981), p. 71.
6 Researches of Hugh Moore.
7 *Records of the Carrick Moore Family*, ed. George Heath (Cobham, 1912; rpt. Ann Arbor, Michigan, 1967), p. 3.
8 British Library Add. MSS. 57321, f. 101.
9 Dr. John Moore, "Sketches of my own Birth & certain circumstances," a

manuscript in the hands of Sir Mark Heath, Surrey. Cited with permission.
10 Henry Grey Graham says that in 1690 the Scottish church borrowed some sixty clergymen from the church in Northern Ireland (*Social Life in Scotland in the Eighteenth Century* [London, 1901], p. 274).
11 Charles Moore's name appears in 1709 on a handwritten class list of students in divinity under the "early Moderate" Professor William Hamilton, Edinburgh University. (Edinburgh University Library MS. I am indebted to Mr. C. P. Finlayson for this discovery.)
12 Moore, "Sketches of my own Birth & certain circumstances."
13 Hew Scott, *Fasti Ecclesiae Scoticanae,* 3 vols. (Edinburgh, 1866–71), vol. 2, pt. 2, p. 679.
14 Even the popular George Mair, whom Moore succeeded, did not draw his salary apparently until November, 1712 (Scottish Record Office, Dunfermline Presbytery Records, CH2/105/4, p. 287), and Erskine was the problem.
15 Dunfermline Presbytery Records, CH2/105/5, pp. 5–13.
16 A. L. Drummond and J. Bulloch, *The Scottish Church, 1688–1843* (Edinburgh, 1973), pp. 39–40.
17 Cited in Shaw, *Management of Scottish Society,* p. 30.
18 Ibid., p. 165.
19 National Library of Scotland MS. 16558, f. 14. Cited with the permission of the Trustees. In 1733–34 the minister was a member of a standing committee on the General Assembly, the "Commission of Some Ministers and Ruling Elders for discussing diverse affairs referred to them"—specifically what to do about Ebenezer Erskine and the Secessionists, who had attracted some sympathy from the Squadrone. The letter refers probably to the winter meeting of this Commission. (I am indebted to Roger L. Emerson, University of Western Ontario, for this note.)
20 See my "Smollett's Apprenticeship in Glasgow, 1736–1739," *Studies in Scottish Literature* 15 (1980): 175–86.
21 According to his "Sketches of my own Birth," the Earl of Albemarle would have obtained for Moore a commission as surgeon in a regiment like the "Green Howards" (19th Regiment of Foot) had not his relatives in Glasgow persuaded him to come home.
22 "Sketches of my own Birth."
23 A. L. Donovan, *Philosophical Chemistry in the Enlightenment* (Edinburgh, 1975), pp. 72–75.
24 *Letters of Tobias Smollett,* ed. Lewis M. Knapp (Oxford, 1970), p. 42.
25 Shaw, p. 58. The authority on patronage in the Scottish universities is Roger L. Emerson, and my work is indebted to his research, though on the question of Black's first Chair we do not wholly agree.
26 This correspondence can be found in the National Library of Scotland, 2524, f. 5, and 4942, f. 152, and it is reprinted in *Selections from the Family Papers Preserved at Caldwell Castle,* 2 vols. (Edinburgh, 1854), vol. 2, pt. 2, pp. 163–66.

27 The fifth Duke of Argyll was the same John Campbell who commanded the North British Fusiliers in 1747, in which Moore served as surgeon's assistant.
28 For the negotiations on this choice see Col. John Stuart to Baron Mure, 20 February 1772 (National Library of Scotland 4945, f. 132); Andrew Stuart to Baron Mure, 21 February (4945, f. 134); Moore to Mrs. Moore, "Tuesday" [25 February] (British Library Add. MSS. 57321, f. 38 [rep. *Records of the Carrick Moore Family*, p. 8]).
29 "Sketches of my own Birth."
30 James Carrick Moore to Moore, 18 October 1781 (MS. in the possession of Martin Heath, Wiltshire; rep. *Records of the Carrick Moore Family*, pp. 43–44).
31 Moore's letters to the Duchess of Devonshire are at Chatsworth and are cited with the permission of the Trustees of the Chatsworth Settlement.
32 *Foreign Office Officials, 1782–1870*, comp. J. M. Collinge (London, 1979), p. 17.
33 Brian Masters, *Georgiana, Duchess of Devonshire* (London, 1981), p. 97.
34 Duchess of Devonshire to Thomas Coutts, 16 September 1789 (Chatsworth Settlement; rpt. *Extracts from the Correspondence of Georgiana, Duchess of Devonshire*, ed. the Earl of Bessborough (London, 1955), p. 161.
35 Dr. Thomas Denman, the Duke of Devonshire's personal physician and an accoucheur (as identified by Masters, *Georgiana, Duchess of Devonshire*, pp. 53 and 83).
36 "My Mind," he wrote, "is so Constituted that I cannot be in the Smallest degree Comfortable unless I think I live within My income—and this I find I cannot do in a decent Manner while I continue to advance £130 to One of [my sons, i.e., Charles], I think therefore it would be becoming if those of my family who can best afford it would relieve me of this burden for the rest of my life" ("Sketches of my own Birth").
37 A. S. Collins, *The Profession of Letters: A Story of the Relation of Author to Patron, Publisher and Public, 1730–1832* (London, 1928).
38 J. Morgan Sweeney, "'Obliging Their Particular Friends': Government, Aristocracy, and *Literati* in Mid-Eighteenth-Century Scotland," a paper read before the East-Central Regional Meeting of the American Society for Eighteenth-Century Studies, Annapolis, October 1984. Cited with permission.

Dryden's Definition of a Play in An Essay of Dramatic Poesy: A Structuralist Approach

CHARLES H. HINNANT

George Watson's opinion that Lisideius's definition of a play in Dryden's *An Essay of Dramatic Poesy* "is bad . . . is shown to be bad" and yet "is none the less accepted" represents but an extreme instance of a prevailing attitude toward Dryden's criticism.[1] This is that his major critical achievements are mainly practical rather than theoretical in character and thus that it is futile to subject critical pronouncements like Lisideius's definition of a play to rigorous scrutiny. There is certainly a good historical explanation for this attitude: much of Dryden's criticism is occasional and even the self-consciously programmatic *An Essay of Dramatic Poesy* is largely concerned with practical issues: to demonstrate the alleged superiority of the Moderns over the Ancients, of Elizabethan drama over the French. Moreover, Dryden is careful throughout his career to cultivate an urbanity that prevents him from ever becoming too deeply involved in the niceties of critical controversy.

Yet, however justified such an attitude may be historically, it is nonetheless too limited if it completely neglects the conceptual premises of Dryden's criticism. Although his prefaces and essays are never purely theoretical, they continually raise issues that have theoretical implications. Ideally, perhaps, a thorough study of these implications should take as its starting point the whole body of his critical writings. But that would raise problems of consistency and development that would extend beyond the confines of a relatively limited essay. Instead, we can take Lisideius's definition in *An Essay of Dramatic Poesy*—certainly the most succinct formulation of a poetics of drama that Dryden ever presented—as a convenient starting point. By looking carefully at such a concise yet well-known definition, we will not be able to account for all the changes which took place in Dryden's criticism during the course of his career.[2] Yet we can draw attention to several significant and hitherto unnoticed distinctions, distinctions which may shed new light on the theoretical dimensions of his criticism.

If we examine Lisideius's definition—"a play ought to be *a just and lively image of human nature, representing its passions and humours, and the changes of fortune to which it is subject, for the delight and instruction of mankind*" (1:25)—we find at the outset that it possesses one very striking feature, a feature that springs from the particular way the terms are arranged. Taken individually, not one of these terms is original; taken together, they constitute a distinctive configuration. Structurally, this configuration is organized in terms of a series of binary oppositions: just and lively, passions and humours, delight and instruction.[3] Nor are these oppositions invalidated by the odd term in the series—changes of fortune. For the odd term has an eccentric function in Dryden's theater; it remains external to the binary structure of the definition and completes it. If we revise the definition to read: "a play ought to be a just and lively image of human nature, representing its passions and humours, for the delight and instruction of mankind," we find that it is static rather than dynamic. Hence the odd term—changes of fortune—has a singular function, variable, multiple and yet basic. In the critical and rationalistic poetics that was gaining favor in Dryden's time, this function would have been performed by the fable or action of the play. But in Dryden's poetics, the term changes of fortune means something quite different, since it refers not to the action as a whole, but to specific events within the action. Dryden defines these events in terms of the disruptions they produce, disruptions that bring about a change or transition from one state of affairs to another. To the extent that these disruptions are viewed from the perspective of the play as a whole, they can be readily assimilated to a larger pattern, a "labyrinth of design" that offers instruction as well as delight (1:61). Yet to the extent that these disruptions are seen from the perspective of the characters within the play, they are unstable and uncertain. Indeed, one might say that in Dryden's theater a play is dramatic insofar as it is erratic. Or to put it rather differently, a play is dramatic insofar as its wayward heroes—its Almanzors and Antonys—appear to be out of control, shifting abruptly from one mood to another—from love, say, to aversion—with little or no apparent motivation—as if to imply the arbitrary workings of the play's changes of fortune.

This does not mean, of course, that changes of fortune are not important in the rationalistic, neo-Aristotelian criticism of the late sixteenth and seventeenth centuries. The prominence given to peripeteias and anagnorises in *Poetics* X and XI is sufficient to prove the contrary. But neither peripeteias nor anagnoreses serve as the basic dramatic units of neo-Aristotelian poetics, and the action or fable is clearly meant to be seen as independent of both.[4] This is almost certainly the way Dryden understood the action in his later neo-Aristotelian "Grounds of Criticism in Tragedy" when he described tragedy "as an imitation of one entire, great, and probable action" (1:243). Defined in terms of a single action, a play is essentially linear in form, its events occurring one after another in temporal sequence. While some of these events may embody changes of fortune, they can be linked, metonymically, by what Crites, the spokesman for a neo-Aristotelian perspective within Dryden's *Essay*, called *la liaison des scènes* (1:29). In this way, they form what Roman Jakobson and Claude Lévi-Strauss described as a syntagmatic chain and they make the spectator's submission to this chain a condition for grasping the play in its entirety.[5] Dryden's earlier definition, by contrast, contains the outline of a system of what Jakobson termed paradigmatic oppositions. Within this system, the syntagmatic order of succession is disturbed not only by the potential elimination of *la liaison des scènes* (1:64), but also by the absorption of the play's episodes into an atemporal design, marked by what Neander later describes as "under-plots" and "by-concernments." If we examine these "under-plots" and "by-concernemnts" in relation to the main plot of a play, then a paradigmatic metaphoric pattern emerges; it becomes apparent that what happens to the characters in the under-plots are metaphoric transformations of what happens to the characters in the main plot.

The distinction between the syntagmatic chains of neo-Aristotelianism and the paradigmatic series of Dryden's definition is not limited to the dramatic action. Its consequences extend into the realm of dramatic illusion. In the neo-Aristotelian tradition, the attempt to eliminate the obstacles preventing an immediate apprehension of the syntagmatic order of the fable contributed to the prominence given to the "rules," especially the rules concerning the unities of time, place, and action.[6] In his defense of the unity of place, Crites affirms that "the scene ought to be continued through the play, in the same place where it was laid in the beginning; for the stage on which it is represented being but one and the same place, it is unnatural to conceive it many, and those far distant from one another" (1:29). Crites bases the superiority of this rule, so vigorously asserted, on the belief that the role of the unities is to enable the spectator to grasp the fable *in praesentia,* that is to say, as if each episode in the chain were actually happening before him on stage. Within Dryden's theory, on the other hand, the syntagmatic relation *in praesentia* is replaced by the paradigmatic relation *in absentia.* In the former, a dramatic impersonation becomes credible only insofar as it is believed to be real;[7] in the latter, it acquires meaning by evoking comparisons with whatever it seeks to represent, even though this must of necessity be absent from the stage. Dryden relies upon this paradigmatic relation *in absentia* when he makes Neander defend on-stage violence in the following passage: "For my part, I can with as great ease persuade myself that the blows which are struck are given in good earnest, as I can that they who strike them are kings or princes, or those persons they represent" (1:62). Neander can only engage in this exercise in self-persuasion through a paradigmatic act in which he compares the actors with the absent persons they are impersonating.[8] He may be aware of the ineradicable differences separating stage kings from real princes, for example, but he is willing to overlook these differences for the sake of the pleasure which the resemblances afford.

Neander's remarks on dramatic illusion are only one aspect of Dryden's attempt to overcome the limits which the noe-Aristotelian argument imposed on the theater. In keeping with his effort to replace a syntagmatic presence with a paradigmatic absence, Dryden tries to find a term that will encompass the visual as well as the verbal. The term "image" rather than "imitation" is upheld as the ideal to which drama should approximate. In Sir Robert Howard's definition, which has its origins in what Plato and Aristotle called "the manner of imitation,"[9] the word play is defined in terms of the organ of hearing: "A Play," Howard tells us, "will still be supposed to be a Composition of several Persons speaking *ex tempore*."[10] Though Howard follows the Aristotelians in acknowledging the existence of visual spectacle, this definition, like Aristotle's classification of spectacle as the last of six parts, gives it in effect only an extrinsic and subordinate position in the theater. Moreover, in spite of his initial, qualified assent to Lisideius's preliminary definition, the neo-Aristotelian Crites virtually reverts to this auditory definition in the debate as to whether rhyme or blank verse is proper for drama.[11] But in Lisideius's definition, the term image implicitly includes not only a Platonic *mimesis* (the imitation of words by actors) but also a *diegesis* (the imitation of costumes, objects and scenes).[12] The latter consists of the sights, allegories, and *tableaux-vivants*, which, as the products of the image-making faculty, are an inseparable part of what constitutes an image of human nature in Dryden's theater. Even language itself becomes more painterly in this definition. Purely verbal forms—epigrams, puns, antitheses—seem to lose their appeal as words seek to move closer to the objects they depict.

At this point we might wonder if the distinction between "image" and "imitation" is not purely verbal, since there are other passages in which Dryden seems to use the terms interchangeably.[13] Yet it would be foolish to overlook the precise usage simply because the terms may be employed more loosely in other, less formal contexts. Moreover, there can be no doubt that precedents exist for this distinction between "image" and "imitation" in earlier seventeenth-century criticism. In *The Advancement of Learning*, for example, Sir Francis Bacon distinguishes between "a meere imitation of *History*" ("Poesie Narrative") and "an Image of Actions as if they were present" ("Poesie Representative").[14] Like Bacon, Dryden employs the term "image" to distinguish a heightened resemblance from a "mere" or "bare" copy. Thus when he defends the use of rhyme in serious drama, he makes Neander argue that while comedy is "the imitation of common persons and ordinary speaking," tragedy—in which "nature" is "wrought up to a higher pitch"—is accustomed "to image to us the minds and fortunes of noble persons" (1:87). In this passage, the "genus" of tragedy and the heroic poem are thus clearly different from that of comedy; inasmuch as the latter is an "imitation," only the former can be described as "a just and lively image of human nature" (1:87).

This distinction between bare imitation and heightened image lies at the heart of Dryden's poetics in *An Essay of Dramatic Poesy*. It is not, however, the only important one. It is also intimately connected with another, latent opposition which lies at the core of Dryden's definition of a play. This is the opposition between imaging and representing. We can bring out this opposition if we revise the definition once again to read: "a play ought to be a just and lively imaging of human nature, representing its passions and humours and the changes of fortune to which it is subject for the delight and instruction of mankind." Although Crites contends that Lisideius's definition is only *a genere et fine* and thus encompasses other forms besides drama, it contains an implicit reference to the dramatic genre. This is because it uses the term representing, a word Dryden employs elsewhere in

An Essay of Dramatic Poesy to refer specifically to the portrayal of characters and events by actors.[15] In Dryden's definition, drama is constituted by the tension between imaging and representing. The exclusive presence of one brings into existence a form which is not yet dramatic. The simple imaging of human nature does not by itself produce theater. The passions and humours and the changes of fortune to which they are subject must also be represented, must be convincingly portrayed by the actors on stage. On the other hand, if there were no images of human nature, there would no longer be a play in Dryden's terms, for there would be nothing for the actors to represent. It follows that Dryden's definition of a play is a union of imaging and representing; it links them together without dissolving them into a single whole. They exist rather in a Janus-faced relation—a relation pointing in two opposite directions, one toward the world, the other toward the world of the stage.

Still another latent opposition is to be found in that critically important pair of terms—human nature and mankind. To what do these two words correspond in our experience as spectators and readers? The word human nature is a term of essence; the word mankind, a term of existence. Human nature is the object of study—the real species as it has been marked, sorted out, and classified by the dramatist in a process of selection and combination. On the other hand, mankind is the subject—the nominalistic aggregate of individuals who comprise the potential audience of the play. In Pope's abbreviated and generalized version of Dryden's definition: "the proper study of mankind is man." But the two terms not only stand in a horizontal relation of object to subject; they also stand in a vertical relation of poetry to history. If the proper study of mankind were mankind, its object would be history—the aggregate of persons and events that comprise the past. But when the proper study of mankind is man, its object becomes poetry—that is to say, mended history—the anthropological rather than the actual—what men might do rather than what they have done.

We might wonder if this interpretation of Dryden's definition in terms of a series of implicit and explicit binary oppositions is not in danger of imposing a fashionable modern schema upon a classic text. Does Dryden provide any justification for interpreting his definition in terms of binary oppositions? Characteristically, like every good author, he offers one—without our suspecting as much. Later in *An Essay of Dramatic Poesy*, he refers in an offhand fashion to "the old rule of logic . . . that contraries, when placed near, set off each other" (1:58). It is clear that by the term logic Dryden refers to an opposition that is more than a mere rhetorical figure, i.e., more than "a poor antithesis"—it is a way of producing meaning from a contrast of ideas rather than a contrast of mere words.

By setting Dryden's definition of a play into the implicit theoretical context of this old rule of logic, we can perhaps come to a better understanding of just how formal and abstract it really is. Two central concerns of Russian formalists and French structuralists have been the definition of a minimal narrative unit and the elimination from critical analysis of character as an uncertain variable. Following Vladímir Propp, Tzvetan Todorov tried to scale narrative structures down to what he called narrative propositions and to reduce characters to what he termed functions of the plot.[16] Dryden might be said to have resorted to similar strategies in his definition. We have already seen how he reduces that loose and baggy monster—the neo-Aristotelian fable—to changes of fortune—minimal dramatic units that really do nothing more than define transitions from one situation or state to another. We should also observe how Dryden replaces the neo-Aristotelian category of character with the phrase "passions and humours." This dichotomy does more than make explicit the modal distinction between comedy and tragedy. It also reduces dramatic characters to pure functions whose actions can be grasped only within the context of the play itself. The only visible analytic categories left in Lisideius's definition are passions and humours. But the extreme mobility of these adjectival qualities in Dryden's theater prevents even them from becoming defining characteristics: Falstaff is described later in *An Essay* as a "miscellany" of humours; Antony shifts as easily from one passion to another as from one costume to another. This is the converse of the decorum of neo-Aristotelian poetics, where characters are defined, not by their attributes, but by their proprietary identities.

The proprietary identities are thus apt to be less important in Dryden's theater than the structural possibilities imposed on the play by the dominance of the passions and humours. There is a tendency on the part of some commentators to equate Dryden's psychology with a rigid doctrine of decorum. But this is not in fact what the prominence of the passions and humours in Dryden's definition implies. For although these attributes are formed out of a finite number of fixed and preexisting elements, they can be arranged and rearranged by the dramatist into an indefinite number of totally different combinations and patterns. What is even more striking, moreover, is that in terms of Dryden's rule of logic the passions and humours are exact "contraries" of one another. There is nothing to suggest that one is psychologically prior to the other. Their relation is not that of a natural to an artificial or affected manner. It is rather between attributes symmetrically the reverse of each other (i.e., courage and cowardice), as if their function is to guarantee the convertibility of themes between different plots or, what is equally important, between different levels of social reality.

We also need to inquire if Dryden's rule of logic allows us, more essentially, to understand his theory of dramatic response. Although his theory of response is summarized in the conventional Horatian formula—delight and instruction—this formula needs to be understood, as seventeenth-century critics probably understood it, in epistemological terms. In such terms, knowledge is the outcome of a combination of the two: delight is constituted by the pleasure that arises from the discovery of resemblances—the comparison of a stage king with an earthly one. Instruction is the result of an act of judgment that discovers differences. To judge is to distinguish, to discern, to differentiate, to mark, to recognize the founding function of difference.[17] It follows that delight and instruction are much more than radically opposed and unrelated ways of apprehending a play. Instead they refer to two coordinate and equally pleasurable activities, activities which permit drama to become a mode of knowing.

Lest we think that this is a purely fanciful interposition of alien categories on an unproblematic Horatian dictum, we should note that the play of differences and resemblances moves across the chain of oppositions in Dryden's definition. It occurs in the opposition of passions—the basis, in Dryden's psychology, of our common identity, our sameness—to humours—the genesis of our difference, of what divides us as human beings. It figures even more prominently in the contrast between just and lively. The originating source of these two attributes are the twin faculties of judgment and fancy, and both are necessary if a dramatic poem is to come into existence. If a play is not lively in Dryden's sense, we are not yet in a theater of genuinely dramatic characters but below it in an inert world of marmoreal, neoclassical statuary. Yet if a work is not just, we find ourselves transported above the theater, as it were, into an airy realm of rococo fictions based entirely upon fanciful resemblances.

What does this kind of analysis hope to accomplish? At the very least, it hopes to bring out aspects of Dryden's conception of a play that have lain embedded for two centuries within its deceptively simple terminology. Much more importantly, however, it also tries to disclose the theoretical implications of Dryden's criticism. In the past, commentators have tended to adopt one of two alternatives in dealing with *An Essay of Dramatic Poesy*. On the one hand, many have simply taken for granted that its critical ideas, though liberal, still lie well within the shadow of that vast and ill-defined system that we once called neoclassicism and therefore hold little interest for us. On the other hand, a few critics have insisted that Dryden is the augur of a kind of preromantic liberation of drama from the shackles of the "rules." But since this liberation is itself only a kind of mindless negativity, it is no more successful than its antithesis in giving Dryden's critical ideas a positive identity of their own. What this perspective tries to do is to advance a constructive alternative to both approaches. By arguing that Dryden is proposing a paradigmatic rather than a syntagmatic system of representation, it tries to give his theory a comprehensible and specific identity. It may be possible of course that Dryden was anticipated in his definition of a play by some obscure French or Italian critic. But if he were not, then I am suggesting that his definition constitutes an original and positive alternative to neo-Aristotelian poetics and one, moreover, that can easily be comprehended within the framework of modern critical ideas.

NOTES

1 John Dryden, *Of Dramatic Poesy and Other Critical Essays*, ed. George Watson, 2 vols. (London: Dent; New York: Dutton, 1962), I:xi. All citations to Dryden's essays in my text are to this edition.
2 Among commentators who argue that Dryden's criticism undergoes a marked shift in emphasis, one might cite Mary Thale, "Dryden's Dramatic Criticism: Polestar of the Ancients," *Comparative Literature* 18 (1966): 36–54; and Robert D. Hume, "Dryden on Creation: 'Imagination' in the Later Criticism," *Review of English Studies* 21 (1970): 295–314; and *Dryden's Criticism* (Ithaca: Cornell University Press, 1970), pp. 187–230.
3 If we examine Dryden's terminology in relation to its sources, we find that "just" and "lively" belong to a much larger rhetorical family that might include Corneille's "just et gracious," and Rymer's "lively, free, elegant, and easy" (quoted from H. James Jensen, *A Glossary of John Dryden's Critical Terms* ([Minneapolis: University of Minnesota Press, 1969], pp. 70, 74). What is noticeable about the terms of Dryden's word pair is that they have been singled out from this family and placed in an implicit opposition to one another within a system of successive dichotomies. Frank Livingstone Huntley observes that Dryden's use of the complementary terms "apt" and "lively" in "An Account of the Ensuing Poem Prefixed to *Annus Mirabilis*" (1667) foreshadows his employment of this opposition in *An Essay of Dramatic Poesy* (*On Dryden's Essay of Dramatic Poesy* [Ann Arbor:

University of Michigan Press, 1951], p. 14). By contrast, "passions" and "humours" do not belong to a larger family but were used to define the objects of imitation in tragedy and comedy during the seventeenth century; here these opposing objects have been yoked together within a framework that posits the coexistence of resemblances as well as differences. Only "delight" and "instruction" have a traditional history as a word pair, deriving as they do from Horace's *Ars Poetica* 334–37, yet even here they gain a new significance in relation to the other oppositions of Dryden's definition. It is noteworthy, in this connection, that no one has been able to establish a specific source for Dryden's definition as a whole; cf. Huntley, *On Dryden's* Essay, p. 22n.

4 This is the point of Aristotle's distinction between simple and complex fables (*Poetics* 10:1–3). Though complex fables are given a privileged position in the *Poetics*, the reversals and recognitions they contain are not allowed to displace the fable as the constituent element of tragedy and comedy. Paul H. Fry has recently drawn attention to the importance of Dryden's shift from the neo-Aristotelian fable to changes of fortune, a shift he describes as decidedly "anti-Aristotelian" (*The Reach of Criticism: Method and Perception in Literary Theory* [New Haven and London: Yale University Press, 1983], p. 111).

5 Roman Jakobson, "Two aspects of language and two types of aphasic disturbances," in *Fundamentals of Language*, ed. Roman Jakobson and Morris Halle (The Hague: Mouton, 1956), pp. 69–96; Claude Lévi-Strauss, "The Structural Study of Myth," *Structural Anthropology* (New York and London: Basic Books, 1963), 1:206–31.

6 The neo-Aristotelianism of Dryden's age can be traced back to critical and rationalistic poetics that began to emerge in Italy and France between 1560 and 1580. In Dryden's time, it would have been well represented in Jules de la Mesnardière's *La Poètique* (1639), Abbé D'Aubignac's *La Pratique du theâtre* (1657) and in the rather grudging concessions to current orthodoxy exemplified in Corneille's *Trois Discours* (1660). On the indebtedness of Crites's exposition to Corneille's *Trois Discours*, see John M. Aden, "Dryden, Corneille and the *Essay of Dramatic Poesy*," *Review of English Studies* 6 (1955): 147–56. For a general discussion of the relation of Dryden's *Essay* to the neo-Aristotelian tradition, see *The Works of John Dryden* (Berkeley: University of California Press, 1956–), vol. 17, *Prose 1668–1691: An Essay of Dramatick Poesie and Shorter Works*, ed. Samuel Holt Monk et al. (1971), pp. 334–46.

7 The relations *in praesentia* and *in absentia* need not, of course, be regarded as mutually exclusive; both can coexist within the same play. Nonetheless, the tendency of neo-Aristotelian criticism is to make the relation *in praesentia* the sole norm for drama. In *La Pratique du theâtre*, for example, D'Aubignac writes of the unity of place, "le Theatre n'est austre chose qu'une representation, il ne se faut point imaginer qu'il y ait rien de tout ce qu nous y voyons, mais bien les choses memes dont nous y trouvons les images. Floridor alors est moins Floridor que cet Horace dont il fait le

Personnage" (*La Pratique du théâtre* [Amsterdam: Bernard, 1715], pp. 87–88). J. E. Spingarn describes the neo-Aristotelian rationale for the dramatic unities in terms of this relation *in praesentia*: "the whole action occurs before our eyes, and is accordingly limited to what we can actually see with our own sense, that is, to that brief duration of time and to that small amount of space in which the actors are occupied in acting, and not any other time or place" (J. E. Spingarn, *A History of Literary Criticism in the Renaissance* [New York: Columbia University Press, 1954], pp. 98–99).

8 On the role of the imagination in assisting the reason in making these comparisons, see *A Defence of an Essay of Dramatic Poesy* (1:72). In the *Preface to Gondibert* (1650), Davenant describes a similar suspension of disbelief, not in terms of a paradigmatic relation *in absentia*, but as a general disposition that could apply equally well to syntagmatic or paradigmatic actions: "For we may descend to compare the deceptions in Poesie to those of them that professe dexterity of Hand which resembles Conjuring, and to such we come not with the intention of *Lawyers* to examine the evidence of Facts, but are content, if we like the carriage of their feign'd motion, to pay for being well deceiv'd" (Spingarn, 2:11).

9 *Republic* 3. 292c; *Poetics* 3.1.

10 Preface to *The Great Favourite or the Duke of Lerma*, in *Critical Essays of the Seventeenth Century*, ed. J. E. Spingarn, 3 vols. (Oxford: Clarendon Press, 1909), 2:107.

11 1:78–79. G. M. A. Grube notes that while Aristotle begins by using the term *mimesis* in the general sense of an imitation of life, he reverts later in the *Poetics* to the Platonic sense of an impersonation of a part by an actor (*The Greek and Roman Critics* [Toronto: University of Toronto Press, 1968], pp. 70–71n).

12 In the definition, Dryden employs the term image, not as part of a theory to be established, but as something to be accepted and as a basis for further elaboration. There is no suggestion that he is using the term "image" in a novel sense; yet clearly he means that the situations actions, and characters of a play must appeal to the sense of sight as well as sound. On the visual implications of Dryden's use of the term, see Jensen, "Image," in *A Glossary of Dryden's Critical Terms*, pp. 62–63.

13 Dryden frequently uses the phrase "imitation of nature" in *An Essay of Dramatic Poesy*; see, e.g., 1:56, 72, 73, 79, 86. On the meaning of the terms "imitation" and "nature" in Dryden's criticism, see Mary Thale. "Dryden's Dramatic Criticism: Polestar of the Ancients," pp. 36–54; and "Dryden's Critical Vocabulary: The Imitation of Nature," *Papers on Language and Literature* 2 (1966): 315–26. Thale suggests that "imitation of nature" is a deliberate substitution for the neo-Aristotelian "imitation of an action" (p. 48).

14 Spingarn, *Critical Essays of the Seventeenth Century*, 1:6–7.

15 It can be found, for example, in Eugenius's handling of the subject of death: "When we see death represented, we are convinced it is but fiction; but when we hear it related, our eyes (the strongest witnesses) are want-

ing, which might have undeceived us, and we are all willing to favour the sleight when the poet does not too grossly impose on us" (1:51). For other instances of this usage, see Watson, 1:29, 48, 52, and 62. On Dryden's usage of representation as the performance of a play or part of a play, see Jensen, "represent," "representation," in *A Glossary of Dryden's Critical Terms*, pp. 99–100. This is also the sense in which D'Aubignac uses the term "representation" in *La Pratique du théâtre*, where he repeatedly pairs it with spectacle: "Tout de même le Poète en considerant dans sa Tragedie le Spectacle ou la Représentation, il fait tout ce que son Art & son esprit lui peuvent fournir pour la rendre admirable aux Spectateurs: car il ne travaille que pour leur plaire" (p. 31). For an interesting discussion of the way in which *mimesis* and representation come to be dissociated in D'Aubignac's theory, see Hugh M. Davison, "Pratique et rhétorique du théâtre: Étude sur le vocabulaire et la méthode de D'Aubignac," *Critique et Creation Littéraires en France au XVIIIe Siécle* (Paris: Centre National de la Recherche Scientifique, 1977), pp. 169–75.

16 Vladímir Propp, *Morphology of the Folktale* (Austin and London: University of Texas Press, 1968); and Tzvetan Todorov, "The Grammar of Narrative" and "Narrative Transformations" in *The Poetics of Prose*, tr. by Richard Howard (Ithaca and New York: Cornell University Press, 1977), pp. 108–19 and 218–33.

17 The connection of delight with the discovery of resemblances and judgment with the discovery of differences was first made in seventeenth-century English criticism by Thomas Hobbes in *The Elements of Law*, 1:10, 4. On the importance of Hobbes's terminology for Restoration criticism, see Spingarn, 1:xxvii–xxix and my "Hobbes on Fancy and Judgment," *Criticism* 18 (1976): 16–20. For a general discussion of the influence of Hobbes on Dryden's early criticism, see John M. Aden, "Dryden and Imagination: the First Phase," *PMLA* 74 (1959): 28–40.

Calista and the "Equal Empire" of Her "Sacred Sex"

J. M. ARMISTEAD

If we look at Rowe's *The Fair Penitent* from the viewpoint of Christian doctrine, as Douglas Canfield has so usefully done in his recent book, we must, I think, come out with a reading very like his: the play is a dramatic essay on the power of forgiveness.[1] And if we look at it with genre uppermost in our minds, then we can hardly dispute Frank Kearful's conclusion that it is an early attempt "to fuse the naturalism of domestic tragedy and the patheticism of 'sentimental' tragedy with a new didacticism."[2] It is only when we keep Calista central to our response, as most critics have always found themselves irresistibly doing, that major difficulties of interpretation arise. Canfield knows he is in the minority when he argues that Calista fully and effectively repents. The prevailing view, in the eighteenth century and now, was concisely stated by Samuel Johnson in his "Life of Rowe"; Calista "shows no evident signs of repentance, but may be reasonably suspected of feeling pain from detection rather than from guilt, and expresses more shame than sorrow, and more rage than shame."[3] Lately, Annibel Jenkins and Richard Dammers have differed as to the reality of Calista's penitence even as they have agreed that, in Dammers' words, "Calista embodies tragic destruction caused by the unreasonable domination of women by men."[4] The most recent readings that I know of, those by Janet Aikins and Jean Hagstrum, shift the emphasis from this social dilemma to the contours of Calista's feelings—Aikins finding that "Rowe is interested in examining the condition of a person in a hopeless situation, not in effecting change in the society that renders such a situation hopeless," Hagstrum concentrating on what he calls the "substructural movement of the play" that pivots on Calista's death wish.[5]

These recent interpretations are not fundamentally wrong, that is, unfaithful to the dynamics of the play itself, but they remain partial so long as they fail to account for the deep integrity of Calista's protest against moral conventions. By examining the literary contexts of that protest we can see that her penitence, though real, does not involve a capitulation to the moral values embodied in her father. What Aikins reads as psychic torment can then be understood as an anguished search for a language and moral code to explain and legitimize unorthodox behavior, and what Hagstrum sees as her death wish can be found giving way to the invocation of a higher law. This higher law is heavenly, even Christian, but is understood only by those who can share Calista's vision of an "equal empire" of her "sacred sex," and it is not operative in the social forms which Sciolto currently "fathers" and which Horatio and Lothario enforce in their antithetical ways. Thus, to some extent Dr. Johnson saw true: while penitence and forgiveness may calm, they cannot cure Calista's "rage," for it springs only secondarily from a sense of the specific sins of individuals, including herself. Its primary source is her tragic recognition, persistent to the play's end, that the dominant institutions and social rituals, albeit supervised by pious men and designed to secure society from mankind's imperfections, cannot fulfill her own most profound, most "soulful" needs.

So the play is very much about psychic torment, the "melancholy . . . woes" of "private" persons trying to socialize and sanctify their fallen natures (Prologue, l. 16).[6] The extent to which they are tragically unsuccessful in doing so is accented by the pervasive shipwreck imagery. Sciolto feels that Calista has "rashly ventured in a stormy sea" (5.1.249). Horatio thinks that Altamont has been "wrecked upon the faithless shore" of his bride (3.1.261). Lothario gives in to a "storm of passion" (4.1.81), but Calista welcomes a different storm that will sink her to the peaceful ocean floor (4.1.133–39). Lavinia, having twice endured the shipwreck of her fortunes, fancies herself a "helpless wanderer" (3.1.368) cleaving "to one faithful plank" (3.1.402). For most of the characters early in the play, the alternative to perilous voyaging is remaining at home, Sciolto's home. To Altamont and Horatio, even to Lothario, Sciolto is the father-creator of a latter-day Eden, sire of Calista/Eve, "author" of Altamont's happiness (1.1.60), and commander of Horatio, a Gabriel figure who fails to protect "yon forbidden place" (2.2.131), the garden, against penetration by Lothario/Satan (see 1.1.19, 22, 35, 67–68, 78; 2.1.131, 167–72; 3.1.267–68). This grand emblem of Eden amidst the storms of passion and fate settles comfortably into the grooves of expectation. Rowe's audience already knew the scenario and could, if they wished, shed sympathetic tears for the devil-possessed Calista and those who suffered by her ruin, even as the ruin itself satisfied their moral scruples: "By such examples are we taught to prove / The sorrows that attend unlawful love" (5.1.288–89).[7]

Probably Rowe catered to these expectations. But perhaps he also wrote for an audience that could respond to variations on convention, to meanings conveyed through allusion and dramatic structure, and to the more complex attitudes of a modern Eve. The Eden myth provides only one of several sources of imagery used to describe the environment of values and institutions fathered by Sciolto in the current moment of history. Sciolto sees himself not as a god—that identity is fastened to him by Altamont and Horatio—but rather as a kind of magician-patriarch, something on the order of Prospero or Merlin. His chief aim is to create and sustain order, a safe haven from the malignant forces of man's fallen nature. He and those around him invoke the language of astrology and classical or folk superstition to signal the sublunar condition of his "power" (1.1.175; 3.1.214). "Let this auspicious day be ever sacred," says Altamont in the play's opening speech (1.1.1); let it inaugurate a "sacred era . . ./ A better order of succeeding days / . . . white and lucky all. / Calista is the mistress of the year" (2.1.83–87).[8] One thinks immediately of Dryden's "times whiter series" in *Astraea Redux* (ll. 292–93), "round of greater years begun" in *Annus Mirabilis* (1.1 71), and "white moment of your fate" in *Conquest of Granada* (part 1, 4.1.33)—all references to Virgil's Golden Age eclogue (4.4–7) conflated with the archetypal significances of "white" as auspicious and pure. To this prelapsarian or millennial trope is linked the reference to Calista as a kind of May Queen, mistress of the new season. "Yes, Altamont," answers Horatio, adding the context of astrology, "today thy better stars / Are joined to shed their kindest influence" (1.1.7–8, and see other astrological imagery in 2.1.99–102, 3.1.6–10).[9] Over all this good fortune and ritual order presides Sciolto, a magus responsible for the enchantment of this special time: "This day," he proclaims, "'Tis yours, my children, sacred to your loves" (2.1.121–22), so let there be music and Dionysian indulgence (2.1.125–27, 141–53).[10]

Eden, then, is sunk into the Golden Age, Eve into an earth mother, and Sciolto-god into an earthly Prospero trying to sustain his temporal paradise amidst the storms of reality. This "vast scheme of joy" (4.1.239) operates through male dominance, reason, and the channeling of passion into rituals of honor, courtship, and marriage. To Sciolto and others who espouse it, this code is sacrosanct, even though quite earthly, and anyone who violates it is regarded as malignant and heretical.[11] Lothario is the diabolical outlaw and uncivilized brute who spurns "sacred order" (1.1.221–24, 2.2.70), and Calista comes in for the full repertoire of misogynistic rhetoric. To Horatio she is a beguiling Eve, a succubus, sorceress, siren (1.1.387–89, 2.1.167–72, 3.1.257–58), a lustful temptress with a "hot imagination" (1.1.314). To Sciolto she embodies the influence of "some malignant planet, / Foe to the harvest" (3.1.6–7) and reincarnates "Helen in the night when Troy was sacked" (5.1.53). As Katherine Rogers has shown, these were all well-established stereotypes by Rowe's time, even the negative allusion to Helen and Lothario's assumption of Calista's basic irrationality (see 1.1.136–38, 149–52, 170–71, 172–78, 200–209).[12] Precisely where Rowe got them would be impossible to pin down, given their conventionality, but that he became aware, at some point, of their potency is indicated in his translation of Claudius Quillet's *Callipaedia*, Book 1 (London, 1720). There we find described a "golden" era giving way to the "impious Age" when Pandora lets loose "mortal Woes" (pp. 12–16). In her study of "The Myth of Feminine Evil" H. R. Hays traces the pre-Renaissance fusion of Pandora and Eve through the "theme of magical misogyny": "On the one hand she is all-giving and has to do with the growth of grain, fruitfulness, and love; on the other, she is responsible for the demonic seduction of men and the death of her lover and is associated with the earth and the chasm of the underworld."[13] Some such composite, mythical figure—May Queen and siren, Harvest Queen and sorceress, Eve and Helen, bride and succubus—is what Calista becomes in the minds of those who try to contain her waywardness within Sciolto's framework of assumptions.

To the extent that Lothario moves within the assumptions of this myth of reason, ritual, and male dominance, he accepts its validity as a model of reality. Rather than reject his role of outlaw and brute, he revels in it like some Restoration rake and dies satisfied that he has "conquered . . . in love" and saved honor through "sweet revenge" (4.1.113–15).[14] But Calista does not affirm Sciolto's paradise; she rejects its magic, its values, its language, and the roles its retainers would cast her in. She and Altamont were "never paired above," she insists, and their wedding day has no sacred significance (2.1.99–106). She regrets her one "guilty night" (4.1.43–46) and will "bless the day" when she escapes from "tyrant man" (3.1.220–21). She affirms neither Sciolto's vision of her as "a cherubim" (5.1.74) nor Lothario's invitation to become "a slave to base desires and brutal pleasures" (4.1.77), and she fights to prevent "warring passions" from deforming her "reason" (2.1.76–80). Moreover, she regards those who represent her father's code in the language of persuasion as bearers of mere tales, legends, riddles, charms (2.1.37–38, 3.1.110, 114, 139, 200, 204), not as the bringers of truth and light.[15]

In fact, Calista finds the antithetical worlds of Sciolto and Lothario equally specious and threatening to her identity. If Lothario has violated her by raping her body when reason was sleeping but passion awake, Horatio has violated her by trying to charm reason while passion was sleeping. That Rowe consciously exploited this parallel is indicated by the verbal analogues in the two pertinent speeches. Lothario's description of what he has done is echoed by what Horatio says he wants to do. Thus Lothario:

> I found the fond, believing, love-sick maid
> Loose, unattired, warm, tender, full of wishes;
> Fierceness and pride, the guardians of her honor,
> Were charmed to rest, and love alone was waking.
> (1.1.149–52)

Later, when Horatio approaches her, he apostrophizes, almost as if calling down a benign demon or astral influence,

> Teach me, some pow'r, that happy art of speech
> To dress my purpose up in gracious words,
> Such as may softly steal upon her soul
> And never waken the tempestuous passions.
> (3.1.54–57)

Calista considers both of these well-wishers to be loose ruffians (3.1.125, 4.1.76–80) and, in rejecting them, rejects the mythical pattern which both represent in opposite ways. Lothario has stolen her virginity, but Horatio tries to rape a more valuable part, her "soul."

Of course, Calista does feel that she has sinned, in the sense that her actions and pride have resulted in injury to individuals whom she loves. And in the final act she does perform an unorthodox penance for these consequences, as well as for her own dissimulation and indignation.[16] But she feels no remorse for violating Sciolto's circle of values and institutions, per se, for they have never nourished what she feels to be her true identity, what she calls her "genius" (2.1.47–

48) or "secret soul" (4.1.91), one of the "high souls" (3.1.50) of her "sacred sex" (3.1.157). Such a soul, in her opinion, should "claim an equal empire o'er the world" (3.1.52), an empire hospitable to female preferences and to love matches which, unlike that of Horatio and Lavinia, rub against the grain of social usage (see 3.1.75–80, 341–42). Perhaps Rowe had in mind the kind of world described by Quillet, in Book 1 of *Callipaedia*, a place where "Love" is "Liking; nor the nuptial League / Be ty'd by Compact," and where "wise Nature" directs "a Couple in their mutual Choice, / . . . by Reason, not by Custom" (p. 29).

Such an empire is not of this world. Calista's incorrigible pursuit of it alienates her from social nourishment and creates discord in the established order. The others, however, find fulfilling retreats or forms of action when this discord breaks down the hierarchy within which their behavior has been classified and pronounced good. Lavinia, armed with trust in Providence (3.1.383–86), transports her sacramental marriage to the cottage of her heart (1.1.396–400) and the bosom of her husband (3.1.380).[17] Sciolto turns to militant revenge (4.1.255–66). And Horatio turns to friendship, "the last retreat . . ./ Secure against ill fortune and the world" (4.1.334–35). But Calista, who has throughout felt herself "captive in a foreign realm" (3.1.78), cannot locate her "native land" (3.1.80), and her only alternative, as Aikins and Hagstrum have shown, is to move from one dismal fantasy world to another and, ultimately, to death beside Lothario's corpse in a black-draped room (see 2.1.18–20, 3.1.221, 4.1.205, 5.1.1–42, 133–36).[18]

Yet death is not finally oblivion for Calista. On the one hand, she does not regard her father's forgiveness as potent in itself; she is merely "Charmed" (5.1.139) by it in an earthly way, so that her acceptance of it is, I think, not to be taken as immersion in his theurgy. In her last speech, however, she senses a blending of his forgiving words with "Celestial sounds" (5.1.257), and her dying prayer appeals not to Sciolto's fatherhood but to that of the God above social and moral systems: "Mercy, heav'n" (5.1.264).

Behind her prideful indignation, rebellion, and special form of penitence lie traditions of thought which, consciously or not, Rowe seems to have expected part of his audience would understand. First is a concept of soul deriving from Christian and pagan demonology. The words "genius" and "soul" are pervasive in the play and, as one might expect, when Horatio and Lothario employ the former, they refer to "the good and bad angels of the Morality plays" (2.2.21, 3.1.150).[19] Perhaps Rowe had recently been reading Sir Thomas Browne's *Religio Medici*, a book in his library, where Browne asserts,

"I could easily believe, that . . . particular persons, have their Tutelary and Guardian Angels. It is not a new opinion of the Church of Rome, but an old one of Pythagoras and Plato."[20] Lothario's dying exclamation, "O, Altamont! Thy genius is the stronger" (4.1.109), refers, however, not to a guardian angel but to the pagan notion of a spirit governing a person's fortunes—a concept which the astrologers associated with a particular set of astral influences on one's personality. Then again, when Sciolto exhorts each member of the wedding party to "indulge his genius" (2.1.143), he means neither guardian angel nor tutelary spirit, but rather the spirit of one's appetites and instincts, a spirit to be propitiated in pagan festivals: "To your glad Genius sacrifice this Day," says Juvenal in Dryden's 1693 translation.[21] This invoking of a pagan demon in a Christian wedding ritual is typical of Sciolto the Christian magician, and it is equivalent to Altamont's linking of Calista the Christian bride with the pagan Queen of May or of the harvest. Rowe may have derived this concept of genius from Pythagoras, whose "Golden Verses" he would soon translate (published in 1707), from the Christian Cabalist John Dee, whose "True & Faithful Relation . . . of Spirits" (1659) he owned, or, perhaps more likely, from the Cambridge Platonist Henry More, whose *Philosophical Poems* (1647) and *Philosophical Writings* (1662) were also in his library. More recognized the Pythagorean levels of genii, corresponding to different orders of virtue, and himself believed that men had separable souls, or "genii," that could assume aerial forms.[22]

More also delineates a theory of ghosts that could have provided Rowe with the doctrine behind Altamont's resolution to follow Calista after death: "Whether our lifeless shades are doomed to wander / In gloomy groves with discontented ghosts, / Or whether through the upper air we fleet, / . . . still I'll pursue thee" (5.1.201–5). According to More, after death unbinds soul from body, the soul moves to a level of existence appropriate to the degree of purity it achieved in mortal life. Thus, while one departed spirit might become a "troubled Ghost" walking its "forewonted coast" in aerial likeness of its former corporeal shape, another, more virtuous, could be invested with a form of perfect beauty and enjoy a higher paradise of intellectual pleasure, hymn singing, and love.[23]

Seen in the context of all this demonology, Calista's pride in her inviolable identity, which she refers to as her "high" soul or "genius" (3.1.50; 2.1.47–48), takes on richer significance. She sees the soul not as a guardian or tutelary spirit, or as the spirit of her appetites and passions, but rather as the species of rational "genius" or "soul" described by More. Regarding the multiple genii of Pythagoras as symbols for different attributes of man's single soul or personality, More speaks of the soul's "selfnesse" when referring to the pristine identity it possessed when it first entered the body by "flowing forth from . . . the World of life," elsewhere called the "life divine." All earthly endeavors toward redemption are attempts to regain this divine "selfnesse" which was lost by the Fall and obscured from our awareness by "long commerce of corporeals." Frustrated mortals like Calista therefore "strike through the Skie / With piercing throbs and sighs" as they seek to recover "the high heaven-born soul" from its double ensnarement by "the dull body" and by fallen social modes.[24]

Whether or not he actually got it from More, Rowe seems to employ this concept of identity and redemption in his portrait of Calista. Her rebellion against Sciolto's system and the female stereotypes it would impose on her amounts to resistance against invasions of the self, of the genius and high soul of her sacred sex. "I the free-born soul to no sect would inslave," writes More.[25] "Let no soothing Tongue," says Rowe in his translation of Pythagoras, "Prevail upon thee . . ./ To do the Soul's Immortal Essence wrong. / Of good and ill . . . Chuse for thy self" (p. 159). But in resisting the soothing tongues of both Lothario and Horatio (see 4.1.27–28), Calista leaves herself no earthly environment in which to realize her "life divine." She is like Virgil's Dido, Shakespeare's and Dryden's Cleopatra, Southerne's Isabella, and Pope's Eloisa—all isolated from the socially ordered life of man by their unorthodox choices. Their impulses are severed from life and "repressed in the dark regions of an individual mind."[26] Hence Calista's death wish is a wish not for oblivion but for a higher empire, the empire of the God above earthly systems, where one's identity, one's genius, flowers forth, at last freed from a fallen world.

The notion of a higher law, indeed a higher reality, than the one prevailing at any given historical moment is a Platonic idea that was Christianized in the early Church. It had fed the parallel ideas of a Golden Age in the past and a millennium in the future, when all imperfectly human social forms and moral rules would dissolve into instinctive harmony. The appropriation of such millenarian notions by reformists and revolutionaries of many ages and climes has been explored and continues to be explored in historical and literary scholarship.[27] Rowe himself could have come across this cluster of concepts in many places. Sir Thomas Browne had spoken feelingly of the God above systems, and Pascal had explained man's restless building of his own environment as an attempt to realize "a true happiness of which there now remain to him only the imprint and empty trace."[28] Dryden, who taught succeeding generations of dramatists how to juxtapose different codes of thought and behavior in different characters, makes Cleopatra the seeker of a transcendent empire.[29] Even the pseudoscientist Thomas Burnet, in another book owned by Rowe, distinguished between a pristine simplicity of life and the "new forms and modifications" that were "superadded by . . . Arts, . . . Religion, . . .[and] Superstition."[30] Again, however, it is Henry More whose articulation of the idea is closest in wording and concept to Calista's expression of her faith: Once "incorporate / Into the higher world," he writes, "Thus do we bud, / True heavenly plants" and "fearlesse sit above all fate."[31]

Toward the end of his life, while translating Lucan's *Pharsalia*, the book through which he was to be remembered for many generations, Rowe put into fluent verse the complex sense of law and order which torments Calista, the sense of "Magick Laws" versus the "Laws, which Heav'n or Nature know, / The rule of Gods above, and Man below."[32] Calista's dying words, "Mercy, heav'n," show her rising above the charms of her father's "Magick Laws," for she now realizes, to quote More again, that "the safest Magick is the sincere consecrating of a mans Soul to God."[33] Likewise, she transcends Lothario's natural law in her quest for an "equal empire" where her "sacred sex" can, in Altamont's phrase, "tread the fields of light" (5.1.204). Presumably, in this supramoral context, the conflicting meanings of that epithet which follow her through the play—"fair," meaning either "beautiful" or "specious"—will resolve themselves into a third meaning, "free from blemish."[34]

I am not arguing that Rowe was a feminist in the modern sense or that he was an occultist, not even that he accepted the curious compromise between occult and empirical thought which Platonizing philosophers like More found so fruitful in the Restoration. He was not, I think, trying to show that Sciolto's worldview is "wrong" or that Calista does not in some sense "repent." What I am arguing is that Rowe, sensitive to contemporary dilemmas faced by females ill-matched in marriage and frustrated by patriarchal social conventions, endowed his Calista with a rather potent vision of her problems, a more metaphysical vision than we have understood heretofore. This vision was based on a loosely related set of philosophical conventions—Platonic, Pythagorean, and Hermetic—which still interested early eighteenth-century writers and readers, and which were strongly affirmed during the Renaissance in Sciolto's Italy. Interestingly enough, many of the early Augustan writers who toyed with such a spirit-informed universe were radicals like Calista, though I can find no evidence that Rowe himself connected her ideas with theirs.[35] Thus, drawing upon the kind of occult metaphysics represented by books in his library, Rowe seems to have provided Calista's understanding of her soul's identity and potential with an established tradition of thought, albeit one hardly in the best repute in 1703, not in order to make her exemplary but to underline the integrity and profundity of her dilemma. I suppose that Rowe himself believed Sciolto's view of social and moral order to be the most practical one for the fallen world at his moment in history, but I think he had read broadly enough, had thought long enough about women's social difficulties, and understood tragedy well enough, to let Calista persist in considering that view hostile to her own development. Her plea for heaven's mercy, together with her remorse over the harm done to her loved ones (including her father's disappointment), becomes in consequence all the more moving.

NOTES

1 J. Douglas Canfield, *Nicholas Rowe and Christian Tragedy* (Gainesville: University Presses of Florida, 1977), see esp. pp. 111, 137.
2 Frank J. Kearful, "The Nature of Tragedy in Rowe's *The Fair Penitent*," *Papers on Language and Literature* 2 (1966): 351-60, p. 360.
3 Samuel Johnson, *Lives of the English Poets*, ed. George Birkbeck Hill, 3 vols. (Oxford: Clarendon Press, 1905), 2:67.
4 Annibel Jenkins, *Nicholas Rowe* (Boston: G. K. Hall, 1977), pp. 53-67; Richard Dammers, "The Female Experience in the Tragedies of Nicholas Rowe," *Women and Literature* 6 (1978): 28-35.
5 Janet Aikins, "To Know Jane Shore, 'think on all time, backward'," *Papers on Language and Literature* 18 (1982): 258-77; Jean H. Hagstrum, *Sex and Sensibility* (Chicago and London: University of Chicago Press, 1980), pp. 117-21.
6 My text is *The Fair Penitent*, ed. Malcolm Goldstein (Lincoln: University of Nebraska Press, 1969). Quotations noted parenthetically in the text are from this edition.
7 In Canfield's treatment of the Eden imagery in *Nicholas Rowe*, he compares Sciolto to Otway's Acasto of *The Orphan* and adds that Altamont eventually displays the "meekness . . . of Christ" (pp. 113-15, 132, 138). For the echoes of Milton, see George W. Whiting, "Rowe's Debt to *Paradise Lost*," *Modern Philology* 31 (1935): 271-79. Storm imagery, of course, pervades Renaissance and seventeenth-century drama, sometimes in association with Eden imagery. Rowe might well have remembered the convention from *Venice Preserv'd*.
8 On the background for understanding Rowe's use of "auspicious day,"

"better order of . . . days," and "White," see *The Works of John Dryden*, ed. H. T. Swedenberg, Jr., et al. (Berkeley and Los Angeles: University of California Press, 1956–), 1:30, 62, 233, 282; 2:36; 10:480; 11:63, 450. See also the *Oxford English Dictionary* under "white." On "mistress of the year" see Sir James Frazer, *The New Golden Bough*, ed. Theodor H. Gaster (New York: Criterion, 1959), pp. 80–90.

9 Astrological lore, as understood by Rowe, may be consulted in William Lilly, *A Prophecy of the White King* (1644) and *Christian Astrology* (2d ed., 1659), and John Partridge, *An Astrological Vade Mecum* (1679).

10 On the magical control of a day, see Stith Thompson, *Motif-Index of Folk-Literature*, rev. ed. (Bloomington: Indiana University Press, 1955–59), D2146.1, D2172.2, V222.12; and C. Grant Loomis, *White Magic* (Cambridge, Mass.: Medieval Academy of America, 1948).

11 "Lavinia" in the "Epilogue" pokes fun at the men who demand obedience to "laws which for themselves they made . . . And huff and domineer by right divine." More seriously, Cardinal Newman aptly describes such thinkers (though he refers specifically to Hume), in whom "imagination usurps the functions of reason; and they cannot bring themselves even to entertain as a hypothesis . . . a thought contrary to that vivid impression of which they are the victims": *An Essay in Aid of a Grammar of Assent*, ed. C. F. Harrold (New York, London, Toronto: Longmans, Green, 1947), p. 62. Sciolto is also like the Gnostic who wants to transform an alien world into something of his own creation; see Eric Voegelin, *Science, Politics, and Gnosticism* (Chicago: H. Regnery, 1968).

12 Katherine Rogers, *The Troublesome Helpmate: A History of Misogyny in Literature* (Seattle and London: University of Washington Press, 1966), see esp. pp. 135–88.

13 H. R. Hays, *The Dangerous Sex: The Myth of Feminine Evil* (London: Methuen, 1966), see esp. pp. 1–121, 158–82; quotations on pp. 79 and 81.

14 Donald B. Clark thinks Lothario combines the fiery personality of Massinger's Romont with the values of a Restoration rake like Rochester or like Otway's Don John ("An Eighteenth-Century Adaptation of Massinger," *Modern Language Quarterly* 13 [1952]: 239–52).

15 Michael McKeon has provocatively explicated man's perennial habit of imposing on history his own patterns "which may constitute fantasy or villainy for those [like Calista] who are not convinced that such patterns accurately describe reality" (*Politics and Poetry in Restoration England* [Cambridge, Mass. and London: Harvard University Press, 1975], p. 259).

16 The best analysis of her profound kind of penitence, which involves rejection of the formal ritual prescribed by the Church, is in Canfield, *Nicholas Rowe*, pp. 119–23, 127–30, 135.

17 Canfield (ibid., pp. 124, 134) has demonstrated how closely Lavinia's ideas of love and marriage correspond to scriptural doctrine. On Lavinia as model for conventional marriage and as moral preceptress, see Richard Dammers, "The Importance of Being Female in the Tragedies of Nicholas Rowe," *McNeese Review* 26 (1979–80): 13–20.

18 Richardson's apparent debt in *Clarissa* to this aspect of Calista's tragedy is discussed by Dammers (*Women and Literature*, pp. 33–34), and Clarissa's death wish is instructively interpreted by R. D. Stock in *The Holy and the Daemonic from Sir Thomas Browne to William Blake* (Princeton: Princeton University Press, 1982), see esp. pp. 279–82.
19 See Canfield, *Nicholas Rowe*, p. 125.
20 Thomas Browne, quoted by Wayne Shumaker, in *The Occult Sciences in the Renaissance* (Berkeley, Los Angeles, London: University of California Press, 1972), p. 241. I do not know that anyone has found Browne a source for Dryden's discussion of "tutelary genii" in his preface to *The Satires of . . . Juvenalis* (1693) which then might have become Rowe's intermediary influence. The sale catalogue for Rowe's library is the appendix of Canfield's *Nicholas Rowe*, pp. 181–94.
21 For each of these meanings see the *Oxford English Dictionary* under "genius."
22 See pp. 179, 198–99, in M. Dacier, *The Life of Pythagoras, With His Symbols and Golden Verses* (London, 1707). Dee's *Relation* was edited and skeptically introduced by Meric Casaubon (London, 1659). For Henry More's concept of "genii" see "An Antidote against Atheism," in *A Collection of Several Philosophical Writings* (1662; rpt. New York and London: Garland, 1978), 1:130–31; hereafter, this two-volume compilation will be cited as *Writings*.
23 More, "Psychathanasia," in *Philosophical Poems* (1647; rpt. and ed. Alexander B. Grosart, 1878; rpt. New York: AMS, 1967), p. 48; "The Praeexistency of the Soul," *Poems*, p. 121; "The Immortality of the Soul," *Writings*, 2:8, 147, 155, 162–63, 180–87. More's ghost lore was exceptional for a Protestant. Most Protestants, explains R. H. West in *The Invisible World* (1939; rpt. New York: Octagon, 1969), receded from "the Roman ghost doctrine" when they renounced purgatory and the intercession of saints (p. 49). Though I think Rowe shared More's "regressive" beliefs, in this play they can be explained by noting that Altamont is meant to be a Roman Catholic.
24 More, "Antimonopsychia," "Praeexistency of the Soul," and "Psychathanasia," in *Poems*, pp. 133, 128, 64, 48, and 58 (following the order of my quotations).
25 More, "Psychathanasia," in *Poems*, p. 47. Another source for Rowe's demonology might have been one of More's own sources, Henry Cornelius Agrippa, the Christian magus whose *Three Books of Occult Philosophy* appeared in English translation by "J. F." in 1651; see p. 410 for Agrippa's definition of the tripartite "demon" of man. Agrippa also promoted women's rights; his *Female Pre-eminence*, translated by Henry Care in 1670, contains sentiments Calista would have found congenial: e.g., "the *tyranny* of Men usurpt . . . all business, and *unjust Laws, foolish Customes*, and an *ill mode* of education, *retrencht* their [women's] liberties. For now a Woman . . . is . . . kept at home; and as incapable of any nobler imployment, suffered only to *knit, spin*, or practice . . . the *Needle*. And when she arrives at riper years, is delivered to the tyranny of a *jealous-pated* Husband, or cloistered up in a Nunnery" (p. 76).

26 For a stimulating discussion of Virgil's Dido and Dante's Francesca, see Maud Bodkin, *Archetypal Patterns in Poetry* (London, New York, and Toronto: Oxford University Press, 1934), pp. 193–216. The quotation is on p. 193. The English drama of the 1690s whet the audience's appetite for alienated women characters, often married women. Southerne's Isabella in *The Fatal Marriage* (1694) became the prototype and could have influenced Rowe nearly as strongly as did Otway's Monimia, Acasto, Polydore (*The Orphan*, 1680) and Don John (*Don Carlos*, 1676). Laura Brown touches upon this subject in "The Defenseless Woman and the Development of English Tragedy," *Studies in English Literature* 22 (1982): 429–43.
27 See Ernest Lee Tuveson, *Millennium and Utopia* (Berkeley and Los Angeles: University of California Press, 1949); Harry Levin, *The Myth of the Golden Age in the Renaissance* (New York: Oxford University Press, 1969); and Christopher Hill, *The World Turned Upside Down* (London: Temple Smith, 1972).
28 Blaise Pascal, *Pensées*, no. 300, quoted in Stock, p. 49. Rowe's contemporary, the popular sacred poet Isaac Watts, often appeals to this God above natural and social systems; see his *Horae Lyricae* (1706).
29 Dryden, *All for Love*, 2.20–22, 5.465–67, in *John Dryden: Four Tragedies*, ed. L. A. Beaurline and Fredson Bowers (Chicago and London: University of Chicago Press, 1967).
30 Thomas Burnet, *The Theory of the Earth*, 2nd ed., ed. Basil Willey (1691; rpt. Carbondale: Southern Illinois University Press, 1965), pp. 178–79.
31 More, "Psychathanasia," *Poems*, p. 69.
32 *Lucan's Pharsalia. Translated into English Verse* (Dublin, 1719), pp. 795, 820, in the section of bk. 6 concerning the sorceress Erictho.
33 More, "Antidote against Atheism," *Writings*, 1:133.
34 All three meanings are given by the *Oxford English Dictionary* as current in Rowe's day.
35 Christian occultism in the Renaissance is surveyed by West, *Invisible World*, and Frances A. Yates, *The Occult Philosophy in the Elizabethan Age* (London, Boston, and Henley: Routledge & Kegan Paul, 1979). The debt of eighteenth-century radical reformers to Renaissance occultism is provocatively discussed by Margaret C. Jacob in *The Radical Enlightenment* (London: George Allen & Unwin, 1981).

Defoe, Political Parties, and the Monarch

MANUEL SCHONHORN

In 1958 Professor Caroline Robbins published a study of the acceptance of party by Englishmen of the eighteenth century.[1] She focused her attention on a host of writers who had not only recognized the existence of party but also "had accepted with varying degrees of enthusiasm or fatalism the role of parties in a free state" (p. 100). Discussing the virtues of party, she cited John Toland, Walter Moyle, and journalists in the reign of George I. She concluded with a writer who, in *Applebee's Journal* in May 1723, "maintained that 'discordant parties' were sometimes the safety of states" (p. 117). Her quotation, and the title of her study, come from the title of that 1723 essay.[2]

That writer was Defoe. Subsequent historians, British and American, have reprinted Defoe's essay and have echoed her conclusion. For example, it is reprinted, and Defoe's positive attitude to party affirmed, in J. A. W. Gunn's collection, *Factions No More, Attitudes to Government and Opposition in Eighteenth-Century England: Extracts from Contemporary Sources*. In his introduction to "Section II: The Uses of Conflict," Professor Gunn writes: "The seemingly paradoxical conclusion that conflict could be valuable appealed in different ways to Shaftesbury and Paterson, Defoe and Gordon."[3]

But the fact is that the title of Professor Robbins' study, which is the putative title of Defoe's essay, and which perhaps prompted her misreading of Defoe's attitude to party, suggesting a paradox, is not and never was Defoe's. The essay from *Applebee's Journal* has been read by all in William Lee's collection of Defoe's voluminous journalism, published in 1869. The titles, Lee wrote in his introduction, "placed above the articles, are my own, prefixed only to correspond with a Table of Contents, and to make every part of each volume conveniently accessible."[4]

If one had paid attention to Lee's introduction, and to Defoe's essays printed a year earlier in which he examined the spirit of party and concluded that it lead to unnatural conduct and corrupt historical writing,[5] Defoe's mature attitude to party and faction in his day would not have been misunderstood; more important, we would have been prompted to reconsider his judgments about the powers and practices of the monarch. For Defoe's essay on "discordant parties" is the second in a series of six successive essays on the subject of parties and kings. The series began with some ambiguous and skeptical remarks on John Toland's *The Art of Governing by Parties* (1701) and concluded with critical and strident answers to a forthright and unambiguous question: What is the main evil of parties?[6]

Now, what is Defoe really saying in these essays, as I read them? Throughout, two ideas are prominent that have significant bearing on his attitude toward monarchy. The first is the metaphor of play. Defoe does accept the fact that there are factions, parties, in the world, but "since Divisions must come, the Politick Statesmen will make their Advantage of it, and make their Market of both. When the subtle Angler fishes for Gudgeons, he takes a long Pole, and rummages and disturbs the Gravel at the bottom of the River, makes an Uproar in the Water, and raises the Stones and Sand; and then the Fish come blindly together, and are caught with the more Ease" (3: 134). This introductory image of an angler playing with "both" is repeated in all subsequent historical-political examples. Thus, Defoe immediately continues, "I have seen a Press Gang, when they have wanted Seamen, set a couple of Fellows to Fight in the Street, thereby drawing a Crowd together; and while one takes Part with JACK, and t'other takes part with GILL, the Press Gang come upon them all, and sweep away from both Parties the People they want" (3: 135).

In his subsequent retelling of Acts 22 and 23, when Paul was in danger of being murdered by the mob in Jerusalem, "the blessed inspired Man, . . . knowing there were Factions and Parties among them, and that they Hated one another . . . immediately turned his speech to the Point in which they disagreed, played the *Pharisees* against the *Sadducees*, . . . and setting the two Factions together by the Ears, made his own Safety the Effect of their Quarrel" (3: 136). This, Defoe concludes, is "certainly a shining Example of the Art of managing Parties" (3: 136).

Modern instances reaffirm the role of the sovereign in the management of competing interests in the state. In his second essay, on the wars in France during the reigns of Henry III and Henry IV, Defoe recounts the growing power of the Catholic princes, led by the Duke of Guise, and the party of the Hugonots. Throughout his reign, Defoe repeats, Henry IV "played the *Hugonots*" against the Guises, "and thereby preserved himself and his Government." When "the greatest part of the Nobility of *France* took Arms against their Sovereign; his Majesty, by the same Policy, Faced about to the *Hugonots*, Plays the King of *Navarre* against the Duke *Du Main*, and so got the better of the Guises." Thus, always by the management of the monarch, "alternately, the Government, and the Person of the King himself, was preserved" (3: 138–39).

Defoe's final example is taken from England's civil wars. First, "the Cavaliers, taking just Measures [of the] two Parties . . . and Playing the Presbyterians . . . against the independents, who were then in the Saddle, knocked the Heads of one against the other; and by this very Thing brought about the Restoration" (3: 140). General Monk, Defoe adds, wisely helped to bring in the King by tickling one faction, the Independents, leaving them in Scotland, and bringing in the King at the head of the Presbyterians (3: 141). It must be noted also that in the next essay, it is the King who, taking advantage of the effects of "Factions and Divisions" between the Presbyterians and Independents, "made them be Instrumental to his Restoration" (3: 143).

To play, to manage: this is the reiterated activity of the monarch that preoccupies Defoe's imagination. It is, I believe, a vision of monarchy that places Defoe in a conservative seventeenth-century milieu. Through all of these essays Defoe has been working with the person of a leader, a statesman, more often a king, managing factions of Aristocracy and People, Guises and Hugonots, Presbyterians and Independents, so as to diffuse the spite, arrogance, and pretensions to power of extreme ideologists. It is always the wisdom of leaders, he writes, "to work the Safety of the Government out of the Mistakes of the People, and out of those very Feuds by which, *if left to an ungoverned* ARISTOCRACY, *they would destroy all Civil Government in the World*" (3: 143; Defoe's emphasis). Defoe later asks if parties are good for anything. Throughout these essays, if there are benefits to parties, it is their management by an astute, gallant, courageous king that overcomes their divisive tendencies and evinces whatever value they have for the health of a kingdom.

Defoe's triads—King, Aristocracy, and People, King, Guises, and Hugonots, King, Presbyterians and Independents—are Defoe's narrative manipulation of the concept of the three estates.[7] It is the concept of the one functioning as a fulcrum, leveraging the other two, able when necessary to protect the legitimate rights of either from the unjustified demands of the other. It is the theory of the mixed constitution. The cardinal document in its history is the *Answer to the Nineteen Propositions of the Parliament,* issued by Charles I in 1642. "In it, Charles completely abandoned the theory of the divine right of kings . . . and declared that the English government was a mixture of monarchy, aristocracy, and democracy, with political power divided among king, lords, and commons."[8]

But Charles continued, and enunciated a principle that would undermine him and his royalist adherents: "The equipoise in the balanced constitution was maintained by the House of Lords, an excellent Screen and Bank between the Prince and People."[9] Nothing is more Roman in the writings of seventeenth- and eighteenth-century political gentlemen than this argument, that the aristocracy, the wise, the landed, learned, and leisured, was the pivotal element guaranteeing English liberty. In 1643, *A Political Catechism,* attributed to Henry Parker, repeated Charles' words.[10] Though Harrington was to voice doubts about the balance, in *Oceania* (1659) his lords were the "isthmus between king and people."[11] It is the language of Denzil Holles, in 1676—"the strength of Government lay in the middle, or Aristocratical part as it ought to do"—an essay reprinted in 1712 and then titled, "*The British Constitution Considered.* . . ."[12]

The Earl of Shaftesbury wrote it in 1675, Commonwealthman Henry Neville in 1681, and John Trenchard in 1697 and 1698.[13] Signal variations appear by Dryden in his last great poem in 1700, where the independent landed gentry "steer betwixt the Country and the Court," "betwixt the Prince and parliament we stand, / The Barriers of the State on either Hand."[14] And in 1701, beginning the radical variation on the theme, Sir Henry Mackworth argued for the infallibility of the Commons. He made it the linchpin of the triad, when he concluded that "Power in this Government is chiefly lodged in the Commons."[15]

Undiminished, the idea and the imaging of the idea were sustained to the end of the eighteenth century. For Burke the House of Lords was "the ballast in the vessel of the Commonwealth."[16] Blackstone began his magisterial *Commentaries on the Laws of England* singing the praises of the nobility and the possessors of landed estates who "support the rights of both the crown and the people, by forming a barrier to withstand the encroachments of both."[17] They are "the pillars, which are reared from among the common people, more immediately to support the throne" (1: 153). And in the final chapter of the final volume of the *Commentaries,* in which he sketched "the rise, progress, and gradual improvements, of the laws of England," the law of primogeniture is "necessary to be supported, in order to form and keep up a nobility, or intermediate state between the prince and the common people" (4: 407).

Defining the chief tenets of Whiggism and Toryism in Defoe's day has been a common and valuable exercise of recent historiography. "To be a Whig was to approve wholeheartedly of the Glorious Revolution, to accept the legitimacy of Protestant dissent, and to support the House of Hanover."[18] To be a Tory was to be steadfast to the Anglican Establishment, to support the interests of the landed gentry, to be hostile to urban finance, and to be committed, in Professor Kramnick's telling phrase, to "the politics of nostalgia."[19] But the inevitably forced simplicity of definition has obscured the subtle and surprising distinctions that are discoverable among the major controversialists of the age. And the insistent demand that Defoe be seen, for better or for worse, as a citizen of the modern world, diametrically antithetical to his "Augustan" contemporaries, has led to questionable conclusions.[20] Once, a political scientist has recently observed, "the well-being of a realm . . . depended on the virtue, the patriotism, and the energetic leadership of the sovereign." The conservatives of Defoe's time, Tories, Professor Kramnick's politicians of nostalgia, continued to accept this traditional idea of national leadership. "Their ideal world view was a seamless web of divine will, moral rectitude, social order, and national dignity symbolized and held together by the person and power of a virtuous monarch." But they now inhabited a chaos, a new world, the cause and consequence of which was the decline of monarchy in their time. "On the other side of the great cultural tension in eighteenth-century Britain, the new world of Daniel Defoe, Robert Walpole, and Adam Smith challenged not only the political economy and ethic of the past but also the foundations and modes of leadership."[21]

Defoe's sustained pronouncements in *Applebee's Journal* in 1723, formulated after a lifetime of political activity and acute political observation that does not need to be detailed here, give the lie to those who wish to markedly distinguish Defoe from his more traditional, and thus less modern, contemporaries.[22] If, in seeking good governance, "Tories looked to the character of the leaders, whereas Whigs, insofar as they shared in republican aspirations, were inclined to search for constitutional devices or mechanisms,"[23] then Defoe's lifelong enunciation of the monarch as the equipoise in the state, his—if not glorification—lifelong commitment to a crown free of the encumbrances of self-seeking advisers and fomenters of faction, invites a skeptical response to those who assert the radical whiggism, the

Lockean republicanism, of this gutter journalist.[24] For Defoe, it would appear, it is not in Parliament that the linchpin of community chiefly lies, it is not in Parliament that the long struggle to preserve the balance of England's ancient constitution has been chiefly carried on, but in the executive and the closet of the monarch.[25]

Defoe's idea of a royal mediatorship, with his significant shift of the point of reference, it must be pointed out, is no late change of an ideological position. Neither a post-Revolution realignment of parties, nor a redistribution of political power, nor the excessively disruptive contentions of the first Hanoverian ministries moved Defoe to this Machiavellian and vestigial tenet.[26] His enunciation of the mediatorship of the monarch appears in his first published tract of 1689 defending the Revolution.[27] This tic of Defoe—if I can use a pathological metaphor—can also be read in pieces as varied as *The Pacificator* (1700), a poem ostensibly on the literary wars of the day, and in *The Quarrel of the School-Boys at Athens*, a satiric allegory on the divisions in George I's ministry in 1717.

In the former, the literary war of "the Men of Sense against the Men of Wit" is given conventional mock-heroic density with martial and political imagery, but the hoped-for resolution of the conflict is both unconventional and untinged with irony:

> Let them to some known Head that strife submit,
> Some Judge Infallible, some *Pope in Wit*,
> His Triple Seat place on *Parnassus* Hill,
> And from his Sentence suffer no Appeal:
> Let the Great Balance in his Censure be,
> And of the Treaty make him *Guarantee*,
> Let him be the Director of the State,
> And what he says, let both sides take for Fate:
> *Apollo's Pastoral Charge* to him commit.
> And make him *Grand Inquisitor* of Wit,
> Let him to each his proper Talent show,
> And tell them what they can, or cannot do,
> That each may chuse the Part he can do well,
> And let the Strife be only to Excel.[28]

In *The Quarrel of the School Boys at Athens* the departure of George I to his Hanoverian dominions from July 1716 to January 1717, and the resultant divisiveness of the Whig leaders that eventually led to the collapse of Whig unity, is reduced to a rollicking allegory of an authoritarian schoolmaster momentarily away from his students and the "meer Bedlam" that ensues. But the schoolmaster returns in anger, appearing at the door with his rod in his hand. The boys "no sooner saw the Master and his Rod, but they all sat down as quiet and as still, as if nothing had happened at all; not a Word was spoken, not the least Noise heard, all was perfectly calm and quiet in a Moment; the Master went peaceably up to his Chair of Instruction, and laid down his Rod; the Scholars fell very lovingly to their Books, and have been very good Boys ever since."[29]

Defoe's principle of political harmony through opposition, a *concordia discors* of government, is, as Earl Wasserman observed, essentially Tory in nature.[30] During James I's reign, in fact, as James Turner's imaginative study of the politics of landscape reveals, this doctrine of balanced opposites became part of the vocabulary of coarse royalism.[31] The earlier dyadic construct of the single prince equal in the balance to the whole weight of his people, of sovereign and subjects, is a constant in the political language of royalists of various hues. In a Spanish emblem book of 1651, the king is the keystone in the arch of commonwealth, one who reconciles opposing political pressures in the state.[32] Marvell has the same image in *The First Anniversary*. His Cromwell, to quote Professor Robbins' elucidative remarks, is a patriot-protector in a balanced government who "does not abolish variety but knits together divergent elements in a stronger structure."[33] In a later reign, in his *Account of the Growth of Popery*, Marvell enhanced the metaphor: "the balance of publick justice [is] so delicate, that not the hand only but even the breath of the Prince would turn the scale."[34]

Perhaps to repair Charles I's thoughtless enervation of kingly powers, Restoration royalists made his son the dynamic ingredient of the triad. With striking frequency these royalists pictured Charles II, as Defoe pictured his monarch, not as one who would banish factionalism but as one who knew the divine art of shaping a political *concordia discors*. Such can be observed in Sir Francis Fane's *Panegyrick to the Kings most excellent Majesty upon his Happy Accession to the Crown;* also in Dryden's *Annus Mirabilis*, Davenant's *Poem to the King's Most Sacred Majesty*, the Restoration reprintings of Denham's *Coopers Hill*, and Otway's elegy on Charles's death, *Windsor Castle*.[35]

Finally, Defoe's monarch is oddly anticipated in a pamphlet written by a supporter of the Stuart court, titled *The Mischief of Cabals: or, The Faction Expos'd*, published a month before Monmouth's rebellion, and carrying an eipgraph from *Eikon Basilike* on its title page:

> when a *Prince* has several *Factions*, whether *Religious* or *Civil* in his *Dominions*, as *Protestant* and *Papist*, *Guelph* and *Gibelline*, which he cannot easily reconcile, 'tis his *Interest*, by employing them indifferently according to their *Parts* and *Loyalty*, to keep the *Ballance* in an

equal *Libration;* that while they are at enmity amongst themselves, they shall have no *Aversion* to him, who impartially rewards them in proportion to their *Deserts*.[36]

To conclude: The point of my argument should not be misunderstood. I am not claiming that Defoe is a Whig or a Tory. He is no adherent of *jure divino* monarchy. But the continual use of Lockean paradigms in the search for his intended meanings in his political pamphlets and, especially, *Robinson Crusoe*, have, I believe, obscured the distinctive aspects of his political imagination. It is my contention that Defoe's political language throughout his career distances him in some significant ways from Revolutionary and Hanoverian whiggism.[37] John Tutchin's whiggism attacked Machiavellian politics, which divided people in order to rule them. It was "one of the known techniques of preserving one-man rulership," and "was widely condemned as Jesuitical."[38] Professor H. T. Dickinson, in an unchallenged response at a recent colloquium, commented that "an essential aspect of Whiggism was its suspicion of the executive."[39] In Defoe's works, in these essays of 1723 and elsewhere, upon the restoration of monarchy, of Charles, of William, of George, all good follows. From the Revolution onward, Defoe surmised that English liberty was endangered by the grasping power of the new parliamentary interests. Perhaps at the end of his political life he might no longer have believed that parties in the state were as irremediable as heresies in the church. His pamphlets, though, do not deal with the virtue of opposition, or the values of political pluralism, or the vitality of diversity. But I cannot believe, as Professor Hill does, that "Defoe found himself a radical in a society in which there was no alternative to the corrupt rule of a gentry Parliament."[40] Rather, Defoe saw, much earlier than 1723, that all the talk of a balance of government in fact screened the supremacy of Parliament. In his eyes, the history of post-Revolution England was the history of English parliaments chipping away at the power of the king.[41] His ideal was to make his king, not absolute, but independent of dictation from parliament. Unlike Bodin's, Defoe's king is not armed for justice but to disperse faction. And opposition groups are not beneficent institutions but countervailing excesses that could only be checked by the manipulative genius of a martial monarch.

NOTES

1 Caroline Robbins, "'Discordant Parties': A Study of the Acceptance of Party by Englishmen," *Political Science Quarterly* 73 (1958): 505–29. Reprinted in *Absolute Liberty: A Selection from the Articles and Papers of Caroline Robbins,* ed. Barbara Taft (Hamden, Conn.: Archon, 1982), pp. 100–120. Page citations continued in the text are from the book.
2 "Discordant Parties sometimes the Safety of States," in William Lee, *Daniel Defoe: His Life and Recently Discovered Writings,* 3 vols. (London, 1869), 3: 136. All further quotations from the essay will be from this volume and cited in the text.
3 J. A. W. Gunn, *Factions No More* (London: Frank Cass, 1976), p. 59; but see p. 253. I should note that Professor Clayton Roberts has also attributed the idea, gained from the title, to Defoe, in a personal communication.
4 Lee, 2: v.
5 Ibid., 3: 30–39.
6 Ibid., pp. 133–46.
7 See Corinne C. Weston, *English Constitutional Theory and the House of Lords, 1556–1832* (New York: Columbia University Press, 1965); Corinne C. Weston, "Concepts of Estates in Stuart Political Thought," in *Representative Institutions in Theory and Practice,* International Commission for the History of Representative and Parliamentary Institutions, vol. 39 (1970), pp. 85–130. See also Corinne C. Weston and Janelle Greenberg, *Subjects and Sovereigns* (Cambridge: Cambridge University Press, 1981).
8 Weston, *English Constitutional Thought,* p. 25. Charles began the nautical image: the three estates "run joyntly in their proper Chanell" (p. 25).
9 Ibid., p. 25.
10 Ibid., p. 40. See also Henry Parker, *Observations Upon Some of His Majesties Late Answers and Expresses* (London, 1642), p. 23.
11 *The Political Works of James Harrington,* ed. J. G. A. Pocock (Cambridge: Cambridge University Press, 1977), p. 198.
12 *A Letter to Monsieur Van——B——de M——at Amsterdam* (London, 1676), p. 4; *British Constitution* (London, 1712), p. 8.
13 Weston, *English Constitutional Thought,* p. 66; Neville, *Plato Redivivus* (1681), in Caroline Robbins, *The Eighteenth-Century Commonwealthman* (Cambridge, Mass.: Harvard University Press, 1959), p. 122; John Trenchard, *An Argument Shewing, that a Standing Army is Inconsistent with a Free Government* (London, 1697), p. 2; see also Trenchard, *A Short History of Standing Armies in England* (London, 1698), preface.
14 "To my Honour'd Kinsman, John Driden, of Chesterton," *The Poems of John Dryden,* ed. James Kinsley, 4 vols. (Oxford: Clarendon Press, 1958), 4: 1533, 1534.
15 *A Vindication of the Rights of the Commons of England* (London, 1701), p. 30.
16 *Reflections on the Revolution in France,* cited in Weston, *English Constitutional Thought,* p. 123.

17 *Commentaries on the Laws of England*, 4 vols. (London, 1769), 1: 153. Further quotations will be cited in the text.
18 Reed Browning, *Political and Constitutional Ideas of the Court Whigs* (Baton Rouge: Louisiana State University Press, 1982), p. 11. See also William A. Speck, *Tory and Whig: The Struggle in the Constituencies, 1701–1715* (London: Macmillan, 1970); H. T. Dickinson, *Liberty and Property: Political Ideology in Eighteenth-Century Britain* (London: Weidenfeld and Nicolson, 1977), pp. 13–90; Linda Colley, *In Defiance of Oligarchy: The Tory Party, 1714–60* (Cambridge: Cambridge University Press, 1982), pp. 85–117.
19 Isaac Kramnick, *Bolingbroke and His Circle: The Politics of Nostalgia in the Age of Walpole* (Cambridge, Mass.: Harvard University Press, 1968).
20 I have suggested some of the problems in "Defoe: The Literature of Politics and the Politics of Some Fictions," *English Literature in the Age of Disguise*, ed. Maximillian Novak (Berkeley: University of California Press, 1977), pp. 15–56; "Defoe, The Language of Politics, and the Past," *Studies in the Literary Imagination* 15 (1982): 75–83.
21 Ralph Ketcham, "The Transatlantic Background of Thomas Jefferson's Ideas of Executive Power," *Studies in Eighteenth-Century Culture*, ed. Harry C. Payne (Madison: University of Wisconsin Press, 1982), 11: 165, 168.
22 Two recent studies that help to place Defoe in his time are Peter Earle, *The World of Defoe* (London: Weidenfeld and Nicolson, 1976), and Laura A. Curtis, "A Case Study of Defoe's Conduct Manuals Suggested by *The Family, Sex and Marriage in England, 1500–1800*," *Studies in Eighteenth-Century Culture*, ed. Harry C. Payne (Madison: University of Wisconsin Press, 1981), 10: 409–28. To see how Defoe was used and "modernized" by later generations consult Jay Fliegelman, *Prodigals and Pilgrims: The American Revolt Against Patriarchal Authority, 1750–1800* (Cambridge: Cambridge University Press, 1982).
23 Browning, *Court Whigs*, p. 21.
24 See J. P. Kenyon, "The Revolution of 1688: Resistance and Contract," in *Historical Perspectives: Studies in English Thought and Society in Honour of J. H. Plumb*, ed. Neil McKendrick (London: Europa Publications, 1974), p. 62.
25 For the ancient constitution see J. G. A. Pocock, *The Ancient Constitution and the Feudal Law* (Cambridge: Cambridge University Press, 1957); and cf. Robert Willman, "Blackstone and the 'Theoretical Perfection' of English Law in the Reign of Charles II," *Historical Journal* 26 (1983): 39–70.
26 See Ernst H. Kantorowicz, *The King's Two Bodies: A Study in Medieval Political Theology* (Princeton: Princeton University Press, 1957), p. 88.
27 *Reflections Upon the Late Great Revolution* (London, 1689), p. 36.
28 In *Poems on Affairs of State: Augustan Satirical Verse, 1660–1714* (New Haven: Yale University Press, 1963–), vol. 6, 1697–1704, ed. Frank H. Ellis (1970), p. 178. As Robert M. Krapp realized earlier, "a pope of wit is a remarkable appendage of a commonwealth" and a strange mediator of peace (*Science and Society* 10 [1946]: 88).
29 (London, 1717), p. 36. See also Geoffrey M. Sill, *Defoe and the Idea of Fic-*

tion, 1713-1719 (Newark: University of Delaware Press, 1983), pp. 121–47; and Archibald S. Foord, *His Majesty's Opposition, 1714-1830* (Oxford: Clarendon Press, 1964), pp. 55–109. Judgments about Defoe, diplomacy, and foreign affairs can be read in William Rossen, "Daniel Defoe: Realist in International Politics," *Studies in History and Politics* 2 (1981–82): 93–111.

30 Earl Wasserman, *The Subtler Language* (Baltimore: Johns Hopkins Press, 1959), p. 107.
31 *The Politics of Landscape* (Oxford: Basil Blackwell, 1979), p. 58.
32 Juan de Solorzano Pereyra, *Emblemata regio-politica* (Madrid, 1651), emblem 48, cited in Wasserman, p. 167.
33 *The Poems and Letters of Andrew Marvell*, ed. H. M. Margolouth, 3d ed. rev. P. Legouis and F. E. Duncan-Jones (Oxford: Clarendon Press, 1971), 1: 110–11; Robbins, "'Discordant Parties,'" p. 109.
34 *Works*, ed. Alexander B. Grosart, 4 vols. (n.p., 1872–1875), 4: 248–49.
35 Fane, *A Panegyrick* (London, 1662), p. 5; Dryden, *Annus Mirabilis*, in *Poems*, ed. Kinsley, 1: 54; Davenant, in *Works* (London, 1673), p. 264; Denham, in Brendan O Hehir, *Expans'd Hieroglyphicks: A Critical Edition of Sir John Denham's Coopers Hill* (Berkeley: University of California Press, 1969), p. 160; *The Works of Thomas Otway*, 2 vols., ed. J. D. Ghosh (Oxford: Clarendon Press, 1932), 1: 454.
36 (London, 1685), pp. 26–27. The "coarse Toryism" returns in some of the more conservative pamphlets published in Queen Anne's reign; see *The Honour and Prerogative of the Queen's Majesty Vindicated and Defended* . . . (London, 1713), pp. 13–14. The work has been attributed to Mary de la Riviere Manley.
37 See n. 20.
38 *Observator*, 7: 15 (3–7 April 1708); also 7: 16 (7–10 April 1708). See Gunn, pp. 7, 8.
39 In *The Whig Ascendancy, Colloquies on Hanoverian England*, ed. John Cannon (London: Edward Arnold, 1981), p. 55.
40 Christopher Hill, "Robinson Crusoe," *History Workshop: A Journal of Socialist Historians* 10 (1980): 16.
41 See Clayton Roberts, "Party and Patronage in Later Stuart England," in *England's Rise to Greatness, 1660–1763*, ed. Stephen B. Baxter (Berkeley: University of California Press, 1983), pp. 185–212. For a more radical view of the shift in power at the Revolution see Lois G. Schwoerer, *The Declaration of Rights, 1689* (Baltimore: The Johns Hopkins University Press, 1981). Useful also is B. W. Hill, "Executive Monarchy and the Challenge of Parties, 1689–1832: Two Concepts of Government and Two Historiographical Interpretations," *Historical Journal* 13 (1970): 379–401.

The Word and the Thing in Swift's Prose

DAN DOLL

In Book III of Jonathan Swift's *Gulliver's Travels* the professors of the Academy of Lagado offer "an Expedient . . . that since Words are only Names for *Things*, it would be more convenient for all men to carry about them, such Things as were necessary to express the particular Business they are to discourse on" (11: 185). Throughout the great variety of discourse Swift produced in his active literary and public career, his "particular business" was often an attempt to overcome the problematical nature of the relationship between words and things, signifiers and signifieds. Swift does occasionally assert that words can clearly and unambiguously represent things, that they can carry a single, reliable meaning. In the first of the *Drapier Letters*, for example, Swift makes his case against Wood by citing an act concerned with coinage from Edward I's statutes and claiming, "That this is the true *Construction* of the *Act*, appears from the plain Meaning of the Words" (10: 9). But Swift's work much more frequently illustrates the ways words fail to fulfill this function. For example, one of the strongest satirical criticisms of the Lilliputians is the bombast of their language and the inequity between word and thing: the six inch tall Emperor is, in all official documents, called "Delight and Terror of the Universe, whose Dominions extend . . . to the Extremeties of the Globe; Monarch of all Monarchs: Taller than the Sons of Men" (11: 43). Often the Lilliputians employ a language in which the word-thing relationship is completely inverted. When Gulliver transgresses Lilliputian law in extinguishing the fire at the Princess' palace, he learns a lesson about Lilliputian (and by implication all) political language: "After the Court had decreed any cruel Execution . . . the Emperor always made a Speech to his whole Council, expressing his *great Lenity and Tenderness, as Qualities known and confessed by all the World*. This Speech was immediately published throughout the Kingdom; nor did anything terrify the people so much as those Encomiums on his Majesty's Mercy; because it was observed, that the more these Praises were enlarged and insisted on, the more *inhuman* was the Punishment, and the *Sufferer more innocent*" (11: 72). Here the word is not merely unequal to the thing, it is exactly opposite.

This concern with and censure of words not properly connected to things occurs not only in *Gulliver's Travels*, but throughout Swift's prose and even in the *Journal to Stella* and Swift's correspondence. He considers the consequences of this failure in three areas of vital interest to him: politics, which Swift generally depicts as the manipulation of words and things for personal and party advantage; literature, which he sees as degenerating into incomprehensibility because of those who use words without clear and consistent referents; and religion, where an unsteady word-thing relationship produces a misreading of the Scriptures and an increase of sects, thereby threatening the Church of England and civil peace. One source of this degeneration and corruption is that the English language is changing its signifier-signified relationship too rapidly as a consequence of the frequent introduction of "fashionable" words from sources like the court and town wits. In his *Proposal for Correcting, Improving, and Ascertaining the English Tongue* Swift claims that the "daily Improvements [of the language] are by no Means in Proportion to its daily Corruptions; the Pretenders to polish and refine it, have chiefly multiplied Abuses and Absurdities" (4: 6). These multiplied terms subvert the proper word-thing relationship because they offer a variety of signifiers for a single signified, too many words for one thing. The various signifiers are not universally interchangeable; rather each social or political group has its own "fashionable" signifier and each group changes its signifier frequently. The result of this variability from group to group and day to day is an utter collapse of communication. In the *Proposal* and in *Tatler* no. 230 Swift focuses on the consequences of this temporal change of the word-thing relationship for the man of letters: "The Fame of our Writers is usually confined to these two Islands; and it is hard it should be limited in Time as much as Place, by the perpetual variations of our Speech" (4: 15).

The rapidity of this change is what Swift fears most because he sees posterity as a true indicator of the value of the word; even in the panegyric part of the *Proposal* this assumption is clear: "The Glory of Her Majesty's Reign . . . ought to be recorded in Words more durable than Brass, and such as our Posterity may read a thousand years hence" (4: 17). In the ironic appeal to Prince Posterity in *A Tale of a Tub* and throughout his prose and poetry, Swift echoes the belief of his age that one of the most important standards of value is the test of time. In the *Proposal* Latin is praised above all other languages because it has best withstood the ravages of time (4: 9), and similar praise occurs elsewhere for objects and institutions of great duration. The English language has proven itself far less durable, however, and its rapid change over time necessarily introduces obscurity and even unintelligibility into the word-thing relationship because of the greater multiplication of words than things; the consequence is that the man of letters finds himself cut off from the past or future. In *Tatler* no. 230 Swift produces a modern letter written by a "wit" and asks, "If a Man of Wit, who died Forty Years ago, were to rise from the Grave on Purpose; how would he be able to read the Letter? And after he got through that Difficulty, how would he be able to understand it?" (2: 175). Similarly, in the *Proposal* Swift argues that this corruption and its consequences might even cause the man of letters to desist entirely from writing: "How then shall any Man, who hath a Genius for History, equal to the best of the Antients, be able to undertake such a Work with Spirit and Chearfulness, when he considers, that he will be read with Pleasure but a few Years, and in an age or two shall hardly be understood without an Interpreter?" (4: 18).

In addition to the rapid change of English, a second cause of degeneration, corruption, and factionalism is one that John Locke strongly criticizes in his *Essay Concerning Human Understanding*, "inconstancy" in the use of words (pp. 492–93). Words are frequently employed to signify different and often opposing things by various political and religious factions. A good example of a word whose promiscuous use and misuse Swift addresses is "Zeal," which he sees as a hypocritical label often adopted by fanatics in religion and partisan politics to excuse their worst excesses. He makes this point with the Calvinist brother Jack in the *Tale of a Tub* of whose "Hatred and Spight" the narrator says, "For this Meddly of Humour, he made a Shift to find a very plausible Name, honouring it with the Title of *Zeal;* which is, perhaps, the most significant Word that hath been ever yet produced in any Language" (1: 86). Calling this improper behavior *Zeal* is a "shift"—a trick, evil masquerading as good. Similarly, in *The Four Last Years of the Queen* Swift criticizes Nottingham's "Rigor and Severity, which his Admirers palliate with the Name of Zeal" (7: 11); here again the thing is given a better name than it deserves. The unsteady word-thing relationship is what allows this deception, this *miscommuni-*

cation. He labels *Zeal* the "most significant Word," by which he means the most abused: zeal is the word that *signifies* the most things. Clearly the one word–one thing ideal of language is being severely violated, for the selfish gain of religious and political factions.

Swift's awareness of the tenuous nature of the word-thing relationship and his anxiety about its consequences draw from him a variety of responses: he prescribes the proper relationship, proscribes abuses of it, and employs a number of strategies to ensure its propriety in his own prose. In those works that might be labeled prescriptive— *Tatler* no. 230; the *Proposal for Correcting; Polite Conversation* and *Hints Towards Polite Conversation;* and *A Letter to a Young Gentleman, Lately Enter'd into Holy Orders*—Swift suggests a number of ways of legislating the relationship between words and things, the most famous of which is, of course, his plan to "fix" the English language by means of an academy on the order of the French Academy, composed of "such Persons, as are generally allowed to be best qualified for such a Work, without any regard to Quality, Party, or Profession" (4: 13–14). What he is arguing is that the only way to avoid the problems occasioned by the rapid change in language is to govern the word-thing relationship by institutionally freezing it in time: "For I am of the Opinion, that it is better a Language should not be wholly perfect, than that it should be perpetually changing; and we must give over at one time, or at length infallibly change for the worse" (4: 14).

As a second prescriptive solution to the problems, especially for religion, of words which mean more than one thing at the same time or mean nothing at all, Swift enjoins the plain style or what he calls "Simplicity, which is one of the greatest Perfections in any Language" (4: 15). Chiefly in the *Letter to a Young Gentleman,* but also in the *Proposal, Tatler* no. 230, the sermons, and even the correspondence, Swift argues for the common and the known: the words to be employed are to be familiar words, words for which there are commonly accepted and acknowledged referents. Here he advocates a language much like that called for by the Royal Society, one which would enable men to deliver "so many *things,* almost in an equal number of *words*" (Sprat, p. 113), and forestall any "useless brangles over words." The assumption underlying the call for such a language is that truth is easily communicated and apprehended by man's reason if only the evidence is expressed plainly. Just as Swift argues frequently that those who pretend politics is difficult do so only for their own gain, he argues that all men have the capability of understanding Christianity unless language obscures this apprehension: "A Divine hath nothing to say to the wisest Congregation of any Parish in this Kingdom, which he may not express in a Manner to be understood by the Meanest among them. And this assertion must be true, or else God requires more from us than we are able to perform" (9: 66). If the language is "simple," in Swift's sense, the word *will* properly signify the thing and the problem of communication and truth will be resolved.

In addition to prescribing the proper word-thing relationship, Swift also proscribes certain abuses of it. His works are filled with attacks on specific "corrupted" words and on those who corrupt them. For Swift it is standard practice to denigrate a foe by denigrating the way he uses words: indeed, he often spends more time attacking an opponent's words than his arguments. He habitually attempts to establish that they irresponsibly use words which are not properly connected to things, that their discourse, and by implication their reasoning or moral character, is not reliable or trustworthy. He calls particular attention to what he labels "Cant" terms, certain stock words and phrases coined by the *beau monde* and applied indiscriminately in discourse. Throughout his work Swift intersperses his responses to others with phrases like "to speak in the Cant of the Times" (10: 132), and "to use their own Cant" (13: 135); he employs the term "Cant" to refute everyone from the Whigs (12: 93, 226), to anticlericals (9: 45), to almanac makers (2: 149). These cant words are what the early 1980s would onomatopoetically call "buzzwords": they carry more noise than signification. Swift allies the user of cant with a kind of madman he describes in "A Digression Concerning Madness" in *A Tale of a Tub*: "One that has forgot the common *Meaning* of Words, but an admirable Retainer of the Sound" (1: 112). He similarly accuses Richard Steele of using cant terminology and claims, "He hath a confused Remembrance of Words . . . but hath lost half their Meaning, and puts them together with no regard, except to their Cadence" (8: 36). Here, as is often the case, Swift's attention to the use of language is more properly attention to the *mis*use of language.

Another set of strategies Swift employs to avert the problems of an unsteady word-thing relationship in his own prose are those which call attention to words as *words* and not things. When the distinction between words and things is ignored, as it is in common discourse, words are often mistaken for things and the result is ambiguity at best and chaos at worst. Swift attempts to avoid this confusion or miscommunication by using what I shall call "word-consciousness," that is, he continually calls his reader's attention to the fact that words are words and not things. In addition, he repeatedly reminds his readers that words are a medium which is not as transparent or reliable as the reader might otherwise assume. In addition to those passages like the one in the *Tale of a Tub* in which the orator's words become physical "things" and drop out of his mouth upon the heads of his auditors, where Swift burlesques the error of confusing words and things, he much more frequently employs a variety of word-conscious devices like definitions, "naming," and literalized metaphors to refute the transparency. These devices appear with great frequency in virtually every piece of prose Swift wrote, and they are finally his strongest line of defense against the consequences of the unsteady word-thing relationship.

The first and most traditional of these methods of word-consciousness is definition: throughout his prose Swift carefully defines any controversial term he is using and at the same time redefines and censures the misdefinitions of others. Many of his sermons, for example, provide a definition or redefinition of a specific word like "Trinity," "moderate," or "subjection," and demonstrate the abuses of religion and politics wrought by that misuse. The opening sentence of *On the Testimony of Conscience* offers a typical example: "There is no word more frequently in the Mouths of Men, than that of *Conscience*, and the Meaning of it is in some Measure generally understood: However . . . it is likewise a Word extreamly abused by many People, who apply other Meanings to it, which God Almighty never intended" (9: 150). Swift then follows with his own definition, by which he seeks not only to establish a one word–one thing relationship, but also to chastise the kind of misbehavior he elsewhere censures in *A Tale of a Tub*: "Is not Conscience a *Pair* of Breeches, which, tho' a Cover for Lewdness as well as Nastiness, is easily slipt down for the service of both?" (1: 47). By paying such careful attention to definition, Swift is himself following the prescriptions of many previous writers who shared his anxieties about the word-thing relationship, especially Hobbes and Locke. Through this careful attention to definition, Swift also alerts his reader to how tenuous the word-thing relationship must be if it needs continual guidance and correction to keep it from deviating into nonsense.

One of the most frequent and characteristic manifestations of Swift's word-consciousness is his attention to words as *names* of things. The phrases "under the name," "is called," and their equivalents appear well over three hundred times in his prose works, and their function is again to deny transparency to the word-thing relationship. More often than not, Swift uses these phrases to signal, usually through an ironic tone, that the name in question is incorrect: the word is not equal to the thing. A typical example is Swift's repeated assertion that what the Whigs denominate "disaffection" is not really disaffection but rather something like loyal opposition: in the *Letter to a Young Gentleman* he warns the aspiring preacher that he lives "In an Age where every Thing disliked by those, who think with the Majority, is called Disaffection" (9: 79). Similarly, in *Intelligencer* no. 19, ostensibly addressed to the Drapier but also written by Swift, the speaker protests that any small shopkeeper who merely expresses the wish that there were enough small coin available to change a guinea for a customer is likely to be prosecuted under the same misnomer: "I have known less Crimes punished with the utmost Severity, under the Title of *Disaffection*" (12: 57). In each case the tone or context makes it clear that these names are not properly connected to the things to which they are applied. But even without the context, Swift's calling attention to "disaffection" as a word through the use of the naming phrases causes us to scrutinize it. Like "conscience," this word has been stretched or even severed from its proper thing in order to make it a *carte blanche* for political oppression. By pointing out that the presence of the word does not necessarily signal the presence of the thing, Swift attempts to avert the danger of confusing the two. At the same time, the illustration of the misuse of the word suggests its proper use: through these word-conscious naming phrases Swift again tries to reassert the correct one word–one thing relationship.

A final method of word-consciousness Swift employs is his much noted tactic of literalizing metaphors: for example, in a letter to Lord Orrery he wonders how much weight the ink of his letter adds to the sheet of paper it was written upon because he has heard "sometimes Words are of much weight, except they be *heavy*" (*Correspondence*, 4: 397). This tactic is part of a larger concern for the special use of the word in figurative language. During the mid- and late-seventeenth-century metaphor came under a heavy attack, no doubt partially as a reaction against the elaborate conceits of the earlier part of the century, and partially as one facet of the plain style advocated by the Royal Society. Sprat, for example, rails against "this vicious abundance of *Phrase*, this trick of *Metaphors*, this volubility of *Tongue*, which makes so great a noise in the World" (p. 112); similarly, Hobbes argues, "Metaphors . . . are like *ignes fatui;* and reasoning upon them is wandering amongst innumerable absurdities" (p. 37). The reason metaphors are seen as especially delusive is that in figurative language the word is even less clearly or securely connected to the thing than in the (already tenuous, at best) word-thing relationship of literal discourse. Swift shares these fears of the "looseness" of metaphoric language but he is not antimetaphor like Hobbes and some members of the Royal Society. Swift nowhere explicitly criticizes or proscribes metaphors nor does he eschew them in his own work. Rather, he employs then straightforwardly, ironically, and playfully. Of course, Swift's well-known addiction to puns and other forms of wordplay is perhaps one reason for his tolerance of figurative language. But in his "serious" prose Swift safeguards against the disconnections of word and thing that can be caused by metaphor through three strategies of word-consciousness: first, he often calls attention to the fact that he is using a metaphor with a phrase like "if I may so speak"; second, he surrounds a metaphor he wishes to puncture with ridiculously inflated diction that calls attention to itself as bombast; and third, he literalizes the metaphor. When he literalizes a metaphor he violates the reader's "suspension of disbelief" about figurative language and thereby calls the reader's attention to a metaphor as a word, or words, far removed from the thing it or they purport to describe.

The implications of Swift's attention to the word-thing relationship affect our readings of virtually all his texts, although some more obviously than others. There is, of course, the most striking of Swift's works about language—*A Tale of a Tub*: if, as Swift says in his famous definition, "Proper Words in proper Places makes a true Definition of Style," a quite plausible estimation of the *Tale* is Improper Words in Improper Places. In the *Tale* Swift explores prescriptions, proscriptions, and abuses of language as he creates his most complex work about the relationship between word and thing. As many critics, especially F. N. Smith in his *Language and Reality in Swift's Tale of a Tub,* have argued, the *Tale* is more *about* language and the word-thing relationship than it is *about* anything else. In the *Tale* the word-thing relationship is a central subject, theme, and even technique.

The same observation can also be made of a number of Swift's other works and an example which is briefer and therefore more manageable for the purposes of this essay is the *Argument Against Abolishing Christianity.* The *Argument* can easily and profitably be approached as a work about a specific word, "Christianity," that has been disconnected from its original "thing," and the consequences of that disconnection. In the *Argument* Christianity is presented as a word that *was* once connected to a proper thing, but which over time has degenerated into something far less proper. The substitution of the possession of the name for the possession of the thing has masked this degeneration and aided its progress; the result is a false, hypocritical society and government, a state where it is conceived necessary to abolish Christianity, in name at least, since the thing has already long since vanished. While ostensibly arguing for the retention of "nominal" Christianity, the *Argument* is clearly a scathing condemnation of modern "Christians," those who pretend to the word only in the absence of the thing. But it is also more: Swift does not attempt to stop this abuse of the name Christianity through his word-consciousness, but rather builds an elaborate edifice of words, the *Argument*, that carries the reduction to nominalism to its logical consequences. An essay about an empty word is written in empty words; as such it is another tale of a tub.

The way the false name "Christianity" both reflects and advances the degeneration of modern England depends upon what Christianity means in the English political system. Given the Test Act and similar legislation, it is clear that politics has misappropriated the religious name Christianity: what is called Christian is supposed to serve the legal and political function of ensuring that men who participate in government and other positions of authority are morally upstanding. This requirement is one reason why what it means to be a "Christian" becomes such a battleground between Whigs and Tories in the war over the dissenters. If the dissenters are regarded as Christians, they can serve in the government and will thereby greatly increase the power of the Whigs. Conversely, the Tories must deny the dissenters a place in Christianity or lose some of their political power. As Irvin Ehrenpreis notes, throughout the *Argument* Swift employs "the synechdoche by which Christianity means Anglicanism" (2: 284): in many of his other works as well Swift deliberately excludes dissenters from Christianity by lumping them with free-thinkers and other "fanatics." In any case, if the "Christianity" required to allow one to serve in government were original, "true" Christianity the system would perhaps work. Because modern man can be called Christian solely on the basis of his political affiliation rather than moral character, however, the system does not work and English society is not protected from greedy and manipulative men. For reasons of political expediency someone less than truly Christian is allowed to masquerade as Christian, and once this process starts it degenerates at a continually accelerating rate: the "Christian" continues his un-Christian ways without reproach because he has the name to cover him. Because political considerations replace religious and moral criteria for judging who is or is not Christian, the name is stretched farther and farther until it becomes so loosely applied as to be meaningless. Because of the corruption of both word and thing, modern Christianity is nothing more than an exploded system, a fashion which has descended, according to the narrator of the *Argument*, through the upper and middle classes and has by now been dropped even by the vulgar (2: 27). Just as the name has been emptied of its real meaning, the institutions and ceremonies of Christianity have been emptied of their original value and significance.

What has replaced the original "thing" underlying the word Christianity is purely and simply politics. The second sentence of the *Argument* cites "the Fundamental Law, that makes the Majority of Opinion the Voice of God" (2: 26): political sanction has replaced divine sanction. Politics is operating under the hypocritical but more honorable name Christianity, and the manipulators of language have been so successful in systematically substituting the wrong "thing" and misappropriating the name Christianity that their subterfuge has changed the perception of the English people. The most deeply rooted feelings in men's hearts are no longer the basic attributes of original or "real" Christianity, such as "Virtue, Conscience, Honour, Justice, and the like" (2: 33); these are now labeled "Prejudices of Education." For the modern nominal Christian the most deeply rooted feelings are "Party and Faction" (2: 32). Primitive, that is uncorrupted, Christianity is dismissed as "utterly inconsistent with our present Schemes of Wealth and Power" (2: 28), but obviously nominal Christianity is quite consistent. In ages past, under real Christianity, the way men conducted their lives was selflessly subservient to the goals and dictates of religion; under nominal Christianity, however, it is just the reverse and religion, or at least its name, is made to serve the selfish way men pursue their material, political goals.

This substitution of politics for religion as the source of value pervades the *Argument* as fully as it pervades English society. The narrator argues that one reason not to abolish Christianity is that it will allow the "wits" to sport with God, an activity less pernicious than sporting with the government or reflecting on the Ministry (2: 29). Political authority is presented here as more "sacred" than religious authority: the Ministry is now the ultimate good. Similarly, religion is presented as a dispensible tool of politics. In his refutation of the claim that banishing terms like High- and Low-Church will eliminate faction, the narrator of the *Argument* asks, "Because Religion was nearest at Hand to furnish a few convenient Phrases; is our Invention so barren, we can find no others?" (2: 32). He then suggests that the names of Italian opera singers in vogue can be used to replace the Christian terms. Here the arguer reduces the importance of Christianity to the level of opera singers enjoying a brief vogue, and thereby denies that there is anything important enough to fight about in true Christianity. This, we surmise, is precisely the reverse of Swift's position; when we correct for the ironic, mocking narrator, we can see

Swift arguing that there *are* things in Christianity worth fighting about, and it is the trivialities of politics and political language that interfere. Within the crazy logic of the *Argument*, however, it is politics that is served by religion: "Is not every Body freely allowed to believe whatever he pleaseth; and to publish his Belief to the World whenever he thinks fit; especially if it serves to strengthen the Party which is in the Right?" (2: 29). Men are encouraged to develop, express, and defend their beliefs not in order to arrive at religious truth, but only to help a political party. One final example of the consequences of substituting politics as the "thing" connected to the word Christianity is the narrator's argument "that the Abolishing of Christianity may perhaps bring the Church in Danger" (2: 36). The only way to secure the Church then would be with a vote of Parliament. This argument emphasizes how politics has taken over for religion: this nominally Christian entity, the Church, in now a purely political entity. The politicians have no more need of the real institution—the Church—than they do of real Christianity, but they need both names to cover and abet their activities. The success with which they have managed to attach their new thing, politics, to the old name, Christianity, demonstrates the power of their manipulation of language.

At both the beginning and the end of the essay the narrator argues that one reason to retain Christianity is that it will give the wits something upon which to work off their destructive energies and thereby divert them from attacking the ministry or state; this is almost exactly the same argument given by the hack for the production of *A Tale of a Tub*, and what is suggested here of Christianity is true of the *Argument* as well. The whole *Argument* is very much a tale of a tub tossed out to divert the wits; no one is really threatening to legally repeal Christianity, nor could they succeed if they tried. Not only is attempting to restore original Christianity a "wild Project": an even wilder project is writing *An Argument To prove, That the Abolishing of Christianity in England, May, as Things now Stand, be attended with some Inconveniences, and perhaps, not produce those many good Effects proposed thereby,* the full title of this work. The *Argument* is neither a defense of nominal Christianity nor a defense of real Christianity. It presents an irresolvable dilemma: to reassert real Christianity "would indeed be a wild Project" (2: 27) and would bring English society and government crashing down, but nominal Christianity is not the answer either because it would simply provide more of the hypocrisy the *Argument* protests. So, like the *Tale*, the *Argument* must concentrate on the negative, the abuse of language and its consequences, rather than offer a positive, medial alternative. Swift begins with the idea that Christianity exists in name only and extends that idea to or even beyond its logical limits. "Christianity" has become language with nothing connected to it, and the only appropriate response is Swift's essay. The *Argument* is like the *Tale* in that it is mostly language about language, or, more properly, clever misuse of language to criticize less clever and more corrupt misuse of language. What the arguer says of the phrase *Prejudices of Education,* "I observe how difficult it is to get rid of a Phrase, which the World is once grown fond of, though the Occasion that first produced it, be entirely taken away" (2: 33), is the import of the whole *Argument:* the occasion that produced the word Christianity has been entirely taken away. The core of the *Argument,* the defense of the "significance" of Christianity, is as hollow as the core of the *Tale.* But like the *Tale,* the *Argument* is a work of apparent nonsense that does make a point, albeit a negative one, not only about religion, but also about language as well. Swift's response to the misuse of words, and the misuse of the name Christianity especially, is in this case not to prescribe or proscribe it; rather he exposes the abuse of words by inflating it into the *Argument* itself and allowing it to collapse of its own weight. This *non*sense, Swift argues, is the inevitable result of words not properly connected to things.

WORKS CITED

Ehrenpreis, Irvin. *Swift: The Man, his Works, and the Age.* 3 vols. Cambridge: Harvard University Press, 1962–83.

Hobbes, Thomas. *Leviathan.* In *The English Works of Thomas Hobbes.* Edited by Sir William Molesworth. London: John Bohn, 1839.

Locke, John. *An Essay Concerning Human Understanding.* Edited by Peter Nidditch. Oxford: Clarendon Press, 1975.

Smith, F. N. *Language and Reality in Swift's Tale of a Tub.* Columbus: Ohio State University Press, 1979.

Sprat, Thomas. *History of the Royal Society.* Edited by Jackson Cope and Harold Jones. St. Louis: Washington University Press, 1958.

Swift, Jonathan. *Correspondence.* 5 vols. Edited by Harold Williams. Oxford: Oxford University Press, 1963–65.

Swift, Jonathan. *The Prose Works of Jonathan Swift.* 14 vols. Edited by Herbert Davis et al. Oxford: Basil Blackwell, 1939–68.

Song Form and the Mind in Christopher Smart's Later Poetry

MARK W. BOOTH

In Christopher Smart's psalms, hymns, and *A Song to David*, all apparently written in or soon after the time of his madhouse confinement, there are consistent formal elements that work to intercept discursive rational thought and to invoke another mentality. The mode of mind dominant in this poetry relies little on continuity through time, to the frustration of the linear apprehension generally hoped for by readers. Rather it turns to the moment of experience and, on the other hand, to a larger geometry of structure. Such a mentality seems often to appear in lyrics written for music, as were these psalms and hymns. Much that is distinctive in *A Song to David*, which was not intended for music, conforms to patterns visible in Smart's singing psalms in particular. Analysis of such patterns and the mentality they serve may also suggest a better understanding of the enigmatic *Jubliate Agno* that Smart produced in brief daily segments through the years of his detention.[1]

Smart's renderings of all the Psalms represent his largest body of verse specifically for music. Through his literary career he had often written song verse. He worked with Thomas Arne, for example, in his early London years, to write Vauxhall music garden songs. It is uncertain how knowledgeable about music Smart was himself, though his stage foolery as "Mrs. Midnight" may have included his singing or playing an instrument. He seems not to have needed a particular tune in mind to write song verse. He did suggest, in the published psalms, specific tunes from among those in common church use as the settings for some but not all of his texts, but in *Jubilate Agno* he recorded his prayer for "a musician or musicians to set the new psalms."[2] He clearly intended them for singing but wrote to the singing occasion rather than adapting details of his verse to details of setting. The following discussion considers, then, not the art of his adaptation of words to particular music, but the character in general of the verse he wrote for the occasion of singing.

A specimen of Smart's song verse is this second of his two versions of Psalm 100.

> HOSANNA! people of all lands
> Unite your voices, lift your hands,
>   And to the Lord repair,
> And thankful fall upon your face,
> And hail with songs the throne of grace,
>   And shew your gladness there.
>
> Yourselves in this belief confirm,
> That man his talent and his term
>   Are God's, and not his own;
> We are the flock he folds and feeds
> With milk and honey in his meads,
>   The Lord is God alone.
>
> O go, but send your song before,
> Into his courts, his temple door,
>   His name in anthems raise—
> Give thanks the soul's immortal food,
> And speak him great, and speak him good,
>   Your hearts with rapture blaze.
>
> For race by race he is renown'd
> In mercies which to peace abound,
>   In truth reveal'd and taught;
> And gracious is the Lord of love,
> Above all estimate, above
>   The flight of time and thought.[3]

This song shares its stanza form and much of its style and matter with *A Song to David*. Setting aside that resemblance for the moment, let us consider these verses on their own, as Smart's new rendering of an old favorite scriptural hymn. For comparison we may consult the Sternhold and Hopkins text that had by Smart's time been the most popular version with English congregations for two centuries:

> All people that on earth do dwell,
>   Sing to the Lord with cheerful voice:
> Him serve with fear, his praise forth tell,
>   Come ye before him and rejoice.
>
> Know that the Lord is God indeed;
>   Without our aid he did us make:
> We are his folk, he doth us feed,
>   And for his sheep he doth us take.
>
> O enter then his gates with praise,
>   Approach with joy his courts unto;
> Praise, laud, and bless his Name always,
>   For it is seemly so to do.
>
> For why? the Lord our God is good,
>   His mercy is for ever sure;
> His truth at all times firmly stood,
>   And shall from age to age endure.[4]

If these psalms are compared, with the understanding that they are texts for congregational singing, Smart's, with its more insistent rhymes and rhythms and its alliterations and other sound effects, seems less didactic of its content and more calculated to strike and elevate. There is less clarity of sense and more play of sound in Smart's version. Smart was also producing a cycle of nonscriptural hymns for the church year, at this time or soon after, and Karina Williamson compares them to other hymns of the time in terms appropriate here as well. She says that the other hymnists showed

> determination to adhere as closely as possible to Scripture; on style their intentions were no less explicit. [They took] their cue from Watts, whose aim was "Ease of Numbers and Smoothness of Sound, and . . . to make the Sense plain and obvious." . . . Smart, unlike them, was not concerned to simplify his poetry to suit "every capacity."[5]

Smart is not very obscure in this psalm, but we may notice what Williamson (p. 423) remarks in Smart, an "arrangement of material on a formal rather than a logical pattern." The alliterative doublets are the most familiar of Smart's sound structures: "man his talent and his term," "the flock he folds and feeds," and "And speak him great, and speak him good" are the pure examples here, while close but not parallel alliterations include "thankful fall upon your face," "milk and honey in his meads," "send your song before," "race by race he is renowned," "truth revealed and taught," "the Lord of love," and "flight of time and thought." Whatever the range of effects possible to such sound relations in various contexts, here they blur the plain sense of statement. In short lines clipped by rapid rhyme, such a phrase as "man his talent and his term" has departed behind its echo before most readers, or singers, have registered the separate senses of "the gifts given to man" and "the limits set to the life in which to enjoy them," which I believe is the sense. It is remarkable that Smart makes the deeply familiar Old Hundredth disappear in something rich and strange, with mostly plain words set into insistent sound patterns. To anticipate a later argument I will notice one further sound detail, the chiastic (l d d l) system of "The Lord is God alone."

Effects such as these were noticed and called typical of the age in which Smart lived in Northrop Frye's seminal essay "Towards Defining an Age of Sensibility": "Our ears are assaulted by unpredictable assonances, alliterations, inter-rhymings and echolalia [Frye quotes Chatterton, Collins, Fergusson, and Blake]. . . . the poetry becomes hypnotically repetitive, oracular, incantatory, dreamlike and in the original sense of the word charming." Frye's brief but wide-ranging remarks sketch a "literature as process" typical of the period, and in the survey his casual references mention Smart eight times and quote him once. The large effect he argues to result from, or at least to correlate with, these formal features, and that appears sustained by other means in works as diverse as Boswell's journal and Blake's *Four Zoas*, is that "emotion is being maintained at a continuous present."[6] We will return to Frye's suggestions in connection with *Jubilate Agno*, below.

Whatever tendency to hypnotic sound and immediacy of emotion Smart's verse shared with a large movement of his day, in his psalms and *Song* we can trace further lineaments specific to the broad family of verse for music, which are not included in, or diverge from, what Frye's description leads us to anticipate. Songs of many kinds share some of the traits of Frye's "literature as process" and are further likely to meet a variety of other expectations.[7] Those noticeable in the present cases are redundancy of the vocabulary of words and phrases, tightly structured stanzaic form, and finally in the *Song* in particular a large symmetrical architecture.

In comparison with Smart's Psalm 100 the older psalm version printed above has some alliteration in "We are his folk, he doth us feed" and "our God is good," but it does not pursue formal beauties or effects. It puts fidelity to text and clarity of message first, with an air of studious inelegance: "For why? the Lord our God is good . . . ," especially set to a rhythm that pauses between the first two words but not between the second and third, is nearly incomprehensible in the isolation each song line momentarily has, and it seems to require an impossible recollection of something in the preceding stanza; but all is less important than the literal and linear pursuit of what the Psalm says, a special and unusual burden for song. Smart, on the other hand, pursued and treasured gems of phrasing, and "his talent and his term" is one of several from Smart's psalms that he used again intact in *A Song to David*:

> Thou art—to give and to confirm,
> For each his talent and his term;
> All flesh thy bounties share
> [st. xli]

Other examples include "multitudes in mail," "good in grain," "the briny broad," "to bless and bear," and "pray'r and praise"—this last phrase used eighteen times, once in *A Song*, ten times in the *Psalms*, and seven times in the *Hymns*. There is a significant degree of recurrence of phrase and of word in Smart's song-and-songlike verse and *Jubilate Agno*. Arthur Sherbo provides an extensive inventory in arguing his case for concurrent composition.[8] The most striking case is that of the motif-word "stupendous," which by Sherbo's count occurs about twenty-five times in Smart's psalms and eight times in the *Hymns*. Even a small degree of such self-quotation is a noticeable feature of any quantity of sophisticated verse in Smart's era or our own; most poets seek to avoid it, but its appearance is much more the rule in song verse—in folk ballad, love lyric, hymn, and popular song.

One way to explain such a tendency towards stock phrasing is that verse to be heard, and heard in music, and apprehended at the rate of the music (much slower than reading or conversational speech) needs a higher level of redundancy or predictability to make itself heard. Stock phrasing is easier to catch. (We will see below a claim that it may also be unavoidable for a writer in a songmaking frame of mind.) In this connection we may raise the next songlike formal feature of this part of Smart's verse, its tight-laced stanzaic regularity, which in song also makes for ready aural apprehension. Frye's observations of the hypnotic sound effects of the Age of Sensibility emphasize their unpredictability, as free play in the moment. These psalm and *Song* stanzas by contrast are intensely and regularly patterned by their meters and rhymes overlaid by alliterative pairs, many of which are further ordered by a syntactic patterning of parallel or opposition.

> He taught the silver moon her way,
> Her monthly and nocturnal sway,
>   Where'er she wanes or grows;
> The glorious globe that gilds the skies
> Is conscious of his early rise,
>   And his descent he knows.
>   [Psalm civ, st. 19]

Sun and moon, an inevitable pair, divide the stanza evenly; the moon "wanes or grows," the sun has "rise" and "descent," and is asserted to be conscious of one and know the other (pairings are iterative as well as oppositional), and the moon's power is felt in the cycles of day and month (rotation and revolution). Every line has a perfectly rhyming companion, and the rhymes fall often, in the short lines: form and content are almost entirely shaped by pairings. "Glorious globe that gilds" is a flourish above this intricate order, but even that phrase satisfies the expectation of the ear because Smart accustoms us to pretty frequent alliterative linking of stressed words. This architecture, tight as that of a Pope couplet, serves the redundancy suggested by repetition of word and phrase—so many pairs, in each of which each element largely specifies the other: Moon, hence sun; rise, hence descent; "way," hence "sway."

Tight patterning is not peculiar to song; couplet or sonnet has it as well. But when the proportion of such patterning to sheer number of words is so high—sound in such a high ratio to sense, and sense so polarized and hence restricted—verse is apt to be closer to the enchanting and further from the descriptive, reflective, narrative, or any species of discourse.

Song proper, of course, has tune, which is a further pattern, the size of a stanza, subtly shaping the sense from outside. A tune that sets several stanzas of a song shapes each of them as a common factor; it is slightly in opposition to whatever is individual in what any stanza says, and works toward making them all alike. It has in itself some shape of departure and return, and as something curved upon itself it stands over against linear progression. Since it recurs identically for each stanza, it exists in the song outside the limits of the stanza (as does the stanza form); as something we see and see again, continually present, it stands opposed to the linear time in which words make sense. Strophic song, compared to other language use, even other poetry, is distinctively overshadowed by standing pattern.

Here we come to the third aspect of song visible in Smart and not embraced by "literature as process," and that is shape. As stanzaic pattern stands over the verses of the psalms, and as tune pattern would stand over them, large patterns loom over the considerable linear length of *A Song to David*. This long poem not properly a song has much of its songlikeness in what critics have usually thought of as its architecture. Some such descriptions are summarized by Robert Brittain:

> Several critics have drawn attention to some of the architectonic features of the poem. . . . Sir Edmund Gosse . . . has remarked on the orchestral effects. . . . Much more sound and thorough is Signor Federico Olivero's investigation of the architectural symbolism of the *Song*. . . ."[The poem] is indeed something of a temple in its precise, symmetrical, architectural structure."

Olivero sees the invocation as steps leading up to an entrance, over which a facade shows twelve views of David; once we enter the temple, "the radiant images that adorn stanzas xviii–xxvi give the impression of nine leaded windows. . . . four on each side of the church and a rose over the entrance. . . . two statues . . . seven pillars . . . a series of bas-reliefs. . . ." More generally, the construction of the poem sustains such fancies by its "perfect symmetry. . . . elegance of the groupings. . . . The images, grouped according to a certain affinity among themselves, are further arranged with well studied gradation" with "distant echoes which chime to each other from strophe to strophe and give unity to the composition."[9] In terms of numbers, Raymond D. Havens found the general divisions "made up almost entirely of stanzas grouped in threes, or sevens or their multiples"; the poem "was constructed with unusual attention to parallelism, formal design, and pattern." Finally, in a book published after Brittain's, Christopher Devlin suggests a correspondence to the particular structure of "Durham Cathedral, which Smart knew so well."[10]

A recent essay by Christopher M. Dennis offers yet another blueprint for the poem, a "structural conceit" shaping the poem around a central series of stanzas which themselves shape the figure of a harp. Quoting Smart's own protestation that the poem has "EXACT REGULARITY AND METHOD," Dennis concludes, "*A Song to David* has eighty-six stanzas and five hundred and sixteen lines. The pattern of the 'harp' is preceded by thirty-seven stanzas and followed by thirty-seven stanzas. . . . The middle of the poem falls between stanzas xliii and xliv, the fifth and sixth 'strings' of the decalogue."[11] Among the descriptions of large pattern in the *Song*, Dennis's is especially interesting in emphasizing purely formal, nonreferential symmetry around the harp shape; he goes even further than his predecessors in isolating abstract, nonprogressive pattern, which grips the sequence of stanzas like an outside caliper measuring and bracing a line of building blocks.

I would like to use the word "appositional" for such pattern, where things made out of language are juxtaposed to each other in a pattern we might lay out in two or three spatial dimensions, to suggest that such pattern fits with the songlike character surveyed above, and to return at last to the notion of "mentality" with which this argument began. A series of medical observations over two centuries, and recent medical experimentation, have shown that the human brain supports two different and complementary kinds of thinking, perception, and even use of words, which are differentially dependent on the two symmetrical halves of the cerebral cortex, but mingled almost inextricably in ordinary mental life. The physiology of their basis in the brain, now being investigated, is of no concern to the present discussion. The terms of distinction of the two mental orders isolated by this research, however, are full of suggestion for the study of Christopher Smart's poetry.

The word "appositional" is used by one investigator, Dr. Joseph Bogen, to describe the functions of mind dependent on the nondominant hemisphere, in contrast to "propositional" for the (usually left side) dominant hemisphere.[12] To instance only a single differentiating phenomenon, some victims of left-hemisphere speech-area stroke, unable to articulate normal forward-moving speech at all, can sing or chant certain verbal wholes learned before the loss: sing songs, pray set prayers, and by some accounts curse in fluent formulas. Verbal constructs, that is, bound by their rhythms, tunes, rhymes, or other patterns not sequential logic or narrative, seem to draw for memory and production on separate apparatus from that dominant when we converse, explain, or relate. There is within the mind a contributing faculty or set of faculties, arising in a separate place, which specializes in other-than-linear perception and grasps other-than-linear patterns even of inherently serial, sequential language—that is, language not merely proceeding in propositions, but patterned as verse is patterned, and as song with its tune is even more highly patterned, to the relative deficit of discursive content. Such constructs have discursive content (unless they are nonsense babble, which we likewise can retain and recall whole when it is patterned by rhythm, rhyme, and tune), and appositional patterns have a linear dimension; discourse conversely has pattern. But the distinction in degree, in tendency, is clear, and, surprisingly, open to even clinical demonstration.

Song is the prime model of language use in this less familiar mentality. Reviewing the evidence, Julian Jaynes remarks that if one attempts to sing one's conversation, one lapses into clichés. Song, among the kinds of language use and even among the kinds of poetry, is perhaps the most patterned in appositional patterns, and among the most likely to resort to common or reiterated phrases, the cousins of clichés. Beyond iteration, language in song seems drawn away from the colorless and businesslike sequences determined, in most prose, by the information they transmit, and toward other shapes determined on other principles: likeness of sound, simple opposition of content, return to the point of departure, "arrangement of material on a formal rather than a logical pattern," to use Williamson's phrase. An example above furnished a small instance of chiasm, sound in the crossed or ring pattern of a b b a. Song lyrics often return—to refrain, to chorus, to closing repetition of the opening stanza—as their tunes typically close where they open.

The description I have been giving of the later poetry of Smart shows these qualities of song in both positive and negative ways. The tendency to recurrence of words and phrases, the heavy overdetermining of language by sound patterns, and similarly on a large scale the symmetrical and other "architectural" patterning, fit with what might be expected to be found in verse by a writer engaged in producing over a hundred and fifty psalms for singing, and a great nonsinging lyric in their mold. Apart from these positive features, Smart's verse shows emphatic aversion from the linear and sequential business it might be tending to: compare above, for example, the dutiful old psalter version following its text, against Smart's psalm turning each Bible verse into a stanza (his usual practice) of worship, arrested from continuity by the degree of its patterning. The psalms and *Song,* in other words, turn continually to the moment, as Frye says such sound-conscious incantation must. To appreciate how fully this turning to the moment imbues Smart's poetry, it is necessary to give brief attention to the large separate issue of the nature of *Jubilate Agno.*

In the manuscript pages called by this name, Smart seems to have written an entry each day during much of his confinement in a Bethnal Green madhouse, from about the beginning until the very end, at the rate of one or two or three doublets of lines a day, on the general pattern, "Let [someone, at first biblical, later contemporary] rejoice with [a creature, flower, or gem] / For [some personal reflection]":

> Let Hushim rejoice with the King's Fisher, who is of royal beauty, tho' plebeian size.
> For in my nature I quested for beauty, but God, God hath sent me to sea for pearls.
>
> [B 30][13]

It is misleading to speak, as the best scholars of Smart do speak, of this record of daily exercises as a "composition," a poem to read as if it were, in Frye's term, literature as product, an aesthetic construct with regrettable incoherences.[14] It is rather the record of a long program of ejaculatory utterances, perhaps spoken, perhaps only written, where utterance is a bringing out from within which is also a creating. In their formal regularity and their sometimes startling discontinuity they represent an accumulation of daily exercises. Smart set himself some rules according to which he would generate a day's exercise in a certain form, and then next day another and so on, at intervals of about twenty-four hours. The discontinuity is the significant ordering principle. The regular isolation of each day's writing (perhaps one pair of lines, perhaps more) from all else, in a setting of great physical and social isolation, radically enforces "writing to the moment"; the phrase recalls Frye's characterization of literature as process, and was coined by Samuel Richardson, whose great heroine is also an imprisoned writer. But in *Clarissa* or Boswell's journal, moments are always defined by narrative context. In Smart's laboratory, moments are purified of all business. The day's utterance has no natural context. Names of men and creatures are fed into a crucible of verbal formula, and verses result. The series of names in a series of Smart's lines has no continuity within that series of lines, but only in the Bible text from which he took them, a resource that is completely external to what Smart writes. Such a series of names represents a subprogram of the overall program, a supply system for continual new creations of utterance, not a structuring device for a composed whole.

The whole experiment is a heuristic of inspiration. Given the "Let . . . rejoice . . . For" formula and a program of names to employ, to be supplemented with another program of names when the first ran out, Smart set himself to find the day's pronouncement.[15] What was produced was a string of exploratory jottings of vision. Within the bounds set, verbal playfulness acted upon broad learning and intense spiritual conviction to bring forth the pearls he seems to speak of in the passage above; another self-reflective demonstration is B 173:

> Let Jona rejoice with the Wilk—Wilks, Wilkie, and Wilkinson bless the name of the Lord Jesus.
> For an happy Conjecture is a miraculous cast by the Lord Jesus.

"Cast" here might be of the net, which could be taken as the *Jubilate Agno* project itself; more likely it is a game, the casting of lots that is the root of "conjecture," where the Lord Jesus governs Smart's play to make it yield truth in divine divination. The commentary line by line in each edition of *Jubilate Agno,* now especially Williamson's, reveals the richness of the fabric of reference now traced in Smart's lines. But "reference" is perhaps the wrong word, implying that something in the text works to take a reader back to some source text, whereas the case here is more the inverse of reference, perhaps "rootedness." What is echoed or employed in a line of *Jubilate Agno* is not thereby invoked by the line or recommended to a reader, it is only where the line partly comes from.

The extreme discontinuity of these daily ejaculations, their spontaneity shaped and enabled by the cues of a program like the rules of a game, allows some comparison to the song verse Smart wrote at this same time, specifically the stanzas of psalms. Like these exercises, the stanzas of psalms, following the program of the English prose (prayerbook) text but freely elaborating and transforming, become moments of realization. They turn toward exaltation one by one, with distinct subordination of continuous discursive content. Versified words set to music is the most common medium by which something like this evocation of moments of exaltation is pursued: an anthem sacred or secular elevates in separate stanzas that have little memory each of the last. In *Jubilate Agno* Smart set himself an analogous course, to punctuate his life and open himself to inspiration for some moments of each day. The project was not musical, but if Smart is imagined uttering aloud what he wrote, it is not hard to hear a kind of recitative chant. In one line, B 80, he thanks God for his sonorous voice; in others he says, "For the AIR is purified by prayer which is made aloud and with all our might"; "For SOUND is propagated in the spirit and in all directions"; "For all whispers and unmusical sounds in general are of the Adversary"; "For it would be better if the LITURGY were musically performed"; "For prayer with music is good for persons [under malignant thoughts of others]" (B 224, 226, 231, 252, 304). The regimen of daily utterances served him as his psalms and hymns were calculated to serve worshippers and as song in general serves, as a program of moments of inspiration, where our awareness of passing time is in abeyance, or where as Frye says of literature as process, "emotion is being maintained at a continuous present."

These reflections of Smart's remind us as well that the little we know of his mental disorder was that it manifested itself in unseasonable public prayer, probably often loud sonorous prayer—

> For I blessed God in St James's Park till I routed all the company
> (B 89)

and perhaps prophetic-sounding chanted, cadenced prayer, rather than reasonable-persuasive discourse. These outbursts turned aside from the practical business of his own and other people's lives, where one thing must be done after another; they stopped people in the sequence of their day's time to turn them toward eternity in the moment. Indeed, in the larger view of Smart's life we see his pursuit of drunken conviviality and heedless expense set to provoke his arrest from everyday proceeding, from the time of his arrest at the suit of a tailor in his Cambridge years to his death in the Rules of the King's Bench Prison for debts: "all this," wrote Thomas Gray of the former incident, "must come to a Jayl, or Bedlam." There was in him the mind to succeed in Cambridge scholarship and then in the London literary market by his fluent production of discursive writing; there was also a mind to turn aside from it and even to subvert it, in clowning, in stupor, in legal confinement. It may be that the prayer behavior was only the starkest instance of a will to turn aside challenging the demands of ongoing responsibility, and that there is something in the discredited romantic fancy that Smart had to repudiate and be repudiated by the world to release his lyric genius.

However that may be, Smart's genius found its expression in his later years in a mentality that at its finest seemed "mad as ever" to Gray's friend William Mason, and that led reviewers to disparage the "ludicrous appearance" of psalm verse they failed to hear as song while they puzzled their reading way through it.[16] At his decisive breakdown and break away from the world, his spirituality called on him to interrupt time and turn to eternity. In confinement his *Jubilate Agno* project set him rigorously to give voice to detached insight welling up in the moment. When he turned to write poetry, to "chaunt praises" (a phrase he had used in one of his earliest Cambridge poems[17]) he wrote in the form and more broadly the mentality of song, the appositional rather than the linear propositional mode of the mind. It is not necessary for these terms to suggest that his art was therefore irrational, unconscious, or of only partial sanity. The mode of mind of these compositions has a congruence with the mission that called him. Psalm C concludes,

> And gracious is the Lord of love
> Above all estimate, above
>   The flight of time and thought.

The psalmist, hymnist, and poet Smart worked to make art that, like Keats's urn, "dost tease us out of thought / As doth eternity." He refrained from using in these lines a word he might have used, the word *stupendous* that Sherbo counted twenty-five times in Smart's psalms but nowhere in the prayerbook text he worked from.[18] Smart repeatedly took occasion to invoke God's grandeur as a stunning and sense-depriving realization. So also in *Song to David:*

> He sung of God—the mighty source
> Of all things—the stupendous force
>   On which all strength depends
>   [st. xviii]

and at the climax,

> Glorious,—more glorious, is the crown
> Of Him that brought salvation down,
>   By meekness, called thy Son:
> Thou at stupendous truth believ'd;—
> And now the matchless deed's atchiev'd,
>   DETERMINED, DARED, and DONE.
>   [st. lxxxvi]

"Sense" is slightly blurred in this high vision. The mantralike chant of "glorious" fourteen times in thirteen lines carries us into an ecstatic last stanza where sleight of syntax leaps from David to Christ and back to David but calls in by the phrasing also God the Father; the lines telescope David's and Christ's and the poet's own time. Believing "at" truth is puzzling—should it be "that . . . truth"?—and this mysterious locution hovers over the transition that Smart collapses. We see what the words do say clearly, however, that what Smart thought he saw in the presence of the stupendous, which overbore certain kinds of rationality and communicative discourse, was truth.

NOTES

1. Time and order of composition of these works is uncertain. The *Jubilate Agno* entries run from about January 4, 1759, to January 30, 1763: see Arthur Sherbo, "The Dating and Order of the Fragments of Christopher Smart's *Jubilate Agno*," *Harvard Library Bulletin* 10 (1956): 201–7, and *Christopher Smart: Scholar of the University* (East Lansing: Michigan State University Press, 1967), p. 128ff; for evidence of concurrent writing of the psalms, hymns, and *Song* see pp. 156–57, and Sherbo's article "The Probable Time of Composition of Christopher Smart's *Song to David, Psalms,* and *Hymns and Spiritual Songs*," *Journal of English and Germanic Philology* 55 (1956): 41–57.
2. *The Poetical Works of Christopher Smart*, vol. I, *Jubilate Agno*, ed. Karina Williamson (Oxford: Clarendon Press, 1980), p. 128, entry or verse D 217. All further references to this work appear in the text.
3. *The Collected Poems of Christopher Smart*, ed. Norman Callan (Cambridge: Harvard University Press, 1949), 2:632; all further references to this work appear in the text by psalm number. Besides the two texts in his published psalms, Smart wrote another version of this psalm, probably earlier, that was printed in a magazine in 1761 while he was confined: "The 100th Psalm, for a Scotch Tune," in a light Scots dialect. See Robert Brittain, *Poems by Christopher Smart* (Princeton: Princeton University Press, 1950), p. 231.
4. *The Hymnal of the Protestant Episcopal Church in the United States of America, 1940* (Norwood, Mass., 1943), no. 278. "All people," first published in the *Psalter* by John Daye, 1560, is probably by W. Kethe. For the history of the "Old," "New," and many other English versions of the Psalms, in which however Smart is barely noticed, see "Psalters, English," in vol. 2 of *A Dictionary of Hymnody*, ed. John Julian (New York: Dover Publications, 1957).
5. "Christopher Smart's *Hymns and Spiritual Songs*," *Philological Quarterly* 38 (1959): 421, 422.
6. Reprinted in *Eighteenth-Century English Literature*, ed. James L. Clifford (New York: Oxford University Press, 1959), pp. 311–18; citations pp. 313–14.
7. I have undertaken to survey some of the formal characteristics of song verse in English in *The Experience of Songs* (New Haven: Yale University Press, 1981), especially pp. 7–14.
8. "Probable Time of Composition"; *A Song to David*, in *Collected Poems*, ed. Callan, 1:357.
9. *Poems by Christopher Smart* pp. 295–97, quoting in his own translation Olivero, "Il 'Canto a Davide' di Christopher Smart," *Studi Britannici* (Torino, 1931).
10. Brittain, pp. 296–97; he quotes Raymond D. Havens, "The Structure of Smart's *Song to David*," *Review of English Studies* 14 (1938): 178–82; Brittain subsumes both Olivero and Havens in his own discussion of "architectonics," pp. 294–98; Christopher Devlin, *Poor Kit Smart* (London: Rupert Hart-Davis, 1961), pp. 138–51.

11 "A Structural Conceit in Smart's *Song to David*," *Review of English Studies* 29 (1978): 266.
12 "The Other Side of the Brain II: An Appositional Mind," *Bulletin Los Angeles Neurological Societies* 34 (1969): 148, 150.
13 See the description by Williamson in the introduction to her edition, pp. xxiii–xxviii. She largely accepts Sherbo's calculation of dates which assumes equal numbers of lines per day for extended stretches; for the view that the number varied irregularly, see C. P. Macgregor, "A Reconsideration of the Dating of Fragments B1 and B2 of Smart's *Jubilate Agno*," *Harvard Library Bulletin* 25 (1977): 322–31.
14 Williamson, *Jubilate Agno*, p. xxiv, says, "At its inception it was clearly intended to be a new Canticle on a grand scale"; John Block Friedman, "The Cosmology of Praise: Smart's *Jubilate Agno*," *PMLA* 82 (1967): 250–56, seeks "any overall design or consistency the poem may have"; W. H. Bond, the discoverer of the Let-For pairings, referred to "an antiphonal composition" and speculated about Smart's intentions for public performance: *Jubilate Agno* (Cambridge: Harvard University Press, 1954).
15 Williamson, *Jubilate Agno*, pp. xxvi–vii: "A begins with a list of patriarchs, followed by priests and Levites, then leaders of Israel; from A33 the names are taken mainly from the historical books (Joshua-Nehemiah), but not according to any apparent system. B starts again with Genesis and Numbers (drawing this time on genealogies and other lists), then moves on to the historical books. . . . At B123 Smart turns to the New Testament, taking names from the Gospels, Acts, and Epistles successively."
16 Mason to Gray, June 28, 1763; Sherbo in *Christopher Smart*, pp. 204–5, quotes the *Critical Review* 20 (September, 1765): 210–11.
17 "Secular Ode on the Jubilee at Pembroke College, Cambridge, in 1743," *Collected Poems*, 1:4, "chaunting her praises."
18 "Probable Time of Composition," p. 51, and *Scholar of the University*, pp. 213–14.

Samuel Johnson, The Vanity of Human Wishes, *and Biographical Criticism*

THOMAS JEMIELITY

When the Johnsonian critic warns that the writings of no other figure in English literature have been so frequently interpreted by recourse to the details of his biography than Samuel Johnson, surely no one would disagree. Patrick O'Flaherty, for example, in his study of Johnson's *Idler,* has sounded a representative caution: "The critic of Johnson," he insists, "has to be especially wary of permitting biographical details to interfere with his business of analysis and judgment."[1] As critics over the past two or three decades have discussed the satiric quality of *The Vanity of Human Wishes,* they have resorted frequently to details of Johnson's life to buttress their positions. Indeed, while preparing and completing an essay which argues that *The Vanity of Human Wishes* succeeds as satire,[2] I was struck not only by the extent to which incidents from Johnson's life were used to support the counterthesis—that the poem fails as satire—but even more by the degree to which that evidence was univocally interpreted and often selectively used.

In this essay I do not object to the use and presence of biographical evidence as such. I do assert, however, that in the case of Johnson's great poem biographical material has often been used very selectively and sometimes with little indication of its really ambiguous quality when seen in the wider context from which this material is drawn. In the first section of this paper, I focus on three portraits in the poem where interpretations have resorted to questionable biographical support: the sketches of Charles XII of Sweden, of virtuous old age, and of the young, fantasy-filled, entering college student. Then, in the second and concluding section of the essay, I consider the manner in which biographical details from Johnson's life have supported the wider but equally questionable claim that Johnson could not write satire at all.[3]

I

In her analysis of *The Vanity of Human Wishes,* Mary Lascelles draws on biography to support her claim that the sketch of Charles XII in the poem appears with tragic rather than satiric insight. Lascelles observes that at the time he published the poem, Johnson "was about to put to the proof his cherished vocation as tragic poet," a claim which the reception of *Irene* "did not vindicate." In the analysis of the sketch itself she says that "'Swedish Charles' had seized Johnson's imagination: he had written, and intended to write further, upon him."[4] The allusion here is to a 1742 letter of Johnson's to his friend John Taylor informing him that "I propose to get Charles of Sweden ready for this winter, and shall therefore, as I imagine be much engaged for some Months with the Dramatic Writers into whom I have scarcely looked for many years."[5] Although Edmond Malone assumed Johnson's project to be either a drama or a history, twentieth-century critics assume only a drama and, specifically, a tragedy. Leopold Damrosch, indeed, calls the sketch in the poem "a miniature tragedy," and adds that "Johnson actually contemplated writing one on this subject."[6] Yet Lascelles admits that, in the poem, Charles XII runs true "to Johnson's lifelong conviction that war must be assessed in terms of its cost in human misery—together with the hope that it may be abolished by satirizing military ambition."[7] In the poem, after all, Charles serves as one of three examples of a military ambition that has found irresistible the attraction, among other things, of "the senate's thanks and the gazette's pompous tale" (177), inducements that appear more ludicrous than dignified. Evidence from Johnson's life and writings warrants hesitation in assuming that tragic colors were necessarily the only hue in which Johnson envisioned this military figure.

Whatever legitimate difference of opinion may surround Johnson's view of Charles XII in *The Vanity of Human Wishes,* his view of Charles in *Adventurer* no. 99 is unmistakably clear. As Damrosch himself observes, the essay describes Charles "as one of those true projectors whose ambitions should be regarded with revulsion." Johnson's own comments express the wish that Charles, along with Caesar, Catiline, Alexander the Great, and Peter the Great, should be "huddled together in obscurity and derision." But what is perhaps most puzzling is Damrosch's wonder that Johnson, for whatever reason, "did not choose, four years earlier, to present Charles in this light in *The Vanity of Human Wishes*."[8] The real question may be whether Johnson, indeed, did present him in another light in the poem.

A key conversation, recorded in Boswell's *Life*, adds more support to the hesitation and skepticism with which a univocally tragic or dignified view of Charles XII should be assumed on Johnson's part. It was 10 April 1778, and Boswell recalls that the company talked "of war." "'Every man thinks meanly of himself for not having been a soldier, or not having been at sea.'" So Johnson insisted in what is surely one of his more memorable conversational remarks. And to illustrate his point, Johnson proceeded to use Charles as an example of the romantic attractions of military service and challenge. He speculated with assurance that were any company presented with the alternatives of following Socrates to a lecture in philosophy or Charles in a campaign to "'dethrone the Czar,'" "'a man would be ashamed to follow Socrates.'" Yet Johnson immediately added that the impression, as universal as he assumed, was, nonetheless, "'strange.'" In the subsequent record of that conversation, both Johnson and Boswell distinguish between the romantic and presumably questionable attraction of warfare and a cooler and more thoughtful consideration of the call to battlefield glory. For Johnson went on to discuss the crowding, filth, and stench that are an inescapable part of the sailor's lot and the distress, danger, idleness, and corruption that fall to the lot of the soldier, as Boswell recalls that Johnson had once observed in a letter. Boswell perceptively judged that Johnson, "warmed and animated by the presence of company," would indeed catch "the common enthusiasm for splendid renown," but the "cool reflection in his study" made him see the attraction in a far more uncomplimentary light.[9] We know also that Johnson often wrote and spoke severely about the human suffering caused by military or colonial activity and that this criticism forms a not unimportant variation of emphasis which he introduced into his first major work, the translation of Father Jerome Lobo's *Voyage to Abyssinia*.[10] We know as well that in the winter and spring months of 1745–1746, some three years after his letter to John Taylor, Johnson may have found himself occasionally crowded off the pages of the *Gentleman's Magazine* by its extensive accounts of the Highland Rebellion and particularly of its suppression, at the Battle of Culloden, by William, Duke of Cumberland. Thirty years later the discretion and care with which Johnson was to treat the Forty-five in the *Journey to the Western Islands* did not obliterate his memory of "the heavy hand of a vindictive conqueror."[11] Since *The Vanity of Human Wishes*, in its general introduction of war as fundamentally at odds with Reason, introduces Charles in that context, biography may very well lend support to the claim that the Swedish conqueror appears in the poem as an example of, not an exception to, the foolhardy pursuit of military glory that can be achieved only by staining "with blood the Danube or the Rhine" (182).

But biographical evidence has figured even more prominently in analyses of the poem's treatment of old age. From Mrs. Piozzi's *Anecdotes of the Late Samuel Johnson*, for example, we derive the information that Johnson had his mother in mind when he composed the lines on virtuous old age (291-98) and, in fact, that the line "The gen'ral fav'rite as the gen'ral friend" (298) alludes specifically to an incident in his mother's life when a neighbor was unable to find an attorney willing to pursue the neighbor's claim against Sarah Johnson.[12] Now Patrick O'Flaherty, who expresses strong dissatisfaction with the failure of earlier critics of the poem to offer a thorough, close analysis of the text, falls into the very pitfall of biographically influenced criticism that he warns about in his later study of Johnson's *Idler*. Were we to look for an extended consideration of the entire passage on old age (255-318) in O'Flaherty's discussion of the poem, we would be disappointed. Except for a passing reference to that entire part of the poem—which he lumps together with the portraits of Charles Albert, Xerxes, the miser, and Wolsey as alike in displaying "the same feeling of compassion" as appears in the portrait of the scholar—O'Flaherty confines his analysis to this single verse paragraph on virtuous old age and observes parenthetically that "Johnson evidently had his mother in mind when he composed the lines." Here, Damrosch's warning is very apropos: "The lines inspired by Johnson's aged mother . . . have frequently been mentioned as if they were the entirety of the section." Damrosch counters that these lines, however, "are an expansion of Juvenal's brief reference to the sorrows of old age *even when* [original emphasis] it is not contemptible; and they are preceded by lines which correspond perfectly to Warton's opinion of the poignancy of Johnson's ridicule." Damrosch finds the entire section "satiric as much as sympathetic."[13]

Johnson's survey of ill-founded human desires devotes five verse paragraphs to the suppliant's prayer for "multitude of days" (255), one of the longest single sections of the poem. The first sketch offered here, worthy in its grotesque quality of Dickens or Waugh, shows a physically and mentally enfeebled miser, manipulated by his prospective heirs, triumphing over crippled joints to count his gold until he dies. Lascelles admits that this is a "terrible picture of old age," but claims that Johnson finally tempers the scene "by changing Juvenal's repulsive dotard among a crowd of parasites into a solitary figure, not without dignity," dying as a superfluous veteran lagging on the stage.[14] But this is the death of Johnson's exemplary old person, not the death of the miser who clearly, in the poem, expires while counting his money. Johnson's discussion of virtuous old age, in fact, is a brief two-paragraph section (291–310) in which the lines inspired by his mother appear only as the first verse paragraph posing a question: does the prospect of an ethically admirable sunset justify the wish for a longer day? The brief paragraph that follows makes clear that virtue does not exempt even the elderly from a load of misfortunes. If the evils mentioned there have any basis in the details of his mother's life, no such information has yet been forthcoming from any sources we have uncovered about Johnson. But then, the poem returns quickly to the grotesque picture of old age with the horrid and culminating examples of Marlborough and Swift (311–18). Johnson, we may hope, did not have his mother in mind when he composed these lines, or, for that matter, the bulk of that section of *The Vanity of Human Wishes* dealing with the folly of praying for long life! The lines on virtuous old age, like the poem itself, were, after all, written a number of years after Johnson's departure from Lichfield, and eleven years before his mother died, never to have seen her son again for the last two decades of her life.[15]

Where the influence of biographical criticism on *The Vanity of Human Wishes* seems most to abound, however, is in critical discussion of the lengthy, four-verse paragraph treatment in the poem (135–74) of the ultimately unfounded hopes for academic success that crowd for attention in the mind of the entering young university student. Here Mrs. Piozzi's *Anecdotes* once again provides an incident that few Johnsonian scholars seem able to resist in interpreting the passage. "When Dr. Johnson," she recalls, "read his own satire, in which the life of the scholar is painted, with various obstructions thrown in his way to fortune and to fame, he burst into a passion of tears one day."[16] The frequency with which this passage is cited strongly suggests that it ranks as Johnson's most famous outburst of tears.[17] And the incident has been central to those arguments that claim a tragic or compassionate quality in the sketch.

Yet as many as are the references to this outburst, so surprisingly few are the critics careful enough to recall that Johnson's poem introduces the academic novice not neutrally and denotatively as "the young scholar," but much more resonantly as "the young enthusiast." Only Larence Lipking, to the best of my knowledge, uses the poem's own precise and pregnant terminology to show how, with "affectionate mockery," the images that introduce the sketch brilliantly convey "the confused, subjective point of view that dooms a fanciful author even before he has begun." In pursuing his analysis of the passage, Lipking goes on to cite more of the incident than any other earlier critic. Drawing on the *Anecdotes,* Lipking observes that George Lewis Scott, who was one of those present, "'clapped [Johnson] on the back,'" and reminded him that he, Johnson, and Hercules "'were all troubled with melancholy.'" As Lipking observes, "Scott's education had prepared him to understand the lines better than most modern critics: he knew the likely progress of the hero, and the end of his labors."[18]

Even Lipking's use of this incident from the annals of Johnsonian biography, however, is not complete. For Mrs. Piozzi not only recollected that Scott clapped Johnson on the back "in a jocose way," but seems unable to shake off a finally comic impression about the entire scene. Scott, she notes, "was a very large man . . . and made out the triumvirate with Johnson and Hercules comically enough." Johnson's reaction? "The Doctor was so *delighted* [my emphasis] at the odd sally, that he suddenly embraced him, and the subject was immediately changed."[19] Does Johnsonian biography leave here an unequivocal impression of tragic quality in the *Vanity's* portrait of "the young enthusiast" at the university, or does it rather demonstrate Johnson's capability of placing his emotional reactions into a serener perspective? Were literary history to uncover an incident of the elderly Swift in tears over his picture of the Struldbruggs, would *Gulliver's Travels* become tragedy?

Johnsonian criticism, however, has even more strongly and frequently claimed that the passage on scholarship in *The Vanity of Human Wishes* is perhaps the most reliably autobiographical part of the poem. Lipking, for example, observes that Johnson here "clearly writes about himself, in a vision that could make any scholar cry." The passage, according to him, takes mocking aim at Johnson's "heroic younger self," in a sketch that has no equivalent in Juvenal's *Tenth Satire,* where the Roman satirist takes aim not at scholarship but at oratory. O'Flaherty calls the passage "an intensely personal piece of writing," and offers no analysis of the lines at all but remains content to remind us about Johnson's later flood of tears when reading it. Such biographical citation seems to lend credence to the claim, often expressed, that Johnson admired learning and therefore would not have subjected scholarly ambition to ridicule of whatever sort.[20] Here, presumably, Johnson the writer is revealing Johnson the person.

But, once again, the references to Johnson's biography pose problems in coming to an understanding of the tone of the passage. The lines of the sketch, particularly in the opening paragraph, strongly convey the sense of an academic setting. The young man envisions a distinguished reputation in what the hideous jargon of our time would call the academic establishment. The references to Galileo, Lydiat, Francis Bacon, and the like are references to professional academicians, men who won their eminence as part of a university community. Even the climaxing mention of Archbishop Laud is, after all, a reference to a professional ecclesiastic. But in 1748, as he was composing these lines, Johnson's situation was hardly academic. Whatever autobiographical quality the lines are assumed to have, they clearly cannot refer accurately to the life Johnson was leading in London for the ten years or so that preceded the composition of the poem. Lipking's speaking of these illusions in the sketch as those of "a fanciful author" do not seem convincing.[21] The sketch is pervasively academic in the suggestions and hints that it inspires, and not at all evocative of the context in which we might assume a struggling hack writer was functioning in the London of the 1740s.

If so, is it likely that the lines are meant to recall sympathetically Johnson's own visions of success when he was a student at Oxford? The problem with this view, however, is that assuming an academically visionary Johnson at that time does not jibe with some of his own recollections about what he was like as a university student. As Boswell informs us, sliding in Christ Church meadow and the "'stark insensibility'" of so informing his tutor Jorden appear to convey a more accurate image of Johnson then than any picture in which he envisions himself in academic regalia.[22] If Johnson was thinking of himself at Oxford when he wrote these lines, he was obviously mocking a very short-lived youthful illusion.

One last possibility for defending a closer autobiographical reading of these lines yet remains, Lipking's reminder that Johnson's lines on the vanity of scholarly ambition have no real precedent in Juvenal's *Tenth Satire*, where the dangers of eloquence, rather than scholarship, are the focus of the Roman original. William Kupersmith, who agrees that the relationship of Johnson's lines to the section on Cicero and Demosthenes "is distant," points out that this variation would seem to justify the view that "the passage [on scholarship] looks like a digression in which Johnson gives an autobiographical discussion of his own early career." But this is only an impression, for, as Kupersmith observes, "even the most personal elements in a neo-classical poem usually have some classical precedent." What Kupersmith proceeds to do is to show how Johnson's lines bear some indebtedness to Juvenal's *Seventh Satire,* where the concern is with "the hardships of poets, scholars, and schoolmasters." Such an awareness does not detract from the poignancy of Johnson's lines—Kupersmith is quick to point this out—but does reinforce our sense that Johnson does not lose his literary instincts however strongly he may be feeling the promptings of autobiography.[23] At best, an autobiographical reading of these lines admits of too many qualifications, too many tenuous applications, to be critically convincing.

Now if it be granted that the biographical evidence used to support nonsatiric readings of this section—and other sections—of *The Vanity of Human Wishes* is not as univocally clear and one-sided as it has sometimes been made to appear, does the selective and debatable use of such material affect our wider understanding of Johnson as a writer of satire? Does his biography have a part to play in explaining why Johnsonian criticism hesitates to award him honors as a satirist?

II

In the many discussions, old and new, that have isolated central features of Johnson's character and personality, his quiet, daily, undemonstrative, and certainly saintly charity has figured prominently. Is it possible that this so often cited feature of his character influences the view that Johnson was not capable of writing satire? In his excellent analysis of Johnson's wit and humor, Walter Jackson Bate, for example, explicitly connects the two. In Bate's view, Johnson refrains from releasing satiric impulses he seems otherwise so very suited for not only because of the strength of these impulses within him, but even more because of "the charity and justice he is always bringing to 'helpless man.'" These more powerful impulses move him to a participation that "sets a bar to satire."[24] Charity compels to a sympathy, compassion, and extenuation which, in Bate's view and that of other critics of Johnson, makes him finally unsuccessful as a satirist.

Yet the very manner in which these critics speak of satire suggests that as this literary mode is examined in Johnson's writings, we are back again in the presence of a centuries-old prejudice—explored as early as Horace's opening poem in the second book of the *Satires*—that satiric writing reflects badly on the character of the satirist, that satire is, at best, a bastard in the family of the arts. As early as his *Achievement of Samuel Johnson*, Bate speaks of Johnson's characteristic inability in *The Vanity of Human Wishes* "to be content *simply* [my emphasis] to document or satirize a thing and then stop." But why the pejorative insistence on *simply*? Writing in the very same year, Henry Gifford speaks of Johnson's poem confronting "an awful possibility that dwarfs the satirical intention," refusing to "abandon himself to the mundane views of the satirist," and going "far beyond satire" to confront, not vice or folly, but "the mystery of human existence," a confrontation which, presumably, satire never achieves. O'Flaherty's study of the *Idler* claims that Johnson "senses that the really significant problems which confront men are *problems beyond satire* [my emphasis]: the terror of death, the anguish of defeated hope, the imperfection of man's knowledge." This claim dovetails very nicely with his earlier insistence that "the pose of the cynical, bitter satirist" which Johnson adopts in the *Vanity* does not allow "his genuine feeling unfettered expression," and, thus, the poem "must be judged finally a failure."[25] The assumptions and attitudes at work here in the final picture of Johnson as the reluctant and ultimately unsuccessful satirist are very clear: he is temperamentally not at home in such a lesser, limited, and demeaning activity as satire. The literary hierarchies have returned.

As seen in the discussions of Bate and O'Flaherty, this view of Johnson draws for support on his aversion to Jonathan Swift, an attitude that Bate is willing to characterize as both "antagonistic and unfair."[26] Mrs. Piozzi again provides the ammunition. No one more than Johnson, she says, "had a more just aversion to general satire," and illustrates her point by drawing attention to the "unprovoked bitterness against the professors of medicine" which Johnson "always hated and censured in Swift." She supplements that example with a comment of Johnson's made in defense of the legal profession on an occasion when an acquaintance of theirs "was one day exclaiming against the tediousness of the law and its partiality."[27] But the entire context of her remarks raises questions about what she meant by the phrase "general satire." Considered against Johnson's own definition of satire in the *Dictionary*, her phrase is redundant, because Johnson defined satire as, in its essence, general, and so distinguished it from the lampoon whose focus is personal and individual. Furthermore, if "general satire" means unqualified attacks against particular professions, it seems trivial to read *The Vanity of Human Wishes* as primarily a satire on various walks of human life. If the primary object of its attack is, rather, vain human desire as illustrated throughout the spectrum of human activity and aspiration, the poem's satiric focus would seem to be more psychological and internal than professional. What Johnson is about in his poem, consequently, is something much more satirically profound than Swift's momentarily seeking, in *Gulliver's Travels*, some humor at the expense of physicians or Evelyn Waugh deciding, in *Decline and Fall*, to have some fun at the expense of the Welsh.

And why must Swift be seen as the only prototype of satire available to Johnson? What of Johnson's very high regard for Alexander Pope, for his poetry and for his character? The praise of neither is unqualified, but surely Johnson was aware that Pope had as great a claim as Swift to the laurels of satire. *The Rape of the Lock* received his unqualified tribute as perhaps the finest specimen of ludicrous poetry yet produced. Despite his reservations, furthermore, about many physically impure ideas in *The Dunciad* and his doubt whether the design was moral, he gave the poem his highest critical compliment: a work of original genius. O'Flaherty has called this "unwilling praise" in excerpts from Johnson's comments that omit the praise for its originality. Given the fact that Johnson recognized the imitative base of *The Dunciad* in Dryden's *Macflecknoe*, and given the fact that he likewise argued that Dryden's poem could at best be considered only a lampoon, his praise of *The Dunciad*'s originality is high praise indeed.[28] In Johnson's opinion, then, Pope successfully transformed his imitative base into a profounder, yet still satirical, poem. Johnson later made a comparable achievement in transforming his Juvenalian model into a much more penetrating and morally sophisticated piece, still satirical in tone. Why assume that Johnson had a monolithic notion of satire's history, traditions, and possibilities? Having mastered and transformed Juvenal in *The Vanity of Human Wishes*, for example, it might be claimed that in *Rasselas*, a decade later, he demonstrated magnificently his mastery of the ironic and indirect method.

Yet, if Bate and O'Flaherty are to be believed, that great decade of Johnson's moral writing can be best interpreted in the framework of his moving away from satiric impulses as early as *The Vanity of Human Wishes* itself. With his supposed lack of satiric success in the poem, Johnson casts off satire and turns to many, many ventures in which the satiric impulse is rebuffed or transformed into something else. "Johnson," O'Flaherty insists, "wrote no satire after *The Vanity of Human Wishes*," a statement intimidating in its absolute quality and clearly implicit in Bate's view of Johnson as the foiled satirist.[29] Surprisingly, however, neither critic deals with the effect on this position of Johnson's *Review of Soame Jenyns' Free Inquiry into the Nature and Origin of Evil* (1757). O'Flaherty ignores the work altogether in his studies of the poem and the periodical essays, and Bate does not take up the work in any context that deals with Johnson as a satirist. Donald Siebert, on the other hand, has seen abundant evidence of Johnson's satiric talents in his edition of Shakespeare and rejects Bate's theory of Johnson as the foiled satirist categorically.[30]

Biographical evidence, then, plays an important role in the arguments that deny satiric quality to *The Vanity of Human Wishes* and to Johnson's writing as a whole. My reservations are not meant to deny the connection between life and art, but, rather, intended to suggest that the two are not as equivalently related in Johnson as some recent criticism assumes. With the range of his mind and the capability of his artistry, Johnson saw deeper, richer, yet still satiric potentiality in much that he undertook as a writer. *The Vanity of Human Wishes* is a major case in point. And if the same debatable use of biography there underlies as well the wider hesitation about assigning him satiric honors at all, perhaps we shall have to be much less confident in asserting that Johnson's impulse to charity could not mix with his inclination to satire. Johnson was capable of distinguishing between life and art. Among the illustrations used in the *Dictionary* for his definition of *satirist*, Johnson includes these lines from Alexander Pope:

> Yet soft his nature, though severe his lay;
> His anger moral, and his wisdom gay:
> Blest *satyrist*! who touch'd the mean so true,
> As show'd vice had his hate and pity too.

Johnson, at least, recognizes here not only that life and art are not equivalent, but, even more, that satire and charity are not necessarily incompatible.

NOTES

1 Patrick O'Flaherty, "Johnson's *Idler*: the Equipment of a Satirist," *ELH*, 37 (1970), 212. All line references to *The Vanity of Human Wishes* are from Samuel Johnson, *The Yale Edition of the Works of Samuel Johnson* (New Haven: Yale University Press, 1958–), vol. 6, *Poems*, ed. E. L. McAdam, Jr., with George Milne.

2 See Thomas Jemielity, "*The Vanity of Human Wishes:* Satire Foiled or Achieved?" *Essays in Literature* 11 (1984): 35–48.
3 The most succinct statement of this position appears in Walter Jackson Bate, *Samuel Johnson* (New York: Harcourt Brace Jovanovich, 1977), p. 493: "Johnson was not and could not be a satirist." Patrick O'Flaherty, who claims that *The Vanity of Human Wishes* fails as satire, contends also that after the publication of the poem, Johnson, "apart from a few minor items in *The Rambler* and *The Idler,* wrote no satire whatever." See "Johnson as Satirist: A New Look at *The Vanity of Human Wishes,*" *ELH* 34 (1967): 89. He pursues this conclusion in the essay on *The Idler* (*ELH* 37 [1970]: 211–25) and in "The Rambler's Rebuff to Juvenal," *English Studies* 51 (1970): 517–27.
4 Mary Lascelles, "Johnson and Juvenal," in *New Light on Dr. Johnson: Essays on the Occasion of His 250th Birthday,* ed. Frederick W. Hilles (New Haven: Yale University Press, 1959), pp. 35, 48. The essay affords as well a biographical reading of Juvenal, based, presumably on the *Satires:* "Juvenal's satires," she writes, "appear to be the work of an embittered and frightened man; a brilliant rhetorician; no philosopher; disappointed in respect of worldly ambition; professing to despise worldly success, perhaps despising himself" (p. 36). But if H. A. Mason is correct in his claim that Juvenal, in the *Satires,* is primarily interested in the display of his rhetorical skills, such biographical inferences about him seem even more untrustworthy. See "Is Juvenal a Classic?" in *Satire: Critical Essays on Roman Literature,* ed. J. P. Sullivan (Bloomington and London: Midland Books, 1968), pp. 93–176.
5 *Letters of Samuel Johnson,* ed. R. W. Chapman (Oxford: Oxford University Press, 1952), 1: 23.
6 Chapman discusses Malone's interpretation in *Letters* (Oxford: Oxford University Press, 1952), 1: 23, n. 3. See the opinion of David Nichol Smith and Edward L. McAdam in *The Poems of Samuel Johnson* (Oxford: Oxford University Press, 1942), p. 40, n. to ll. 191–222; of Donald J. Greene in *The Politics of Samuel Johnson* (New Haven: Yale University Press, 1960), p. 265; and of Leopold Damrosch in *Samuel Johnson and the Tragic Sense* (Princeton: Princeton University Press, 1972), p. 145.
7 Lascelles, p. 48.
8 Damrosch, p. 147, where the citation from *Adventurer* no. 99 appears.
9 *Boswell's Life of Johnson,* ed. George Birkbeck Hill, rev. ed. L. F. Powell (Oxford: Oxford University Press, 1934), 3: 265–67.
10 See Joel Gold, "Johnson's Translation of Lobo," *PMLA* 80 (1965): 50–61.
11 Samuel Johnson, *The Yale Edition of the Works of Samuel Johnson* (New Haven: Yale University Press, 1958–), vol. 9, *A Journey to the Western Islands of Scotland,* ed. Mary Lascelles (1971), p. 89.
12 Hester Lynch Thrale Piozzi, *Anecdotes of the Late Samuel Johnson, LL.D., During the Last Twenty Years of His Life,* in *Johnsonian Miscellanies,* ed. George Birkbeck Hill (1897; rpt. New York: Barnes & Noble, 1966), 1: 151.
13 O'Flaherty, "Johnson as Satirist," pp. 86–88. In his study of the *Rambler*

essays, however, O'Flaherty claims that the sketch of the miser is not compassionate but "ridiculous." See "The Rambler's Rebuff to Juvenal," p. 519. Damrosch, p. 151.

14 Lascelles, p. 53.
15 George Irwin is only one of a number of critics who have commented on the very thorny problem of Johnson's relationship with his mother. See his "Dr. Johnson's Troubled Mind," in *Samuel Johnson: A Collection of Critical Essays*, ed. Donald J. Greene (Englewood Cliffs: Spectrum Books, 1965), pp. 25–29, and his *Samuel Johnson: A Personality in Conflict* (Auckland: Auckland University Press, 1971).
16 Piozzi, 1: 180.
17 See O'Flaherty, "Johnson as Satirist," pp. 86–88; Frederick W. Hilles, "Johnson's Poetic Fire," in *New Light on Dr. Johnson: Essays on the Occasion of His 250th Birthday*, ed. Frederick W. Hilles (New Haven: Yale University Press, 1959), p. 73; Lawrence Lipking, "Learning to Read Johnson: *The Vision of Theodore* and *The Vanity of Human Wishes*," *ELH* 43 (1976): 530.
18 Lipking, pp. 529–31; Piozzi, 1: 180.
19 Piozzi, 1: 180.
20 Lipking, pp. 529–30; O'Flaherty, "Johnson as Satirist," p. 86; Francis G. Schoff, "Johnson on Juvenal," *Notes and Queries* 198 (1953): 295; George T. Amis, "The Style of *The Vanity of Human Wishes*," *Modern Language Quarterly* 35 (1974): 18.
21 Lipking, p. 529.
22 *Life*, 1: 59–60.
23 William Kupersmith, "Declamatory Grandeur: Johnson and Juvenal," *Arion* 9 (1970): 60–61.
24 Bate, *Samuel Johnson*, p. 493.
25 Walter Jackson Bate, *The Achievement of Samuel Johnson* (New York: Galaxy Books, 1961), p. 20 (first published in 1955); Henry Gifford, "*The Vanity of Human Wishes*," *Review of English Studies* n.s. 6 (1955): 164–65; O'Flaherty, "Johnson's *Idler*," p. 220; O'Flaherty, "Johnson as Satirist," p. 91.
26 Bate, *Samuel Johnson*, p. 493; O'Flaherty, "Johnson as Satirist," pp. 88–90.
27 Piozzi, 1: 223.
28 Samuel Johnson, "Swift," in *Lives of the English Poets*, ed. George Birkbeck Hill (New York: Oxford University Press, 1905), 3: 38, 10; *Life*, 2: 318–319; "Pope," in *Lives*, 3: 104, 241–242; O'Flaherty, "Johnson as Satirist," pp. 88–90.
29 Bate first presented his view in "Johnson and Satire Manqué," in *Eighteenth-Century Studies in Honor of Donald F. Hyde*, ed. W. H. Bond (New York: Grolier Club, 1970), pp. 145–60, and later incorporated this material into the chapter "Humor and Wit," in *Samuel Johnson*, pp. 480–99; O'Flaherty, "Johnson as Satirist," p. 89.
30 Donald T. Siebert, Jr. "The Scholar as Satirist: Johnson's Edition of Shakespeare," *Studies in English Literature* 15 (1975): 483–503. See, in particular, his concluding paragraph.

Johnson and Hume: Of Like Historical Minds

JOHN A. VANCE

The very title of this essay could find me guilty on two counts of heresy in the court of literary history. As "everyone" knows, few figures from the eighteenth century have been perceived as any more different than Johnson and Hume—philosophically, the period's cobra and mongoose.[1] According to Johnson, the Scot was a "modern infidel," a "vain man," a "rogue," a "blockhead," a "Hobbist," and a man devoid of all principle.[2] Regarding count two, again as "everyone" knows, Johnson had little use for history. Hester Thrale noted in memorable passages that Johnson was never less pleased with a conversation "than when the subject was historical fact or general polity." "What shall we learn from *that* stuff," he supposedly barked. And let no one discuss with him the Punic Wars or the Catiline Conspiracy: such talk was "lost time," and when Charles James Fox spoke to him at the Club about Catiline Johnson "withdrew [his] attention, and thought about Tom Thumb."[3]

But in defiance of the authority of literary history, I will argue that Johnson and Hume shared a deep respect for the uses and potential of history, wrote with facility and purpose on historical events and personalities, and agreed on many important aspects of historical inquiry and composition reflective of the growing "Rationalist" movement in British historiography. This essay does not afford me the space to explain Johnson's remarks quoted in Thrale's *Anecdotes* or Boswell's *Life* that seem to disparage history or demonstrate through a careful examination of his writings how often he employed and even wrote history,[4] but I hope to show by comparing his and Hume's historical minds just how perceptive and *au courant* Johnson was in his historical thinking. I moreover cannot do justice to Hume's splendid intellect by condensing his views on history in an easily comprehensible form, but I do so to help overturn the verdict of literary history regarding the dissimilarity of Johnson's and Hume's thought and Johnson's supposed disregard for history.

On 5 January 1753 David Hume wrote to John Clephane that "there is no post of honour in the English Parnassus more vacant than that of History. Style, judgement, impartiality, care—everything is wanting to our historians."[5] The comment is especially interesting in that it serves as both an impetus and a justification for the completion of Hume's historical project, the first part of which, the *History of Great Britain (1603–1649)*, would appear in November of the following year.[6] But Hume's lament over the state of British Historiography was similarly stated nearly two years earlier by Samuel Johnson, who wrote in *Rambler* no. 122 (18 May 1751), "It is observed, that our nation, which has produced so many authors eminent for almost every other species of literary excellence, has been hitherto remarkably barren of historical genius."[7] Certainly, Johnson was not the first to publicize the void, but the remark's wide circulation in that respected periodical surely had more impact than, say, Peter Whalley's pamphlet, the *Essay and Manner of Writing History* (1746), which also noted that few in Britain had distinguished themselves in historical writing.[8] Whereas one cannot argue with any confidence (although the possibility exists) that a reading of Johnson's essay prompted Hume's response to Clephane or stimulated his efforts toward completing the first volume of his proposed history, a comparison of the observations indicates that both men knew enough about recent historical composition to voice their frustrations over its shortcomings and that both Johnson and Hume saw the significance of good history to a nation proud of its heritage and literary accomplishments. And in *Rambler* no. 122 Johnson encourages a new commitment to excellent historical writing by first shaming his countrymen: "if we have failed in history, we can have failed only because history has not hitherto been diligently cultivated." Suggesting his respect for history and its potential, Johnson calls for historical works that will rise to "the majesty of history."

One might add, however, that Hume did something about the dearth of good historical composition; Johnson did not. Such an assertion fails to consider Johnson's frequent employment of his impressive historical knowledge[9] in his varied writings—at times even assuming the mantle of historian himself. His translations, reviews, prefaces, dedications, early biographies, miscellaneous pieces for the *Gentleman's Magazine*, periodical papers, poems *London* and *The Vanity of Human Wishes*, the *Dictionary*, the edition of Shakespeare and its preface, the political pieces of the late 1750s and early 1770s,[10] *Rasselas*, his assistance—whatever its nature—to Robert Chambers's Vinerian Law Lectures of the late 1760s,[11] the *Journey to the Western Islands*, and the *Lives of the Poets* all bear irrefutable testimony to Johnson's strong historical interests and sense.[12] And a good number of these pieces appeared before the popular reception of Hume's *History of England* and therefore before the "flowering" of British historiography in the second half of the eighteenth century.

Careful readers of Johnson and Hume should note, besides the men's sharing of an impressive knowledge and a strong appreciation of history, their like views on such matters as the "barbarity" of medieval (and even Renaissance) learning and taste on the one hand and the significance to the present of medieval laws and customs on the other.[13] Also readily apparent is their belief that mankind has shown a marked progress, not a decline as some would have it, from classical times to the present. As Johnson said, "I am always angry when I hear ancient times praised at the expense of modern times. There is now a great deal more learning in the world than there was formerly."[14] And for a man who professed not to have read Hume's *History of England*,[15] Johnson's estimations of the English monarchs from Elizabeth to James II are strikingly similar to Hume's—estimations that reflect Johnson's and Hume's judicious interpretations of historical evidence rather than a repetition of historical commonplaces. Both men praised, as did all England, Elizabeth's leadership qualities, policies, and achievements, but they also offered harsh criticism of her treatment of Mary Queen of Scots. Sensitive to the romantic side of Mary, Johnson and Hume wrote of Elizabeth's vengeful and hypocritical motives and behavior during the Queen of Scots' trial.[16] Each man noted the learning of James I but also stressed his timidity, vanity, and unsuitability for the important matters of state. James's "timidity and indolence fixed him, during most of his reign, in a very prudent inattention to foreign affairs," Hume argued—as did Johnson: "James quietly saw the Dutch invade our commerce; the French grew everyday stronger and stronger and the protestant interest, of which he boasted himself the head, was oppressed on every side, while he writ, and hunted, and dispatched ambassadors."[17]

Regarding Charles I and the events and personalities that marked his reign and the years immediately afterward, Johnson and Hume emphasized the religious zeal and fanaticism of the time, the inability of Charles to gauge correctly the mood of his people, and the tragedy of Charles's execution, which Hume called the "height of all iniquity and fanatical extravagance" and "the most atrocious of all [Cromwell's] actions" and Johnson termed "murder of the most atrocious kind."[18] Both men agreed as well that Cromwell was a complex man with many attractive qualities but who ultimately must be judged a tyrant whose fanaticism "rendered him the most dangerous of hypocrites."[19] A few other passages from Hume's *History* and Johnson's works demonstrate further the men's like thinking about the Civil War years:

> Every man, as prompted by the warmth of his temper, excited by emulation, or supported by his habits of hypocrisy, endeavored to distinguish himself beyond his fellows. . . . Government is instituted in order to restrain the fury and injustice of the people, and being always founded on opinion, not on force, it is dangerous to weaken, by these speculations, the reverence which the multitude owe to authority. (Hume)[20]

> It is scarcely possible, in the regularity and composure of the present time, to image the tumult of absurdity and clamour of contradiction which perplexed doctrine, disordered practice, and disturbed both publick and private quiet in that age, when subordination was broken and awe was hissed away; when any unsettled innovator who could hatch a half-formed notion produced it to the publick; when every man might become a preacher, and almost every preacher could collect a congregation. . . . To change the constituent parts of Government must be always dangerous, for who can tell where changes will stop. A new representation will want the reverence of antiquity, and the firmness of Establishment. (Johnson)[21]

Johnson and Hume also shared a basic assessment of Charles II as a charismatic and social king who nevertheless neglected the responsibilities of his office: "his love of [social] pleasure," Hume noted, "was not attended with proper sentiment and decency," and Johnson remarked that "many frailties and vices" marked the king's character.[22] Both men thought his "bounty" was more show than substance[23] and that, more importantly, he was by nature of his temperament ill-equipped for the more weighty concerns of domestic and foreign affairs. In 1742 Johnson stated that Charles "betrayed and sold" his country in his dealings with the French, and fourteen years later Hume wrote that the king "had actually in secret sold his neutrality to France." Hume blamed Charles for not preserving the balance of power in

Europe, "which it has since cost this island a great expense of blood and treasure to restore"—a point seconded by Johnson in the same year: although public reaction compelled him at times to actively oppose French designs, Charles "never persevered long in acting against her, nor ever acted with much vigour."[24]

Finally, Johnson and Hume reminded their readers of James II's doomed policy of religious readjustment. As Johnson observed, James "was not ignorant of the real interest of his country; he desired its power and its happiness, and thought rightly, that there is no happiness without religion; but he thought very erroneously and absurdly, that there is no religion without popery."[25] Hume characterized James's tampering with English Protestantism a "violent and dangerous innovation"—sentiments echoed at that time and later by Johnson, who wrote of the "dangerous bigotry" and "violence of his innovations."[26] As commentators on English history from 1586 to 1688, Johnson and Hume were not only similar in their assessments but also in the way they phrased their historical observations.

On more philosophical grounds, Johnson and Hume held like views on how history should be written, studied, and employed. As noted, in the 1753 letter to Clephane, Hume asserted that "Style, judgement, impartiality, [and] care" were wanting in British historians. Johnson could not have agreed more. Regarding style, his commentary in *Rambler* no. 122 is in large part concerned with the historian's skill with prose. For all his favorable assessments of Clarendon, Johnson described the historian's style as "the effusion of a mind crouded with ideas and desirous of imparting them." In the same number he praised the efforts of William Knolles, who he believed wrote in a clear style and avoided tedious minuteness in his digressions. Elsewhere, we find Johnson justifying to Edward Cave a new English translation of Father Sarpi's *History of the Council of Trent* primarily on the grounds that the style of Nathaniel Brent's 1620 translation was "capable of great Improvements." Johnson harshly criticizes Thomas Blackwell's style in the 1756 review of the latter's *Memoirs of the Court of Augustus:* "His great delight is to show his universal acquaintance with terms of art, with words that every other polite writer has avoided and despised." Readers of Boswell's *Life* may recall that Johnson labeled Gilbert Burnet's style "mere chit-chat." A more telling remark would be Johnson's response to Lord Hailes's *Annals of Scotland* (1775): "The narrative is clear, lively, and short. . . . It is in our language, I think, a new mode of history, which tells . . . all that is known, without laboured splendour of language, or affected subtilty of conjecture."[27]

We sense in the remarks on Hailes's *Annals* a commentator who, like Hume, understood the relationship between the presentation and the success and utility of history. And one might note the similarity of style as well as content between Johnson's assessment of the *Annals* and Hume's review of Robert Henry's *History of Great Britain* (1773): "His narration is as full as those remote times seem to demand; and at the same time, his inquiries of the antiquarian kind, . . . omit nothing which can be an object, either of doubt or curiosity. The one as well as the other is delivered with great perspicuity and no less propriety, which are the true ornament of this kind of writing: All superfluous embellishments are avoided: And the reader will scarcely find in our language, except in the work of the *celebrated* Dr. Robertson, any performance that unites together so perfectly the great points of entertainment and instruction!"[28]

Johnson did not come to agree with those like James Moor who believed that the "proper Art, and method, of Composition, in which a good Historian must excel, requires, perhaps, not much less genius and skill, to execute in perfection, than that of any other kind of writing; without excepting Poetry itself,"[29] because Johnson feared an overactive imagination and inordinate concentration on style would distort the truth and lead to "romance" rather than good and accurate history. But as he got older he appears to have shed some of his conservatism in this matter, for in the "Life of Milton" he wrote that the historian is to "improve and exalt" his material by a "nobler art" and animate it by "dramatick energy."[30]

Hume also lamented the lack of judgment in British historians. Like the Scot, Johnson disdained the naiveté, blithe optimism, and sheer ignorance of those who accepted without question all that has passed for written history. Certainly, both Johnson and Hume reflected the tradition of "exemplary" history, as George Nadel deftly terms it.[31] Hume, we might recall, observed in his *Enquiry Concerning Human Understanding* (1748): "It is universally acknowledged, that there is a great uniformity among the actions of men, in all nations and ages, and that human nature remains still the same, in its principles and operations. . . . Mankind are so much the same, in all times and places, that history informs us of nothing new or strange in this particular." History's "chief use," Hume continues, "is only to discover the constant and universal principles of human nature."[32] In agreement with this humanist historian's credo was Samuel Johnson: "We are all prompted by the same motives, all deceived by the same fallacies, all animated by hope, obstructed by danger, entangled by desire, and seconded by pleasure. . . . human nature is always the same, and every age will afford us instances of public censures influenced by events."[33] A reading of *The Vanity of Human Wishes*, many of the periodical papers, and some of the sermons—in which Johnson, as does Hume in the *History* and *Treatise of Human Nature*, employs such wording as "history will inform us," "every page of history will furnish us," and "Let us be warned by the calamities of past ages"—moreover emphasizes the educative and moral use to which Johnson put his historical examples.

Comparing several of Johnson's periodical papers, particularly *Adventurer* no. 99, with sections of Hume's *Treatise* demonstrates the facility with which both men employed historical figures and events to adorn and enrich their moral observations. Johnson would have undoubtedly seconded Hume's argument that history and historians were (or should be) the "true friends of virtue" and that history was "the great mistress of wisdom."[34] Hume wrote in his early essay, "Of the Study of History" (1741), "I must think it an unpardonable ignorance in persons of whatever sex or condition, not to be acquainted with the history of their own country, together with the histories of ancient Greece and Rome"—a point Johnson embellishes brilliantly in *Rasselas:* "If we act only for ourselves, to neglect the study of history is not prudent; if we are entrusted with the care of others, it is not just. Ignorance, when it is voluntary, is criminal; and he may properly be charged with evil who refused to learn how he might prevent it."[35]

But like Hume Johnson was aware of and responsive to the growing scientific approach to history and to the legacy of seventeenth-century skepticism, forwarded most notably by Pierre Bayle and the French Pyrrhonists. Both Johnson and Hume realized that the scope of historical investigation must be broadened beyond the religious, military, and political realms for a more accurate and complete understanding of the past. Johnson's writings suggest the catholic nature of his historical tastes, and he enjoyed numbering the streaks of the tulip as far as his historical inquiries were concerned. He saw the significance of the subtle as well as the grand. Johnson evinces, for example, the historian's interest in exploration, colonization, and trade and in the evolution of learning and the law—topics on which Hume also commented.[36] And Johnson thought with Hume that a knowledge of the facts, as unglamorous as they might be, was crucial if one hoped to discover the truth: "History is little more than romance to him who has no knowledge of the succession of events, the periods of dominion, and the distance between one great action and another."[37] But again like Hume, Johnson advised that the historian select his facts carefully.

Johnson and Hume looked closely at the common people whom

historians frequently ignore in their accounts. Johnson's commentary on migration and customs marks the achievement of his *Journey to the Western Islands*,[38] and Hume's "Of National Characters," "Of the Populousness of Ancient Nations," and parts of the *Treatise* and the *History* speak to the importance he placed on these matters. Hume's appreciation of the particulars of history may be nowhere better evident than in his *History of England*. At the year 1660 he ceases his narrative to "take a general survey of the age, so far as regards manners, finances, arms, commerce, arts, and sciences. The chief use of history is, that it affords materials for disquisitions of this nature."[39] Johnson told Boswell that the "history of manners is the most valuable" and remarked that Robert Henry's *History of Great Britain* would have done better to focus its attention not so much on the civil, military, and religious realms but rather on "the history of manners."[40] Johnson's thoughts on customs are numerous and spread throughout his canon, and much of what he writes agrees with Hume's observations in the *History* and the *Treatise*.[41] In addition, both men rejected unhesitatingly the authority of oral tradition: it is, Johnson believed, "but a meteor, which, if once it falls, cannot be rekindled"—to which Hume added, "the history of past events is immediately lost or disfigured when entrusted to memory and oral tradition."[42]

Hume wrote that the "first Quality of an Historian is to be true and impartial"; Johnson that the "first law of History" is the "Obligation to tell truth."[43] Neither Hume nor Johnson was advancing something novel, but in Johnson's case his regard for truth was passionate—reflected best, perhaps, by Thomas Percy's remark that no man had a "more scrupulous regard for truth; from which . . . he would not have deviated to save his life" and by Johnson's own comment in *Idler* no. 20 that "no crime" is "more infamous than the violation of truth."[44] Anyone who has studied Hume intimately knows of his response to seventeenth-century skepticism, which Isaac Kramnick considers "at the heart of the Enlightenment's attitude to history."[45] Johnson's response is much less known and appreciated, but as early as 1742 he was advocating an active skepticism in historical research and calling "distrust" a "necessary qualification" of the student of history.[46]

The influence of Pyrrhonian skepticism on historical thinkers such as Bolingbroke, Hume, and Gibbon is too complicated and rich to be discussed adequately here, but like these men Johnson dismissed what one might see as the intemperate negativism in the view that history was nothing more than the distorted perception of partisan historians and that, with their limited perspectives, men and women could never know the truth about the past. Like Hume, who came to "yield to the current of nature, in submitting to [his] senses and understanding,"[47] Johnson applied his active skepticism to a working historical method, which put all written evidence and oral testimony through a rigorous examination regarding the authenticity and reliability of that evidence and the bias, self-interest, and reputation of the author or eye-witness. For Johnson such an approach led one closer to the truth, and he believed historical truth could be attainable—at least to the degree that it would justify an investigation of the past. Johnson and Hume of course knew that history has often been the prisoner of those who wrote it, but they also saw that the modern historian has the means by which to let the truth of history escape and speak accurately and relevantly to the present. Therefore, when we read of Johnson's criticisms of earlier and contemporary historians and his comments to the effect that "What are all the records of history, but narratives of successive villanies, of treasons and usurpations, massacres and wars?," we should evaluate them in the context of Johnson's historical skepticism. They should not be seen as evidence that he disliked history or considered its uses negligible.

Related to these matters is Hume's assessment that "impartiality" was also wanting in British historians. The irony here is that his *History of England* was *perceived* as a partisan account—for example by Catharine Macaulay—even though he took much pain to claim his freedom from fashionable views of the past (usually Whig views) and especially from any political pressures. In the *History,* Hume censures contemporary partisan historians who "have been extolled and propagated and read as if they had equalled the most celebrated remains of antiquity":

> No man has yet arisen who has paid an entire regard to truth, and has dared to expose her without covering or disguise to the eyes of the prejudiced public. Even that party among us which boasts of the highest regard to liberty has not possessed sufficient liberty of thought in this particular [the reigns of the Stuarts], nor has been able to decide impartially of their own merit, compared with that of their antagonists.[48]

And in his writings and observations concerned in whole or in part with historical matters, we find Johnson, much to the disbelief of many, the impartial historian with thoughts like Hume's on the shortcomings of politicized accounts of the past. If one pieces together Johnson's remarks on the Stuart monarchs, one finds him, as one finds Hume, more a critic than an apologist, but whose criticism stems from his independence, not prejudice, as a historical thinker. Johnson's commentary on exploration and colonization in the political pieces moreover reveals his independence as a historian—a writer willing to cast aspersions at current policy and fashionable thought in order to set straight the historical record.[49]

As a parallel to the passage from the *History* quoted above, we might look to Johnson's review of William Tytler's *Historical and Critical Enquiry* (1760). "When an opinion has once become popular," Johnson writes, "very few are willing to oppose it. Idleness is more willing to credit than inquire; cowardice is afraid of controversy, and vanity of answer." As if nodding in Hume's direction, Johnson continues, "It has now been fashionable, for near half a century, to defame and vilify the house of Stuart, and to exalt and magnify the reign of Elizabeth. The Stuarts have found few apologists, for the dead cannot pay for praise; and who will, without reward, oppose the tide of popularity? yet there remains, still, among us, not wholly extinguished, a zeal for truth, a desire of establishing right, in opposition to fashion."[50] Like Hume, Johnson angrily denounces and clearly removes himself from the crowd of historians echoing party lines. Both men saw as the best kind of historian the one who stands alone, answering to neither political pressure nor the social mood.

In his letter to Clephane, Hume also regretted the lack of "care" in previous British historians. Here too Johnson was in strong agreement. Johnson thought that many historians relied too heavily on the larger, more popular accounts, and he accordingly criticized Francis Bacon, who in his writing of the *History of Henry VII* seemed not to have consulted any records but rather took "what he found in other histories, with what he learnt by tradition."[51] No doubt influenced by his early work on the Harleian collection and Harleian miscellany, Johnson saw the need of consulting manuscripts, records, memoirs, diaries, and other smaller sources to supplement and correct the larger histories: "many Advantages may be expected from the Perusal of these small Productions, which are scarcely to be found in that of larger Works."[52] As his *Journey to the Western Islands* informs us, Johnson, like Hume, rejected oral history as historical fact, and he placed more faith in those, like Clarendon, who first witnessed and then wrote about historical events—or in those, like Voltaire for his *History of Charles XII*, who interviewed and corresponded with the actual participants. At the very least he argued that all history, "so far as it is not supported by contemporary evidence, is romance."[53]

And like Hume, Johnson understood the complexity and contradictory nature of historical causation.[54] He did not believe that only one or two determining factors explained historical occurrences. Nor did he relegate causation to "providential" explanations ("God's will"). Rather he was cognizant of a number of forces at work—from the catastrophic event to the influence of dynamic personalities (the "great man" theory of causation). In addition, he thought, as did Hume in the *History*, that much was determined by "chance," by which he often meant the complex interaction among several causes, which blend so agreeably that their individual parts lose their identities and thus defy simplistic explanation. Johnson scorned those historians who believed that "every effect has a proportionate cause."[55] He appreciated with Hume those great moments in time—such as the execution of Charles I and the Revolution of 1688—when profound change was set in motion, but also like Hume he saw history as the result of slow and usually painful growth, affected by natural laws, human virtue and vice, and fortuitous circumstance. Arthur Murphy was quite accurate in his observation, then, that "no man better understood the nature of historical evidence than Dr. Johnson."[56]

Johnson and Hume—of like historical minds. Two of the best historical thinkers of their age. And yet Johnson has long suffered the onus of Thomas Babington Macaulay's pronouncement that he spoke of history "with the fierce and boisterous contempt of ignorance."[57] And as a major piece of evidence Macaulay presented Johnson's antipathy for Hume and refusal to read his history. It is impossible, I suppose, to avoid this matter, especially since Johnson's reaction to Hume seemingly runs counter to the thesis of this essay, so by way of conclusion we might again consider Johnson's estimation of Hume and attempt to reconcile it to the men's similar historical minds.

First of all, one must suppress the temptation, when looking back on literary history, to assume that one writer's personal dislike of another always encompasses the kind of work the other did. That is, Johnson could hate Hume and still love history. (And the same would apply to Johnson's apparently strained relationship with Gibbon.) Second, there is evidence that Johnson did in fact read Hume's *History*: Thomas Campbell, for example, related in 1775 that Johnson liked Hume "better" than Robertson.[58] I would argue that Johnson not only read the *History* but enjoyed it and appreciated many of its moral evaluations and surely, as we have seen, its estimations of the seventeenth-century monarchs and the English Civil War.

But why then did Johnson say in 1773 that he had not read the *History* if, as evidence suggests, he already had? And considering his and Hume's like historical minds, why did he not praise it? Hume told Boswell in 1776 that Johnson "should be pleased with my History"[59]—a remark that I believe reflects Hume's sense of Johnson's historical knowledge, interests, and sophistication more than any "Tory" political preferences. By this time, Hume had had the opportunity to read almost all of Johnson's canon, which amply testified to the Englishman's strong grasp of history. But Johnson did not appear pleased, and I attribute his seemingly negative or indifferent reaction to the *History* to both his habit of tormenting Boswell with his anti-Scots pose and his disdain for Hume's reputation and writings as a *religious* skeptic.

As readers of Boswell's *Life* should know, Johnson let few occasions slip by without making light of Scotland's intellectual elite: "You *have* Lord Kames. Keep him; ha, ha, ha! We don't envy you him."[60] Johnson's unfavorable evaluations of William Robertson have also been dragged forth as evidence of his antihistorical bias. But here again the criticism of Robertson's historical work was offered to Boswell, who this time was not fooled and pointed out that Johnson's view was most likely insincere.[61] Johnson thought far more highly of Robertson's character and historical efforts than the comments in the *Life* could ever suggest.[62] We therefore cannot ignore the possibility that Johnson's "antipathy" for Hume's *History* was, at least in part, more deception than reality.

There can be little doubt, however, that Johnson rejected Hume's religious skepticism and a philosophical position which argues, "So that, upon the whole, we may conclude, that the *Christian Religion* not only was at first attended with miracles, but even at this day cannot be believed by any reasonable person without one."[63] According to Ernest Mossner, Johnson's "hatred of Hume was grounded on fear—on the fear that Hume might conceivably be right, and if right, that immortality itself was unsure."[64] Although this assumption is compatible with the Johnson who emerges from Bate's acclaimed biography, I cannot agree with Mossner's conclusion. If "fear" is the operative word, then it was a fear of Hume's influence on others to think as he did. Hester Thrale once noted that Johnson was often apprehensive that a quotation from a controversial writer might "send People to look in an Author that might taint their Virtue."[65] Johnson respected Hume's intellect—and certainly his historical sense—but because Hume's brilliant mind was in the service of the "enemy" Johnson considered him dangerous and accordingly refused to endorse *anything* Hume wrote, for singing the praises of the *History of England*, Johnson believed, might be misconstrued as an approval of Hume's other, more controversial, work. Regardless of who is right, Mossner or I (Macaulay most certainly is wrong), it is a fascinating irony that Johnson refused to praise, publicly anyway, a man with whom he agreed on so many aspects of historical composition and thought—a man with whom he should share the distinction of having one of the most perceptive historical minds of the age.

NOTES

1 Comparison studies, some stressing similarities as well as differences, would include: William Agutter, *On the Difference between the Deaths of the Righteous and the Wicked, illustrated in the instance of Dr. Samuel Johnson and David Hume. A Sermon, preached* . . . *July 23, 1786* (London: Philanthropic Society, 1800); [William Howison], "Samuel Johnson and David Hume," *Blackwood's* 3 (August 1818): 511–13; Ernest C. Mossner, "Hume and Johnson" in *The Forgotten Hume* (New York: Columbia University Press, 1943), pp. 189–209; Edward Ruhe, "Hume and Johnson," *Notes & Queries*, n.s. 1 (1954): 477–78; Charles E. Noyes, "Samuel Johnson: Student of Hume," *University of Mississippi Studies in English* 3 (1962): 91–94; A. R. Winnett, "Johnson and Hume," *New Rambler* (June 1966): 2–14; Donald T. Siebert, Jr., "Johnson and Hume on Miracles," *Journal of the History of Ideas* 36 (1975): 543–47.
2 James Boswell, *The Life of Samuel Johnson, LL.D.*, ed. G. B. Hill, rev. L. F. Powell, 6 vols. (Oxford: Clarendon Press, 1934–64), 1: 444; 4: 194; James Boswell, *A Journal of a Tour to the Hebrides with Samuel Johnson, LL.D.*, ed. Frederick A. Pottle and Charles H. Bennett (New York: McGraw-Hill, 1961), pp. 17, 239. These works will be abbreviated *Life* and *Tour* in subsequent citations.
3 *Johnsonian Miscellanies*, ed. G. B. Hill, 2 vols. (Oxford: Clarendon Press, 1897; rpt. 1966), 1: 201–3. This work will be abbreviated *Misc* in subsequent citations. The quotation is from Thrale [Hester Lynch Piozzi], *Anecdotes of the Late Samuel Johnson, LL.D.* (1786).
4 See John A. Vance, *Samuel Johnson and the Sense of History* (Athens: University of Georgia Press, 1984).
5 David Hume, *The Letters of David Hume*, ed. J. Y. T. Greig, 2 vols. (Oxford: Clarendon Press, 1932), 1: 170–71.
6 Hume had apparently been collecting materials from as early as 1745. The six volumes of Hume's history, the collected edition titled *The History of England*, were published from 1754 to 1762.
7 Samuel Johnson, *Works of Samuel Johnson* (New Haven: Yale University Press, 1958–), vol. 4, *The Rambler*, ed. W. J. Bate and Albrecht B. Strauss (1969), pp. 288–89.
8 Peter Whalley, *Essay on the Manner of Writing History*, ed. Keith Stewart, Augustan Reprint Society Publication no. 80 (Los Angeles: William Andrews Clark Memorial Library, 1960).
9 See Vance, *Samuel Johnson and the Sense of History*, pp. 5–30.

10 Especially the *Introduction to the Political State of Great Britain* (1756).
11 See Thomas M. Curley, "Johnson's Secret Collaboration" in *The Unknown Samuel Johnson*, ed. John J. Burke, Jr. and Donald Kay (Madison: University of Wisconsin Press, 1983), pp. 91–112.
12 Nor should we forget the historical projects Johnson once contemplated, such as translations of De Thou's *Historia sui temporis*, Herodian's *History*, Benzo's *New History of the New World*, and Machiavelli's *History of Florence*; and his desire to write a history of the state of Venice, a body of chronology in verse with "historical notes," a dictionary of ancient history, a history of the British Constitution, and a history of the revival of learning in Europe (*Life*, 4: 381–82).
13 See the early chapters of Hume's *History of England* and his "Of the Populousness of Ancient Nations" and Johnson's preface to the Shakespeare edition (1765) and the sections of the Vinerian Law Lectures attributed to him by E. L. McAdam, Jr. in *Dr. Johnson and the English Law* (Syracuse: Syracuse University Press, 1951).
14 *Life*, 4: 217.
15 *Ibid*, 2: 236.
16 See Johnson's review of William Tytler's *Historical and Critical Enquiry* (1760) in *The Works of Samuel Johnson, LL.D.*, 16 vols. in 8 bound vols. (Cambridge: Harvard Cooperative Society, 1903), 13: 260–71; and Hume, *History of England*, 6 vols. (New York: Harper and Brothers, 1879), 4: 68, 69, 85. All subsequent quotations from Hume's *History* will come from this edition.
17 Hume, *History*, 4: 283; Johnson, *Introduction to the Political State of Great Britain* in *Works of Samuel Johnson* (New Haven: Yale University Press, 1958-), vol. 10, *Political Writings*, ed. Donald Greene (1977), p. 133.
18 Hume, *History*, 4: 478; 5: 59, 283, 417; Johnson, Sermon no. 23 in *Works of Samuel Johnson* (New Haven: Yale University Press, 1958–), vol. 14, *Sermons*, ed. Jean Hagstrum and James Gray (1978), pp. 246–47; *Political Writings*, p. 134.
19 Hume, *History*, 5: 330. Johnson wrote in the "Life of Milton" that Cromwell dismissed Parliament "by the authority of which he had destroyed monarchy." Cromwell, Johnson summarized, was "a tyrant, of whom it was evident that he could do nothing lawful." "Life of Milton" in *The Lives of the English Poets*, ed. G. B. Hill, 3 vols. (Oxford: Clarendon Press, 1905), 1: 115–16. See also Vance, *Samuel Johnson and the Sense of History*, pp. 58–60.
20 *History*, 5: 184, 296.
21 *Lives of the Poets*, 1: 214–15; Samuel Johnson, *The Letters of Samuel Johnson*, ed. R. W. Chapman, 3 vols. (Oxford: Clarendon Press, 1952), 3: 5.
22 Hume, *History*, 5: 505; Johnson, *Life of Thomas Browne* (1756) in *Works*, 15: 75.
23 Hume, *History*, 5: 505; Johnson, *Lives of the Poets*, 1: 13, 74, 205–6.
24 Hume, *History*, 6: 81, 88; Johnson, *Account of the Conduct of the Duchess of Marlborough* in *Works*, 13: 167; *Introduction to the Political State* in *Political Writings*, p. 139.

25 Hume, *History*, 6: 248–97; Johnson, *Introduction to the Political State* in *Political Writings*, p. 142.
26 Hume, *History*, 6: 283; Johnson, *Introduction to the Political State* and *The False Alarm* in *Political Writings*, pp. 142–43, 342; *Lives of the Poets*, 1: 233–34, 305, 384.
27 *Rambler* no. 122, 4: 289–90; *Letters*, 1: 8; *Works*, 13: 175; *Life*, 2: 213; *Letters*, 1: 409; 2: 83.
28 Printed in David Fate Norton and Richard H. Popkin, eds., *David Hume: Philosophical Historian* (New York: Bobbs-Merrill, 1965), p. 388.
29 James Moor, *An Essay on Historical Composition* (1759), ed. J. C. Hilson, Augustan Reprint Society Publication no. 187 (Los Angeles: William Andrews Clark Memorial Library, 1978), p. 127.
30 *Lives of the Poets*, 1: 170.
31 George Nadel, "Philosophy of History before Historicism," reprinted in Nadel, ed., *Studies in the Philosophy of History* (New York: Harper and Row, 1965), p. 73.
32 From sec. 8, "Of Liberty and Necessity," reprinted in Norton and Popkin, *David Hume: Philosophical Historian*, p. 52. Nineteenth- and twentieth-century theorists have of course found this passage to be antihistorical, but as John J. Burke, Jr., has cautioned us, Hume qualifies his assertions about the uniformity of human nature. See Burke, "Hume's *History of England*: Waking the English from a Dogmatic Slumber," *Studies in Eighteenth-Century Culture*, ed. Roseann Runte (Madison: University of Wisconsin Press, 1978), 7: 245–47.
33 *Rambler* no. 60, 3: 320; *Adventurer* no. 99 in *Works of Samuel Johnson* (New Haven: Yale University Press, 1958–), vol. 2, ed. W. J. Bate, J. M. Bullitt, and L. F. Powell (1963), p. 431.
34 Hume, "Of the Study of History" (1741) in Norton and Popkin, p. 38; *History*, 5: 298.
35 Norton and Popkin, pp. 37–38; Johnson, *Rasselas*, ed. Warren Fleischauer (Woodbury: Barron's Educational Series, 1962), pp. 117–18.
36 See, for example, *Introduction to the Political State of Great Britain*, the Introduction to *The World Displayed* (1759), *Thoughts on the Late Transactions Respecting Falkland's Islands*, *Taxation No Tyranny*, *Journey to the Western Islands of Scotland*, preface to the Shakespeare Edition, and the passages of the Vinerian Law Lectures attributed to him.
37 Preface to Du Fresnoy's *Chronological Tables* (1762) in Allen T. Hazen, *Samuel Johnson's Prefaces and Dedications* (New Haven: Yale University Press, 1937), p. 88.
38 Samuel Johnson, *Works of Samuel Johnson* (New Haven: Yale University Press, 1958–), vol. 9, *A Journey to the Western Islands of Scotland*, ed. Mary Lascelles (1971), pp. 46–52, 91–99, 134–35, 142; Boswell's *Tour*, pp. 190, 260–61. See as well *Taxation No Tyranny*, *Idlers* nos. 11, 22, 90, and *Adventurer* no. 131.
39 *History*, 5: 451.
40 *Tour*, p. 55; *Life*, 3: 333.
41 See Johnson's commentary in works cited in n. 38 and Hume's in bk. 3,

pt. 2, sec. 10, "Of the Objects of Allegiance," of the *Treatise* (Norton and Popkin, pp. 22–34).
42 Johnson, *Journey to the Western Islands*, p. 111; Hume, *History*, 1: 1–2.
43 Hume *Letters*, 1: 210; Johnson, Introductory Essay to the *Universal Chronicle* (1758) in Hazen, *Prefaces and Dedications*, p. 211.
44 *Misc*, 2: 218; *Idler* no. 20, p. 62.
45 Isaac Kramnick, *Lord Bolingbroke: Historical Writings* (Chicago: University of Chicago Press, 1972), p. xxx. See also Popkin's "Skepticism and the Study of History" and Norton's "History and Philosophy in Hume's Thought" in Norton and Popkin, pp. ix–l.
46 *Account of the Conduct of the Duchess of Marlborough* in *Works*, 13: 165.
47 *Treatise*, bk. 1, pt. 4, sec. 7.
48 *History*, 6: 333–35. See also Burke, "Hume's *History of England:* Waking the English from a Dogmatic Slumber."
49 See especially, *Introduction to the Political State of Great Britain*, *Observations on the Present State of Affairs*, *Thoughts on the Late Transactions Respecting Falkland's Islands*, and *Taxation No Tyranny*.
50 *Works*, 13: 260, 261.
51 *Tour*, p. 181.
52 *Introduction to the Harleian Miscellany* in Hazen, p. 55.
53 *Tour*, p. 392. See as well *Life*, 2: 237; 3: 404.
54 Hume's theories on causation reflect both the historian and the philosopher, as his *Treatise* and *Enquiry* reveal. See Tom L. Beauchamp and Alexander Rosenberg, *Hume and the Problem of Causation* (New York: Oxford University Press, 1981).
55 *Thoughts on the Late Transactions Respecting Falkland's Islands* in *Political Writings*, pp. 365–66.
56 *Misc*, 1: 479.
57 Macaulay's review of Croker's edition of Boswell's *Life of Johnson* in *Edinburgh Review* (September 1831), reprinted in James T. Boulton, ed., *Johnson: The Critical Heritage* (New York: Barnes and Noble, 1971), pp. 428–29.
58 *Misc*, 2: 48. Johnson's review of Tytler's *Historical and Critical Enquiry* suggests a knowledge of at least the first volume of Hume's *History*. G. B. Hill believes that Johnson might be borrowing from Hume's *History* in the "Life of Milton" (*Lives of the Poets*, 1: 127).
59 Charles McC. Weis and Frederick A. Pottle, eds., *Boswell in Extremes, 1776–1778* (New York: McGraw-Hill, 1970), p. 13.
60 *Life*, 2: 53.
61 *Life*, 2: 238.
62 See Vance, *Samuel Johnson and the Sense of History*, pp. 164–67.
63 *Enquiry*, sec. 10, "Of Miracles," in Norton and Popkin, p. 76.
64 Ernest Mossner, *The Forgotten Hume*, p. 207. This view is seconded by A. R. Winnet in "Johnson and Hume," p. 12.
65 Katharine C. Balderston, ed., *Thraliana: The Diary of Mrs. Hester Lynch Thrale*, 2 vols. (Oxford: Clarendon Press, 1942), 1: 191.

Images of the Orient:
Goldsmith and the Philosophes

SAMUEL H. WOODS, JR.

    Goldsmith's Oriental pieces, especially *The Citizen of the World* and also some shorter, journalistic pieces like "The Proceedings of Providence Vindicated" are among the very few eighteenth-century British Oriental works still actively read and studied by undergraduates, graduate students, and professors, with Samuel Johnson's *Rasselas* about their only rival. The great mass of other eighteenth-century British writings with Oriental settings lie mouldering unread, except when they attract the attention of the student of some specialized feature of eighteenth-century life and culture. In addition, Goldsmith is, I believe, the only major British writer of the period to use both Chinese and Persian material, although as is well known, he drew heavily on Montesquieu, Voltaire, and especially the Marquis d'Argens, as well as Louis Le Comte and J. B. Du Halde, as R. S. Crane, Arthur Lytton Sells, Hamilton J. Smith, Arthur Friedman, and others have clearly shown.[1] Thus, his writing, especially *The Citizen of the World*, served as a principal conduit for British readers to receive ideas from the French *Philosophes*, the older generation of deists like Montesquieu and Voltaire, but even more extensively from the younger generation of atheists, especially d'Argens, although most of these works were also quickly translated into English so that the general ideas of the *Philosophes* were directly available to the eighteenth-century British reader. Goldsmith's images of both China and Persia differ markedly from those found in Montesquieu, Voltaire, and d'Argens in that

Goldsmith presents China especially as a despotic, cruel tyranny, not a benevolent monarchy governed by a philosopher-god-king and administered by mandarin sages.

William W. Appleton and especially Basil Guy have carefully traced the way the *Philosophes* used the material compiled by the Jesuits Louis Le Comte and J. B. Du Halde to support an image of China where benevolent authority and morality prevailed with a minimum of dogmatic religion or even no religion at all.[2] Appleton notes that by the eighteenth century, "In the character of Confucius they [the English] had found an amalgam of the qualities of the good man of the eighteenth century: the detachment of the Spectator, the personal devoutness of William Law, and the compassion and understanding of Parson Adams."[3]

A close examination of Arthur Friedman's notes to his edition of *The Citizen of the World* shows that Goldsmith's three principal sources for specific Chinese material were Le Comte, Du Halde, and d'Argens. He used Louis Le Comte's *Nouveaux mémoires sur l'état présent de la Chine*, Paris, 1697; the 1724 English translation of Du Halde's *Description of China and Chinese-Tartary*, and the 1755 edition of d'Argens' *Lettres Chinoises, ou Correspondance philosophique, historique & critique, entre un chinois voyageur à Paris & ses correspondans a la China, en Muscovie, en Perse & au Japon*, first published at La Haye, 1739, 1740. Though Goldsmith used the 1755 edition of this last work, Friedman's citations are to the 1751 edition (2: x and 2: x, n. 3). George Sherburn describes the eighteenth-century prevailing European image of China:

> Long before d'Argens such writers as Le Comte and Du Halde had started a Chinese tradition that was invaluable to both d'Argens and Goldsmith. As this tradition developed, the Chinese were made into a race of philosophers, embodiments of simple reason and common sense; people who lived in a patriarchal society or under an absolute but perfectly benevolent emperor. They honored men of letters above conquerors and military heroes, and were in religion rationally devout, tolerant—and altogether void of bigotry and "superstition." In a word, the Chinese traveler embodied the pure light of reason, and his mind played effectively over the customs of England and of Christendom in an impartial and at times devastating fashion. To him nothing established had an absolute validity: in the Orient, as these essayists all loved to remark, polygamy was perfectly respectable; in Christendom the marriage customs were frequently shocking. All things were relative. The *philosophe* had quite emancipated himself from the ecclesiastical interpretation of the universe. The excellence of all customs was to be estimated according to human

Goldsmith and the Philosophes / 259

and common-sense standards. If Goldsmith's "Chinese Letters" are less brilliantly trenchant than the best of his French models, it is in part due to the fact that England was, by definition almost, the land of liberty, and the English, unlike the French, did not have "God and the King to pull down"—to borrow Walpole's phrase. Goldsmith is more playful, more relaxed, more superficial, more of the literary man, less of the revolutionary.[4]

Sherburn's account is an extremely cogent description of what Montesquieu, Voltaire, and d'Argens had done in criticizing French society, but his conclusion seems to imply somewhat faint praise for Goldsmith. Goldsmith may be "less trenchant than the best of his French models," but he far surpasses them in creating brilliant comedy throughout his series, especially through parody of the general European image of China and the Chinese and in suffusing his work with a cosmopolitanism that denies any glorification of oriental or English culture, that recognizes the particular differences between different cultures, and that finds human nature pretty much the same in all civilizations.[5]

As Sherburn implies, Goldsmith does not offer a programmatic critique of English society, especially of two of its fundamental institutions, the monarchy and the Church of England. Unlike the *Philosophes*, especially Voltaire and d'Argens, Goldsmith favored a strong monarchy, arguing that it needed more power against the Whig magnates who dominated Parliament.[6] Goldsmith's attacks on practices in the Church of England are limited to relatively venial abuses like the greed of the verger-guides in Westminster Abbey in Letter 13 or the gluttony the clergy show at a visitation dinner in Letter 58. The most frequent targets for Voltaire's and d'Argens' satire of the Roman Catholic Church are its censorship of the press and the abuses of the monastic system, neither of which existed in Goldsmith's England, censorship of the press having lapsed in the late seventeenth century and monastic institutions having disappeared during the Reformation.

D'Argens' use of Chinese material Guy describes as "a flimsy but convenient fiction to criticize French manners and customs," with the Chinese serving merely as thin disguises for d'Argens to vent his opinions: "The Chinese find virtue attractive and attempt to live according to it because a scant half century after Bayle, it is more and more publicly admitted that public morality is independent of theology."[7] Guy adds that "It seems that after 1740 Chinese atheism was considered an acknowledged fact," preferable to the Jesuits' claims that their Confucianism was just one step short of Christianity: "even as he protests that almost all Chinese are good deists, he cannot deny at least one mandarin was a professed atheist,"[8] and thinks it necessary to have another of his Chinese refute the atheist's arguments to avoid outraging his readers.

When we look at *The Citizen of the World* to see the extent to which it does express two of the principal ideas of the *Philosophes*, the attacks on absolute monarchy and on Christianity, either its theology or its institutions like monasticism, the clearest example of adverse criticism of European customs and praise of Chinese customs occurs in Letter 42, written not by Lien Chi Altangi, Goldsmith's philosophical traveler, but by Fum Hoam, his teacher-master, who has remained in Peking. He argues that even though European countries may be more advanced technologically, China's great empire is founded on the principle of filial obedience transferred to the emperors, "who in general consider themselves as the fathers of the people, a race of philosophers who bravely combated idolatry, prejudice, and tyranny, at the expense of their private happiness and immediate reputation" (2: 177). Friedman points out that most of the material praising China Goldsmith took from Du Halde, while d'Argens is the source for the section discussing European disorder (2: 177, n. 2; 2: 178, n. 3, n. 4). Even though this letter in isolation might seem to show Goldsmith presenting the main *Philosophe* criticisms of Europe and an idealized China, even the casual reader of the whole series will recall Letter 7, in which Fum Hoam writes Lien Chi that the emperor has had Lien Chi's entire family executed, except for his son Hing Po, whom Fum helped escape, for Lien Chi's breaking the rule against leaving China without imperial permission. Thus, Fum Hoam's *Philosophe* commonplaces have a very hollow ring to them, and this letter serves as a splendid and typical example of the way Goldsmith uses *Philosophe* commonplaces to attack, even though indirectly, China as tyranny-ridden and bigoted, not the ideal civilization, showing an almost total inversion of the general *Philosophe* position presented, especially by d'Argens. Goldsmith further informs his reader of the emperor's cruelty in Lien Chi's Letter 22 to the Amsterdam merchant and added details about his son's having made his way to Persia, where he has been enslaved.

Goldsmith's criticism of the *Philosophe* image of China appears very early in his writing career. As Robert H. Hopkins points out, his review of Arthur Murphy's *Orphan of China* in the May 1759 *Critical Review* attacks the taste for *chinoiserie* as an absurdity, a mere preference for novelty, and a "perversion of taste" (1: 170). He praises Voltaire, whose 1755 play Murphy had adapted, for "deviating from the calm insipidity of his Eastern original," adding that the Chinese literary "productions are the most phlegmatic that can be imagined . . . and therefore improper for literary imitation" (1: 171).[9] Though his series was popularly called the "Chinese letters" during its publication in the *Public Ledger*, the early letters stress both cosmopolitanism and the relativity of many notions in the realm of customs, fashion, and taste, not the inferiority of English culture to the *Philosophe* Chinese image. In Letter 3 Lien Chi accepts a relative standard of beauty,[10] an idea that Goldsmith had previously argued for vigorously in Chapter 7 of his *Enquiry into the Present State of Polite Learning in Europe*, 1759. The opening sentences of Letter 4 briefly contrast the English with non-Chinese Orientals like the Japanese and Siamese. In Letter 6, as just noted, Fum Hoam describes the Chinese emperor's brutal tyranny. Lien Chi's reply in Letter 7 shows Goldsmith ridiculing him as a philosopher-sage, since Goldsmith added this headnote to the letter: "The Editor thinks proper to acquaint the reader, that the greatest part of the following letter, seems to him to be little more than a rhapsody of sentences borrowed from Confucius, the Chinese philosopher" (2: 39). To the contemporary reader the word *rhapsody* was a clear signal that he was not to swallow whole whatever Lien Chi might have to say, since the *OED*, meaning 4, current in the 1760s, defines *rhapsody* as "an exalted or extravagantly enthusiastic expression of sentiment or feeling; an effusion (e.g., a speech, letter, poem) marked by extravagance of thought and expression, but without connected thought or sound argument." Lien Chi defends his original plan to achieve happiness through philosophy, concluding, "For my part, my greatest glory is, that travelling has not more steeled my constitution against all the vicissitudes of climate, and all the depressions of fatigue, than it has my mind against the accidents of fortune, or the accesses of despair" (2: 41).

In Letter 8, a prostitute deceives the naif Lien Chi with her fancy dress and steals his watch, leading to his comparison in Letter 9 between Chinese legal polygamy and English illegal, but nonetheless real, sexual promiscuity. The attack on faddish *chinoiserie* appears most specifically in Letter 14, in which a fashionable lady entertains Lien Chi, who comes dressed in European clothes to her disappointed astonishment. She wants him to eat with chopsticks and displays her collection of what she and her friends believe is extremely fine *chinoiserie*. Lien Chi finds nearly all her valuables being used for purposes different from their original functions in China, or like her pagods [idols] related to non-Confucian religion, or simply ugly—"sprawling dragons, squatting pagods, and clumsy mandarines" (2: 65)—and tolerantly leaves without trying to disabuse the lady of her misguided notions and grotesque collection.

Goldsmith's most important way of showing his readers that his image of China was not that of the *Philosophes* came when he collected the series his contemporaries had known as the "Chinese letters" and chose his new title, *The Citizen of the World*. This change significantly stresses not only Goldsmith's own cosmopolitanism, but Lien Chi's too. However, in the "Editor's Preface," Goldsmith carefully distinguishes his views from at least some of Lien Chi's:

> The distinctions of polite nations are few: but such as are peculiar to the Chinese, appear in every page of the following correspondence. The metaphors and allusions are all drawn from the East. Their formality our author carefully preserves. Many of their favourite tenets in morals are illustrated. The Chinese are always concise, so is he. Simple, so is he. The Chinese are grave and sententious, so is he. But in one particular, the resemblance is peculiarly striking: the Chinese are often dull; and so he is. Nor has my assistance been wanting. . . . Thus in the intimacy between my author and me, he has usually given me a lift of his Eastern sublimity, and I have sometimes given him a return of my colloquial ease (2: 14)

Thus, with the publication of the letters in book form, Goldsmith made clear how his image of the Orient differed from that of the *Philosophes* because of his cosmopolitanism, his genuine cultural relativism, and his belief in a human nature much the same in all cultures.

Letter 7 also offers a particularly good example of how Goldsmith uses his three major French sources. The second paragraph derives largely from Du Halde and Le Comte, though of course Du Halde's image of the Wheel of Fortune with its ups and downs is a commonplace one and is used by many other writers. The last sentence of the paragraph, "Our greatest glory is, not in never falling, but in rising every time we fall," (2: 39), Friedman identifies as "the twelfth maxim of Confucius given by Le Comte, 1: 350" (2: 39, n. 3). The long sentence concluding paragraph three, "let European travellers cross seas and deserts merely to measure the height of a mountain, to describe the cataracts of a river, or tell the commodities which every country may produce; merchants or geographers, perhaps, may find profit by such discoveries, but what advantage can accrue to a philosopher from such accounts, who is desirous of understanding the human heart, who seeks to know the *men* [Goldsmith's italics], who desires to discover those differences which result from climate, religious education, prejudice, and partiality," (2: 40) and the opening sentence of the next paragraph, pointing out particular contrasts between Chinese customs and English ones, such as ladies wearing longer clothes than men, Friedman identifies as a fairly close translation of a passage from d'Argens' *Lettres chinoises*, lettre 79 (2: 40, n. 1). The material from Du Halde and Le Comte, of course, expresses none of the usual *Philosophe* attacks, as indeed we should expect from two Jesuit writers. The material from d'Argens likewise presents relatively commonplace eighteenth-century ideas, but aside from the cultural relativism, none of d'Argens' frequent attacks on French society. Indeed, this translation is fairly typical of almost all of Goldsmith's use of material from the thirty-two d'Argens' *Lettres chinoises* that Friedman shows Goldsmith drew from, in whole or in part.[11] Generally, Goldsmith uses d'Argens in much the same fashion he did Le Comte and Du Halde, mostly for local-color details, though reversing d'Argens' views on monarchy, since Goldsmith supported the British limited, but strong monarchy as a balance to the Whig magnates of the time, and the letters on religion deal with matters other than d'Argens' favorite targets, since these characteristic features of d'Argens had no application to British society. It is true that Goldsmith does satirize the priest-ridden Daures in Letter 10, and one paragraph might seem to show d'Argens' views, though Friedman found no source for it in d'Argens: "In every country, my friend, the bonzes, the brachmans, and the priests deceive the people; all reformations begin with the laity; the priests point us out the way to heaven with their fingers, but stand still themselves, nor seem to travel towards the country in view" (2: 49). However, these views occur in Lien Chi's description of the barbaric regions he has traversed from Pekin to Moscow and apply in this context to the primitive kinds of religion he has found among these savages. In addition, Lien Chi's emphasis on the role of the laity in bringing about reformation perfectly fits the Church of England, with the corruptions of early Renaissance Roman Catholicism, especially the monastic system, purged by the Tudor monarchs and other laymen. These general remarks, then, are not to be taken as an indictment of the Church of England; if anything, they constitute an endorsement of it, a strong contrast to d'Argens' anticlericalism.[12] This letter confirms the analysis of Letter 7 concerning Goldsmith's use of d'Argens' *Lettres chinoises*, showing that what may seem to be anticlerical remarks in the spirit of d'Argens, even if not based on any specific passage, assume a different meaning in *The Citizen of the World*.

Letter 25, dealing with the rise and fall of the kingdom of Lao, north of China, presents a state in which conflict develops between two factions, the artisans and the soldiers. When the Tartars attack the kingdom, the soldiers defeat them, but from this victory "historians date their down fall," (2: 106) because Lao embarked on an expansionist colonial policy rather than trading with their neighbors as in the past. As a result, "the state resembled one of those bodies bloated with disease, whose bulk is only a symptom of their wretchedness" (2: 107).[13] None of the material in this letter derives from d'Argens, according to Friedman's notes, but instead it would seem to represent Goldsmith's own view of the dangers of the expansionist colonial policy Britain began by taking over the former French colonies in India and Canada as part of the spoils of her victory in the Seven Years' War with France.

Goldsmith's presentation of Persian materials occurs in the cluster of letters, 35–37, in which Hing Po traces his attraction to Zelis, his beautiful fellow-slave, which develops into love, though she is fated to marry their brutal owner. The Hing Po-Zelis romance serves chiefly to provide what Hopkins calls "narrative continuity"[14] in the *Citizen* and helps characterize Lien Chi as the typical apprehensive father in Letter 44, the delay occurring, because of the time required for an exchange of letters, urging his son not to be carried away at the prospect of immediate pleasure at hand. These letters from Hing Po do not give a comprehensive analysis of Persian society, just a picture of one household in it. Hing Po does, however, comment incidentally on Persia's tyranny: "A nation once famous for setting the world an example of freedom is now become a land of tyrants, and a den of slaves.... Thousands pine here in hopeless servitude, and curse the day that gave them being" (2: 152).

None of this material appears in d'Argens, and the narrative thread is, as most critics grant, Goldsmith's invention and his major device for providing a continuity in his series, rather than discussing random topics as most of the essay serials do, though Montesquieu's *Lettres persanes* do have a slight narrative element. Further, Goldsmith's Persians never appear as enlightened, satirical commentators on European civilization, if only because we never see them except on their home ground, where tyranny and slavery are the hallmarks of their society, all reported by Hing Po, a victim of their barbarity.

One might expect that Letter 43, occasioned by a false report of Voltaire's death, but kept in the work because of Goldsmith's admiration for Voltaire, might show anticlerical sentiments, and it does to some extent in one paragraph, describing famous men who have been persecuted for opposing their societies' received ideas, like Socrates and Galileo; but Galileo was persecuted by the Roman Catholic Church, a body as abhorrent to Anglicans like Goldsmith as it was to *Philosophes* like Voltaire. Locke is mentioned briefly as one who "escaped not without reproach," (2: 182) which Friedman believes may derive from *Lettres chinoises,* lettre 36. The qualities Lien Chi praises in his eulogy are Voltaire's genius, his courageous resistance to his persecutors, his condemnation by "the journalists and illiterate writers of the age" (2: 183), but praise from the writers of his own quality, praise of his "good nature, humanity, greatness of soul, fortitude, and almost every virtue," with "the royal Prussian [Frederick the Great], Dargens [sic], Diderot, Dalembert [sic] and Fontenelle" cited as his eulogists (2: 183). Lien Chi concludes: "Between Voltaire and the disciples of Confucius there are many differences; however, being of a different opinion does not in the least diminish my esteem, I am not displeased with my brother, because he happens to ask our father for favours in a different manner from me" (2: 184–85). The key point here is that Lien Chi, and Goldsmith, distinguish Voltaire from the Confucians: he represents virtue, but a different kind of virtue from that of the Confucians, though both exemplify the qualities of the good man in their different ways.

Thus, as these representative selections show, Goldsmith drew very heavily on the French *Philosophes* for material about China and even more heavily on the Jesuits Le Comte and Du Halde. But Goldsmith's image of the Orient is not the common one we find in the *Philosophes,* especially d'Argens, using. Indeed, Goldsmith's Orient is the opposite of d'Argens', who condemns absolute monarchy circumspectly, but praises the benevolent autocracy of China, while Goldsmith's condemns the Chinese emperor as cruel and tyrannical, arguing for the strong, but limited monarchy he hoped would emerge under George III, just then come to the throne. In religion, Goldsmith seldom uses Confucianism as the ideal against which Anglicanism is measured and found wanting. Goldsmith's letters criticizing the Church of England hit at relatively minor matters and never really touch Christian theology, which, by implication, he seems to support in *The Citizen of the World.*[15] This point alone makes his image of the Orient almost the polar opposite of the image of China constructed by the *Philosophes.* The repeated attacks, especially by d'Argens, on the corruptions of the monastic system never appear in *The Citizen of the World,* since England had eliminated such institutions at the Reformation. Goldsmith's image of the Orient does not serve as the standard against which he measures eighteenth-century Anglicanism to subject it and other English institutions to a searching, trenchant critique. The whole body of Goldsmith's ideas expressed here appears in the general body of his work: the state is best ruled by a strong, but limited monarchy as a balance against the great lords who dominate Parliament, and in religion, the Church of England as reformed under the Tudors represents an institution with few if any major problems needing drastic change.[16] As in all institutions, a gap exists between the ideal and the reality, but the problems were minor compared with those in Roman Catholicism. Thus, he drew on the *Philosophes* for particular details, but not for their image of an idealized Orient. Like Swift, Pope, and Johnson, Goldsmith defends the central institutions of his society, as they exist, even with their flaws. His comedy remains genial, concentrating on the follies and foibles of men, because, at bottom, he approved of the established, traditional, tried and true institutions of his society and remained deeply skeptical, unlike the French writers from who he drew so heavily, of radical social innovation, and was especially skeptical of the colonial expansion on which England had just embarked and of any radical shifts in the structure of the Church of England. Again, like Swift, Pope, and Johnson, Goldsmith remained a profound social conservative, mourning the loss of the older England even as Imperial Britain was emerging.

NOTES

1 See especially Ronald S. Crane and Hamilton J. Smith, "A French Influence on Goldsmith's *The Citizen of the World*," *Modern Philology* 19 (August 1921): 83–92; Ronald S. Crane and James H. Warner, "Goldsmith and Voltaire's *Essai sur les moeurs*," *Modern Language Notes* 38 (February 1923): 65–76; Arthur Lytton Sells, *Les Sources françaises de Goldsmith*, Bibliothèque de la Revue de la littérature comparée, no. 12 (Paris: Champion, 1926); Hamilton J. Smith, *Oliver Goldsmith's The Citizen of the World: A Study*, Yale Studies in English no. 71 (New Haven: Yale University Press, 1926); and Arthur Friedman's annotations in his edition of *The Citizen of the World* in *Collected Works of Oliver Goldsmith*, 5 vols. (Oxford: Clarendon Press, 1966), 2: passim; the particular articles in which Friedman and others published their identifications later incorporated in Friedman's edition of *The Citizen of the World* are indexed in Samuel H. Woods, Jr., *Goldsmith: A Reference Guide* (Boston: Hall, 1982).

Nearly all these scholars show Goldsmith's use of material from various *Philosophes*, especially d'Argens, but except for Crane and Smith's 1921 article, few of the scholars have concerned themselves with how Goldsmith used these sources. Smith's 1926 study especially must be used with great caution since it contains many errors.

Goldsmith used the 1755 edition of d'Argens' *Lettres chinoises*, though English translations were in print under the titles *The Chinese Letters*, 1741, and *The Chinese Spy*, 1752. See Phillip Harth, "Goldsmith and the Marquis d'Argens," *Notes and Queries* 198 (1953): 529–30.

All quotations from Goldsmith's works are from Friedman's 1966 edition of *Collected Works of Oliver Goldsmith* and appear parenthetically, citing only volume and page number. Works of Goldsmith other than *The Citizen of the World* are named either in the body of the paper or in the notes.

2 See especially William W. Appleton, *A Cycle of Cathay: The Chinese Vogue in England during the Seventeenth and Eighteenth Centuries* (New York: 1951), and Basil Guy, *The French Image of China before and after Voltaire,* Studies on Voltaire and the Eighteenth Century, vol. 21 (Genève: Institut et Musée Voltaire, 1963). One study of d'Argens in English exists: Newell R. Bush, *The Marquis d'Argens and his Philosophical Correspondence: A Critical Study of d'Argens' Lettres juives, Lettres cabalistiques, and Lettres chinoises* (Ann Arbor, Mich.: Edwards Brothers, 1953). Bush treats these series analytically: d'Argens' attack on the Church, Deism and Natural Ethics, Physics and Metaphysics, and Cosmopolitanism. I have used for the full text of the *Lettres chinoises* the 1751 edition, as did Friedman, and Bush's study. Bush himself remarks: "The Marquis d'Argens has generally been known best for the somewhat dubious distinction of having been a prominent figure among the satellites of Frederick II of Prussia, for whom he served as chamberlain and literary factotum for a period of over twenty-five years" (p. 2). D'Argens did not acquire his Prussian appointment until 1742, well after the publication of the *Lettres chinoises* in 1739–40 and his other essay series, the *Lettres juives* and the *Lettres cabalistiques.* D'Argens has been known to Goldsmith scholars as a possible source at least since J. W. M. Gibbs' edition of Goldsmith's *Collected Works* in Bohn's Standard Library, 1884, and, as n. 1 indicates, the object of careful scholarly study since 1921.

3 Appleton, p. 124.

4 George Sherburn, "The Restoration and Eighteenth Century" in *A Literary History of England,* ed. Albert C. Baugh (New York: Appleton-Century-Crofts, 1948), p. 1059. Appleton, pp. 138–39, presents a similar view: "Goldsmith did use these works [Le Comte, Du Halde, and d'Argens], but for their materials alone. Their air of panegyric is gone. Had his examination of English society been more slashing, more doctrinaire, he might have, for purposes of contrast, measured English beliefs and manners against those of an older civilization. But Goldsmith was content with a less trechant analysis pursuing absurdities and follies as his predecessors Addison and Steele had done. Though he at first tried with some success to pose as a genuine philosophical traveler, the role did not become him."

5 Robert H. Hopkins, *The True Genius of Oliver Goldsmith* (Baltimore: The

Johns Hopkins Press, 1969), pp. 100–101, points out that Sherburn's "judgment tends to blur the sharp differences between the ideologies of the French and English satirists by trying to find similarities." Hopkins' point is sound, although as I have noted in my text, I believe Goldsmith uses mainly comedy, not satire.

For one view of the complex problems of Goldsmith's intentions in *The Citizen of the World*, see Wayne Booth, "The Self-Portraiture of Genius: *The Citizen of the World* and Critical Method," *Modern Philology* 73 (May 1976, part 2: A Supplement to Honor Arthur Friedman): S85–S96.

6 See Goldsmith, *The Traveller*, 1764, 11. 381–92:

> But when contending chiefs blockade the throne,
> Contracting regal power to stretch their own,
> When I behold a factious band agree
> To call it freedom, when themselves are free;
> Each wanton judge new penal statutes draw,
> Laws grind the poor, and rich men rule the law;
> The wealth of climes, where savage nations roam,
> Pillag'd from slaves, to purchase slaves at home;
> Fear, pity, justice, indignation start,
> Tear off reserve, and bare my swelling heart;
> 'Till half a patriot, half a coward grown,
> I fly from petty tyrants to the throne.
>
> (4: 265–66)

7 Guy, p. 150.
8 Ibid., p. 152. See also Bush, pp. 32–114.
9 Hopkins, *True Genius*, pp. 98–99. Most of the specific points quoted here appear in Hopkins.
10 Friedman, 2: 22, n. 1, points out that two paragraphs of Goldsmith's letter are very similar to a passage in d'Argens' *Lettres chinoises*, lettre 53, in which Sioeu-Tcheou writes from Paris to Yn-Che-Chan in Pekin, describing his realization that Chinese and French standards of female beauty are only relative. However, Sioeu-Tcheou's other comments in the letter, which Friedman does not quote, chiefly satirize Frenchwomen's reliance on cosmetics and wigs, while most of Goldsmith's letter describes different details in English and Chinese ideas of female beauty. Thus Lien Chi's letter raises the more general idea of the cultural relativity of notions of beauty. D'Argens letter centers on far more limited satire of Frenchwomen's efforts to improve on nature.
11 Letters in *The Citizen of the World* drawing material from d'Argens' *Lettres chinoises* are Nos. 1, 3, 4, 5, 6, 7, 9, 10, 12, 13, 15, 16, 19, 20, 33, 35, 37, 39, 41, 42, 43, 51, 56, 58, 64, 74, 81, 89, 111, 118, according to Friedman. Goldsmith also used d'Argens' *Lettres juives*, though of course not for Oriental material. See Friedman's notes.

12 Bush, p. 94, notes that d'Argens in his *Lettres cabalistiques*, 1737, had endorsed the Anglican rejection of clerical celibacy, but no evidence exists that Goldsmith used or knew this publication by d'Argens. It does not appear in the list of books he owned at the time of his death. See James Prior, *The Life of Oliver Goldsmith, M.B.* (London: John Murray, 1837), 2: 577–84.

13 Goldsmith uses virtually the same image for politically diseased states in *The Deserted Village*, 1770, 11. 389–94:

> Kingdoms by thee [luxury], to sickly greatness grown
> Boast of a florid vigour not their own.
> At every draught more large and large they grow,
> A bloated mass of rank unwieldy woe;
> Till sapped their strength, and every part unsound,
> Down, down they sink, and spread a ruin around
> (4: 302).

14 Hopkins, *True Genius*, p. 102.

15 What Goldsmith's personal religious views were remains quite uncertain. Boswell was shocked by what he thought was Goldsmith's indifference (see James Boswell, *The Life of Samuel Johnson, LL.D.*, ed. George Birkbeck Hill, revised and enlarged by L. F. Powell (Oxford: Clarendon Press, 1934–64), 2: 214–15), but Goldsmith's character of the village parson in *The Deserted Village* is full of praise, and of course Goldsmith himself was the son and brother of priests of the Church of Ireland. Ricardo Quintana, *Oliver Goldsmith, A Georgian Study* (London: Macmillan, 1967) finds only one direct statement by Goldsmith of his religious views, in his March 1760 review of the Works of the Rev. Mr. W. Hawkins, published in the *Critical Review*, which Friedman considers a probable, but not completely certain ascription. Concerning the immortality of the soul Goldsmith writes, "we are obliged to revelation alone for any evidence in this matter" (1: 226). In "A Resverie," *Bee* no. 5, 3 November 1759, the coachman of the Fame Machine at first dismisses "a gentleman" generally identified as Hume for offering "rhapsodies against the religion of my country" as his ticket for the ride to the Temple of Fame. "Right or wrong (said the coachman) he who disturbs religion, is a blockhead, and he shall never travel in a coach of mine," (1: 448) though he accepts the first volume of Hume's *History of Great Britain* as an acceptable substitute. The coachman may very well represent Goldsmith's personal opinion, since Friedman's note on his speech refers to Goldsmith's statement in the *Enquiry:* "A man, who with all the impotence of wit, and all the eager desires of infidelity, writes against the religion of his country, may raise doubts, but will never give conviction; all he can do is to render society less happy than he found it" (1: 303). A very wide variety of opinion exists among recent scholars about Goldsmith's portrayal of the Rev. Dr. Charles Primrose, the protagonist-narrator of *The Vicar of Wakefield*.

16 Goldsmith wrote three separate essays in which he criticized the lack of

emotional appeal in contemporary Anglican preaching: "Of Eloquence," *Bee* no. 7, 17 November 1759 (1: 475–83); "A Sublime Passage in a French Sermon," *Weekly Magazine* no. 3, 12 January 1760 (3: 49–51); and "Some Remarks on the Modern Manner of Preaching," *Lady's Magazine*, December 1760 (3: 150–55), reprinted in *Essays*, 1765 as Essay no. 17. During his whole writing career, 1759–74, Britain was, of course, undergoing enormous social and demographic changes which actively engaged his interest, as *The Deserted Village* also shows. All three of his essays on Anglican preaching praise the Methodist preachers for their ability to involve their audiences emotionally, though he shows little sympathy for the content of what they were preaching.

Is God Really Omniscient? or What Does God Know about Pain?

GEORGE B. WALL

Der gute Bishop Berkeley, as Immanuel Kant was wont to refer to the eighteenth-century philosopher George Berkeley, developed one of the most novel, astonishing forms of theistic philosophy ever to hit Western man, a form of philosophy which, if it had ever taken root, would at the very least have had the salutary effect of providing strong job security for Berkeley, as well as all other bishops and clergymen. That is, the position of bishop would be extremely tenuous in a world rampant with atheism. However, if Berkeley is right, atheism is simply impossible, for according to Berkeley the world consists entirely of spirits and their ideas—no material objects whatsoever—including Infinite Spirit (God) and his ideas.

Of the many astonishing views of Berkeley none is more astonishing—at least at first glance—than his view of God's knowledge of pain, a view expressed in the following exchange between Hylas and Philonous, the two characters in Berkeley's *Three Dialogues*.

> Hyl. But you have asserted that whatever ideas we perceive from without are in the mind [God] which affects us. The ideas, therefore, of pain and uneasiness are in God; or, in other words, God suffers pain: that is to say, there is an imperfection in the Divine nature: which, you acknowledged, was absurd. So you are caught in a plain contradiction.
> Phil. That God knows or understands all things, that He knows, among other things, what pain is, even every sort of painful

sensation, and what it is for his creatures to suffer pain, I make no question. But, that God, though He knows and sometimes causes painful sensations in us, can Himself suffer pain, I positively deny. . . . God, whom no external being can affect, who perceives nothing by sense as we do; whose will is absolute and independent, causing all things . . . it is evident, such a Being as this can suffer nothing, nor be affected with any painful sensation, or indeed any sensation at all. We are chained to a body: that is to say, our perceptions are connected with corporeal motions. . . . This connexion of sensations with corporeal motions means no more than a correspondence in the order of nature, between two sets of ideas, or things immediately perceivable. But God is a Pure Spirit, disengaged from all such sympathy, or natural ties. No corporeal motions are attended with the sensations of pain or pleasure in His mind. To know everything knowable, is certainly a perfection; but to endure, or suffer, or feel anything by sense, is an imperfection. The former, I say, agrees to God, but not the latter.[1]

Thus, Berkeley maintains that although God knows painful sensations, he never *suffers* them, for to suffer painful sensations, indeed, to suffer sensations of any sort—sight, sound, smell, taste, touch— is to be affected by something external. More exactly, to suffer sensations is to have sensations which are connected with the body, "with corporeal motions," as Berkeley quaintly puts it. (Corporeal motions are, as Berkeley reminds us, nothing but a certain order of ideas.) Obviously, since God does not have a body, "no corporeal motions are attended with the *sensations of pain and pleasure in his mind*" [italics mine].

Now a problem of interpretation arises here. Does Berkeley really mean to say that God *has* sensations of pain and pleasure? Does he mean to deny only that God *suffers* the sensations? That seems to be all Berkeley denies in the passage cited. (We may observe in passing that if corporeal motions are not connected with God's sensation of pain, then God's sensation of pain would apparently not be like our sensations of physical pain—pain in the neck, in the big toe, in the side, in a tooth, and so on.) Yet surely Berkeley should deny more. Since pain is something negative, something to be avoided, something to be eliminated as much as possible from life, experiencing pain has to be an imperfection. Experiencing pain would especially be an imperfection in the case of God, a being without a body and thus a being in which pain would not, in contrast to the case of humans, have any function. As a consequence, Hylas' objection should be stated as: "The ideas, therefore, of pain and uneasiness are in God, or, in other words, God experiences pain; that is to say, there is an imperfection in the Divine nature." Whatever Berkeley intended for Hylas to say, the objection just raised is definitely one which Berkeley should have considered.

We may say, then, that if Berkeley grants that experiencing pain is an imperfection, all he may ever hold is that God has an idea of pain, not the sensation of pain. Moreover, Berkeley would have to say that God knows pain by way of the idea of pain, not by way of having pain. The same would go for the sensations of sight, sound, smell, taste, and touch, for, as we have seen, Berkeley puts these sensations in the same bag as pain and pleasure.

Two questions immediately arise. (1) How could God have an idea of pain apart from the sensation of pain? (2) Even if God could have the idea of pain apart from the sensation of pain, would he know pain? Berkeley does not explicitly discuss the first question. For a discussion and answer to the question we have to go to David Hume. Hume's answer is found in the following principle: *"All our simple ideas in their appearance are deriv'd from simple impressions* [sensations], *which are correspondent to them, and which they exactly represent."*[2] Of course, Hume makes his famous exception to this principle, maintaining that one might very well imagine some shade of color he has not seen. For example, a person presented with a color scale having all the shades of blue except one might imagine the missing shade of blue. However, Hume does not make much of this exception, believing that it does not require an abandonment of the general principle.[3]

The question is whether Hume's principle need apply to God. Would Berkeley have to accept the principle in the case of God? Could not Berkeley hold that ideas do not arise in God but are eternally present? Thus, God would eternally have the idea of pain, as well as the ideas of all the other sensations. Even so, would the ideas be sufficient to let God know pain, as well as the other sensations?

First of all, we need to be clear about the sorts of knowledge Berkeley is claiming for God. Two sorts of knowledge are claimed. (1) God knows *that* his creatures are in pain, including *that* they are having pain of a certain sort. (2) God knows *what* pain is like. Knowledge of the first sort is knowledge which practically anyone would claim at one time or another. For example, while standing as an official at a broadjump pit, I see a broadjumper twist his ankle as he hits the board, and now he lies writhing and groaning in the sand pit. I would have little hesitation in saying: "I know that the jumper is in pain, that his ankle is killing him." Since I would say this, I must reject the view which raises knowledge to a kind of absolute or ideal level, namely, the view that only the person having a pain really knows whether or not he is having it. In this view of knowledge God could never know that we are in pain and would, as a consequence, not be omniscient. We should observe that few people hold to such an absolute or ideal form of knowledge. Berkeley certainly did not, although he might have held to a modification of it, namely, that only the person having pain, *along with God,* knows that he is having it. We shall not try to determine what Berkeley's actual view was.

Supposing, then, that we may rightly claim knowledge of another's pain, we surely should be willing to grant the same favor to God. Moreover, we should be willing to grant the favor to God, without granting that God ever has pain or without reducing pain to behavior. We could maintain that God infers pain both from pain behavior and human reports of pain, including the reports that pain is not identical with behavior. To be sure, if pain were identical with certain neural events (a position Berkeley decidedly does not take), God would be in an ideal position, for God could easily read off the neural events occurring in his creatures. Or so all the above seems—until we remember that for Berkeley the physical world is nothing but an order of ideas (sensations), ideas (sensations) which are in the same bag as pain, raising the same questions with respect to God's knowledge, namely, how can God, apart from any experience of sensations, know what they are like, and how can God, if he does not know what sensations are like, know that we are having them? In addition, we must remember that for Berkeley the sensations constituting the corporeal order of nature are caused in us by God. The question above all questions, then, is how God could, without ever having had a sensation and hence, presumably, without knowing what sensations are like, cause the "corporeal" sensations in us, as well as the sensations of pain and pleasure.

Thus, our discussion of whether God knows *that* his creatures are in pain has led us to the question of whether God knows *what* pain is, whether God's eternal idea of pain—assuming he has such an idea—is sufficient to let God know what pain is like. Yet how could the idea be sufficient? Clearly, an idea of pain is a pale imitation of an actual sensation of pain. We may, for example, recall our experience in the dentist's chair, saying: "When he hit my nerve, I jumped two miles out of the chair. I mean, I can just feel it now." Only we would take a thousand I-can-feel-it-now's instead of the actual experience of having the nerve hit. In short, the person who has an idea of pain does not experience any pain.

The reply is that nobody, certainly not Berkeley, ever claimed that an idea of something is equivalent to the experience of that something. All that Berkeley need claim is that an idea of pain conveys sufficient information concerning pain for God to know what pain is like. What is wrong with this claim? Is it logically impossible, the denial of a necessary truth?

On its face the claim does not look logically impossible. However, it does run counter to some of our most deeply held beliefs about sensations, ideas, and knowledge. If a person were to question us about pain, ask us how we really knew what pain was like, our response would likely be either "What makes you ask a question like that? Do you think I've never had pain?" or "Listen, friend, you don't think I've had pain? Let me tell you about the time I had a kidney stone." Normally, people do not raise questions about how we know what pain is like; however, they often do raise questions about whether we appreciate some particular level or form of pain. Thus, someone might say: "You just don't know what I'm going through. You've never had pain like this." Our likely reply would be: "No, maybe I've never had pain in my back as you say you do; but I'll tell you, I've had pain that would knock over a horse." Our answer here, as in the first case, reveals that we take our knowledge of pain to rest on experience—no experience of pain, no knowledge of pain. Whatever ideas a person may have of or about pain, they are simply insufficient as long as they do not hark back to the actual experience of pain. We are saying, then, that even the imagination of pain ultimately refers back to the actual experiences we have had. For example, when I imagine the pain of a pulled hamstring, I am, in effect, simply projecting from the pain I have experienced of having a pulled hamstring. In a word, an idea of pain not backed by the experience of pain, an idea not referring back to the actual experience of pain, is simply an empty idea, empty of the actual qualities of pain and thus inadequate to bring us knowledge of what pain is really like. Hume's principle holds!

Obviously, if sensory ideas cannot convey knowledge of sensations as long as sensations have not been had, God cannot know what pain is like. The result is big trouble for Berkeley. First of all, he would have to give up on God's omniscience, for God would not know some knowable things. Of course, Berkeley could always just bite the bullet and say that God experiences pain, or at least forms of pain or uneasiness. To say this would really not be to step outside the Biblical tradition, especially the tradition of the Hebrew Scriptures, where God is represented, for example, as being grieved at the spiritual harlotry of his people. Whether being grieved, psychologically pained, would be sufficient to let God project the full gamut of physical pain is a question of considerable significance; however, Hume's exception to his principle certainly leaves us an opening.

The second problem, the main one, a problem already mentioned, concerns Berkeley's account of the physical world. Obviously, if God does not know what pain is—or any other sensation—he cannot cause sensations in us. Yet since the whole order of the world depends on God's causing sensations in us (including the sensations of pain in connection with the sensations of the physical), the whole order of the world comes crashing down—a result not especially shattering to the orthodox faithful, both philosophers and lay persons, who have never taken with alacrity to Berkeley's system.

To be sure, Berkeley could say that the world began with considerable experimentation on God's part; that is, God did not know how to cause particular sensations but discovered how through a process of trial and error, a process which included conversing with early man in order to discover what man was experiencing. Perhaps this view is absurd; then again, perhaps it is not. At any rate, it is not Berkeley's view and would, once more, entail limitations on God's omniscience.

The least troublesome course for Berkeley would simply be to stick with the thesis that God's eternal ideas of sensations are sufficient for God to know what the sensations are like. This thesis would seem especially plausible in the case of the sensations of sight and sound. An idea of color may be an image of color—that is, I can imagine various colors or picture in my mind various colors I have seen; likewise, I can "hear" in my mind a particular section of music, say, a passage from Mozart's *Jupiter Symphony*. Although my ideas here, my "imagings," are not equivalent to the sensations they represent, we would surely say that they represent the sensations as they are, conveying, as a result, sufficient information for knowing what the sensations are like. Why not say the same for all the other ideas of sensations, including the ideas of pain? May not the idea of a pain, say, the idea of having the nerve in a tooth hit, be as much an "imaging" of pain as an idea of color or sound is an "imaging"? Further, why not say that God, without having any sensations, has all the ideas of sensations from eternity, ideas which are in part, anyway, similar to our "imagings"? Unquestionably, saying all this would run counter to our deeply held beliefs about the necessity of having sensations in order to know what they are really like; that is, we are left with the mystery of how God's ideas can be so sufficient without experience when ours are so insufficient without experience. Yet neither saying that the ideas are sufficient without experience nor saying that God has the ideas from all eternity seems logically impossible. Berkeley certainly did not think so. Undoubtedly, saying either thing would astonish most people, but Berkeley seemed to be immune to the astonishment of the public over what he said. Moreover, der gute Bishop could easily contend that the mystery concerning the eternal ideas of God is really no greater than the mystery of such a simple matter as how sensations give rise to ideas in us—in short, the mystery inherent in Hume's principle. We give little thought to the latter mystery only because we are used to it, having given it, as did Hume, the status of a principle.

NOTES

1 George Berkeley, *Three Dialogues between Hylas and Philonous*, in *Berkeley's Philosophical Writings*, David M. Armstrong, ed. (New York: Collier Books, 1965), pp. 202–3.
2 David Hume, *A Treatise of Human Nature*, ed. L. A. Selby-Bigge, (Oxford: Clarendon Press, 1949), p. 4.
3 Ibid., p. 6.

Learning, Virtue, and the Term "Bluestocking"

SYLVIA H. MYERS

Mid-eighteenth-century Englishwomen were uncomfortable about being known as learned ladies. This discomfort reflected their awareness of the taboo against learning for women which had been imposed intermittently since classical times. The attitude of Jemima, Marchioness Grey, a friend of the "bluestocking" Catherine Talbot, is a case in point. In the winter of 1744–1745 Jemima was eating a solitary dinner in her London house when the Bishop of Oxford, Thomas Secker, called on her. Secker was Catherine's "foster father," and had been a mentor of both young women. He offered to send Jemima a new translation of Horace. The book, in four thick octavos bound in blue paper, came while she was making tea next morning for "Fine Gem'men." (She used these words herself in describing the incident to Catherine.) Naturally, the books were first presented to her husband, Philip Yorke, eldest son of Lord Chancellor Hardwicke, but he disowned them and referred them to Jemima, who had to confess that the Bishop had said he would send them. She was rather alarmed at this accident:

> An English Translation is always one should think Unexcceptionable [sic],—but then it had Latin of One Side, & *which* I read you know may be doubtful: besides an Old Latin Poet in any Dress I fear by no means belongs to a Fine London Lady.[1]

Then Mr. Wray, another gentleman at the breakfast, talked about "Electrical Experiments" and setting a day for Jemima to observe them.

She swallowed her tea and escaped, hoping she did not leave behind her "the Character of *Precieuse, Femme Scavante,* Linguist, Poetess, Mathematician, & any other name that any Art can be distinguished by."[2]

Jemima did not use the term "bluestocking" because its meaning in the sense of a woman with intellectual interests had not yet been invented. The term dates from the late 1750s. Elizabeth Montagu and her friends—later called the bluestocking circle—first used the term to refer to a particular man with intellectual interests, Benjamin Stillingfleet. Then they used the term both for men with intellectual interests and for the idea that women needed intellectual interests. Gradually over a twenty-year period they began to use the term for both the men and women of their circle. It was critics of the female bluestockings who limited the term to women. This shift in gender indicates contemporary awareness that the "bluestockings" had in fact broken the taboo against learning for women.

Of course, the taboo against learning for women had never been enforced equally in all times and all places. At times, in various parts of the Continent and England, individual women had dedicated themselves to learning and persisted in their own paths. During Queen Elizabeth's reign it had become accepted, even praiseworthy, for some aristocratic women to know both classical and modern languages. But in the course of the seventeenth century in England learning for women had again fallen into disrepute; at the close of the century scholars like Bathsua Makin and Mary Astell were again trying to convince the public that it was both useful and respectable for a woman to be educated.[3] Although, as we have seen, certain mentors might encourage women to read the classics, learn French, study history, women themselves hesitated to have their learning publicly known.

This reluctance was surely a response to the kinds of arguments that were so often offered against learning for women. A single woman with intellectual interests might be considered a prime target for a medical case of hysteria. A learned lady might be, as was Narcissa's aunt in Smollett's *Roderick Random,* unkempt, unclean, out of touch with reality.[4] More significantly, perhaps, learning might encourage sexual laxity. An example of this sort of argument are the admonitions given by Alessandro Tassoni, an Italian poet of the seventeenth century. His harsh view of learned women was quoted in an article on Guarini, the author of *Pastor Fido,* in Bayle's *General Dictionary* as late as 1737:

> there is no doubt, but that study is an occasion of exciting lust, and of giving rise to many obscene actions; because together with the

reading of amorous adventures and stratagems in loose books, and especially in the solitude and leisure which study requires; obscene images present themselves, with unchaste thought and desires, under the appearance of pleasure and delight, to which the inquisitive mind abandons itself. Hence as I suppose, it is, that we find, in Euripides and Juvenal, that the learned women of antiquity were accused of immodesty, who, by perusing loose books, and conversing, upon the specious pretence of learning, more freely with men than was proper for the weakness of their sex, grew bold; so that their lust became inflamed by Idleness, and the utmost sagacity of their wit was employed to apologize for their libidinous conduct.[5]

A similar suspicion that learned women are lewd crops up in Aubrey's *Brief Lives*, where the author describes the learned atmosphere of Wilton House and adds slanderous remarks about the supposedly immoral conduct of Mary Sidney Herbert, Countess of Pembroke.[6]

If one wished to promote learning for women, how would it be possible to counter the deep-seated anxiety which probably gave rise to the taboo? As Makin and Astell well knew, it would be necessary to offer an opposing viewpoint which reassured both men and women of the irreproachable conduct of learned women. In order to pursue a life of the mind, and begin to deal with men on something more like an equal footing, it would be necessary for women to be of impeccable reputation, countering suspicions that such women might be immodest and unchaste. The women who came to be called "bluestockings" provided the needed model.

In the 1740s and 1750s some writers were encouraging women to break the double standard that had prevented them from developing sustained intellectual interests. Richardson's novels, Johnson's *Rambler* essays, the poems of Thomas Seward and John Duncombe all contributed to a changing atmosphere. Thus the "bluestockings" actually asserted a right which was being recommended to women at that time—the "female right to literature," and on the terms on which this right was being offered—that women might be learned if they were virtuous. Fulfilling these terms, the bluestockings established their access to a life of the mind, and to friendships between men and women.

The term "bluestocking" first appears in Elizabeth Montagu's correspondence in 1756. The use of the term began with a joke about Benjamin Stillingfleet, scholar and botanist, a well-educated but eccentric gentleman (he was the grandson of a bishop) who lacked preferment. He seems to have worn blue worsted stockings to gatherings where white hose might have been expected. "An elegant leg in a white silk stocking was an important part of fashionable appearance."[7] White silk hose was the mark of the gentry, or of a successful London tradesman; blue knitted wool hose was the dress of the working man.[8] Blue was the dye which was least expensive to produce, and was used for the uniform of such charity schools as the Bluecoat School.[9]

There was a certain amount of teasing about Stillingfleet's blue stockings among Mrs. Montagu's friends of the late 1750s. Samuel Torriano wrote to Mrs. Montagu (November 13, [1756]):

> pray Madam be so good as to tell Stillingfleet I neither can nor will answer his questions till he returns to Clarges Street. Monsey swears he will make out some story of you & him [i.e., Stillingfleet], before you are much older. You shall not Keep Blew stockings at Sandleford for nothing.—[10]

The tone of this letter suggests the jocularity of a spa friendship; Torriano seems to imply that Dr. Messenger Monsey, an eccentric physician who wished to ingratiate himself with Mrs. Montagu, was jealous of Stillingfleet, who was then visiting at Sandleford, Mrs. Montagu's country home. In March 1757, Mrs. Montagu wrote to Dr. Monsey that Stillingfleet "is so much a man of pleasure, he has left off his old friends and his blue stockings, and is at operas and other gay assemblies every night."[11]

But if Stillingfleet had even temporarily abandoned his blue stockings, the term itself remained alive, and was used in the letters of Mrs. Montagu and her friends during the 1760s in two different ways. Most frequently it was applied to men with intellectual interests whose friendships were valued by the women as helping to sustain a life of the mind. Writing to George, Lord Lyttelton on November 22, 1763, from Newcastle-upon-Tyne, where she had gone with her husband to oversee his extensive holdings in estates and coal mines, Mrs. Montagu contrasts her visitors in Newcastle and London:

> I have not stirr'd out of my room for some days, & the fireside, which if in London would be incircled with beaux esprits & blue stocking philosophers, is now filled by stewards & people who are in the business of the Mines. Virgil, Milton, & Fingal are forgotten, of the sublime & beautifull I have at present no taste. (MO 1428)

Elizabeth Vesey (called by her friends The Sylph), one of Mrs. Montagu's favorite companions when both were in London during the season, enjoyed the term and used it in her letters written from her home in Ireland. Mrs. Montagu's reply to a letter in which Mrs. Vesey described bluestocking activities in Ireland, [February] 17, [1764], plays with meanings of the term:

> I receive such charming letters from the blue stocking Lodge, that I begin to be jealous for the Original Society. You seem to imitate the Jesuits of Paraguay, who became infinitely more rich & great than the Country from whence they went out a small colony. The imitation of Dr. Young is admirable, I may say the imitation is inimitable for it has all possible marks of resemblance and yet is not mere mimickry & that is hard to hit. I find Mr. O'Hara reveres as he ought the blue stockings of the Peripatetick philosophers; Mr. Caulfield the blue hose which encircles the nimble & taper leg of une jolie paisanne. I am not sure therefore that he is worthy of our society, however as he may be only an elegant spectator of forms, or consider blue stockings as the least deviation from the simplicity of the golden age, I am glad he is received into the Lodge, & I think we may admit him of the Colledge in time. (MO 6375)

Evidently Mrs. Montagu was skeptical of the nature of Mr. Caulfield's interest in the blue stockings of a "pretty peasant," but was at least willing to consider him capable of platonic attitudes.

The blue stocking philosophers were a source of entertainment and learning. On February 2, 1768, Mrs. Montagu in London wrote to Mrs. Vesey:

> Mr. Montagu passd ye Xmass at Sandleford, I with the blue stocking philosophers. I had parties of them to dine with me continually, & had my Sylph been of ye party, nothing had been wanting. I have got a new blue stocking with whom I am much pleased, a Mr. Percy who publish'd ye Reliques of ye ancient Poetry, he is a very ingenious man, has many anecdotes of ancient days, historical as well as Poetical. (MO 6393)

During these years the friends had also begun to use the term to indicate a point of view—"blue stocking doctrine" or "blue stocking philosophy." Writing presumably in 1764 Mrs. Montagu forwarded to Elizabeth Carter a letter from Mrs. Vesey in Ireland:

> I introduce la chere Sylph to you, she has nobly discharged the postage to me by half a sheet of excellent epistle, she longs to be again with the blue stocking Philosophy; she was not made for ordinary society. (MO 3061, prob. after June 26, 1764)

Writing to Elizabeth Carter, [August] 17, [1765], Mrs. Montagu speaks of Mrs. Vesey's problems and their cure:

> She complains of stomach, & says she is languid, but I hope the late hot weather may have occasiond her languor more than any thing else. Philosophical blue stocking doctrine apply'd to her ear is the best cure for all her complaints. Sensible & ingenious minds cannot subsist without variety of rational entertainment; & then the languor of mind is charged on that most innocent Hulk ye body. If a person is robust enough to bear a course of hard study they may live in any place, with dull society sometimes, or in retirement without any society at all; but in a delicate state of health it wont do. . . . Poor Vesey complains of want of rational conversation. (MO 3151)

Mrs. Montagu saw blue stocking philosophy as detached from politics. After a long account to Mrs. Vesey of Parliamentary debates, Mrs. Montagu says, "I design for the future to addict myself intirely to the Blue stocking philosophy which treads not the paths of ambition" (MO 6387). To this remark Mrs. Vesey replied that she thought her friend's character "too animated to retire to blue Stocking or any other exclusive Philosophy" (MO 6276).[12]

At the end of one London season Mrs. Montagu bewailed the dispersion of her friends:

> & oh barbarous cruel desertion. Some blue stocking philosophers went to fish for polypes in ditches, others to cull simples in the fields; the Poets to gather new blown similes in the meadows & gardens; Prose writers to meditate & reason in solitude. (MO 6376, June 5, 1764, to Mrs. Vesey)

In the 1760s therefore, Mrs. Montagu and Mrs. Vesey were using the term "bluestocking" to refer to men with intellectual interests with whom they had friendships, and to the idea that women needed rational entertainment. But by 1774 Mrs. Montagu could refer to the bluestocking circle without seeming to restrict the term to men. In a mood of disenchantment with literary interests, Mrs. Montagu wrote to Mrs. Vesey on August 6, 1774, that she was temporarily giving up her interest in the Muses for a concern with Hygea, "sweet Goddess of unthinking Mien," at least until Mrs. Vesey would return to London. At the moment Mrs. Montagu is choosing simple health, "let ye delicate aspire to the more elegant joys of the blue stocking circle" (MO 6439). At this point Mrs. Montagu seems to be thinking of both men and women as members of the "Muses Coterie." In "Bas Bleu, or Conversation," published in 1786, Hannah More referred to men and women of the circle. As late as 1791 Hester Chapone was still using the term in this sense—symbolizing the intellectual companionship of men and women:

> Are you in Town my dear Miss Burney? & do you remember an old Soul that used to love your Company? if you will give it me next Thursday Eveng you will meet Pepyss—Boscawen & so you may put on your blue Stockings. if you have got any *boots* to walk about in the mornings, *I* shall like you as well in *them*.[13]

Mentioning a male friend (Pepys, or she may mean a married couple), and a female friend (Boscawen), Mrs. Chapone was suggesting that the term itself was not something she took seriously.

But commentators on the bluestockings had begun to focus on the feminine gender by the late 1770s. Hester Thrale's references to the "blues" in *Thraliana* are all to women. In 1779 she noted that Fanny Burney's play "The Witlings" was not staged because of "fear of displeasing the female Wits—a formidable Body, & called by those who ridicule them, the *Blue Stocking Club*."[14] In April 1781, describing the events just before her husband's death, Mrs. Thrale recounted a visit to go to see "Webber's Drawings of the S: Sea Rareties—we met the Smelts, the Ords, & numberless *Blues* there, & displayed our Pedantry at our Pleasure" (1: 488, and n. 3—she is referring to John Webber's work as an artist on Cook's third voyage). On May 17, 1781, after her husband's death, Mrs. Thrale wrote resentfully that Mrs. Montagu was encouraging her to continue with her duties at the brewery: "the *Wits* & the *Blues* (as it is the fashion to call them) will be happy enough no doubt to have me safe at the Brewery—*out of their way*" (1: 494).

Why did the term "bluestocking" change its gender? Why did it not at least continue to refer to men *and* women, as it seems to have done in the late 1760s and early 1770s? The problem goes back to the taboo against learning for women. A significant number of the women of the bluestocking circle achieved publication between 1758 and 1775: Elizabeth Carter's translation of Epictetus (1758), her *Poems* (1762), Elizabeth Montagu's *Essay on the Writings and Genius of Shakespeare* (1769), Catherine Talbot's posthumous *Reflections on the Seven Days of the Week* (1770) and her *Essays on Various Subjects* (1772), and Hester Chapone's *Letters on the Improvement of the Mind* (1773), and her *Miscellanies* (1775). Their "fame" as scholars and writers, discussed in newspapers and periodicals, combined with interest in and gossip about their social gatherings, brought the idea of eminently respectable women with intellectual interests into public notice; the change in gender reflected an uncomfortable awareness of the breaking of a taboo. Henceforth, used sometimes in a complimentary way, often in a derogatory one, the term "bluestocking" would refer to women with intellectual interests.

For the bluestockings themselves, learning and virtue *were* inextricably linked. In their own eyes to be a bluestocking meant to be an impeccable member of an intellectual community. Although when we read their writings, we may think that they left themselves open to charges of sanctimoniousness or pedantry, they were in fact rather daring in their self-direction, although orthodox in religion and conduct. Elizabeth Montagu wrote to Mrs. Vesey (September 21, 1781):

> We have lived much with the Wisest, the best, & most celebrated Men of our Times, & with some of the best, most accomplish'd, & most learned Women of any times. These things I consider, not merely as pleasures transient, but as permanent blessings, by such Guides & Companions we were set above the low temptations of Vice & folly, & while they were the instructors of our Minds they were the Guardians of our Virtue. (MO 6566)

The propriety of the bluestocking circle made it impossible to attack them on the grounds of libertinism; in general, affectation became the ground for attack. Essays, poems, plays, even a comic opera were written about bluestockings. In *M. P. or the Blue-Stocking*, performed in 1811, Thomas Moore presented Lady Bab Blue. Educated by her father, who had no son, she carries a telescope, spouts chemical terms, and is writing a poem on the "Loves of Ammonia."[15] In *The Blues* (1823) Byron complained that women were crowding into lecture halls.[16] He satirized women who try to be literary leaders—his Lady Bluebottle is a faint portrait of Elizabeth Montagu. On the other hand, William Pitt Scargill, in a three-volume novel called *Blue-Stocking Hall* (1827), tried to show that well-educated women make more sensible wives and mothers than ignorant, worldly ones.[17] In this novel the characters discuss the term "bluestocking," define it, and demonstrate that education is a right of women as well as of men.

Writing in 1852, Thomas De Quincy suggested that it was time to put the term "bluestocking" to rest.[18] He thought that the "order of ladies called *Blue-stockings* by way of reproach" had become extinct. He recognized that in earlier generations any intellectual interest by women "carried with it an air of something unsexual, mannish and (as it was treated by the sycophantish satirists that ever humour the prevailing folly) of something ludicrous." But he felt that such a treatment was possible only when literary ladies formed a "feeble minority." The vast increase in educated men and women had rendered the term "not simply obsolete, but even unintelligible to our juniors."

Still the term appears in contemporary dictionaries and contemporary writing. Even the connotation of moral rectitude has persisted. In 1982, in a review in *The Times Literary Supplement,* Anthony Holden, writing about Diana Trilling's *Mrs. Harris: The Death of the Scarsdale Diet Doctor,* expressed the thought that the trial of Mrs. Harris for the murder of her lover gained special interest because Mrs. Harris was "a bluestocking headmistress, symbol of chaste community propriety."[19] Chastity and the bluestockings! Evidently the association of the term "bluestocking" with virtue (which enabled the bluestockings to make learning accessible to women) has not completely died.

NOTES

I wish to thank the Huntington Library, San Marino, Calif., for permission to quote from the Montagu Collection, and Lady Anne Lucas for permission to quote from the Lucas papers at the Bedford Record Office. I gratefully acknowledge the Ellen Moers Fellowship granted me by the Tulsa Center for the Study of Women's Literature, University of Tulsa, for research in England.

1 Jemima, Marchioness Grey to Catherine Talbot (copy), January 18, [1745?], Bedford County Record Office, L30/9A/4, 31.
2 Ibid., 32.
3 See *Female Scholars: A Tradition of Learned Women Before 1800,* ed. by J. R. Brink (Montreal: Eden Press Women's Publications, 1980).
4 *The Adventures of Roderick Random* (Oxford: Oxford University Press, 1979), chap. 39. John F. Sena, "Smollett's Portrait of Narcissa's Aunt: The Genesis of an 'Original,'" *English Language Notes* 14 (June 1977): 270–75 gives the medical sources for the aunt's condition.
5 *De Pensieri Diversi* (Venetia: Per il Barezzi, 1646), 227–28. Bayle quotes this passage in the original Italian in the article on Baptiste Guarini in the *Dictionaire historique et critique* (Rotterdam, 1697). The passage appears in Italian in the 1710 English edition of the *Dictionary*. In the English version of Bayle's *General Dictionary,* ed. Thomas Birch et al. (London, 1734–41) the passage appears in vol. 5 (1737) both in Italian and in English as above. The index contains an entry, "Women, why several learned women among the ancients were very lustful."
6 *Aubrey's Brief Lives,* ed. with a Life of John Aubrey by Oliver L. Dick, 2d ed. (Ann Arbor: University of Michigan Press, 1957), p. 138.
7 Anne Buck, *Dress in Eighteenth-Century England* (New York: Holmes & Meier, 1979), p. 31.
8 Ibid., pp. 138, 149.
9 Elizabeth Ewing, *History of Children's Costume* (New York: Scribner, 1977), p. 35.

10 MO 5153, The Elizabeth (Robinson) Montagu Collection, Henry E. Huntington Library, San Marino, Ca. Further references to this collection are in the text.
11 John Doran, *A Lady of the Last Century* (London: Richard Bentley, 1873), p. 270. I have not found this letter to Dr. Monsey in the Montagu Collection in the Huntington Library.
12 MO 6387 is dated by the Huntington Library Feb. 4 [1766]; Mrs. Vesey's letter (MO 6276), which is the reply, is dated Feb. 11 [?1765].
13 Hester Chapone to Francis d'Arblay BL Eg. 3698, f. 119, dated Dec. 27 [1791].
14 *Thraliana*, ed. by Katherine C. Balderston, 2d ed. (Oxford: Clarendon Press, 1951) 1: 381, n. 3. Further references are in the text.
15 Thomas Moore, *M. P. or The Blue-Stocking, A Comic Opera in Three Acts* (London: Printed by W. Clowes for J. Power, 1811).
16 George Gordon, Lord Byron, *The Blues: A Literary Eclogue,* in *Works,* ed. by Ernest Hartley Coleridge (London: John Murray, 1901), 4: 567–88.
17 William Pitt Scargill, *Blue-Stocking Hall* (London: Henry Colburn, 1827).
18 Thomas De Quincy, "Autobiography," in *Collected Writings,* ed. by David Masson (London: A & C Black, 1896) 1: 322, n. 1.
19 Anthony Holden, "The Homicidal Headmistress," *Times Literary Supplement,* 14 May 1982, p. 526.

Executive Board, 1984–85

President: HARRY C. PAYNE, Professor of History and Director of the Division of Social Sciences, Colgate University

Past President: JEAN A. PERKINS, Susan W. Lippincott Professor of French, Swarthmore College

First Vice-President: GITA MAY, Professor of French and Chairman, Department of French and Romance Philology, Columbia University

Second Vice-President: RONALD PAULSON, Professor of English, The Johns Hopkins University

Executive Secretary: R. G. PETERSON, Professor of English and Classics, St. Olaf College

Treasurer: RENÉE WALDINGER, Professor of French, The Graduate School and University Center of the City University of New York

Members-at-Large: JEFFREY BARNOUW, Visiting Associate Professor of English and Comparative Literature, The University of Michigan (1985)

BARBARA MARIA STAFFORD, Professor of Art History, University of Chicago (1984–85: Woodrow Wilson Fellow at the Smithsonian Institution, Washington, D.C.) (1985)

FREDERICK CUMMINGS, New York, New York (1986)

ENGLISH SHOWALTER, JR., Executive Director, Modern Language Association (1986)

PATRICIA BRÜCKMANN, Professor of English, Trinity College, University of Toronto (1987)

JANE PERRY-CAMP, Associate Professor of Music Theory, School of Music, The Florida State University (1987)

Business Manager: BRIAN ANDERSON

Institutional Members

*of the American Society
for Eighteenth-Century Studies*

Arizona State University
National Library of Australia
University of Calgary
University of California, Davis
University of California, Irvine
University of California,
   Los Angeles/William Andrews
   Clark Memorial Library
University of California, San Diego
California State University, Long Beach
Carleton University
Case Western Reserve University
Art Institute of Chicago
University of Cincinnati
City College, CUNY
Claremont Graduate School
Cleveland State University
Colonial Williamsburg Foundation
University of Colorado,
   Denver Center
University of Connecticut
Dalhousie University
Delta State University
Detroit Institute of Arts,
   Founders Society
Emory University
University of Evansville
Folger Shakespeare Library,
   Washington, D.C.
Fordham University
Georgia Institute of Technology
Georgia State University
University of Georgia
Gettysburg College

Herzog August Bibliothek,
   Wolfenbüttel
University of Illinois, Chicago Circle
Institute of Early American History and
   Culture
John Carter Brown Library
The Johns Hopkins University
University of Kansas
University of Kentucky
Kimbell Art Museum, Fort Worth
Lehigh University
Lehman College, CUNY
The Lewis Walpole Library of Yale University
Los Angeles County Museum of Art
University of Massachusetts, Boston
McMaster University/Association for
   18th-Century Studies
University of Michigan, Ann Arbor
Mount Saint Vincent University
State University of New York,
   Fredonia
University of North Carolina,
   Chapel Hill
Northern Illinois University
Northwestern University
The Ohio State University
University of Pennsylvania
University of Pittsburgh
Purdue University
University of Rochester
Rockford College
Rutgers University, New Brunswick
Smith College

292 / *Institutional Members*

Smithsonian Institute
University of Southern Mississippi
State University of New York,
 Binghamton
Swarthmore College
Sweet Briar College
University of Tennessee
University of Texas, Austin
Texas A & M University
Texas Tech University
Toledo Museum of Art
Towson State University
Tulane University
University of Tulsa
University of Utrecht,
 Institute for Comparative
 and General Literature
University of Victoria
University of Virginia
The Voltaire Foundation
Washington University
Washington and Lee University
Westfälische Wilhelms Universität,
 Münster
The Henry Francis Dupont Winterthur
 Museum
University of Wisconsin,
 Milwaukee
Yale Center for British Art and British
 Studies
Yale University

Sponsoring Members

of the American Society

for Eighteenth-Century Studies

Stephen J. Ackerman
G. L. Anderson
Mark S. Auburn
Mary-Margaret H. Barr
Pamela J. Bennett
Carol Blum
Timothy R. Bovy
T. E. D. Braun
Patricia Brückmann
Max Byrd
Joseph A. Byrnes
W. B. Carnochan
David W. Carrithers
Richard G. Carrott
Ellmore A. Champie
Henry S. Commager
Brian Corman
Howard J. Coughlin
Philip Daghlian
Robert A. Day
John Dowling
E. L. Eisenstein
Lee Andrew Elioseff
Robert Enggass
John Irwin Fischer
Elizabeth Fox-Genovese
Frank J. Garosi
Morris Golden
Walter Grossmann
Leon M. Guilhamet
H. George Hahn
Roger Hahn
Phillip Harth
Donald M. Hassler

Alfred W. Hesse
Stephen Holliday
Robert H. Hopkins
Adrienne D. Hytier
Margaret C. Jacob
Shirley Strum Kenny
Gwin J. Kolb
Carl R. Kropf
Colby H. Kullman
I. Leonard Leeb
J. A. Levine
Herbert Livingston
J. Robert Loy
Albert M. Lyles
David Macaree
H. W. Matalene III
Donald C. Mell, Jr.
Paul H. Meyer
Earl Miner
Sven Eric Molin
Catherine E. Moore
Nicolas H. Nelson
Melvyn New
Robert C. Olson
Hal N. Opperman
Harry C. Payne
Jean A. Perkins
Leland D. Peterson
J. G. A. Pocock
John V. Price
Irwin Primer
Clifford Earl Ramsey
Thomas J. Regan
Walter E. Rex

Jack Richtman
Ronald C. Rosbottom
Constance Rowe
E. L. Ruhe
Peter Sabor
Robert Shackleton
English Showalter
Oliver F. Sigworth
Henry L. Snyder
Robert Donald Spector
Mary Margaret Stewart
E. J. Thomas, Jr.

James Thompson
Connie C. Thorson
James L. Thorson
Teri Noel Towe
Betty Perry Townsend
Daniel D. Townsend
David M. Vieth
Morris Wachs
Renée Waldinger
Howard D. Weinbrot
Raymond Whitley
Samuel H. Woods

Patrons

of the American Society for Eighteenth-Century Studies

Chester Chapin
Louis Cornell
Sara Cornell
Charles N. Fifer
Basil Guy
J. Paul Hunter
Kathryn Montgomery Hunter
Annibel Jenkins
Judith Keig
J. Patrick Lee
Helen L. McGuffie
R. G. Peterson
Edgar V. Roberts
J. E. Stockwell
Robert W. Uphaus
Calhoun Winton